(157834)

Condition: NF/VG

Edition: 1st   Printing:

17 B/W Photos, 2 Maps

Jacket: w/DJ   NO   Pages: pp(Index)

Comments: DJ ncl htos, fcs, bre,
cloth lt rd at same sput, 115

Keywords: KB 2/4 AZ   NATO, Military Strategy
Military Logistics Europe, Military Policy 260 95
Military Pacts, UP

ONE FOR ALL

ONE FOR ALL

NATO Strategy and Logistics through the
Formative Period, (1949–1969)

James A. Huston

NEWARK: UNIVERSITY OF DELAWARE PRESS
LONDON AND TORONTO: ASSOCIATED UNIVERSITY PRESSES

Associated University Presses
440 Forsgate Drive
Cranbury, NJ 08512

Associated University Presses
25 Sicilian Avenue
London WC1A 2QH, England

Associated University Presses
2133 Royal Windsor Drive
Unit 1
Mississauga, Ontario
Canada L5J 1K5

Library of Congress Cataloging in Publication Data

Huston, James A. (James Alvin), 1918–
  One for all.

  Bibliography: p.
  Includes index.
  1. North Atlantic Treaty Organization—Military policy.
2. North Atlantic Treaty Organization—Armed Forces—
Procurement.   3. North Atlantic Treaty Organization—
Armed Forces—Supplies and stores.   I. Title.
UA646.3.H85   1984   355.′.031′091821   82-49305
ISBN 0-87413-231-2

Printed in the United States of America

Contents

Preface

Although one of the most significant, if complex, aspects of NATO is the international logistics associated with it, this also is an area least regarded by the general public. In a sense it is the effort at logistic cooperation that more than anything else has given meaning to NATO as a functioning international organization. Strategy too is important, since strategic assumptions provide the bases for logistic planning, but this part of NATO's discussions and activity has, by its nature, attracted a great deal of public attention. At all events, it should be recognized that strategy and logistics, together with tactics, form a continuum in which each has such effects on the others that none can be regarded in isolation.

B. H. Liddell Hart has pointed to the central position of logistics in an alliance:

> The weakest spot of any force is its administrative area. . . . This weakness has increased with technical progress. . . . That complexity, and weakness, would be vastly multiplied in any force composed of national contingents intent to maintain their "national character"—each requiring different rations to feed its men; different calibres of ammunition to feed its weapons; different spare parts and tools; and each functioning on a different staff-system. [*Deterrent or Defense: A Fresh Look at the West'sMilitary Position* (New York: Frederick Praeger, 1960), p. 242]

The broad scope of logistics in providing the material resources to make armed forces effective may be seen in the NATO definition: "The marshalling and employment of the military resources of Nations in support of military operations; embraces the five functions of: supply and maintenance, casualty evacuation and hospitalization, movement and transportation, construction and facilities, and communications and administrative management" (NATO Definition, SHAPE, AG 1228.11 LOG of 1 August 1955). Another definition follows closely that used by the Joint Chiefs of Staff of the United States: "The science of planning and carrying out the movement and maintenance of forces. In its most comprehensive sense, those aspects of military operations which deal with (1) design and development, acquisition, storage, movement, distribution, maintenance, evacuation and disposition of matériel; (2) movement, evacuation and hospitalization of personnel;

(3) acquisition or construction, maintenance, operation, and disposition of facilities; and (4) acquisition or furnishing of services" (NATO Glossary of Military Terms and Definitions, 15 November 1963, p. 76).

Perhaps the most significant aspect of the North Atlantic Treaty Organization in making it an effective alliance—and the one most neglected in public interest and awareness—has been the development of structure, procedures, and facilities for mutual logistic support. Most of these developed and took their present form during NATO's first twenty years—what now may be regarded as its "formative" period. Most of the deficiencies apparent at the end of that period still persist. There have been many modifications and refinements, but the general pattern then was pretty well set. A history of the attempts at international logistics in that period should be helpful in the consideration of the current situation and of possible further improvements.

Here the attempt has been to provide some perspective and context for readers to make critical judgments on recent trends and proposals for future change in NATO, to give some background for students who wish to study further the role of the United States in international logistics, to offer some points of departure for staff studies by officers and others who find themselves in assignments relating to these areas, and finally to help fill a gap of neglect—the elements of logistics—common to the study of military history. The international dimension, mutual support in coalition welfare, is a consideration of special significance for the United States in the twentieth century.

This study was begun as a result of a NATO fellowship for the summers of 1963 and 1964, and I am especially indebted to Mr. John Vernon, NATO Cultural Affairs Officer, for his cooperation and friendly counsel in directing the fellowship program.

Visits at various times—and frequent return visits in a number of instances—to several divisions and offices of NATO's International Staff and with liaison officers and national representatives of several nations, to SHAPE at Rocquencourt and at Casteau, to AFCENT at Fontainebleau and at Brunssum, to AFSOUTH at Naples, BALTAP in Denmark, to NAMSSO at Neuilly and to NSC at Chateauroux, to MAS in London, to SACLANT at Norfolk, to the Military Committee in Washington, and with current and past officials and military leaders in many places, always found a cordial reception and most understanding cooperation. In thanking all of them, however, I wish to avoid any personal reference that might in any way compromise personal and private conversations, for I wish to make it clear that opinions expressed here are altogether unofficial and do not necessarily represent the views of NATO or any agency related to it or of any government. All statements of fact or opinion rest fully on my own responsibility.

For assistance in preparation of the manuscript, special thanks are due Dr. Anne Marshall, Miss Lois Daniel, and Mrs. Shirley Moore.

Lynchburg, Virginia

ONE FOR ALL

Part 1
Evolution of Coordinated
Logistic Efforts

1
Antecedents

A shadow has fallen upon the scenes so lately lighted by the Allied victory. Nobody knows what Soviet Russia and its Communist international organization intends to do in the immediate future, or what are the limits, if any, to their expansive and proselytizing tendencies. . . .

From Stettin in the Baltic to Trieste in the Adriatic, an iron curtain has descended across the Continent. Behind that line lie all the capitals of the ancient states of central and eastern Europe. Warsaw, Berlin, Prague, Vienna, Budapest, Belgrade, Bucharest, and Sofia, all these famous cities and the populations around them lie in what I might call the Soviet sphere, and all are subject, in one form or another, not only to Soviet influence but to a very high and in some cases increasing measure of control from Moscow. Police governments are pervading from Moscow. But Athens alone, with its immortal glories, is free to decide its future at an election under British, American, and French observation. . . .

However, in a great number of countries, far from the Russian frontiers and throughout the world, Communist fifth columns are established and work in complete unity and absolute obedience to directions they receive from the Communist center. . . . These are sombre facts for anyone to have to recite on the morrow of a victory gained by so much splendid comradeship in arms and in the cause of freedom and democracy, but we should be most unwise not to face them squarely while time remains.

—Winston Churchill, Fulton, Missouri,
5 March 1946

Tranquility did not automatically succeed the formal combat operations of World War II. Signs of new tensions to replace the old were appearing in the very efforts to meet the latter. Few problems in human affairs can be disposed of permanently. Solutions to major social problems frequently carry secondary problems, which in turn may grow to primary importance. Already in 1945 and 1946 dark clouds, even if "no bigger than a man's hand," were appearing on the horizon. It was almost inevitable that reasons for international tension should remain in the wake of so gigantic a struggle as World War II.

Though dimmed for Americans in the carefree abandon of the Roaring Twenties by an enviable confidence that war had been banished from the earth, this backwash of war had been hardly less evident after World War I. An advertisement for *Current History* in the spring of 1919 listed its contents as: "The Civil War in Germany," "The Peril of Bolshevism," "The Revolution in Hungary," "The Conflicts in Poland," "The Warfare in Russia," "The Problems of Yugoslavia," and "The Unrest in Egypt."[1]

That such tensions would continue after World War II should have come as no surprise. In fact, it was no surprise to the many officers who had applied themselves to clear analyses of the situation. Probably consequences of a victory by the Soviet Union were clear to some from the very beginning. In a remarkable staff study in April 1942—only four months after Pearl Harbor and nearly three years before the Yalta Conference that would realize so many of its predictions—an officer of U.S. Army Ground Forces had written:

> In case of a Soviet victory, or of Soviet participation in an allied victory, Russian domination of Eastern Europe is certain. Probably minimal demands would be the Baltic States, large portions of Finland, Poland, and Rumania, and control of the Dardanelles. In the Middle East, the Sovietization of Iran and possibly Afghanistan is very likely. China would be subject to heavy Russian pressure; she would have to recognize the "independence" of Outer Mongolia and possibly Sinkiang, as well as granting major economic and political privileges in Manchuria. Japan would be forced to cede the Kurile Islands, Southern Sakhalin, and probably the Tsu and Saishu Islands.[2]

The major concern of American forces remaining overseas after V-J Day, aside from the demobilization, was the military occupation of Germany, Austria, Japan, and Korea. Logistically this involved not only the supply of the troops assigned to that duty, but it called for substantial contributions to the sustenance of the local civilian populations as well.

In Germany the occupation began under policies laid down in a Joint Chiefs of Staff directive, known as JCS 1067, which General Eisenhower had received in April 1945. The principal objectives were to prevent Germany from making war again and to root our nazism. This meant disarmament, demilitarization, trials of war criminals, removal of Nazis from important positions, limitation of industry, and encouragement of democratic institutions. But first it was necessary to round up remnants of the *Wehrmacht,* look after several million displaced persons, set up local governments, and restore essential services. General Joseph T. McNarney succeeded General Eisenhower as commanding general of United States Forces European Theater and military governor of Germany. He served there from 1945 to 1947, when his deputy, Lt. Gen. Lucius D. Clay, became military governor and commander-in-chief of the European Command. In September 1949 civil government replaced military government in Germany; the Office of the U.S. High Commissioner for Germany, under the State Department, took over the responsibilities of the Office of Military Government for Germany the same day that the Western Federal Republic of Germany came into being.[3]

Austria supposedly was to be treated as a "liberated" state rather than as an ex-enemy state, but this seemed to make little real difference in the nature and the duration of the occupation there. Like Germany, it was divided into zones of occupation, and the capital again was divided into sectors for each occupying power. In May 1947 Lt. Gen. Geoffrey Keyes succeeded Gen. Mark W. Clark as commander of United States Forces in Austria.[4]

In Japan, on the contrary, the occupation was unified under General of the Army Douglas MacArthur, Supreme Commander for the Allied Powers and commander in chief of the Far East Command. There the basic policy directive, prepared by the State, War, Navy Coordinating Committee, like the policy in Germany, called for complete demilitarization, the encouragement of democratic institutions, and changes in the economic structure that would destroy the industrial bases for military power and would permit the payment of reparation. Within a few weeks the occupation forces had carried out their first tasks of rounding up and demobilizing about four million Japanese soldiers and of repatriating about one million allied nationals. By March 1947 General MacArthur declared that the military purposes of the occupation had been accomplished, and he looked forward to an early termination of his mission.[5]

After the Japanese surrender, the XXIV Corps, then on Okinawa preparing for the planned invasion of Japan, received orders to land in Korea to receive the surrender of Japanese troops south of the 38th Parallel. Landing at Inchon in September 1945, the corps, under the command of Maj. Gen. John R. Hodge, fell heir to the military government of the southern half of the country. To handle the specific matters of civil affairs General Hodge set up in January 1946 the United States Military Government in Korea as an element of his overall command, now known as U.S. Army Forces in Korea. Succeeding Maj. Gen. Archibald V. Arnold in January 1946, Maj. Gen. Archer L. Lerch served as military governor until his death in September 1947. A few weeks later Maj. Gen. William F. Dean became military governor. General Hodge's command in Korea was subordinate to General MacArthur's Far East Command, but after 26 July 1947 General Hodge reported directly to the Joint Chiefs of Staff on military government matters. In September 1948 the new government of the Republic of Korea took over civil responsibilities for South Korea.[6]

Continuing Crises

Certainly the support of the military occupation demanded the major part of overseas logistic commitments immediately after the war, but the irony in the situation was the changing orientation of security measures under which that logistical support continued. Initial occupational policies apparently were aimed almost wholly against a possible resurgence of power on the part of Germany and Japan. This too was the tenor of the United Nations Charter, for the machinery of international peace enforcement had been designed to operate smoothly only when operating against the former enemies. That a recovery of power and the creation of a new threat to world security was possible had been demonstrated in the rise of Nazi Germany out of the defeat of World War I. But if anything at all was clear in world affairs in 1945, it must have been that Germany and Japan, prostrate under the heavy blows of aerial bombardment and complete defeat on land and sea, constituted no immediate threat to the security of the United States. Only one country in the world—whatever policies it might pursue—had the physical capacity to pose such an immediate threat to the United States, and that was the Soviet Union. Neglect of the realities of power politics led to some disillusionment when threats to the national security began to appear from the actions of an erstwhile ally. But those actions led to an important change of emphasis in the occupation policies. More and more it became evident that American forces were being kept in Germany, Austria, and Japan less for keeping those countries down than to block possible aggression on the part of that former ally.[7]

In March 1945—before the United States had yet had a chance to begin its precipitous demobilization—the Soviet Union began to pressure Turkey with an announcement that the Soviet-Turkish treaty of neutrality and friendship of 1925 would not be renewed. Reviving an expansionist policy that the Russians had pursued off and on for over a century and a half, the Soviet Union now sought joint control of the Turkish straits—the Bosporus and the Dardanelles—and the annexation of Turkey's northeastern provinces of Kars and Ardahan. In November 1945 the United States suggested that the international convention governing the straits be revised. While willing to accept the Soviet proposals on navigation through the straits, the United States resisted any arrangement for joint Soviet-Turkish defense of that area. This, in the view of American officials, would lead inevitably to Soviet domination of Turkey and would create a serious threat to the strategically important Near East. The differences led to a diplomatic impasse, but Turkey remained in control of the straits, as well as of the northeastern provinces.[8]

Now the U.S.S.R. turned its attention to Iran and Greece, where internal weaknesses might permit relatively easy domination, which would isolate Turkey as well as gain command of the important strategic positions and resources of these two countries themselves. In November 1945 the pro-Soviet Tudeh Party merged with the Democratic Party to stage a revolt in Iran's northern province of Azerbaijan, and Soviet troops there refused to permit the entry of Iranian forces to put down the revolt. The Soviet troops were there as a result of a joint occupation with the British in August 1941 aimed at protecting the Baku oil fields of the Soviet Union and the holdings of the Anglo-Iranian Oil Company in southern Iran. By a treaty of January 1942 those powers had agreed to withdraw their troops within six months after the termination of hostilities. When Soviet troops failed to depart during the next few weeks, Iran lodged a complaint with the United Nations

Security Council on 19 January 1946. In March, Iran further complained that the Soviet Union still was maintaining troops in Iran in violation of the treaty. Then, strangely enough, while the Security Council was debating the question, Iran suddenly withdrew the complaint. At the insistence of the United States, however, the Security Council kept the Iranian question on its agenda. In May the Iranian government reported that Soviet troops apparently had withdrawn, but it was not until December that Iranian troops were able to enter Azerbaijan and reestablish control over that province. Before the withdrawal of their troops, the Soviet Union had negotiated an oil agreement with Iran by which a joint Soviet-Iranian oil company was to be formed on the basis of fifty-one percent Soviet control for a period of twenty-five years—and then the Iranian parliament refused to approve the agreement.[9]

Just two days after Iran brought its complaint to the Security Council, the Soviet delegation—doubtless to attract attention away from Iran—charged that the presence of British troops in Greece constituted interference in the internal affairs of that country. On a proposal of the United States, the council rejected that contention. Then in August 1946 the Ukrainian S.S.R. brought a further complaint before the Security Council on affairs in Greece. They argued that Greek armed forces were provoking incidents along the Greek-Albanian border. On the very face of it this was a situation fraught with danger. Yet when the United States proposed that the Security Council establish a commission to investigate the facts of the matter, with authority to call upon Albania, Bulgaria, Greece, and Yugoslavia for information, the Soviet Union vetoed the resolution.[10]

Abolition of the Yugoslav monarchy in November 1945 in favor of a Federal Peoples' Republic indicated the subservience of Yugoslavia to the Soviet Union. Communist ascendancy there and vociferous demands for the Italian port of Trieste, then occupied by British and American forces, led to a period of uneasy relations between the United States and the government of the communist dictator, Marshall Tito. These relations reached a crisis in August 1946 when two U.S. Army transport planes were shot down by Yugoslav fighters over Yugoslavia. The occupants of the first plane were taken into custody; five men on the second were killed. Feeling ran high in the United States. Secretary of State James F. Byrnes, then in Paris for a peace conference to conclude treaties with the former German satellite states, sent an ultimatum to Yugoslavia. He demanded the release of the men being held within forty-eight hours—or the case would be taken to the United Nations. This was a new kind of ultimatum, but it got results. Tito had backed down both on the question of Trieste and on holding the American fliers. But the Trieste situation was far from cleared up. In the fall of 1946 the Council of Foreign Ministers arrived at a compromise solution on Trieste: the port city and the surrounding territory would be made a free territory, independent of both Italy and Yugoslavia, to be guaranteed by the Security Council. Although the Security Council was to choose the governor, it was unable to make a choice, and as a result the territory remained under the control of occupational military forces—American and British in the northern zone, Yugoslav in the southern zone.[11]

Elsewhere in the world promises of peace and security were scarcely more reassuring. In China, where Communist forces had been waging civil war sporadically since 1927, the danger of Communist domination seemed to be as great as ever. As a result of the Yalta agreement and the Sino-Soviet Treaty of 1945, the Soviet Union had returned to about the same advantageous position in Manchuria that Czarist Russia had enjoyed before 1904. According to a report of Edwin W. Pauley, who headed a mission to inspect conditions there, the Soviets stripped Manchurian industry to the extent of direct damage estimated at $858,100,000, and total damage, including deterioration and cost of replacement, was estimated at over $2 billion. In November 1945 President Truman named General of the Army George C. Marshall his special emissary to go to China to try to work out an agreement that would put an end to the civil strife there. At first it appeared that the general might be successful. In January 1946 the warring parties agreed to an armistice and Marshall set up headquarters in Peiping to try to work out an effective agreement. But in succeeding months negotiations degenerated to a complete break. General Marshall returned in January 1947 with little hope of reconciling the Chinese Communists to a democratic regime, or of finding effective resistance to communist expansion in the Nationalists of Chiang Kai-shek. A mission of Lt. Gen. Albert C. Wedemeyer in July 1947 offered little more reason for hope.[12]

Warfare also was continuing in the Dutch East Indies where Indonesian leaders were seeking to establish a republic independent of the Netherlands. This gave to the Soviet Union another opportunity to attract attention away from Iran, and perhaps to exploit growing Asiatic nationalism. On 21 January 1946 the Soviet Union asked the Security Council to make an investigation of the situation in Indonesia where, it was claimed, British and even some Japanese troops were being used against the native population. Noting that negotiations between Netherlands and Indonesian leaders then were in progress, the United States led a move that blocked the investigation.[13] Later, a United Nations team did go out to the Indies in order to promote a truce.

In the Philippines the United States continued to have a special interest—mainly defense—after the Islands became independent on 4 July 1946. The Philippine Military Assistance Act of 1946 provided not only for the transfer of substantial quantities of matériel to the Philippines, but it provided for the maintenance and repair of military equipment and for training and instruction in its use. A military assistance agreement, signed 21 March 1947, gave effect to the act. Though such a program was the natural consequence of concern for security in a country where it now was necessary to build up local forces to defend their independence, this became but one in a long series of military assistance programs that soon would become a keystone of

American policy. By an agreement signed 14 March 1947 the United States retained Fort Stotsenberg, near Manila, as its chief military base in the area, together with ten other Army bases and four naval "operating areas" in the Philippines.[14]

During the last half of 1947 and early 1948 even the appearance of free choice disappeared from most countries behind the Iron Curtain. In a series of swift seizures of total authority, the Communists moved to consolidate their control. On 31 May 1947 Communists ousted Premier Ferenc Nagy of Hungary, whose Smallholders party had won an absolute majority in the election of 1945; shortly thereafter they broke up his party and drove Nagy into exile. In October Stanislaw Mikolajczyk, vice premier of Poland and leader of the Peasant party, had to flee for his life when the Communists moved in to take complete control. And that same month Communist leaders met in Warsaw to organize their Communist Information Bureau (Cominform) as successor to the old Communist International (Comintern). In November 1947 Ana Pauker became foreign minister of Romania, and her Communist regime dissolved the National Peasant Party and imprisoned its leader, Iuliu Maniu; King Michael went into exile in December. In Bulgaria the Agrarian Union Party was broken up and its leader, Nikola Petkov, was hanged. Bulgaria adopted a new Soviet-type constitution in December.

Then came the final blow. So far Czechoslovakia had been able to hold on to something of its tradition of democracy, and its leaders still hoped that it might be a bridge between the East and the West. But in February 1948 this country too came under full Soviet sway. Foreign Minister Jan Masaryk fell to his death from a window. Shortly thereafter Eduard Benes, a sick and broken man, gave up the presidency. Benes had served as foreign minister under Masaryk's father in the hopeful days after the founding of the Republic out of World War I. He had seen his country parceled away at Munich. Now his dream of a return to independence and democracy had been shattered. Perhaps more than any other action up to that time, the coup détat in Czechoslovakia indicated the real danger that Soviet policies posed. As the Brookings Institution reported in 1949, "When Czechoslovakia, which had done everything possible to conciliate the Soviet Union, was seized by the Communists in February 1948, little doubt remained in Western minds that the Communist ambitions could be checked only through the evidence of superior power."[15]

The Marshall Plan

From the end of World War II the United States had been contributing substantial economic assistance throughout the world by export-import bank loans, support of the United Nations Relief and Rehabilitation Administration, and through a post-UNRRA relief program. This aid had done much to alleviate immediate economic distress, but it had done little to stimulate basic industrial recovery. Conditions in Europe in the winter of 1946–1947 suggested that much more would have to be done if lasting economic stability were to be restored. This economic stability had important implications for the long-term economic well-being of the United States. And to the extent that economic instability created conditions and weakness that invited the spread of Communism, it had important implications for the security of the United States.

After Under Secretary of State Dean Acheson had anticipated it in a speech at Cleveland, Mississippi, on 8 May 1947, Secretary of State George C. Marshall presented the broad outline of a new policy in a commencement address at Harvard University on 5 June 1947. At the moment this amounted to little more than an invitation to European nations to get together on an integrated economic program to which the United States could lend its support for European industrial recovery.[16] European statesmen lost little time in taking the cue.

Marshall adopted a cooperative, nonbelligerent attitude. What came to be viewed as one of the greatest bulwarks against the spread of Communism in Europe was not couched in anti-Communist terms at all. Marshall said: "Our policy is directed not against any country or doctrine, but against hunger, poverty, desperation, and chaos. Its purpose should be the revival of a working economy in the world so as to permit the emergence of political and social conditions in which free institutions can exit."[17]

Representatives of European states met on 27 June in Paris to prepare a response to the American offer. V. M. Molotov arrived from Moscow with a retinue of eighty-nine experts and clerks, but after studying the matter, he announced that the Soviet Union could have no part of such a program. This provided the cue for any of the states behind the Iron Curtain that might have entertained hopes of sharing in the proposed American aid. In July sixteen nations agreeing to the plan began working out concrete programs. As it evolved, the Marshall Plan was a four-year program for coordinated economic assistance to the sixteen European nations accepting it. Its economic objective was to achieve equilibrium in the international balance of payments by 1952.[18]

After passing an interim measure, the Foreign Aid Act of 1947, to tide over France and Italy, Congress took up consideration of the Marshall Plan early in 1948. Title I of the Foreign Assistance Act of 1948, approved 3 April, put the plan into effect and set up the Economic Cooperation Administration (ECA) to administer it.

The objective of the Marshall Plan was economic recovery. Even had there been no Communist threat, something of its kind would have been necessary. The Communist threat made it urgent. Insofar as its effect was to stem the tide of Communism in Western Europe, the plan could be considered an economic corollary to the Truman Doctrine. Yet even in this economic program, important implications for Army logistics were to be found. When it came to the actual delivery of relief supplies and industrial goods, the Army's logistical system had an important part to play in supporting the Economic Cooperation Administration.

Berlin Blockade

General Lucius D. Clay, commander in Chief of the European Command and military governor of Germany, on 5 March 1948 sent a message to Lt. Gen. Stephen J. Chamberlin, Director of Intelligence (G-2), Army General Staff:

> For many months, based on logical analysis, I have felt and held that war was unlikely for at least ten years. Within the last few weeks, I have felt a subtle change in Soviet attitude which I cannot define but which now gives me a feeling that it may come with dramatic suddenness. I cannot support this change in my own thinking with any data or outward evidence in relationships other than to describe it as a feeling of a new tenseness in every Soviet individual with whom we have official relations. I am unable to submit any official report in the absence of supporting data but my feeling is real.[19]

At the end of that month General Clay received notice from the Soviet commander that under a new system of inspection being inaugurated on 1 April it would be necessary for Russian soldiers to board Allied military trains to inspect the shipments going through the Soviet Zone. When General Clay refused to permit this inspection, the Russians stopped the trains. Again the American commander's reaction was to hold firm. He advised that the withdrawal of the 7,000 American military personnel and their 1,000 dependents from Berlin likely would result in hysteria among the German population, and abandonment of Berlin would lead to a serious weakening of the American position not only in Germany but in all of Europe. General Clay's solution was to supply the American forces in Berlin by air. After eleven days of this airlift the Soviet authorities rescinded their inspection order, and military supply by rail could be resumed, subject only to the normal inspection of shipping documents.[20]

During the next several weeks Soviet needling tactics interfered with some highway traffic, attempted to regulate air traffic, and slowed the clearance of trains. In the last week of June the Soviets cut off all traffic between the western zones and Berlin. On 23 June the Western Powers announced plans for currency reform in their zones. On the 24th the Russians stopped all rail shipments to Berlin. This time the blockade was complete—it applied to civil as well as to military shipments. On the 25th the Western Powers began issuing their new currency and the Russians announced that they would not supply food to the German population of the western sectors of Berlin. Already the president had made it clear to Secretary of Defense Forrestal that the policy would remain fixed: the United States would stay in

Berlin. A meeting of State Department and military officials at the Pentagon on Sunday afternoon, 27 June, upheld this view. On this same day Lt. Gen. Curtis E. LeMay, commander of the United States Air Forces in Europe, was meeting with General Clay in Berlin to discuss plans for an airlift. The next day General LeMay announced that he was going to send air freight to Berlin at maximum capacity, twenty-four hours a day, seven days a week, on a wartime basis, with no holidays. Four squadrons of C-54 transport planes, on the way to reinforce air units in Germany, were due to arrive about 5 July.[21]

Already—on 21 June—the airlift for the supply of military forces in Berlin had begun. The experience of the April airlift had permitted thorough planning and rapid action. Tonnage jumped from 5.88 tons in three C-47 planes on 21 June to 156.42 tons in sixty-four planes on 24 June. But the supply of the civilian population of western Berlin was another matter. Headquarters of the European Command first learned of such a project on 26 June, and the first civilian supplies went into Tempelhof Airfield, Berlin, on 28 June. This called for hasty planning and improvisation.[22]

The maximum air effort needed to carry out these missions of civilian as well as military supply called for essential support from Army logistical agencies of the European Command. It was up to them to furnish and repair necessary trucks, to provide quarters for the air crews, to expand the air terminal facilities, to provide communications, to bring in gasoline. They had to deliver to the airports the supplies destined for the military forces in Berlin, to receive them at the Berlin end, and to distribute them to the Berlin garrisons. In the beginning of the civil supply program—which became known as Operation Vittles—the Army forces had the responsibility of finding the supplies and getting them to and from the airplanes. Later (28 July) the Bipartite Control Office took over responsibility for getting the German food to the airports. Then civilian agencies of military government and of the German local governments handled the procurement, storage, financing, and movement to the airfields of the civilian supplies. But the Army had to continue important logistic activities in order to keep the airlift going.[23]

Through the winter the Berlin airlift continued, carrying food, clothing, coal, raw materials, and medicines to the 2,500,000 people of the western sectors of Berlin. By the spring of 1949 the American and British allies had reached an average daily air delivery rate of 8,000 tons. On the record day (16 April 1949) they delivered nearly 13,000 tons—more than was being brought into Berlin by rail and water before the imposition of the blockade. The results suggested that the air supply operation might go on indefinitely, and American leaders seemed determined to do just that if it were necessary. At last on 4 May 1949 the Western Allies arrived at an agreement with the Russians for lifting the blockade, and on 12 May all transport, trade, and communication services between the eastern and western zones of Germany were restored. Nevertheless, the airlift continued in order to build up a reserve against a possible renewal of restrictions. It gradually reduced in scope until the last load was flown from Rhein-Main to Tempelhof on 30 September 1949.[24]

Western European Union

The forerunner of the North Atlantic Treaty Organization was the Western Union Defense Organization, which developed under the Treaty of Economic, Social, and Cultural Collaboration and Collective Self-Defense, signed at Brussels on 17 March 1948 by Belgium, France, Luxembourg, the Netherlands, and the United Kingdom—states thereafter referred to collectively as the "Five Powers." Like the Treaty of Alliance and Mutual Assistance that the French and British had signed at Dunkirk a year earlier, the Brussels pact was intended to remain in force for fifty years. The pact declared that in the event of an armed attack in Europe against one party, all the others would give all military and other assistance in their power in accordance with the provisions for collective self-defense of Article 51 of the United Nations Charter. To carry out the aims of the Brussels Treaty, the Five Powers established elaborate machinery for consultation and coordination. The Five Powers agreed to the pooling of equipment and resources, subject to the outside commitments that they already had undertaken, but all together their equipment was very scant.[25]

While determined to fight against aggression with whatever they had, the leaders of the Brussels Treaty Powers recognized that they had to depend on the United States for a great part of the support that would make resistance more than token. In reply to a question from the Defense Committee, the Permanent Military Committee on 12 May 1948 stated firmly and frankly:

> In the event of an attack by Russia, however soon it may come, the Five Powers are determined to fight as far east in Germany as possible. If Russia overruns the countries of Western Europe, irreparable harm will be done before they are liberated, owing to the Russian policy of deportation and pillage. Their preparations are, therefore, aimed at holding the Russians on the best position in Germany covering the territory of the Five Powers in such a way that sufficient time for American military power to intervene decisively can be assured.[26]

From the time of the adoption of the Vandenberg Resolution by the United States Senate in June 1948 until the following spring, representatives of the Brussels Treaty Powers, Canada, and the United States met in Washington for informal discussions on the feasibility of expanding the idea of Western Union to include the participation of these two North American powers. One immediate result of these conversations was the acceptance by both Canada and the United States of invitations to send observers to the conferences of the Permanent Military Committee in London. In July 1948 the U.S. Delegation to the Military Committee of the Five Powers (DELWU), headed by Maj. Gen. Lyman L. Lemnitzer, arrived in London and set up an office at the headquarters of the Eastern Atlantic and Mediterranean-commander in chief on Grosvenor Square. The delegation was a joint mission operating under the control of the Joint Chiefs of Staff. American representatives sat in on meetings of the Defense Committee, the Military Supply Board, the Supply Executive, the Security Committee, the Principal Administrative and Planning Committee, frequently the Chiefs of Staff Committee, and occasionally the Commanders in Chief Committee. In September the delegation was made a permanent organization, manned by thirteen Army officers, three Air Force officers, and one Navy officer. In December the Joint Chiefs of Staff designated Lt. Gen. Clarence R. Huebner as U.S. Representative to the Western Union Chiefs of Staff Committee.[27]

A Summary of Inventories of Military Forces and Resources submitted to the Western Union Military Committee in August 1948 revealed pathetic weaknesses. All the ground forces that these once-mighty powers now could raise among themselves for 1949 were ten divisions and thirteen brigades "in being," and a hope that another twelve divisions and nine brigades could be mobilized within three months. Americans had been used to abolishing practically their entire ground force in peacetime, but not the French, who had boasted the greatest army in the world in the 1930s. Worse of all was the equipment situation. Lists showed serious deficiencies in tanks, antiaircraft artillery, engineering equipment, most types of ammunition, and motor transport. Except for light weapons such as rifles, machine guns, and anti-tank guns, little or no equipment was available to supply additional forces on mobilization. Much of the World War II equipment was not serviceable, and it could not be rehabilitated soon because of shortages in spare parts and technicians. Most of the difficulties preventing complete mobilization of trained reserves could be traced to the shortage of matériel.

Consideration of furnishing arms for Western European nations had begun with the talks of a North Atlantic pact. At a conference with Secretary of Defense Forrestal in October 1948, General Marshall, then Secretary of State, returned repeatedly to the importance of getting equipment to the European nations. He described those nations as being "completely out of their skins, and sitting on their nerves." The conclusion was that any kind of an immediate shipment—even of rifles—would have an "electrifying" effect.[28]

The French were the first to press requests for matériel assistance from the United States. They submitted to General Clay a list of items needed to bring up to combat effectiveness three divisions then in the French occupation zone of Germany. Clay was sympathetic to the request, and he urged that it be granted. In September 1948 the president of the United States approved a recommendation of the U.S. National Security Council to make the equipment available. That which was available in the European Command—stocks of spare parts and accessories remaining after the bulk transfer of surplus property in Germany—was turned over to the French immediately. The remainder was shipped from stocks in the United States. Officials in Washington recognized the need for matériel assistance to European countries, but at the same time they feared that if they continued to entertain unilateral requests for such assistance, the result might be to undermine the attempts to coordinate Western Union requests for supplemental assistance. In return the United States would expect reciprocal assistance to the extent practicable.

After some drastic revisions, the Joint Chiefs of Staff in February 1949 approved a general program of assistance based on a Western Union interim supply plan. That plan had shown a requirement for Army equipment sufficient to equip the ten division slices existing in 1949 plus the mobilization and maintenance of another twelve division slices within ninety days after D-day. The Joint Chiefs of Staff reduced this to the minimum equipment necessary for nine division slices in being in 1949 plus the minimum equipment for training purposes only of a force equal to twelve division slices capable of being mobilized within ninety days. They reduced the estimated cost of the program from $2.097 billion to $731 million. The Joint Chiefs asked that the Five Powers indicate the priorities in which requested equipment should be made available. If assistance were requested formally, and if agreements could be reached within the Western Union countries, the president was prepared to present to Congress a program of assistance for the fiscal year ending 30 June 1950.

The lists from the participating governments were returned to the U.S. Delegation, which now developed specific programs for each of the Western Union countries. Teams sent from Washington to Denmark, Norway, and Italy prepared the initial programs for those countries. They too had the assistance of the U.S. Delegation to the Military Committee of the Five Powers in refining their programs.

North Atlantic Treaty

By 1948 consolidation of Soviet hegemony in eastern Europe and the possibilities of further aggrandizement at the expense of Western Europe suggested that it would not be enough to meet each new crisis with full confidence that it be overcome. The obvious response to the consolidation of a Soviet bloc in the East seemed to lie in the direction of integrated policies in the West.

Already the United States had, in September 1947, committed itself to a defensive alliance with the Latin American republics by the Treaty of Rio de Janeiro. But that had amounted to a promise of military aid in an area where an attack by an outside power seemed least likely. To accept such a commitment in Europe would be a revolutionary departure from an American policy that traditionally had sought to isolate itself from European affairs, and that had consistently refused to have any part of a formal military alliance. But in April 1948 the U.S. National Security Council discussed the possibility that the United States might consider a new regional defense arrangement under the provisions of Article 51 of the United Nations Charter, which permitted members to participate in collective measures of self-defense whenever assistance from the United Nations itself would be inadequate.

In June 1948 the Senate passed the Vandenberg Resolution, which amounted to such a statement. This paved the way for the negotiation of the North Atlantic Treaty. While negotiations were in progress, the Soviet Union did not hesitate to make known its displeasure. In particular, the U.S.S.R. inquired of Norway, in January 1949, what the latter proposed to do about signing the treaty. The implication was that signature would be an unfriendly act toward the Soviet Union. In a second note on 5 February, the Soviet Union referred to the "aggressive aims" of the treaty and proposed to Norway a nonaggression pact. But the Norwegian representative, together with those from the United Kingdom, France, Belgium, Luxembourg, Netherlands, Italy, Denmark, Iceland, Portugal, and Canada, and the Secretary of State for the United States, signed the North Atlantic Treaty in Washington on 4 April 1949.[29]

The treaty provided that an armed attack against the territory, occupation troops, vessels, or aircraft of any of the parties, in North America, Europe, Algeria, or the Atlantic Ocean north of the Tropic of Cancer would be regarded as an attack against all. The signatories agreed that they would "assist the Party or Parties so attacked by taking forthwith, individually and in concert with the other Parties, such action as it deems necessary, including the use of armed force, to restore and maintain the security of the North Atlantic area."[30] The Senate gave its approval on 22 July, and the president ratified the treaty three days later.

Coming into force on 24 August 1949 with the deposit of the ratifications of France and the Netherlands, the treaty brought the United States into active participation with the Western European nations in developing plans and programs for defense. Most significantly, the United States, together with those European states and Canada, had committed itself not only to come to the assistance of any member attacked in the North Atlantic area, but to contribute to a program of mutual matériel assistance.[31] "For the first time," said the Secretary of Defense in his semi-annual report, "we have to face the security problems of our allies, in peace time, and to accept responsibility in quarters where in the past we gave only advice."[32] Even yet Americans generally displayed a remarkable reluctance to grapple with problems of global strategy and mutual support. Even after the North Atlantic Treaty had been signed, and while high officials were developing the Mutual Defense Assistance Program, unwillingness of Americans to admit the possibility of another war seemed to be holding back considerations of rearmament. Books and articles touching this subject were rare in 1949 and the first half of 1950.[33]

The United States had accepted an unprecedented military commitment in Europe. Doing so was a recognition that control of the population and industrial plant of Western Europe—greater than those of the Soviet Union itself—by a hostile power would be a serious threat to the security of the United States.

Even as the North Atlantic Treaty was being discussed, the implication was clear that American matériel assistance to the participating countries would be necessary if the new organization were to have any real effectiveness as a deterrent to aggression. But President Truman waited until the day after he signed the instrument of ratification to follow it up with a formal request for military assistance. Calling for $1.45 billion, this proposal would consolidate in one act the existing programs for Greece and Turkey, Iran, Korea, the Philippines, and the Western Hemisphere, with a new program for North Atlantic Treaty countries. It envisaged three types of assistance: (1) direct transfer of American military equipment; (2) expert guidance in using the equipment and in production of equipment; and (3) dollar aid to increase direct military production in Europe. Ten weeks later Congress approved the program in the Mutual Defense Assistance Act.

Initially the assistance was to go to eight signatories of the North Atlantic Treaty, Greece, Turkey, Iran, Korea, and the Philippines, and for assistance "in the general region of China." Congress made the availability of $900 million for the North Atlantic Treaty countries contingent upon the formation of an integrated defense plan by the North Atlantic Treaty Organization. Economic recovery in Europe still was to have priority over rearmament.[34]

The North Atlantic Treaty was open, by unanimous invitation, to the accession of other European states. The first extension of membership was to Greece and Turkey, effective 18 February 1952.[35] For some, this strained the designation "North Atlantic," but British and French leaders long had regarded the eastern Mediterranean as a critical area for their own security, and Greece and Turkey had been the first recipients of the kind of aid from the United States that developed into the Mutual Defense Assistance Program. The forces of the two countries, being built up with the assistance of American matériel and advisers, were welcome additions to the strength of the Western European Powers.

Notes

1. Frederick Lewis Allen, "This Time and Last Time," *Harper's Magazine* 154 (1947): 195.
2. Russian Combat Estimate, Staff Study, April 1942, G-3, Army Ground Forces (AGF), Plans. Adjutant General's Office (AGO) Historical Records Section, 163.
3. Lucius D. Clay, *Decision in Germany* (New York, 1950), 51–83, 227–44; Harold Zink, *American Military Government in Germany* (New York, 1947); John C. Campbell, *The U.S. in World Affairs, 1945–47* (New York, 1947), 164–75; U.S. Dept. of Army, *The Army Almanac* (1950), 758–63; Office of the U.S. High Commissioner for Germany, *First Quarterly Report on Germany*, Sept.–Dec. 1949, 2; James K. Pollock and James H. Meisel, *Germany Under Occupation, Illustrative Materials and Documents* (Ann Arbor, 1947); U.S. Forces European Theater, *Occupation* (Germany, n.d.), 25; U.S. Dept. of State, *Occupation of Germany, Policy and Progress*, State Dept. Publ. 2783, Aug. 1947, passim.
4. Campbell, *The U.S. in World Affairs, 1945–47*, 198–205; Military Government, Austria, Report of the U.S. Commissioner, Feb. 1947; *Army Almanac* (1950), 763–66.
5. Selected Data on the Occupation of Japan (prepared by GHQ, SCAP, and FECOM); Campbell, *The U.S. in World Affairs, 1945–47*, 254–73; U.S. Dept. of State, *Occupation of*

Japan, Policy and Progress, State Dept. Publ. 2671; *Army Almanac (1950)*, 769–74.

6. E. Grant Meade, *American Military Government in Korea*, (New York, 1951), 76–78; George M. McCune and Arthur L. Grey, Jr., *Korea Today* (Cambridge, 1950), 47–51; Campbell, *The U.S. in World Affairs, 1945–47*, 273–80; *Army Almanac* (1950), 774–78.

7. See Clay, *Decision in Germany*, 317–42, and Campbell, *The U.S. in World Affairs, 1945–47*, 194–98.

8. Brookings Institution, *Major Problems of United States Foreign Policy 1948–49* (Washington, D.C., 1949) 70; Harry N. Howard, "Some Recent Developments in the Problem of the Turkish Straits, 1945–1946," *Department of State Bulletin* 16 (Jan. 1946): 143–51, 167; Campbell, *The U.S. in World Affairs, 1945–47*, 149 ff.

9. Brookings Institution, *Major Problems in U.S. Foreign Policy, 1948–49*, 71–72; U.S. Dept. of State, *The United States and the United Nations; Report Series No. 7, Report by the President to Congress for the Year 1946*, State Dept. Publ. 2735, 33–34.

10. *The United States and the United Nations, Report Series No. 7*, 35–36; Campbell, *The U.S. in World Affairs, 1947–1948* 30.

11. Campbell, *The U.S. in World Affairs, 1945–47*, 155–56; Mary E. Bradshaw, "Military Control of Zone A in Venezia Biulia," *Department of State Bulletin*, 16 (June 1947): 1257–72; Brookings Institution, *Major Problems in U.S. Foreign Policy, 1948–49*, 61–62.

12. Campbell, *The U.S. in World Affairs, 1945–47*, 280–99; Brookings Institution, *Major Problems of U.S. Foreign Policy, 1948–49*, 80–81.

13. *The United States and the United Nations, Reprint Series No. 7*, 35.

14. Edward W. Mill, "One Year of the Philippine Republic," *Department of State Bulletin* 16 (June 1947): 1280; Campbell, *The U.S. in World Affairs, 1945–47*, 306–14.

15. Brookings Institution, *Major Problems of U.S. Foreign Policy, 1949–50*, 99; see also Campbell, *The U.S. in World Affairs, 1948–49*, 104–16.

16. Dean Acheson, *Present at the Creation* (New York, 1969), 227–34; Harry S. Truman, *Memoirs*, vol. 2: *Years of Trial and Hope* (Garden City, N.Y., 1956), 112–16.

17. Quoted in Acheson, *Present at the Creation*, 233.

18. Campbell, *The U.S. in World Affairs, 1947–48*, 49–59, 422–31; Brookings Institution, *Major Problems of U.S. Foreign Policy, 1949–50*, 104–7, 221–29.

19. Quoted in Walter Millis, ed., *The Forrestal Diaries* (New York, 1951), 387.

20. Ibid., 407; Clay, *Decision in Germany*, 358–61; Elizabeth S. Lay, "Berlin Airlift, 1 January–30 September 1949," Occupation Forces in Europe Series, European Command, Hqrs., Hist. Div. Copy in Office of Chief of Military History, Dept. of the Army, Washington, 2–3; U.S. Dept. of Army, *Annual Report of the Secretary of the Army, 1948*, 15.

21. *Annual Report of the Secretary of the Army, 1948*, 53–55; Lay, "The Berlin Airlift," 1:9–11; Millis, *Forrestal Diaries*, 451–54.

22. Lay, "The Berlin Airlift," 1:7, 10–12.

23. Ibid., 1:12–13, 129.

24. Clay, *Decision in Germany*, 381; Lay, "The Berlin Airlift, 2:3, 78, 107–8; Campbell, *The U.S. in World Affairs, 1948–49*, 133–49; U.S. Dept. of State, *Germany 1947–49: The Story in Documents*, State Dept. Publ. 3556, March 1950; *Annual Report of the Secretary of the Army, 1948*, 147–50; Military Government of Germany, monthly report of military governor, U.S. Zone, 1949; Millis, *Forrestal Diaries*, 469–70.

25. U.S. Dept. of Defense, "History of the Joint American Military Advisory Group," mimeo 1:1–54; *The NATO Handbook* (London, 1952), 3–7.

26. Quoted in U.S. Dept. of Defense, *History of Joint Military Advisory Group*, 1:13.

27. U.S. Secretary of Defense, Directive 49, "Functions and Responsibilities within the Department of Defense for Military Assistance," Appendix A, JCS Information Memo 697, 1 December 1949; Millis, *Forrestal Diaries*, 425–34, 520–25; Campbell, *The U.S. in World Affairs, 1948–49*, 512–17; "History of Joint American Military Advisory Group" (typescript), vol. 1: "Background Information," 222–37.

28. Millis, *Forrestal Diaries*, 500.

29. Brookings Institution, *Major Problems of U.S. Foreign Policy, 1949–50*, 430–38; Campbell, *The U.S. In World Affairs, 1948–49*, 527–41; Millis, *Forrestal Diaries*, 243.

30. North Atlantic Treaty, Article 5.

31. See Bernard Brodie, "Strategic Implications of the North Atlantic Pact," *Yale Review* 39 (Winter 1950): 193–208; Royal Institute of International Affairs, *Defense in the Cold War: The Task for the Free World* (London, 1950).

32. U.S. Dept. of Defense, *Second [Semiannual] Report of the Secretary of Defense, 1949*, 24.

33. Library of Congress, *The United States and Europe, A Bibliographical Examination of Thought Expressed in American Publications during 1959*, Reference Dept. European Affairs Div., Library of Congress, 144.

34. Brookings Institution, *Major Problems of U.S. Foreign Policy, 1950–51*, 3, 132; Richard Stebbins, *The U.S. in World Affairs, 1949* (New York, 1950), 79–84.

35. Protocol to the North Atlantic Treaty on the Accession of Greece and Turkey, signed 17 Oct. 1951, printed in SRE special publication, *North Atlantic Treaty and Related Documents*.

2
NATO and the Mutual Defense Assistance Program

Probably the greatest stimulus to the unification of policy among neighboring states is an awareness of a common external threat to the security of each of them. But if that threat appears to be too overpowering, the result is more likely to be a feeling of helplessness and a hope for individual accommodation such as that which enabled the armies of Hitler to overrun European states one by one in 1940 and 1941. Given the strength to back up the determination expressed by nations of Western Europe in the Brussels Treaty of 1948, a drive toward unity of purpose seemed the immediate consequence of the peril of Communist expansion toward the West. It was possible that future generations would be grateful for a Soviet threat, which stimulated a unity in Europe that resulted in better living for all concerned. But for the moment the prospect seemed hopeless without the early and effective logistical support of the United States. Even when large-scale programs of American assistance became certain, possibilities of violent Soviet counteraction as well as the recognized military advantage that the Soviet then held in Europe left only the most stouthearted free from pessimism.

The Soviet Position in Europe

General Eisenhower's first annual report as Supreme Allied Commander in Europe stated the problem this way:

> There was serious question as to the state of public morale among the European members of the North Atlantic Treaty Organization. They were living daily under the shadow of a powerful Soviet striking force, stationed in East Germany and Poland, and pressing the obvious capability of over-running much of Europe. It was extremely difficult for the average European to see any future in an attempt to build defensive forces which might offset this real and formidable threat. There seemed to be too much of a lead to be overtaken. The doubts of the European peoples gave birth to the false but glittering doctrine of neutralism, through which they hoped to

preserve the things they had always held dear. Their fears were stimulated by ugly overtones of threat from Communist propaganda organs, and from traitorous outriders already in their own midst. Beyond all this, the cumulative effects of repeated failure to make any headway in conferences with the Soviets produced an intellectual defeatism, in some quarters bordering upon despair.

* * * * *

Beyond the Iron Curtain, deployed from the Arctic Ocean to the Adriatic Sea, the forces menacing the free world were formidable. Just beyond the Iron Curtain in Eastern Europe lay thirty divisions with their supporting squadrons of aircraft. These were only a fraction of the Soviet strength; yet their employment was significant of the whole Communistic philosophy of force. While the Western Powers reduced their active forces to small occupation units which were concerning themselves with peacetime training, and becoming identified more and more with the communities where they dwelt, the numbers and the status of the soldiers of the Soviet had remained unchanged since shortly after the end of the war. They were still confined in sullen isolation within their barracks and compounds; they were still deployed and poised for war.

* * * * *

Each side, the West and the East, possessed outposts beyond the frontier of the other. Albania remained in the Soviet orbit, though isolated from it by the regained sovereignty of Yugoslavia. West Berlin and Vienna, with their devoted populations and garrisons of French, British and Americans, were still impervious to Soviet threats and blandishments alike. Apart from these exceptions, the Iron Curtain divided the continent into regimented and free Europe. East of it were 175 Soviet line divisions, one-third of which were either mechanized or armored, and an Air Force of 20,000 aircraft. The Navy at the same time stood at twenty cruisers and some 300 submarines. Behind all this was a vast, sprawling economy, still largely harnessed to war. Though inefficient by Western technical standards, Soviet industry had already demonstrated that it was producing atomic weapons.[1]

In contrast to the United States, demobilization of Soviet armed forces proceeded gradually after the end of World War II combat. Soviet Army strength dropped to about 2,500,000 early in 1947, and there it remained at least for the next six years. In addition to regular army troops, the Russians maintained some 400,000 security police. Also to be counted were some sixty-eight divisions in the satellite countries of eastern Europe, and twenty-four regiments of East German "police" forces.[2] Not to be discounted were the Communist "fifth columns" to be found in the countries of Western Europe. Communists were infiltrating the armed forces, interfering with the logistical operations of ports and lines of communication, and hampering industrial production; it was not unlikely that their effect would be considerable in wartime.

In building up the strength of satellite armies to support Soviet policies, the Russians had a military assistance program of their own. Increasing quantities of Russian-made heavy and medium equipment were being found in the hands of satellite troops early in 1952. Most of the satellites received

T-34 medium tanks; Bulgaria and Hungary boasted Stalin tanks. Standard Russian artillery, antitank and antiaircraft guns, and self-propelled guns all continued to arrive in these armies. Soviet advisory groups and training missions varied in size from 500 in Albania to 2,000 in Bulgaria and Czechoslovakia. Instructors from the regular Soviet garrisons in East Germany, eastern Austria, Poland, Hungary, and Romania served the forces of those countries.

Russian troops had a reputation for living off the country. To some extent this was exaggerated, since ammunition, weapons replacements, and gasoline generally were not to be found in any countryside short of captured enemy supply dumps. But Russian soldiers had displayed a remarkable capacity for resistance under most unfavorable conditions. Whenever expedient, Russian soldiers of almost any arm or service would be assigned to labor—harvesting crops, tending herds, or other tasks for the subsistence support of Army units.

Again in contrast to the action of the United States, the Soviet Union did not dissipate its stockpiles of military equipment after V-J Day, but on the contrary steadily added to them over the next seven years. By mid-1952 Soviet stockpiles of most kinds of equipment appeared to be far above the mobilization requirements for 320 divisions at M plus 30 days. Some observers speculated on the deterioration and obsolescence of all this equipment, and some saw a further immediate danger to the security of Europe in a supposition that Soviet leaders might be tempted to provoke a war in order to put this equipment to use before it should become completely obsolete. But indications were that Soviet maintenance was keeping the equipment serviceable, and showings in Korea attested that it was not yet obsolete. The maintenance system included a periodic turnover of equipment for return to the factory for complete rehabilitation. Soviet research and development was going forward, but there was no inclination to abandon equipment just because an improved model could be made. Much of the stockpiled equipment had functional interchangeability, and this, together with other measures of standardization, made production and repair relatively simple. The Russians were in the position of being able to concentrate their research and development on any given item, and then to place that item into large-scale production whenever they chose. Huge stockpiles of finished equipment, strategically located near potential war areas, not only provided the basis for rapid mobilization on a large scale; they also would ease the burden on transportation. Moreover, stockpiles of finished goods would delay the effectiveness of strategic bombing directed at industrial plants rather than at supply depots.[3]

Backing up this huge stockpile of military equipment was a munitions industry that was turning out sufficient matériel during these peacetime years to replace completely within five to eight years many of the major items needed for the 320-division mobilization force. That production included a yearly output of approximately 6,000 tanks and self-propelled guns, and 10,000 to 12,000 artillery pieces. Steel production in 1951 was three times the World War II peak. With this increasing steel capacity, with available standby facilities, a trained labor force, and stockpiles of raw materials, it was likely that Soviet munitions production could return to the peak production rates of World War II within two years of any given time—a peak that included the manufacture of 30,000 tanks in 1944. By the end of 1952 the war-devastated Ukraine was producing more coal, iron, steel, and electric power than before the war. The Soviet economy seemed better prepared for war, and less vulnerable, than ever before. In addition, industries in the satellite states were being integrated with the Soviet economy, and output appeared to be climbing in those eastern European countries too.[4]

Sums allocated directly for military purposes in the Soviet budget rose steadily from the postwar low of 66.3 billion rubles in 1948 to 82.9 billion in 1950, 96.4 billion in 1951, and 113.8 billion in 1952. (The official rate of exchange was four rubles to the dollar.) The budget announced in 1953 showed a reduction of 3.5 billion rubles from that of the previous year, but the fact that there had been some decline in prices, and the fact that all funds allocated in 1952 had not been spent indicated that real expenditures in 1953 would be as great as ever.

Undoubtedly the Achilles heel of Soviet logistics—and so of overall military potential—was the transportation system. Military transportation, as all transportation in the Soviet Union, relied mainly on the railways. Though taxed severely, Russian railroads had been able to bear the burden of major operations during World War II, and improvements since that time gave reason to assume that future performance would be even better. The U.S.S.R. had only one-third the railway mileage of the United States in an area twice as large, but the density of freight traffic on Soviet railroads was more than double that of the United States in 1949. Highways inside the Soviet Union were few and far between, and as late as 1945 at least half of the entire Soviet motor truck pool consisted of American lend-lease vehicles. But here too notable improvements had been made since the war. Emphasizing trucks at the expense of passenger cars, the Soviet automotive industry was producing some 430,000 motor transport vehicles a year in the early 1950s.[5]

In the post-World War II period, Soviet forces, and stockpiles of equipment, had the advantage of jumping-off places in the satellite countries and East Germany, where relatively dense rail and highway networks were available to them. Though horse-drawn transportation still probably would be found in the event of mobilization, nearly all Soviet units in occupied areas of eastern Europe were motorized or mechanized. Here the troops had an opportunity to learn to use their motorized equipment. Some observers would point to the long lines of communications upon which a Soviet offensive in central Europe would have to depend, the implication being that such an offensive thus would be much more difficult for the Russians to maintain than had been their World War II operations. But this overlooked the advantages of the stockpiles, the industries, and the transportation system in the satellite states. Up to a certain point, military operations would be easier to support from this area than in Russian territory itself, while deep in the rear, out of reach of the battle area, the large-scale Soviet industry would be replenishing the stockpiles. In the event of war in Europe it was unlikely that the Russian Achilles heel of limited transportation facilities would be exposed very early in the conflict unless widespread defection developed in the satellites.

The Structure of NATO

Article 9 of the North Atlantic Treaty provided for a council as the supreme body of the North Atlantic Treaty Organization (NATO) to give effect to the treaty. The article also directed the council to establish a defense committee and such other subsidiary bodies as might be necessary. The structure that developed followed closely that which had grown up earlier under the Brussels Treaty for Western Union. In the beginning the foreign ministers of the member states were the council representatives, and the council was to meet annually, or more frequently when necessary. As under the Brussels Treaty, the Defense Committee was made up of the defense ministers of all the members, and under this committee a Military Committee, composed of chiefs of staff of all the members (Iceland, having no military establishment, was represented by a civilian), was organized. Since the Military Committee was intended to meet only once a year ordinarily, a subcommittee of military representatives of the United Kingdom, France, and the United States was organized as the Standing Group to function continuously, with headquarters in the Pentagon. Five regional planning groups engaged in defense planning for specific regions of Europe, the North Atlantic, and North America. Also subordinate to the Defense Committee was the Military Production and Supply Board. Another agency made up of ministerial representatives was the Defense Financial and Economic Committee. It was organized in December 1950, and its staff was established in Paris where it could be near the Organization for European Economic Cooperation. Permanent staffs and working committees for the various agencies carried on continuous activities in London and Paris.[6]

It was not long until experience in NATO showed a need for some kind of central body, set up on a permanent basis, to coordinate the various agencies and to follow up agreed plans. The first step in this direction was the establishment of the Council Deputies in May 1950. Acting as representatives of the foreign ministers, the Council Deputies after July 1950 met in continuous session in London. As activities became more complex, organization needed to be simplified. The need was for fewer committees and more fulltime operating agencies with clearcut lines of authority. Following a Canadian proposal for reorganization in the autumn of 1950, the council at its December meeting authorized the deputies to study and recommend further changes in organizational structure. The permanent international staff began functioning in February 1951 under the direction of the Council

Deputies. In May 1951 the council adopted recommendations for reorganization of the principal consultative bodies. Now the North Atlantic Council was broadened to include the Defense Committee (defense ministers) and the Defense Financial and Economic Committee (finance ministers) as well as the foreign ministers. Representation at council meetings might be by heads of governments themselves or by the foreign, defense, and finance ministers, or by any one of them, depending upon the nature of the agenda. A new Financial and Economic Board, with headquarters in Paris, took over the responsibilities previously belonging to the permanent working staff of the Defense Financial and Economic Committee, the Advisory Group of Raw Materials, and the Economic and Financial Working Group. Already, in December 1950, the Defense Production Board had been established in London as a permanent agency to replace the Military Production and Supply Board. Except for the absorption of the Defense Committee into the council, the military structure remained unchanged.

The Lisbon meeting of the council resulted in further reorganization effective in April 1952. This provided that the council should function in permanent session through the appointment of permanent representatives, and that a single integrated and strengthened international staff should be organized under a permanent secretary-general. Under this arrangement the council assumed the responsibility for the tasks previously performed by the Council Deputies, the Defense Production Board, the Financial and Economic Board, and by two special committees—the Temporary Council Committee and the North Atlantic Community Committee. Ministerial meetings of the council would continue to be held two or three times a year, but the council would be able to function continuously through the permanent representatives. Chairmanship of the council was rotated annually according to alphabetical order of the member states, but the secretary-general was vice-chairman of the council, and he presided at all the meetings other than those attended by the ministers. Lord Ismay of Great Britain became the first secretary-general. Permanent headquarters of NATO now were centralized in Paris.

Certain other specialized agencies continued to function. The Petroleum Planning Committee, organized by the Council Deputies in January 1952, retained its responsibilities for assessing the total wartime military and petroleum requirements of member countries in relation to availabilities, and for recommending what measures should be taken in peacetime and what plans should be adopted to meet wartime requirements. Two other groups were responsible for planning for wartime transportation coordination—the Planning Board for European Inland Surface Transport, and the Planning Board for Ocean Shipping.

The general structure of NATO has remained substantially the same since the reorganization of 1952, though modifications in specific bureaus, committees, and agencies have reflected changes in administrative procedure or changes in emphasis as conditions and plans change.

Since 1957 the secretary-general has served as chairman of the council, while the foreign minister of each member state in turn has been designated president of the council.

A series of principal committees that the council established served to consider particular areas of interest in developing plans and studies. One group of a dozen committees operated directly under the council, and at least ten of these had a significant function in NATO logistics. These included the Committee of Economic Advisers, Annual Review Committee, Armaments Committee, Science Committee, Committee of European Airspace Coordination, NATO Pipeline Committee, Civilian Budget Committee, Military Budget Committee, and Infrastructure Committee and its subcommittee on infrastructure payments and progress. In addition the Committee on Information and Cultural Relations had to deal with logistical subjects, and the Committee of Political Advisers was bound to be involved in discussions on political relations that have important implications for logistics.

A second category of council committees, operating under the general direction of the Senior Civil Emergency Planning Committee was concerned altogether with the development of plans relating to the economic mobilization and civil defense aspects of logistics. This group included the long-established Planning Board for European Inland Surface Transport as well as the Civil Communications Planning Committee, Civil Defense Committee, Civil Emergency Coordinating Committee, Medical Committee, Petroleum Planning Committee, Industrial Planning Committee, Food and Agriculture Planning Committee, Manpower Planning Committee, and Civil Aviation Committee.

Divisions and offices of the International Staff/Secretariat worked closely with the council committees and with the various special agencies of NATO in plans and operations. The division most obviously concerned with logistic matters was the Division of Production, Logistics, and Infrastructures, which operated under the direction of an assistant secretary-general. This division had the responsibility of promoting efficient use of resources for the equipment and support of forces. In particular it studied problems relating to the standardization, development, production, supply, and maintenance of weapons and equipment in conformity to military plans. The division promoted the exchange of information on logistic problems among member nations, attempted to assure technical and financial supervision over the infrastructure programs, and studied problems relating to the operation of the NATO Pipeline System, the NATO Maintenance Supply Services System, and the various NATO production organizations.

In addition it was clear that the work of the Division of Economics and Finance was closely related to logistic matters, the Division of Scientific Affairs frequently touched these matters, and again, the Division of Political Affairs was concerned with questions often closely related to logistics. The Civil Emergency Planning Office came under the supervision of the executive secretary, who also served as secretary of the council and as coordinator of the activities of the council committees. His office provided secretarial staff for the committees and maintained their records.

The Problem of Germany in NATO

An immediate difficult problem was the bringing of Germany into full partnership in European defense. The whole North Atlantic alliance was concerned. Plans for rearming the enemy, only five years after "unconditional surrender," aroused serious misgivings in neighboring states. The problem was how to bring German economic and military potential into the defense of Western Europe without reconstituting a military power that in the eyes of other peoples in that area might itself threaten their security.

At the same time that he proposed the organization of a supreme headquarters for allied forces in Europe, at the meeting of the North Atlantic Council in September 1950, Secretary of State Dean Acheson presented an American proposal for seeking units from the Federal Republic of Germany for NATO forces. France was reluctant to see Germany rearmed in any way before the French were able to rebuild their own strength. At a meeting of the North Atlantic Defense Committee in Washington in October, Jules Moch, the French defense minister, proposed a far-reaching innovation. The French could entertain no suggestions for reconstituting German divisions or a German general staff, but, said he, why not bring the Germans in as part of a unified European army? The proposal received further consideration at the Brussels meeting of the North Atlantic Council in December. French representatives met with those of Italy, Belgium, Luxembourg, and western Germany to work out the details. Later the Netherlands joined in the planning. After a year's preliminary work, the six nations developed a comprehensive plan for a European Defense Force, within the framework of a European Defense Community, under which forces would be integrated for the common defense of Western Europe.

Groupements, the basic ground units for the integrated force, would be made up of about 12,000 men of one nationality. At higher levels, they would be mixed. Integration also would extend to air and sea units. Troops required to meet commitments outside Europe would remain under national control. Once formed, the European Defense Force would come under SHAPE, as had the force of the United States and those of Canada and the United Kingdom that had been allocated to that command. The effect would be to make Germany an "associate member" of NATO. All the North Atlantic Treaty powers approved the European Defense Community plan at the Lisbon meeting of the North Atlantic Council in February 1952. But early promise of success began to give way to doubts as delays developed on the ratification of the pact to give effect to the plan.[7]

Having proposed it, the French now killed the project when their parliament refused to ratify the agreement. Though Secretary of State John Foster

Dulles warned that there was no alternative, Foreign Minister Anthony Eden of Great Britain immediately set out to look for one. He found it in a revitalization of the Western European Union, to which both Italy and Germany then were admitted, and shortly thereafter (May 1955) the Federal Republic became a member of NATO, and German units were added to the NATO forces. This paved the way for American military assistance and for full German participation in NATO strategic and logistic planning.[8]

Military Organization

The North Atlantic Treaty itself provided for consultation among the parties, but it had not envisaged an active military organization. Probably it took the Communist coup d'état in Czechoslovakia and the Berlin blockade to bring the North Atlantic Treaty Organization fully into being. Two further events changed its character—the announcement in September 1949 of an atomic explosion in the Soviet Union, and the Communist attack in Korea on 25 June 1950. The French inquired in August if the United States were prepared to contribute ground forces for the defense of Western Europe and whether forces of the allies should be integrated under a supreme commander. The American reply was an unprecedented affirmative on both counts. In Europe the Joint American Military Advisory Group (JAMAG) had prepared a study recommending the organization of the European area as a single combined theater, with certain subordinate commands, and the appointment immediately of a theater commander designate. At the meeting of the North Atlantic Council in September 1950, Secretary of State Acheson presented the American proposal for an integrated command in Europe under a supreme commander, and the representatives approved the plan on 26 September. General Eisenhower, then serving as president of Columbia University, learned in October that he might be recalled to active duty to take over the Allied Command in Europe. Meeting again in Brussels in December, the North Atlantic Council approved a recommendation of the Defense Committee for the establishment of Supreme Headquarters, Allied Powers, Europe (SHAPE), and to ask General Eisenhower to take the Supreme Command. In February 1951—as the United States Senate debated the president's plans for sending four additional divisions to Europe—SHAPE was established in temporary facilities at the Astoria Hotel in Paris. On 2 April the new command became operational.

As the supreme directing body, the North Atlantic Council was analogous in certain respects to the meetings held at various times during World War II by Prime Minister Churchill and President Roosevelt to give top-level direction to the common war effort. Now holding a position somewhat similar to that of the wartime Combined Chiefs of Staff, which coordinated Anglo-American strategy, the standing Group of the Military Committee, made up of chiefs of staff representatives of France, the United Kingdom, and the United States, sitting in Washington and working closely with the Military

Representatives Committee organized there to give all the member states a voice in the activities of the Standing Group, assumed greater importance with the establishment of operational commands for the European and the North Atlantic Ocean areas.

Major military commands established by NATO were Allied Command Europe, with headquarters at Paris, where General Eisenhower first served as Supreme Allied Commander and was succeeded in turn by Generals Matthew B. Ridgway, Alfred M. Gruenther, Lauris Norstad, and Lyman L. Lemnitzer; Allied Command Atlantic, with headquarters at Norfolk, for which Admiral Lynde D. McCormick was appointed Supreme Commander in February 1952, and the Channel Committee, composed of chiefs of staff of states bordering the English Channel and southern North Sea and with an operational Allied Commander in Chief Channel, also organized in February 1952.

Of the five regional planning groups that had been included in the original structure, only one remained. This was the Canada–United States regional planning group. Of the others, the functions of three had been absorbed by SHAPE and the other by the new Atlantic Command.

Several subordinate commands were organized within the area of SHAPE. These included Allied Forces Northern Europe, with headquarters at Oslo, Allied Forces Central Europe at Fontainebleau, Allied Forces Southern Europe at Naples, and, later, Allied Forces Mediterranean, with headquarters on Malta, and U. K. Air Defense Region at Stanmore, England.

Major subordinate commands of Allied Command Atlantic were the Western Atlantic Area (headquarters at Norfolk, Virginia), Eastern Atlantic Area (Northwood, England), and Striking Fleet (New York).

The Supreme Allied Commanders ordinarily received their instructions from the Standing Group, though they had the right of access to the military chiefs of any of the member countries, and even, in certain instances, to the ministers of defense and the heads of government. Under the general direction of the Standing Group, they were responsible for the defense of allied territory, forces, vessels, and aircraft within their respective areas. They had the duty of making recommendations to the Standing Group and to individual nations on matters of training, priorities, for the organization and equipping of assigned and earmarked forces, and for the construction of facilities to support them. Certain forces of member nations were assigned to the Supreme Allied Commander Europe (SACEUR) in peacetime, while others were earmarked for assignment in case of war. The Supreme Allied Commander Atlantic (SACLANT) had no assigned forces in peacetime, though forces were earmarked for wartime assignment. Earmarked forces were assigned from time to time to the respective commands for training exercises to enable the commanders to develop all forces available to them into effective integrated forces. On becoming operational, SHAPE took over all the responsibilities that previously had been assigned by the five Brussels Treaty Powers to their commanders-in-chief committee, and at that time,

Field Marshal Montgomery, who had headed the "Uniforce" organization, became the first Deputy Supreme Allied Commander Europe.

Four other NATO organizations of international military cooperation operating under the Standing Group were the Military Agency for Standardization, the NATO Defense College, Communications Agencies in Europe, and the Advisory Group for Aeronautical Research and Development. Organized early in 1951, the Standardization Agency, in London, comprised an Army Board, Navy Board, and Air Force Board, each consisting of a member from France, Great Britain, and the United States, and with accredited liaison representatives from each of the other NATO countries. The NATO Defense College was established in the fall of 1951 at the Ecole Militaire, Paris, mainly for the purpose of training officers and key civilian workers for assignments on NATO staffs.

The Communications Agencies included the European Military Communications Coordination Committee, the European Naval Communications Agency, and the European Long Line Agency, all established in Paris in August 1951, and the European Radio Frequencies Agency established in London to collect information and prepare plans for the allocation and assignment of radio frequencies. The Advisory Group on Aeronautical Research and Development (AGARD) was set up in Paris in January 1952 to advise on the coordination of the use of facilities and research workers of the NATO countries in aeronautical research and development activities of common interest.

An inevitable weakness of the international military structure was in provisions for logistic support. Initial emphasis on the creation of combat units resulted in serious shortages of service troops and of certain critical equipment necessary for the support of combat units. Each nation retained responsibility for the logistic support of its forces, and the result was a lack of flexibility in the supply system. In October 1952 SHAPE offered recommendations for an approved overall supply organization, but no organization could overcome the current lack of operational reserve stocks. Truly a coordinated international military command structure in peacetime was in itself no mean achievement. Already, with the appointment of a supreme commander for Europe, the Allies had accomplished even before the outbreak of a possible European war what had taken three and one-half years to bring about in World War I, and, so far as the United States was concerned, two years (although an embryonic headquarters had been established eight months earlier) in World War II. Shortcomings of Western European defense were chiefly logistical. Success or failure of the North Atlantic Treaty hinged immediately on the availability of matériel resources to back up plans for defense.[9]

Mutual Defense Assistance Program

Late in 1949 the United States began a long-range program of providing military equipment and technical assistance to foreign countries. Once more the program was a broad, coordinated effort, and once again it operated on the basis of grants rather than loans. Its peculiarity was that it had not depended upon a shooting war to bring it into being. Now the objective was to build up the strength of peacetime allies in order to deter further aggression if possible or to stop it more effectively if it came.

Through the whole eleven-year period, 1940–1951, the total outlay of the United States for foreign assistance of all kinds, economic as well as military, aggregated $82 billion. Seven-eighths of this amount had been in grants, the remainder in loans and credits.[10]

If the Korean attack had in fact been planned deliberately in the Kremlin, it might have been done to detract matériel assistance from other countries. If so, the result in the long run had been the opposite. While demands for equipment in Korea delayed shipments to Europe and other areas, the attack there also served to magnify the importance of the general programs of assistance, so that objectives tended to be raised rather than lowered because of it. From June 1950 to the end of December 1952 the United States furnished $12.9 billion in aid to foreign countries. Military grants amounted to over $4.6 billion of that total. For the first year since 1945 grants for military assistance exceeded those for economic assistance: in 1952 $2.7 billion went for military assistance and $2 billion for economic assistance.[11]

Noting the danger to the security of the United States arising from the aggressive expansionist policies of the Soviet Union on the one hand, and the lack of military strength in the non-Communist nations on the other, the National Security Council in July 1948 recommended to the president that consideration be given to the development of a comprehensive program of military assistance. The president accepted this recommendation and asked the secretary of state to explore ways of strengthening foreign nations, particularly those of Western Europe, with which American security was closely identified. This action undoubtedly was a response to the rising apprehensiveness of Soviet intentions, which had sprung up anew with the Communist coup d'état in Czechoslovakia in February 1948 and reached its climax with the imposition of the Berlin Blockade in June. Already the Vandenberg Resolution, which the Senate had adopted in June, had encouraged the formation of regional and other collective security arrangements "based on continuous self-help and mutual aid."[12] Earlier in July American representatives had begun informal talks toward that end with representatives of Canada, Great Britain, France, and the Benelux countries.

Early in January 1949 the secretary of state, secretary of defense, and Economic Cooperation administrator agreed to establish a committee, composed of a representative of each of them, to go into the details of the problem. Designated the Foreign Assistance Correlation Committee (FACC), this group had the job of surveying the world situation to determine the nature and the extent of the threat to American security arising from military weakness abroad, of evaluating the ability of the United States to provide assistance and the ability of foreign nations to use it, and of recommending the type and amount of assistance needed and the relative priorities in which it should be granted. With the assistance of the staffs of the three agencies involved, the committee reviewed the objectives of national policy on a global basis. It then had the task of developing a single program to cover all military assistance projects and of drafting and guiding through Congress the necessary legislation.

A few days after the signature of the North Atlantic Treaty (4 April 1949), the president announced his intention to ask Congress for a military aid program. The treaty itself in its third article provided, in language adopted from the Vandenberg resolution, "in order more effectively to achieve the objectives of this Treaty, the Parties, separately and jointly, by means of continuous and effective self-help and mutual aid, will maintain and develop their individual and collective capacity to resist armed attack." On the same day that he signed the instrument of ratification (25 July 1949), the president sent his recommendation to Congress for legislation to establish a mutual aid program.

In his letter of transmittal the president said, "The Soviet Union, with its violent propaganda, its manipulation of the conspirational activities of the world Communist movement, and its maintenance of one of the largest peacetime armies in history, has deliberately created an atmosphere of fear and danger."[13] He went on to refer to the troubles in Greece, the pressures on Turkey and Iran, the coup d'état in Czechoslovakia, and the Berlin Blockade. He said further that the Republic of Korea was menaced by the Communist regime in the northern part of that country. Already "many anxious governments" had requested military assistance. "Our objective," said the president, "is to see to it that these nations are equipped, in the shortest possible time, with compact and effectively trained forces capable of maintaining internal order and resisting the initial phases of external aggression." Again he said, "Helping free nations to acquire the means of defending themselves is an obligation of the leadership we have assumed in world affairs." The president requested authorizations totaling $1.4 billion for the current fiscal year.

In supporting the proposed assistance program General Bradley explained, "The strategy of deterring a potential aggressor for our own protection is the backbone for the Joint Chiefs' endorsement of this arms aid."[14]

As finally approved on 6 October, the Mutual Defense Assistance Act of 1949[15] provided for military assistance on a grant basis to parties to the North Atlantic Treaty who had requested such assistance before the passage of the Act,[16] continued the Greek-Turkish program, and provided for assistance to Iran, the Philippines, the Republic of Korea, and in the "general area" of China. Actually the program involved four types of assistance: (1) Grants of military supplies and equipment; (2) technical and training assistance; (3) provision of raw materials and machine tools with which recipient nations could increase their own production of military equipment; and (4) procurement of equipment through American military procurement agencies for cash.

The subsequent appropriation act, approved 28 October, provided $1.314

billion in appropriations and contract authority to carry out the provisions of the basic act. Additional appropriations provided for in regular and supplementary appropriation acts in September 1950 brought the total appropriations approved during the first calendar year of the new program's operation up to $6,536,510,000—approximately $5.5 billion for the North Atlantic Treaty countries, about $535 million for Greece, Turkey, and Iran, and not quite $500 million for the Far East.[17]

The Mutual Defense Assistance Act carried the proviso that economic recovery was to have priority over programs of military assistance. By 1951 the economic recovery of European nations, with the benefit of the Marshall Plan, had progressed notably, but external threats to security seemed as dangerous as ever. The Marshall Plan came to an end officially with the enactment of the Mutual Security Act, approved 10 October 1951, which brought economic and technical assistance as well as military assistance programs under the general supervision of a single director for Mutual Security. From this time the emphasis was upon military assistance. Even the economic programs frequently had to be justified as contributing toward the effective military defense of the countries concerned. The program was to end 30 June 1954.[18] The Mutual Security Act of 1952, approved 20 June, made a number of additions and amendments to the original law, but retained its principal provisions.[19]

The sending of American assistance groups to the countries designated to receive aid was one of the distinctive features of the Mutual Defense Assistance Program. Under lend-lease and other programs the United States had depended originally upon the foreign governments themselves to compute their requirements, and for representatives of those governments in Washington to make their presentations. Lend-lease missions sent overseas after late 1941 were the forerunners of the Military Assistance Advisory Groups (MAAG), which appeared upon the scene nearly a decade later. Now from the outset the impetus was to be in the other direction, and at the same time supervision on the part of the United States would be much closer. In general the military assistance advisory groups consisted of army, navy, and air force sections, each headed by a senior officer of the respective service. The senior officer, whatever his service, was chief of the MAAG. His responsibility on general policy matters was to the American ambassador or minister in the country where located, but on questions of military programming, supply, and related questions he reported, in Europe to the Joint American Military Advisory Group in London (later Military Assistance Division of U.S. European Command) and in other areas, directly to the Department of the Army as executive agency for the Joint Chiefs of Staff. Section chiefs were authorized direct communication with the ambassador, with their respective military departments in Washington, and with corresponding components of the recipient country's armed forces on questions affecting their service alone. By the end of 1950 military assistance advisory groups had been established in the United Kingdom, France, Belgium (serving also Luxembourg), Denmark, Norway, the Netherlands, Italy, and Portugal. These were in addition to the groups already established, with similar functions, in Greece and Turkey.

Procedures

Planning for annual mutual defense assistance programs began ten to twelve months before the beginning of the fiscal year in which the particular program was to be put into effect. The U.S. Joint Chiefs of Staff was the agency responsible for determining the forces to be equipped and for setting up the criteria to govern the supply programs. From the total forces approved for a country by the Joint Chiefs of Staff, the government concerned and the military assistance advisory group assigned would develop a list of overall requirements. Matériel already in the hands of that government, goods that it would be able to purchase economically, and that which would be in the process of manufacture during the time being considered would then be subtracted from the requirements. The United States would then try to provide assistance based on the net deficiency. For the fiscal year 1953 program, for example, the Joint Chiefs of Staff in July 1951 developed a time schedule for foreign nations and the respective military assistance advisory groups to present their requests and recommendations. At the same time the Joint Chiefs issued the criteria that would determine the types and number of forces they would consider eligible for military aid and the types of equipment that could or could not be included.[20]

As with the initial programs, the Office of Military Assistance reviewed and consolidated the revised tentative programs and again passed them on to the director for Mutual Security. With his approval they became a part of the Mutual Security Program for presentation to Congress. Proposed legislation to authorize the program in the House of Representatives was referred to various committees and representatives from the Department of Defense and the military services were called upon to explain and defend the proposed programs. It was common for hearings to go on before the committees of both Houses simultaneously and at times an individual would testify before both on the same day. After all this testimony had been completed and the legislation, changed in varying degrees, finally had been approved by both Houses of Congress and by the president, the end was still not yet in sight. Evidence again had to be marshalled to convince members of the two appropriations committees that the funds authorized in the previous legislation really ought to be appropriated. The appropriation bill was likely to embrace another round of cutting and usually some delays in making the funds available. For the fiscal year 1953 program Truman requested $7.9 billion for military assistance. In the Mutual Security Act of 1952, approved by the president on 20 June 1952, Congress authorized $6.431 billion. The Mutual Security Appropriation Act, 1953 (Title III of the Supplemental Appropriation Act, 1953) passed by Congress on 7 July and approved by the president on 15 July 1952 reduced the amount to $5.995 billion—a reduction of 22 percent from the president's request.[21]

In the case of the fiscal year 1953 program, the Joint Chiefs of Staff were unable to reach agreement on the apportionment of the funds that Congress appropriated and the director for Mutual Security allocated. In August 1952 the secretary of defense had to resolve the impasse by recommending apportionment of the full appropriation on a percentage basis without approving specifically the programs of any of the services. After all the months of close figuring, screening, and revising, programs now had to be based on an arbitrary division of available funds.

After approval of adjusted ceilings, the secretary of defense (Office of Military Assistance) would order the military departments to prepare refined country programs. After more consultation and after approval by the foreign governments, at last the refined programs—the fourth round of programming—would be forwarded by the military departments to the Office of Military Assistance for review and consolidation and submission to the director of Mutual Security. Still the programs could not be finally set until funds became available. After approval of the programs, the director for Mutual Security allocated the funds for military assistance to the Department of Defense, which in turn allocated them to the military departments.

Four or five cycles of programming and screening through half a dozen or more headquarters and staff agencies often were not enough. At times the compulsion to revise followed country programs to the very ships carrying the matériel away. The Oversea Supply Division at the New York Port of Embarkation reported that between 7 January and 31 March 1953 it received eighty-seven telephone calls relating to hold orders, change orders, or the remarking of MDAP cargo.[22]

The very nature of military activities, where emergencies must be accepted as normal and adjustment to changing conditions as routine, requires flexibility in execution as well as in planning. Yet the complexities of military activities also require firm planning and resolute execution in order to reduce the imponderables and the unforeseen eventualities to a magnitude that can be met without sacrificing major objectives. Constant change in plans and orders for the shipment of matériel was costly in time and money—and in the frayed nerves of people caught in the backwash of countermands. In a caustic letter to the chief of the Supply Division of G-4, Colonel Charles C. Peterson, Chief of the Oversea Supply Division at the New York Port of Embarkation, wrote that constant change "places this Division, which is a direct G-4 Representative, in an untenable position with the Technical Services, as we are the ones to give them instructions and then when we constantly change and revise, they become suspicious as to whether or not we know what we are doing."[23]

As was the case under the lend-lease program during World War II, appropriations for foreign military aid were made to the president.[24] During the earlier experience the War Department had insisted that it would have been preferable to have appropriations made directly to the technical services concerned in the manner of regular Army appropriations.[25] But the old system remained in effect. With the appointment of a director of Mutual Security, the president ordered that funds appropriated to the president should "be deemed to be allocated to the Director for Mutual Security without further action by the President."[26] The president retained authority to transfer funds from one area to another. Now the director for Mutual Security in effect held a position analogous to that of the lend-lease administrator after establishment of that office in October 1941. But the newer effort at military aid was more closely coordinated and its execution was more closely bound with the regular procurement and supply procedures. Appropriations still were separate, but in effect MDAP amounted to a separate bank account against which the procurement agencies could draw checks in financing an integrated overall procurement program. During World War II manufacturers at times had to satisfy foreign purchasing agencies who had placed contracts directly with them and the lend-lease administrator or the president for lend-lease commitments, as well as the various U.S. military agencies having procurement responsibilities. Now all procurement went through the same people, whether the eventual purpose was for the U.S. forces or for foreign military aid.

General Policies

Objectives and conditions for foreign military aid programs that the National Security Council had laid down in 1948 remained valid in 1953. These included the assumption that aid programs should not interfere with the fulfillment of mobilization reserve requirements as determined by the Joint Chiefs of Staff, and that they should be consistent with approved joint strategic plans. The council recognized, however, that conditions might develop into overriding political considerations—involving the morale or internal security of recipient nations, or the protection of specific American interests abroad—that would make it advisable in exceptional cases to modify the strict application of those principles. A further general policy was that assistance programs should be based upon assumptions of self-help and reciprocal assistance on the part of recipient nations, but also that continuing support on the part of the United States should be planned to include the supply of spare parts, replacement, and ammunition for as long as it was in the interest of American security to do so. Military aid programs were to be integrated with programs of economic assistance and carried out in such a way that they would not jeopardize the economic stability either of the United States or of other participating nations. The other countries participating in the programs would be encouraged to develop their armaments industries with a view to supplying their own equipment when economic conditions permitted. At the same time they would be encouraged to standardize their weapons and other equipment, and, insofar as practicable, to conform to types accepted by the United States. In return for military assistance, the recipient countries would be expected to furnish strategic raw materials to the United States when practicable.[27]

Before supply action could begin on the original fiscal year 1950 MDAP, several policy decisions had to be taken. As mentioned previously, a bilateral agreement had to be signed with each recipient country before it could receive grant aid. Nine hundred million dollars in appropriations and contract authority remained frozen until the president could approve an integrated defense plan for the countries of the North Atlantic Treaty Organization. The Departments of State and Defense had to make agreements covering the details of local administration and operation in the various countries such as railway transportation, the operation of motor pools, local communications, and other questions. It had to be determined whether newly manufactured equipment or World War II types would be furnished foreign nations, and on this point the secretary of the army decided in June 1949 in favor of sending World War II equipment and using new equipment to replace it. The technical services had to adjust their personnel to handle the increasing workloads that would result from the new programs. An executive order had to be agreed upon between the State and Defense departments and submitted to the president for signature to direct the execution of the act. Funds had to be allocated. Programs had to be approved.[28]

The original pricing pattern established by the law authorizing aid to Greece and Turkey was retained under the Mutual Defense Assistance Act. This provided that surplus property should be furnished without cost except for rehabilitation and delivery charges. According to the original policy, items taken from stocks needed for maximum retention level requirements but not needed for minimum retention levels were to be charged at the 1945 price plus delivery costs. However, in order to prevent the Army from being short-changed, the policy was changed by a provision that for all issues from stocks the charge against MDAP funds would be the estimated actual current replacement cost plus packing, handling, transportation, and administrative costs. Still, it was difficult to arrive at accurate estimates of current replacement costs. This was particularly true in cases where a new or modified model had replaced an older item being provided under aid programs. Later G-4 established the policy that the estimated current replacement cost would be computed as 170 percent of the gross average acquisition cost of the item except in cases where a modern version of the item was being acquired at a less cost in which case the latter price would apply.[29]

Title to all MDAP supplies remained with the Army until the goods reached shipside at the port of embarkation if they were to be transported on foreign vessels. In cases where the Department of the Army was responsible for the oversea shipment of the supplies in American vessels, title remained with the Army until the equipment was delivered in the foreign country at the end of the ship's tackle.[30] The law required that at least fifty percent of the gross tonnage of MDAP cargoes should go in American ships.[31] Actually about seventy-three percent of the MDAP supplies shipped during the period up to 1 June 1953 were transported in American commercial shipping.[32] In addition, the Department of the Army carried no insurance on MDAP cargoes. All losses or damage during shipment, prior to the transfer of title, were chargeable to MDAP funds.[33]

The Army's policy was that MDAP equipment should be new or it should have the appearance and serviceability of new equipment. The department was sensitive about reports of unsatisfactory equipment arriving in foreign countries, because such occasions, even if infrequent, were likely to provide effective ammunition for unfriendly propaganda.[34]

A bigger problem in many ways that of keeping equipment serviceable after it had been delivered to foreign forces. The imposition of American nomenclature and supply procedures on people untrained in their use led to confusion as assorted pieces of equipment and parts began to arrive in faraway places. The old problem of spare parts appeared again, with the added complications of storage and cataloging, which made it difficult for local supply personnel to locate the parts when needed—or even to be sure of what they had. Under the fiscal year 1950 and 1951 programs, a year's supply of spare parts (concurrent) for each programmed end item was shipped as much as possible with the item. Additional spare parts had to be shipped for the maintenance of World War II equipment that the countries had received prior to MDAP. The 1951 program originally included an additional six months' supply of parts for the maintenance of equipment programmed under the previous year's program, but this was eliminated in June 1951. Some advisory groups, particularly those in Greece and Turkey, had maintained that the policy on shipping parts would result in unbalanced stocks and the buildup of unneeded parts. The experience of 1951 seemed to bear this out. Differences in use, storage, maintenance standards, climate and other local conditions led to considerable differences in requirements for specific parts, and excesses did begin to build up in various areas. A new policy announced in November 1951 provided that for the fiscal year 1952 and later programs a year's supply of concurrent spare parts still would be programmed for all end items in the program. But maintenance spare parts, i.e., those other than the ones provided for in the concurrent programs, would be supplied only on the basis of requisitions forwarded to the Oversea Supply Division at the port of embarkation. Once the supply of parts was exhausted in the United States it would be necessary for them to buy parts on the world market if they could not arrange for local manufacture.[35]

In addition to provision for furnishing finished military items, the mutual security program also included aid intended to stimulate the local production of arms in foreign countries. The policy of Director for Mutual Security Harold E. Stassen was that when aid was to be given for the production of specific military equipment, that equipment would have to meet the standards of NATO in quantity and quality or would have to be acceptable to the military assistance advisory groups concerned. This type of aid would be deemed economically and militarily justifiable both according to criteria of NATO and to those of the Joint Chiefs of Staff. The United States would furnish only such materials and other assistance as had to be obtained from dollar sources in order to meet delivery schedules.[36] One type of item in high demand under this "Defense Support Program" was machine tools. The Army's policy, however, opposed releasing machine tools from its reserve for foreign aid programs.[37]

The Mutual Defense Assistance Program was not adapted to furnishing military equipment to allies under wartime conditions. War would not wait for the months of programming, reprogramming, revision, coordination, and multilateral approval. It was ironic that when the Korean War came, the farreaching program of foreign military aid that was just beginning to become effective offered no help in supplying allies willing to participate in the collective action in Korea. Plans and programs aimed solely at building strength for war left void the area of serious consideration on what action should be taken in case the war against which all this preparation was being taken should in fact break out. A year after the Korean attack had pointed so forcibly to the need for such plans, none had yet been drawn up. In March 1951 G-4 had stated, "Up-to-date guidance for war-time aid to allies is required at earliest practicable date by G-4 and Technical Services."[38]

The Scope of Mutual Defense Assistance

The Mutual Defense Assistance Program got off to a slow start. Most foreign aid actually delivered during fiscal year 1950 was that which already had been scheduled under previous programs. It was obvious from the beginning that a large part of the funds appropriated for fiscal year 1951 could not be committed for specific programs before the end of that fiscal year. The original act itself had not been approved until 6 October 1949, the appropriation act was approved three weeks later, and the required bilateral agreements were not completed with the European countries until 27 January 1951.[39] The fiscal year was half gone and supply action had not even commenced. Foreign requirements brought back by preliminary survey teams could not be reprogrammed until the State and Defense departments agreed upon criteria. The military assistance advisory groups would be able to contribute little to reprogramming for fiscal year 1950 in the time left to them after their arrival in foreign countries. Procedures still had to be worked out for meeting all the administrative problems involved in such a complex undertaking. Considering all these things, General Larkin recommended that fiscal year 1950 funds be carried over to the next fiscal year. The 1951 MDAP should be limited, in his view, to provide necessary training, the replacement of training ammunition and other consumed items, spare parts, and administrative expenses; new funds requested for the next fiscal year he felt should not exceed $100 million. Any further substantial program of reequipping selected foreign armies should be deferred to fiscal year 1952.[40] Actually the General Appropriations Act passed in September 1950 contained $1.223 billion for MDAP (for all services), and already, a month after the commitment of ground forces to action in Korea, President Truman had asked Congress for additional funds for foreign military aid. Here was clear testimony of the stimulus to foreign aid that the Korean attack had provided. The Supplemental Appropriations Act, passed less than three weeks after the General Appropriations Act, included an additional $4 billion for the Mutual Defense Assistance Program—nearly a billion more than that provided in the act for the expansion of the Army itself and for its conduct of operations in Korea. In addition, nearly $300 million (for all services) remained unobligated from the 1950 appropriation. At the end of June 1950 the Army had obligated $470 million and spent only $25.6 million of the $524.8 million in MDAP funds that had been allocated to it.[41]

Actual shipments under the Mutual Defense Assistance Program did not begin until March 1950. By the time of the Korean attack the Army had programmed $1.0326 billions' worth of equipment for MDAP, had initiated supply action on $155.1 million of this, and had shipped $19.2 millions' worth—of which $2 million was from excess stocks not charged against the MDAP appropriation. Total tonnage shipped by all services up to that time was about 139,000 measurement tons. Ordnance equipment and Quartermaster supplies made up the bulk of Army shipments. Shipments rose considerably in succeeding months, but deliveries fell several months behind approved programs.[42] Still, all deliveries other than aircraft and ships delivered under their own power reached a total of 1.6 million measurement tons by the end of June 1951. This included 4,480 tanks and other combat vehicles, 2,930 artillery pieces, 18,837 general purpose vehicles, and about 400,000 small arms and machine guns. Sixty-two percent of the tonnage went to Western Europe, twenty-four percent went to the Near East, and fourteen percent went to the Far East. Only about $1.2 billion of the $5.22 billion appropriated for the year were used in fiscal year 1951. About one-fourth of that year's grant assistance represented deliveries from reserve stocks.[43]

The total of MDAP funds made available to the Army through 31 December 1952 amounted to $8.3 billion. Disbursements up to that time totaled only $2.89 billion, and unpaid obligations totaled $4.14 billion.[44] Total Army shipments through 30 April 1953 included supplies and equipment valued at $3.66 billion (including surplus property not chargeable to MDAP funds). By this time these shipments included 25,810 tanks and combat vehicles, 77,515 pieces of electronics and signal equipment, 136,114 motor transport vehicles, 24,397 artillery pieces, 1,459,228 small arms and machine guns, 725,729,000 rounds of small arms ammunition, and 18,279,000 rounds of artillery ammunition. Army shipments of approximately five million measurement tons comprised about seventy-five percent of all MDAP shipments. All this was in addition to the 25 million tons of supplies and equipment that had been shipped by this time to Korea.[45]

The cumulative value of matériel recorded as requisitioned (i.e., called forward) as of 31 May 1953 totaled $5.058 billion—sixty-one percent of the total fiscal years 1950–1953 programs of $8.3 billion. A growing backlog of materiél requisitioned but not shipped reached a value of $1.225 billion at the end of May 1953.[46] By early 1953 it was clear that fulfillment of mutual defense assistance programs was running at least eighteen months behind— about the lead time required for initial procurement of items most difficult to manufacture. The hope was that the total shipments by 31 December 1953 would be equal in value to the fiscal year 1950–1952 programs ($6.246 billion). This did not mean that all items included in those programs would be shipped by that time, but only that the monetary value, made up by the shipment of available items from the 1953 program, would be equivalent. Similarly G-4's estimate was that cumulative shipments through December 1954 might be equal in value to the fiscal year 1950–1953 programs ($8.293 billion). But it was expected that the 1950–1953 program itself would be only about ninety percent completed by the end of 1954. Some items already programmed probably could not be shipped before late 1955. But time pushed even those tentative goals further into the future.[47] By 1 June 1953 estimates had been revised to assume completion of shipments equal in value to the 1950–1952 program no sooner than March 1954, nor of the whole 1950–1953 program before June 1955. Even the shipping rates that had been calculated to meet that schedule were not being kept.[48]

Delays in completing mutual defense assistance programs could be attributed to the fact that current military production in the United States had not yet reached the point where it could provide all the equipment needed both for foreign aid and for operations in Korea at the same time. Closely related to this were the increasing worldwide matériel requirements for the Army's own forces in these critical times and the relative priority that had to be assigned to MDAP. Now with the signing of the truce in Korea on 27 July 1953, the outlook suddenly became brighter for completion of foreign aid programs ahead of previously estimated target dates. Now that combat consumption would not be claiming huge quantities of ammunition and losses of tanks, trucks, radios, and other equipment, it was reasonable to expect that MDAP would be the beneficiary to much of the equipment that Far East Command would not be needing. This at least would provide a cushion against the accumulation of large stocks of surplus property for a while.

In addition to the grants of military equipment discussed above, other equipment was going to foreign governments during this period on a cash purchase basis under the provision of the Mutual Defense Assistance Act (Section 408e) that in effect put the procurement machinery of the Army and the other military services at the disposal of allied governments for their purchases in this country. Over 1,000 requests from forty-nine foreign countries for reimbursable assistance of this kind had been received through the end of June 1952. As of 31 October 1952 forty-one foreign governments had made purchases of equipment valued at $601 million, of which $185 million was for Army equipment. By 30 April 1953 arrangements had been completed with forty-five countries for the purchase of $654 millions' worth of equipment, including $224 million in Army equipment. This called for no financial outlay on the part of the United States, but it was an additional claim on matériel resources of this country.[49]

Another objective of the Mutual Security Program was to stimulate the buildup of local defense industries in participating countries. One of the aspects of the original Mutual Defense Assistance Program was provision for furnishing tools and materials to foreign countries under what was referred to as "Additional Military Production" projects. MDAP appropriations for fiscal years 1950 and 1951 each contained about $500 million for these projects. The hope was that by a small American contribution aimed at eliminating bottlenecks such as shortages of materials and machine tools, European production facilities that otherwise would be idle might add many times the value of that contribution in finished military goods. Each project went through a long process of screening for military suitability, technical feasibility, availability of licenses and patents, availability of labor and technical skills, production resources, and other factors. Indeed the screening was so fine that little got through it. Only about $26 million of assistance for this purpose had been granted by 31 May 1951. While the value of the final production expected from the projects approved was about $321 million, this clearly was not putting much of the European industrial capacity into military production. By the end of 1951 "Additional Military Production" practically was defunct. Some American planners felt that European countries were "dragging their feet" in pushing local military production in anticipation of receiving finished items from the United States under the grant assistance program.[50]

But there were other ways of achieving the same end. One of these was through "offshore procurement." This was a part of the regular end-item grant program, but the procurement orders were placed in foreign countries instead of in the United States. It thus was possible to kill two or three birds with one stone. The finished equipment being furnished a foreign government would be the same type and quality as though it had been manufactured in the United States. But since it was being produced in foreign countries, military production in those countries would be stimulated. Moreover, the drain on American resources and industrial facilities at a time when so many demands had to be met would be relieved. By 31 December 1951 the three services had programmed over $500 million for the offshore procurement of ammunition, spare parts, and auxiliary vessels. Over half of this amount was for Army procurement, and the Department of the Army was designated executive agency for the coordination of offshore procurement activities among the three services. The commander in chief, Europe, in turn became the executive agent for the European area. In May 1952 the Army, Navy, and Air Force commanders in Europe established the Joint Coordinating Board for Offshore Procurement, and they joined with the U.S. Special Representative in Europe in setting up a secretariat in the latter's office to serve as a central statistical office on offshore procurement.[51]

A detailed study of the fiscal year 1953 Mutual Defense Assistance Program by the U.S. Special Representative in Europe submitted in September 1952 carried with it recommendations for a far-reaching offshore procurement program in Europe. The Army's share of this procurement for the fiscal year would have been $731.8 million. Now the pendulum was swinging the other way. Army planners pointed to the necessity of retaining sufficiently large orders in the United States to maintain its production base. Pressure for additional offshore procurement brought a proposal for the Ordnance Corps to absorb for U.S. Army use some $209.5 million worth of ammunition items that had been overprocured for the MDAP 1952 program and then had been listed in the fiscal year 1953 program. To this G-4 objected, but was overruled. Charging these items against Army appropriations now made the funds available for further MDAP procurement. Instructions for procurement of ammunition, some other ordnance items, and some Signal Corps items in December 1952 brought the total fiscal year 1953 offshore procurement program for U.S. Army, Europe to $605.5 million. In December 1952 the Department of the Army also authorized the procurement of $5 million worth of ammunition in Formosa for the Nationalist Government of the Republic of China, and in February 1953 authorized the procurement in Japan of forty-seven items at a cost of $35.6 million for mutual defense assistance in the Far East. Offshore procurement contracts actually placed under the fiscal year 1952 and 1953 Mutual Defense Assistance Programs totaled $1.757 billion for all services on 31 May 1953; the Army had placed $993 million of these contracts. Nearly half of the contracts, in value, had been placed in France. Great Britain and Italy were the next most important sources. Only $34 million of the amount so far contracted had been placed in the Far East—$28.6 million in Japan, and $5.8 million in Formosa.[52]

Yet another approach to encouraging the development of local military production in friendly foreign countries was the broad program of economic assistance known as "defense support" administered by the Mutual Security Agency. In effect this was a successor, on a much broader basis, to the Additional Military Support projects. Virtually all economic aid now had to be justified as contributing to defense support. It was administered in much the same way as the previous economic assistance given under the Economic Cooperation Administration, but the emphasis had been shifted away from economic recovery per se to the building of production for military support. This made the objective of the former Additional Military Support program—the providing of scarce materials and tools—the major objective while avoiding the tangle of screening for individual projects that had contributed to the suffocation of the earlier effort.

Offshore procurement was the responsibility of the military. Defense support was the responsibility principally of the Mutual Security Agency. Secretary of Defense Lovett explained the difference between these two approaches as follows:

> Offshore procurement, as used by the military departments, refers to the purchase outside of the continental limits of end items which we are permitted to deliver to the NATO groups or to other friendly countries around the world.
> Military support, or defense support, or economic aid, as you choose in

this matter, applies to that form of procurement which deals mainly with raw materials or similar items which when delivered to an ally, permit that ally to do the work himself on the manufacture of certain forms of and items needs.

The difference, therefore, is essentially between the procurement by this country of the completed end item abroad, which is offshore procurement, whereas defense support, as used in this act, applies to the provision of raw materials, tools in some instances, and similar items which go into the manufacturing process by which the foreign ally uses his own labor, carries his own overhead and produces an end item for his particular use.[53]

Programs of offshore procurement and defense support were not without their objectionable features. It was possible that the emphasis being placed upon military production instead of upon general economic improvement might have unfortunate long-term consequences in which apparent economic health would be found to be without solid foundations. Under certain circumstances, where idle industrial plans and manpower were to be found, and a country was unable to expand its own military budget, there was an opportunity for American military buyers to place dollar contracts and thus to stimulate the use of idle resources, increase employment, and provide much needed dollar exchange while obtaining the required military equipment. But often the economic and political objectives of improved conditions and higher morale were in conflict with the military procurement objective of obtaining certain needed equipment of good quality at reasonable prices. In a situation such as that found in England, where the economy already was working at near capacity and the local military budget already was at a satisfactory level, the effect of American offshore procurement was to divert industrial capacity and raw materials away from production for civilian consumption or long-range, dollar-earning export markets. In those circumstances the result was likely to be a net lowering of the standard of living, and to that extent, a nullification of the effects of the earlier Marshall Plan. One leading British industrialist told a member of a Mutual Security Program survey team: "We're converting some of our very scarce capital structure to get your OSP dollars. We are willing to do it, if your people feel it essential, but we're worried. We know that as soon as your own munitions production lines catch up on their contracts and need more to keep them going, neither your Congress nor your military will want to justify placing contracts here for goods you can make in the United States."[54]

Some observers saw in the growing offshore procurement program a danger of too-prominent participation of military officers in foreign economic policies. Clearly procurement implied certain controls. It was more than a matter of going out to buy something on the open market. Specifications had to be met, delivery schedules set up, inspections entertained. American military advisers appearing in most of the countries of the free world, military procurement officers dealing with foreign industrialists, military officers, and government officials might, unless handled with skillful restraint, contribute to a certain measure of popular acceptance of the Communist propaganda that American intentions were purely imperialistic. Some Europeans thought that Americans still had their eyes too close to the present and were seeking quick results at the expense of more fundamental long-range objectives.[55] Whether such interpretations were valid or not, they had to be taken into account in developing an effective American policy. Subsidies granted with conditions implying ulterior motives could defeat their own higher purposes. Even gifts freely given, if too obviously granted as alms from the powerful to the weak, might injure national pride more than they helped national defense. Only a mutuality of purpose and effort, based upon national self-respect, could be expected to turn the resources of the free world to common defense. Such was the appeal of an arrangement like the North Atlantic Treaty Organization.

By 1960 France, Germany, and the United Kingdom had become militarily self-supporting. No further grant aid was programmed for those countries other than small amounts to complete earlier commitments. Soon the only U.S. military aid still going directly to NATO countries was that for Greece and Turkey. All the rest was for American participation in various cost-sharing programs—for the construction and operation of facilities, contributions to combined development programs, and the maintenance of international headquarters. In the eleven years from the founding of NATO in 1949 through fiscal year 1960, total expenditures of the United States for military assistance to NATO countries amounted to $14 billion, while expenditures of other NATO countries on their own defenses totaled $114 billion. Whatever the difficulties in the military aid program, it clearly was serving the stated purposes: (1) modernization of the NATO defense forces while maintaining the effectiveness of forces already developed; (2) inducing countries capable of doing so to assume responsibility for their own matériel and training needs; and (3) encouragement of multilateral joint efforts in the coordinated development, standardization, and economical production of the best available modern weapons.[56]

Notes

1. *First Annual Report,* Supreme Allied Commander, Europe (Paris, 2 April 52), 9–11.
2. *Statement of General Alfred M. Gruenther, CofS SHAPE, 25 March 52, Hearings before House Committee on Foreign Affairs Mutual Security Act Extension,* 82d Cong., 2d sess., 237; for comparison of equipment of Soviet and U.S. divisions, see Louis B. Ely, *The Red Army Today* (Harrisburg, Pa., 1951), 261.
3. U.S. Dept. of Army, *Handbook on the Soviet and Satellite Armies,* March 1953, pamphlet no. 30-50-1, 1:79–85; Drew Middleton, "Soviet Re-Equips Force in Germany," *New York Times,* September 11, 1952, 4-C.
4. See Harry Schwartz in *New York Times,* 27 October 1952, 6-C; 2 November 1952, 38; 6 January 1953, 49-C.
5. Harry Schwartz, *Russia's Soviet Economy* (New York, 1950), 332–42, 347–50; idem, *The Red Phoenix: Russia Since World War II* (New York, 1961), 106–90; George Kish, *Economic Atlas of the Soviet Union* (Ann Arbor, Mich., 1960), 1–10c.
6. Unless otherwise noted, this section is based on the following: *The NATO Handbook,*

(London, 1952), 18–29 and the 1963 *Handbook* edition, 20–36; *NATO, Facts about the North Atlantic Treaty Organization* (Paris, 1962), 3–60; U.S. Dept. of State, *NATO: North Atlantic Treaty Organization, Its Development and Significance*, State Dept. Publ. 4630, Aug. 1952, 17–20; *Statement of William H. Draper, Jr., U.S. Special Representative in Europe, 24 Mar. 52, Mutual Security Act Extension, Hearings before House Committee on Foreign Relations*, 82d Cong., 2d sess., 215–34; *Statement of Frank C. Nash, Asst. Secy. of Defense, 19 Mar. 53, Mututal Security Act Extension, Hearings before House Comm on Foreign Affairs*, 83d Cong., 1st sess., 23–26; *Statement of General Alfred M. Gruenther, CofS, SHAPE, 25 Mar. 52, Mutual Security Act Extension, Hearings before House Comm on Foreign Affairs*, 82d Cong., 2d sess., 235–67; *Testimony of General Alfred M. Gruenther, CofS, Allied Powers Europe, 9, 22 July 1951, Hearings before a Subcommittee of Committee on Foreign Relations, U.S. Senate*, 82d Cong., 1st sess., on U.S. Economic and Military Assistance to Free Europe, 1–11, 265; "Annual Report to Standing Group NATO," Supreme Allied Commander, Europe, (Paris, 30 May 53), 17–18; U.S. Dept. of Defense, "Semiannual Report of the Secretary of Defense," 1 Jan.–30 June 1951, 59–60; Thorsten V. Kalijarvi and Francis O. Wilcox, "The Organizational Framework of the North Atlantic Treaty," *American Journal of International Law* 54 (Jan. 1950): 155–61.

7. "First Annual Report," Supreme Allied Commander, Europe (Paris, 2 Apr. 52), 21–26; Protocol of North Atlantic Treaty and Tripartite Declaration Regarding the European Defense Community; "U.S. Will Help Arm Bonn After Europe Implements Face," *New York Times*, 10 Apr. 53, p. 1 plus; "Germans Go Ahead on Army Planning," *New York Times*, 19 Apr. 53, p. 17.

8. *NATO Facts and Figures* (Brussels: NATO Information Service, 1969), 34–37.

9. Kalijarvi and Wilcox, "Organizational Framework of NATO"; Semiannual Report of the Secretary of Defense, January 1–June 30, 1951, 59–60; *The NATO Handbook* (London, 1952), 18–29; *NATO: Facts about the North Atlantic Treaty Organization* (Paris, 1962), 3–60.

10. U.S. Dept. of State, *Foreign Aid by the United States Government, 1940–51*, (Nov. 1952), v, vi, 1–2.

11. U.S. Dept. of Commerce, *Foreign Aid by the U.S. Government, Basic Data through December 31, 1952*, i.

12. Quoted in U.S. Dept. of State, *NATO: North Atlantic Treaty Organization, Its Development and Significance*, State Dept. Publ. 4630, Aug. 1952, 8–9.

13. *Message of the President of the United States Transmitting Recommendation for the Enactment of Legislation Authorizing Military Aid to the Nations of Western Europe*, 81st Cong., 1st sess., 25 July 1949, House Doc. 276.

14. *Statement of General Omar N. Bradley, CofS USA, 29 July 49, Hearings before House Committee on Foreign Affairs, Mutual Defense Assistance Act of 1949*, 81st Cong., 1st sess.

15. P.L. 621, 81st Cong. (S. 3809).

16. I.e., The United Kingdom, France, Belgium, the Netherlands, Luxembourg, Denmark, Norway, and Italy; Canada, Iceland, and Portugal so far had made no requests for military assistance.

17. "Third Semiannual Report to Congress on the MDAP" (6 Oct 50–31 Mar 51), 82d Cong., 1st sess., House Doc. 179, D/S Publ. 4291, Gen. For. Pol. Series 59, released July 1951, 1–2.

18. P.L. 165, 82d Cong., 10 Oct. 51.

19. P.L. 400, 82d Cong., 20 June 52.

20. *Statement of General of the Army Omar N. Bradley, Chairman, JCS, 13 Mar. 52, Hearings before House Committee on Foreign Affairs, Mutual Security Act Extension*, 82d Cong., 2d sess., 24–25; *Statement of Maj. Gen. George H. Olmsted, Dir. Office of Military Assistance, OSD, 26 Mar. 52, Hearings before Senate Committee on Foreign Relations, Mutual Security Act of 1952*, 82d Cong., 2d sess., 324–26; SR 795–200–1, "General Procedure for Furnishing Military Assistance to Foreign Governments." 9 Jan. 50, and Change 1, 7 Feb. 50, Change 2, 27 Mar. 50, Change 3, 14 Apr. 50, Change 4, 31 July 50, Change 5, 1 Feb. 51, and Change 6, 15 Feb. 51, and other Special Regulations in the SR 795–200 series relating to specific countries; John O. Bell, lecture, Industrial College of the Armed Forces,, 13 Feb. 50, L50–91, 7–9; *Testimony of General J. Lawton Collins, CofS, 31 July 51, Hearings before Committee on Foreign Relations and Committee on Armed Services, U.S. Senate, Mutual Security Act of 1951*, 82d Cong., 1st sess., on S. 1782, 199–200, 270–74; Stanley L. Scott, "The Military Aid Program," *Annals of the American Academy of Political and Social Science* 278 (Nov. 1951): 52–53.

21. *Hearings before Committee on Foreign Relations and Committee on Armed Services, U.S. Senate, Mutual Security Act of 1951*, 82d Cong., 1st sess.; *Hearings before Senate Committee on Foreign Relations, Mutual Security Act*, 82d Cong., 2d sess.; *Mutual Security Appropriation Act*, 1953; P.L. 547, 82d Cong., 15 July 1952.

22. OSNYP, Col. Charles C. Peterson, Chief Oversea Supply Div. NYPE, to Chief Supply Div. OACofS G-4, attn Colonel Richard K. Boyd, 3 Apr. 53: "Excessive Holds and Remarks," and 1st ind, Colonel J. B. Corbett, Chief FMA Br, to Chief Oversea Supply Div. 29 May 53. Copies in G-4 FMA hist. files, no. 15, "Delayed Shipments."

23. Colonel Charles C. Peterson to Chief Supply Div. OACofS, G-4, 3 Apr. 53.

24. Mutual Security Appropriation Act, 1953, Title III, P.L. 547, 82d Cong., 15 July 52.

25. See Richard M. Leighton and Robert W. Coakley, *"Global Logistics and Strategy:* 1941–43," chap. 3 in U.S. Army in World War II," Office of the Chief of Military History, Dept. of Army, Washington, D.C.

26. Executive Order 10300, 1 Nov. 51, as amended by Exec. Order 10368, 30 June 53; see statement of Robert A. Lovett, Secty. of Defense, 21 Mar. 52, *Mutual Security Act Extension, Hearings before House Committee on Foreign Affairs,* 82d Cong., 2d sess., 182; and presentation by Mr. Burton, Conference brief, 15 Sept. 49, U.S. Dept. of Army.

27. U.S. Dept. of Army, "Basic Policies of the Department of the Army" (DA-PB-50), Change 11, May 1953, 24, Change 10, Jan. 1953, 25.

28. U.S. Dept. of Army, Memo for record, 3 Nov. 49, conference in office of the assistant secy. of the army.

29. Mutual Defense Assistance Act of 1949. Sec. 403 (c); presentation by Lt. Col. Offer, conference brief, 15 Sept. 49, U.S. Dept. of Army; U.S. Dept. of Army, "Supply Supplement to the Troop Program and Troop List," 1 Aug. 50, 55, U.S. Dept. of Army, "Logistics Policies and Priorities," 1 Nov. 52, 71–72.

30. SR 795-200-1, par. 20.

31. Mutual Defense Assistance Act of 1949, Sec. 409.

32. U.S. Dept. of Army, "Army Foreign Military Aid," Supply Planning Branch, G-4, 1 June 53, 24.

33. SR 795-200-1, par. 21.

34. DF G4/D3–32627, Brig. Gen. Sam C. Russell, DACofS G-4 FMA, to chiefs of technical services, 28 May 53: "Shipment of Unserviceable MDA Equipment," and memo for record, Lt. Col. Oppelt, 27 May 53.

35. Included with Memo G4/D3, Chief FMA Branch, for DACofS G-4 FMA, 9 Jan. 53, "MDAP Spare Parts Policy"; Operation M-DAP, FY 1953, OS Div, 5; Seminar, ICAF, 17 Dec. 51; Interview with Colonel Emons B. Whisner, formerly member of Joint American Military Mission for Aid to Turkey, and formerly executive officer of MAAG—IndoChina, 29 July 53; U.S. Dept. of Army, "G-4 Critical Problems," Problem No. 35, 16 Mar. 51; U.S. Dept. of Army, "Report of Critical Problems," 31 Dec. 52, and Problem No. G-4-72, "Responsibilities of Foreign Governments for Maintenance of MDA Matériel."

36. DMA D-2/2A, Office of the Director for Mutual Security, 18 Feb. 53, "Criteria for Determining Supply and Financing Responsibility for Assistance to European Production of Military Equipment, Offshore Procurement."

37. U.S. Dept. of Army, G-4 Memo of Important Action G4/B1 36480, 19 July 50.

38. U.S. Dept. of Army, G-4 Critical Problems Report, 9 Mar. 51.

39. "U.S. Dept. of Defense Operations Under MDAP," June 1952, v.

40. DF, Lt. Gen. T. B. Larkin, director of logistics, to director of plans and operations Ops, 22 Dec. 49: "Continuation of MAP, and incl Staff Study."

41. "U.S. Dept. of Defense Operations Under MDAP," June 1952, v.

42. "U.S. Dept. of Defense, Semiannual Report of the Secretary of Defense," 1 Jan.–30 June 1950, 11; G-4 Memo of Important Actions, 3 Aug. 50, 1; U.S. Dept. of Defense, Report of Operations, MDAP, prepared by Progress Reports and Statistics Office, Secretary of Defense, 28 Aug. 50, 28, 34, 42.

43. "Third Semiannual Report to Congress on the MDAP (Oct 6, 1950–Mar 31, 1951)," House Doc. 179, 82d Cong., 1st sess. D/S Publ. 4291, General Foreign Policy Series 59, released July 1951, 4; "U.S. Dept. of Defense, Semiannual Report of the Secretary of Defense," 1 Jan.–30 June 1951, 66; *Foreign Aid by the U.S. Govt 1940–51,* 68; John D. Morris, *New York Times,* 4 May 1952, 1.

44. U.S. Dept. of Army, Progress Report 16-A, Financial Statement, D/A, Dec. 1952, 9, 33, 57.

45. "U.S. Dept. of Defense Operations Under MDAP," May 1953, ix, 33; Statement of General J. Lawton Collins, CofS, quoted in *U.S. Army Combat Forces* 3 (July 1953): 41.

46. U.S. Dept. of Army, "Army Foreign Military Aid," a monthly report prepared by Supply Planning Branch, G-4, 1 June 53, 2–3; DF, Chief FMA Branch, OACofS G4 to CofOrd, 19 June 53: "Rate of MDAP Shipments."

47. Brief, included with DF, Brig. Gen. G. C. Stewart, DACofS G-4 FMA, for Chief Control Office, 2 Jan. 53: "G-4 Problems of Major Importance, Obligations of MDAP Funds."

48. U.S. Dept. of Army, "Report of Critical Problems," 31 Dec. 52, Problem No. G4–45, "Progress of MDAP Deliveries"; *Analysis of MDAP Working Capital, Mutual Security Act Extension, Hearings before the House Committee on Foreign Affairs,* 83d Cong., 1st sess., 1287–88.

49. "The Mutual Security Program," second report of the president to Congress for the six months ending 30 June 1952, 48; ibid., six months ending 31 Dec. 1952, 14, "U.S. Dept. of Defense Operations Under MDAP," May 1953, xi.

50. Scott, "The Military Aid Program," 50; U.S. Dept. of Defense, "Semiannual Report of the Secretary of Defense," 1 Jan.–30 June 1951, 66; Seminar, ICAF, 17 Dec. 51; G-4 History Summary, 13 Dec. 51, Procurement Division: Foreign Procurement.

51. DA G-4 Historical Summary 1951–1952, Purchases Branch, Procurement Division, 3–11; "U.S. Dept. of Defense Operations Under MDAP," Dec. 1951, viii–ix.

52. Army Foreign Military Aid, 1 June 53, 9; "U.S. Dept. of Defense Operations Under MDAP," May 1953, X, 35; DA G-4 Historical Summary 1951–1952, Tab G, Purchases Branch, Procurement Division, 3–11.

53. *Statement before House Committee on Foreign Affairs, 21 Mar 52, Mutual Security Act Extension,* 82d cong., 1st sess., 180.

54. Herman Miles Somers, "Civil-Military Relations in Mutual Security," *Annals of the American Academy of Political and Social Science* 288 (July 1953): 29–30.

55. Ibid., 27–34; see also Richard M. Bissell, "Foreign Aid. What Sort? How Much? How Long?" *Foreign Affairs* 31 (Oct. 1952): 15–38.

56. U.S. Dept. of State, *Report to Congress on the Mutual Security Program for the Fiscal Year 1960,* State Dept. Publ. 7099, 1961, 20, 75.

3
U.S. Lines of Communication in Europe

Perhaps too when they begin to see that we are getting ready, and that our words are to be interpreted by our actions, they may be more likely to yield. . . . Our hopes ought not to rest on the probability of their making mistakes, but on our own caution and foresight. . . . We can afford to wait, when others cannot, because we are strong.

—Thucydides

Forces stationed in Europe, whatever their size and purpose, had to be assured supply lines that would provide them with the food, clothing, and equipment necessary for their existence and for the performance of their mission. That mission was conceived to be one of occupation and military government in Germany. In those circumstances the setting up of a line of communication was principally a problem of administration to be worked out in the way that would be most economical and efficient. Little thought, supposedly, had to be given to tactical considerations in the disposition of troops and facilities or the supply line serving them. But as soon as the military problem in Europe was seen as one of meeting threats of new aggression from the East more than one of controlling the Germans, it was necessary to revise the thinking on delivering supplies. Now thought had to be given to the continuation of effective supply in the event of a renewal of war in Europe.

Bremerhaven

In order to provide port facilities for civil and military needs in the American occupation zone of Germany after the conclusion of World War II, the United States arranged for an enclave including Bremen and Bremerhaven to be set aside under American control, and for goods to move from those ports southward across the British zone to Hesse. Bremerhaven became the military port serving American occupation forces. The line of communication connecting Bremerhaven with American installations in southwest Germany ran through Bremen-Hanover-Kassel to Frankfurt. From Frankfurt one line branched southwest to Wurzburg and Nuremberg, while another continued south through Mannheim to Karlsruhe and then turned to the southwest to Stuttgart, Augsburg, and Munich. Running generally north and south as it did, this line of communication was parallel to the boundary of the Soviet zone, and thus it lay athwart the route of advance of any major attack from East Germany. At Kassel this line of communication was within twenty miles of Soviet-occupied Thuringia. No defensible barrier protected it against possible attack from the East.[1]

For purposes of the occupation this arrangement seemed logical and satisfactory. The United States did not have to depend upon the port and transportation facilities of any other country, and the costs involved were borne by German mark funds provided under the occupation statutes. Then the Russian blockade of Berlin in 1948 opened the eyes of everyone concerned to the reality of the danger of a Communist attack. And if this needed further emphasis, the Communist attack in Korea provided it. With complete dependence on the Bremerhaven line of communications (schedules in 1951 called for the unloading of an average of 79,000 and a peak of 100,000 long tons a month by the Bremerhaven Port of Embarkation) commanders had visions of the whole American army in Germany being imperiled by a sudden thrust of Communist forces across their supply route. Now security had to supersede economy and convenience in logistical thinking, and friends had to be called upon to make other facilities available.[2]

The opening of the American line of communication across France relieved some of the pressure on Bremerhaven, and logistical dispositions began to reflect emergency war plans. With the coming into effect of the "Peace Contract" with Germany expected in 1953, at which time the German economy would be relieved of bearing the costs of military occupation, some of the financial advantages for the United States of maintaining this route of supply rather than other possible routes through Holland, Belgium, or France would be lost. The Army considered closing down the Bremerhaven Port of Embarkation altogether, but it was retained for the time being for the movement of nonrisk supplies and military personnel and their dependents, while the bulk of military supplies now would move through the French ports. The shorter overland haul from Bremerhaven still made that the more economical route, and it still seemed desirable to have an alternate evacuation port available in case of emergency.[3]

Across France

Under the stimulus of the Berlin blockade, the Logistics Division of the European Command in 1948 and early in 1949 set about investigating the possible establishment of a line of communication across France. In November 1949 the Joint Chiefs of Staff approved such a move, and straightway the European Command appointed a team under the leadership of Colonel

Mason J. Young to survey the proposed route and to meet with French military representatives to determine what installations, facilities, and services would be required. The initial plan called for the unloading of only five vessels a month, including one tanker, at La Pallice and Bordeaux, whence the cargoes would be shipped by rail to storage facilities in France or Germany. Based on a forty-five-day level of supply for 100,000 men, 100,000 tons of supplies, according to these plans, would be stored in France. It was the task of the survey team to find facilities to handle this tonnage as well as to find shop space for servicing equipment in France and a headquarters for the logistical organization that would operate the line of communication. Before the end of January 1950 the team tentatively selected, in agreement with French military authorities, facilities and storage areas in or near the port areas of Bordeaux, Rochefort, La Rochelle, and La Pallice, and forward to Fontainebleau, Verdun, and Metz. The French General Staff also recommended acceptance of American plans for stationing 2,500 officers and men of the U.S. Army in France, the use of 750 Polish guards for American installations, and the location of 4 radio teletypewriter stations in the country. Initial estimates of the cost were $19,645,912 for rehabilitation and operation of the facilities during the year, and then an annual operating cost of $10,114,756 thereafter. The planned route extended for nearly 600 miles, by road, from Bordeaux and La Pallice on the southwest coast, northeast across France to the Saar.[4]

There remained the matter of concluding an agreement with the French government. This introduced a situation almost without precedent in recent international military affairs where the army of one nation negotiated to set up a complete line of communication across the territory of another fully sovereign, friendly state in peacetime. It was to be expected that the strong Communist elements in France would exploit the novelty fully in order to show that the United States was establishing military bases in France in preparation for war and in violation of French sovereignty. For this reason it was essential that the negotiations proceed most carefully and diplomatically. Both sides were anxious to avoid political repercussions in France, to limit the inflationary pressure resulting from large-scale local spending that might dislocate elements of the French economy, and to discourage situations that might lead to ill-feeling and clashes between the local civilian population and the troops that soon would be arriving. In addition the U.S. Army was anxious for the French to assume a major share of the costs of the line of communication.[5]

By the end of February 1950 U.S. Army representatives had completed preliminary military discussions with French officers, and the stage was set for the opening of diplomatic negotiations. The State Department designated Charles E. Bohlen, minister of the embassy in Paris, to conduct the negotiations. Of the problems to be settled the most troublesome in the beginning was that of finance. The position of the Department of the Army was first of all to ask the French to bear all of the costs outlined in the original estimates; failing that, the French should be asked to bear all costs possible, in order of priority, for rehabilitation, railway transportation, civilian labor, port operations, and all other costs; as a minimum position the French should be expected to pay all rehabilitation costs plus at least $6 million on the other costs. In no case should the American contribution exceed $6 million. Bohlen considered this approach to be unrealistic as well as mercenary, but when State Department instructions arrived, after several weeks' delay he proceeded to raise the question of France making a substantial contribution to the costs. This led to restudies in the French ministries and to a long series of diplomatic discussions. But these had little more than begun when the French cabinet resigned on 24 June. With that rare sense of timing that had come to characterize postwar France, the French government had paralyzed itself in a cabinet crisis on the eve of the Korean attack. Military conversations continued in the interim until a new ministry could be formed, and then diplomatic negotiations were resumed on 13 July. But further delays ensued. Bohlen himself was absent from Paris during much of the summer, and subordinates had to carry on what negotiations could be conducted. Early in August the French made an offer to contribute the equivalent of about $5,714,000 toward the costs of the line of communications. Amounting to about twenty percent of the costs as then estimated, this was but a fraction of what the Department of the Army was asking for, even as a minimum. But General Handy, whose conviction was growing that the establishment of the line of communication without delay was absolutely essential to American security, urged acceptance. After repeated inquiries from the American Embassy, the State Department on 30 August cabled acceptance of the offer, and by 14 September it was possible to complete the financial terms of the agreement.[6]

Questions now remaining to be settled included the American proposals for the stationing of troops and Polish guards in France for setting up radio stations, and for obtaining headquarters and other facilities. A Civil Affairs Agreement signed in 1948 to govern the status of troops stationed in France would continue in effect for the time being so that the problem could be postponed without interfering with the work now being undertaken.[7]

Eleven months after the first military discussions on the subject and five months after the opening of diplomatic negotiations, Ambassador David Bruce of the United States and Alexandre Parodi, secretary-general of the French Ministry of Foreign Affairs, on 6 November 1950 signed the agreement on the line of communication. The basic agreement provided very simply that a line of communications would be established from the La Pallice-Bordeaux area to the German frontier, over which the principal means of movement would be by railways. Procedures for the establishment and operation of the line of communication were to be worked out by the military authorities of the two countries. The agreement was to remain in effect for five years, and then would be renewed automatically unless terminated by six months' advance notice by one of the parties.[8]

Three annexes and two letters of understanding by the American Ambassador attached to the agreement amplified certain specific points. The first provided for the continuation of Civil Affairs Agreement of 1948 pending the conclusion of a new treaty to govern the juridical status of American troops stationed in France. The second annex provided for financing the line of communication o the basis of a French contribution of two billion francs, payable after 1 January 1951, toward the estimated first year's total cost of ten billion francs for installation and operation. The United States was to bear the remaining costs including all costs arising out of operations prior to 1 January 1951. The third annex authorized the U.S. armed forces to install and operate radio facilities along the line of communication in accordance with technical arrangements worked out between U.S. military representatives and competent French authorities.

Supplementary agreements were necessary to cover further details of procurement procedures and financial arrangements. General Yount, representing the European Command, and the chief of the French Liaison Mission signed two agreements on this subject on 14 December. Already differences in interpretation had arisen on the role of the French governmental agency mentioned in Annex 2 of the basic agreement in procurement matters. The negotiators had assumed that this "intermediary," in accordance with French usage, would act as the agent for the U.S. Army in making contracts with French firms—that is, the Army itself would be a party to the contracts. The Department of the Army, on the other hand, expected the agency referred to in the annex to act as coordinator with the U.S. Army, but that the French Government would be the party to the contracts by which it would provide the needed goods and services to the U.S. Army on a reimbursable basis. In the agreement of 14 December the latter view prevailed.[9]

Negotiations had not even been completed on the line of communication agreement of 6 November 1950 when it already had been made obsolete by an expansion of plans that made further negotiations necessary. Originally making its plans on the basis of supporting an American force of 100,000 men in Germany, the European Command by October 1950 was drawing up plans for expanding the line of communcation to support a total troop strength of 150,000 in Phase 2 of its development, and ultimately to support an Army and Air Force strength of approximately 309,000 in Phase 3. In January 1951 the commander in chief of the European Command asked the 7966 EUCOM Detachment to inform the French Liaison Mission of plans for expansion. Instead of the approximately $20 million expenditure for the first year estimated in the original agreements, planned expenditures now were put at $50 million by 30 June 1951. Instead of 2,500 troops and 750 Polish guards to be brought into France, the new plans called for the use of 10,000 troops, 1,500 displaced persons, as well as 6,000 French civilians by 30 June 1951. It was estimated that port and railroad traffic, including petroleum products, would reach 20,000 tons a month by 30 June 1951 and 40,000 tons a month by 30 June 1952. This would require three general cargo berths—one of which European Command asked to be located at Saint Nazaire or Nantes on the Loire—one berth for ammunition and one for petroleum products.

Further, the new plans called for the laying of a ten-inch pipeline from Donges on the Loire estuary to Montargis, 270 miles to the east.[10]

All this required further negotiations. The French government adopted a policy that all requests for facilities in addition to those that already had been agreed to would have to be submitted through the American Embassy to the Foreign Office, and then would have to have the approval of the National Defense Committee. This would include agreements on financial implications of the expanded line of communication, the proposed pipeline, and the request for a general cargo berth at Saint Nazaire or Nantes. The Foreign Office considered that other aspects of the expansion plans could be settled by agreements between military representatives.[11]

After the major outstanding questions had remained at a standstill for several months, the Department of the Army in November 1951 moved to obtain a revision of the agreement that had been signed a year earlier. In it the Department of the Army sought to establish the principal that the French would contribute twenty percent of the increased costs and to obtain from the French an undertaking to furnish all real estate for the line of communication without cost to the United States. In addition the Department of the Army recommended revision of the supplementary agreements of 14 December 1950 to permit the United States to use military personnel and equipment for certain construction, to make direct contracts for construction services, and to eliminate the French taxes on materials being used. These proposals gained greater force when the secretary of state and the secretary of defense, meeting in Paris, tied them to other plans for the expenditure of some $650 million in France for military and economic assistance. But finance and political sensitivity interposed long delays before the major problems could be settled.[12]

One of the most baffling of these problems was the proposed pipeline now planned to run from Donges to Melun. It developed that the pipeline would have to be built by a French semipublic corporation known as the Societé des Transports Pietroliers par Pipeline (TRAPIL), which the French government previously had organized for the development of pipelines in France. But then in June the French government asked that the size of the pipeline be increased from ten to twelve inches and that they share in the peacetime and wartime flow of the completed pipeline. Negotiations remained deadlocked at that point for the next several months. In December 1951 the Departments of State and Defense agreed that the French offer to meet one-half of the increased costs should be accepted, but they also agreed that the United States should press for elimination of taxes on work and materials used in the construction and for a method of disposing of the pipeline upon the withdrawal of American troops from France. But negotiations lagged until in 1952 the French withdrew their offer of sharing in the cost of construction. At the end of 1952 the Department of the Army was preparing to seek congressional approval for financing the pipeline with United States funds alone. The Commander in Chief, U.S. Army, Europe, was becoming increasingly concerned over the vulnerable position in which the lack of pipelines and gasoline storage facilities placed his forces.

By the spring of 1953 the plans were revised and the pipeline was extended all the way to Metz. Without such a line it was estimated that in the event of a general European war U.S. forces would have to construct 1,684 miles of six-inch pipelines within the first few months of such a war, and perhaps as much again subsequently. Finally an agreement was reached and at the end of May the State Department authorized signature. Briefly this agreement provided for the construction of a twelve-inch pipeline from Donges to Châlons-sur-Marne, where storage facilities would be located, and for a ten-inch line from Chalons to the vicinity of Metz, where additional storage facilities would be established. The French government would designate TRAPIL as the agency responsible for the construction, operation, and maintenance of the line. Thus the operation as well as the construction would be purely a French proposition without the direct participation of American military units. The French would be granted up to five percent of the pipeline's capacity a month for the transportation of fuel for their own military requirements. No products going through the line would be used for commercial purposes except by special agreements. The United States would reimburse the French government for the expense of materials, construction, and operation; the French government would make available the land.[13] About the same time the French agreed to make available port facilities at Saint Nazaire.[14]

Given enough time, it appeared that agreements ultimately could be concluded on the principal questions affecting the line of communication. But it had taken two years to get these matters settled, and some—notably the amount of the French financial contribution—had not yet been settled. What had started in an atmosphere of extreme urgency now had slowed to the cumbersome pace of peacetime bureaucracy. It was clear at the outset that the political situation was very touchy and that it would be necessary to proceed with caution. But other factors had contributed delays far beyond what might have been expected. In the beginning the lack of overall coordination among American representatives and the lack of a unified command permitted many difficulties to develop. Then it took some time to realign the military command channels and to set up new agencies to coordinate negotiations. Again the close supervision over negotiations by Washington appeared to slow the process.[15]

Delays did not end with the negotiation of the high-level and general agreements. The red tape involved in the actual selection and approval of sites for line of communication installations and in initiating rehailitation and construction work made yet more remote the day when the line of communcation across France could be relied upon for the support of forces in Germany.[16]

For its part the French government was reluctant to take agricultural land or commercial establishments out of production, and it was unwilling to exercise the right of eminent domain in condemning private property as long as it could be avoided. Consequently sites offered for line of communication installations were on public property, such as at French military installations, national forests, and beach areas. This probably could have served the relatively small-scale operations at first planned for the line, but with its expansion, private facilities had to be rented or leased.

It was especially difficult for the French to understand the necessity for finding subsidiary facilities for American forces. They discovered that providing sites suitable for installations and troop barracks soon involved as well requests for areas for baseball fields, post exchanges, snack bars, theaters, and service clubs. Such facilities seemed essential to Americans to overcome the boredom of living in rural areas of a strange land. But the French *poilu* had been able to get along for years without all this peripheral development, and to the French it was not always clear why these special services were so important for American morale.[17]

Soon after the signing of the line of communication agreement on 6 November, a U.S. Army motor convoy of 300 trucks and 100 trailers crossed from the Saarland into France to be the first elements of service troops assigned to getting the line of communication into operation. By 11 November they had arrived in the port area to prepare for receiving military supplies. South of Bordeaux at Captieux, they found themselves facing a sea of mud and thousands of acres of desolate, water-logged wasteland. There they set up pyramidal tents on what dry spots they could find, got ready to organize a large ammunition depot, and waited for French construction to catch up with them. Several weeks before the signing of the agreement, G-4 had instructed the Technical Services to ship from the United States the minimum essential equipment necessary for activating the line of communication.[18]

The fact that the French had no modern construction industry capable of meeting the immediate demands for military construction, that a number of the installation sites were poorly drained, and that administrative procedures were cumbersome made it inevitable that rehabilitation and construction projects could not be completed speedily. The military casernes at Orleans, Fontainebleau, and Verdun still needed extensive renovation. Forest areas and wastelands had to be drained and access roads built, as well as new buildings raised for storage and troop housing. As plans for the line of communication grew while construction lagged, it soon became clear that several years would pass before all planned construction could be completed.[19]

In Septembr 1951 the European Command approved a program for prefabricated buildings to be erected for troop housing and for warehouses at a number of sites where permanent structures obviously would not be completed for many months. Undertaken as a measure to speed getting shelter for men and supplies, this program too fell far behind schedule. Some ten French firms contracted to erect forty-eight company-sized units at eighteen sites where no housing was available. By the completion target date of 1 January 1952 only nine percent of the buildings had been erected. An unusually wet winter—which made living conditions even less bearable for the troops—as well as the French system of separate contractors working independently at each task in a given area, close controls, and administrative red tape, held back the entire prefabricated building program. In 1953 some 10,000 Army troops faced the prospect of spending their third winter in tents.[20]

World War II and the difficult period of economic readjustment following the war had left the French themselves with a serious housing shortage in many areas. At the same time French laws that controlled rents and protected tenants from eviction had discouraged the construction of housing for American families because the length of their stay was highly uncertain. Officers and noncommissioned officers moving from Germany to France were permitted, and advised, to leave their families in Germany until they could find housing in France. Obviously special measures were necessary if any new housing were to be obtained for these families in France. After several months of negotiations and discussions, the only feasible course seemed to be that the United States would guarantee occupancy for a period of years at a stated rate of rent in return for a building program by French private enterprise. After another year's delay Congress authorized a program under which the United States would guarantee full occupancy for at least five years of 2,000 new apartment units that French builders would erect at their own cost near Army concentrations at Bordeaux, Saint Nazaire, Chateauroux, Orleans, Toul, and Verdun. But it would be another twelve to eighteen or more months before the new apartments would be ready. By May 1953 about 5,000 wives and children of officers and noncommissioned officers already were reported to be in France.[21]

In spite of vexatious administrative details and local methods, and in spite of the delays that characterized the whole construction program, notable achievements were to be found. It took time to overcome the difficulties, but they usually could be worked out. Eventually the mud and water at Captieux gave way to hardstands, roads, and walks paved with crushed stone or other materials; clean, well-built barracks replaced tents for thr 800 men on duty, and a snack bar, service club, and theater appeared on what previously had been a great bog. Reconstruction at Caserne Coligny at Orleans transformed war ruins to a collection of attractive headquarters buildings, mess halls, and quarters. Steel prefabricated huts appeared at Jeumont, adjacent to La Rochelle, prefabricated buildings rose in the Foret de Haye, and the Nancy Ordnance Depot had ninety-two percent of its facilities completed by May 1953. The Fontainebleau Medical Depot was turned into a virtual showplace. Slowly the line of communications across France was reaching the state where it could support major military operations.[22]

Another source of irritation to American leaders in France was the full imposition of French taxes on line of communications construction and other activities. The production tax, transaction tax, contract registration tax, special taxes, and certain local taxes together ate away what European Command estimated to be as much as twenty percent of the total construction budget. This meant that the French contribution of twenty percent or less to the cost of the line of communication would be completely canceled out by the taxes that the French government would collect. At last in June

1952 the French agreed that these taxes should not apply to expenditures made in France by the Government of the United States "in the interest of common defense."[23]

What set the direction of the line of communication across France was the selection of the ports. The ports chosen depended upon strategic considerations, the needs of other members of the North Atlantic Alliance in supporting their forces under war conditions, and the availability of local facilities. The agreement signed with France on 6 November 1950 stated specifically that the ports to serve the American line of communication would be in the area of Bordeaux and La Pallice. Located about sixty-five miles up the Gironde and up the Garonne River from the open sea, Bordeaux offered good protection and had extensive mechanical cargo handling equipment. But access of deep-draft vessels depended upon the tides, and loaded vessels had to be lightened in midstream before they could move into the docks to complete the discharge of their cargoes. Then space for sorting and storage near the docks was scarce. The only place that permitted deep-draft dockside berthing in the entire area was the Mole d'Escale at La Pallice, but there facilities for unloading were limited. The decision to use the ports of La Pallice, La Rochelle, and Bordeaux already had been made when the original 7966 EUCOM Detachment line of communication survey team was appointed in December 1949. After the ports had been selected, Engineer staff officers determined how much port capacity could be expected from them. In order to avoid arousing the anxieties of the French or British, and in order not to disturb the negotiations then in progress with the French, the Office of the Chief of Engineers made a study upon the basis of information available in Washington. Seriously questioning the highly optimistic conclusions of this study, the Engineer section of the 7966 EUCOM Detachment decided to make one of its own. Its conclusions differed from those of the Chief of Engineers by nearly fifty percent. In December, after the agreement with the French had been concluded, a special European Command survey team was able to make a more accurate study. Its findings were even less optimistic than those of the 7966 EUCOM Detachment. Allowing for needs of the French civilian population, the survey team put the combined military tonnage capacity that could be expected for the ports of Bordeaux and La Pallice at approximately 140,000 tons. This was just sufficient to satisfy what had been calculated to be the peacetime operating requirements for the line of communication, but those ports offered little opportunity to expand for wartime operations. The total military tonnage capacity of Saint Nazaire and Nantes was twice that. Here, and perhaps later Brest and Cherbourg, were the ports that would have to be assume the major share of wartime unloading of cargo for the support of American forces.[24]

French agreement to the use of facilities at the port of Saint Nazaire provided the basis for expanded capacity that would be critical if war should come. For the time being the United States was granted berths for two ships, transit shed, warehouses, and outdoor storage space. An advance party from the 188th Port Company already was there before the French gave their formal consent, and the *Waltham Victory* discharged its cargo on 10 April—two weeks before the oral agreement for use of the port.[25]

Recognizing that ports would be attractive targets for attacks by aircraft and guided missiles, logistic planners developed plans for over-the-beach operations to feed the line of communication across France. Freeing itself at last from the concept that peacetime should be considered normal for the Army, the Department of the Army in September 1951 directed the commander in chief, European Command (later U.S. Army, Europe) to establish an amphibious support organization capable of unloading one ship a month across the beaches of France. This would provide the nucleus for wartime expansion if necessary. By actually unloading military cargo over the beaches, the Army exploited a rare opportunity to train men in new techniques and to test new field equipment designed to improve the efficiency of such operations. The actual program began when the first ship discharged its cargo over the beaches near Point de Grave, at the mouth of the Gironde estuary, in June 1952. By the end of the year seven ships had discharged a total of 27,146 long tons (or about 49,170 measurement tons) of cargo over the beaches at Point de Grave or near La Pallice.[26]

One of the serious logistic bottlenecks in Korea was the movement of supplies from the ports. In contrast, France had excellent systems of railways and highways. Under the line of communication agreement signed in November 1950, the United States agreed that the principal means of movement of supplies across France would be by rail. Coordination with the French national railroads, the Société Nationale Chemin de Fer (SNCF), was through the French General Staff. The French Liaison Mission designated an officer of the French Transportation Corps to remain at headquarters of the 7966 EUCOM Detachment (later Communications Zone) to handle rail traffic for the U.S. forces in France. Only the limited clearances of some routes, loading and unloading capacities at points of origin and destination, and considerations of safety limited what American military forces could ship on the French railroads. The French SNCF and the German Federal Railways (Bundesbahn) had established a common freight car pool of 100,000 cars in order to facilitate freight movements between the two countries. For mobile storage of certain supplies in railroad yards and on spurs where they would be available for rapid dispatch when needed, the U.S. Army provided a number of freight cars of its own. American military shipments included those from the French ports direct to depots in Germany, those from the ports to storage areas and depots in France, those from depots in Germany to depots in France in accordance with the new dispositions of the supply system, and the movement of stocks being rotated from French depots to the American Occupation Zone of Germany. The United States of course had to bear the cost of all this transportation.[27]

Highway transportation supplemented the railroads only to a very limited extent. In early 1953 a small-scale revival of the wartime Red Ball Express was operating a fleet of some ten ten-ton trucks and dolly-trailers to give transportation units experience in long-distance hauling, and again to provide a nucleus for rapid expansion in an emergency.[28]

From Bordeaux to Orléans the line of communication crossed a section of France where the population was somewhat sparse and the commercial development relatively unadvanced. As a consequence the military forces could not depend upon highly developed commercial telephone and telegraph systems. In response to a request for fifty pairs of line for the exclusive use of the headquarters in Orléans, the 7966 EUCOM Detachment (Communications Zone) received only eight from the French Ministry of Post, Telegraph, and Telephone (PTT). In the agreement of 6 November 1950 the French authorized American military forces to install and operate necessary radio facilities, but technical details had to be worked out between the U.S. forces and the French authorities. It was clear that PTT could not provide all the needed facilities for a major expansion program. Plans of European Command Signal Division called for a microwave radio system to provide necessary facilities beyond those that the French PTT could guarantee. The system was to include six main or terminal stations and nineteen relay stations on the line between the Base Section headquarters at La Rochelle and Kaiserslautern, Germany. But the system remained in the planning stage from late 1950 to early 1953, when Secretary of Defense Wilson was able to obtain French approval for a single microwave system for the Army and Air Force in France.[29]

Supply activities on the line of communication began concurrently with the furthering of negotiations and the development of storage, headquarters, and quartering sites. Some supplies came into the forward areas of France from Germany. Others went in by the ports and followed the routes that would be more or less normal in emergency operations. By freight train and truck American military supplies and equipment moved from the wine country of Bordeaux and the coastal town of La Pallice north and northeast, across the battlefield where Edward of England, the Black Prince, defeated King John of France in 1356, to Poitiers, through the fields where in 732 Charles Martel stopped the Moors who had been advancing over this same route, to Tours, where this route joined another coming from Saint Nazaire and Nantes up the picturesque valley of the Loire; then to Orléans, set in a countryside little changed since Joan of Arc led her French troops to raise the siege of the city in 1429. Eastward the routes diverged along two main lines. The northern route ran through Fontainebleau, historic home of French royalty; across the plains where Romans and Visigoths combined to turn back Attila and the Huns in 451 to Châlons-sur-Marne; across grim battlefields of World War I and World War II to Verdun and to Metz, and across the German border at Saarbrücken. The southern route continued east from Orleans through Montargis, Sens and Troyes to Toul and Nancy, and across the German border at Sarreguemines; the two routes then rejoined in the Saar and continued through Kaiserslautern and Ludwigshafen to Mannheim.

Storage areas in France by no means were arranged in a single or double line across the country; they were well distributed over large areas of both the base section and the advance section. But supplies moving across the country generally followed the axis here described.[30]

Tanks and engines went to a storage farm near Toul; bulldozers, graders, bridging sections and tractors went to the Engineer depot at Chinon; trucks, jeeps, ambulances, and parts went to the Ordnance depot at Angoulême; bulk supplies of food and clothing went to Ingrandes and Metz; Signal Corps switchboards, field wire, telephones, and radios went to Sammur and Verdun.[31] These and other supplies went to a dozen other depots and storage areas. Supplies moved along one of the principal routes that the American Expeditionary Force's Services of Supply had used in 1917–18. Trucks on long hauls followed the same routes that the spearheads of General Patton's Third Army had followed in the celebrated race across France in 1944. Now heavy Army trucks rumbling through the narrow streets of medieval towns, double-clutching up the slopes, and keeping up a steady hum on open highways awakened in French citizens the bittersweet nostalgia of liberation and the dread of occupation. Veteran officers and men felt the sensation of having been through all this before; newcomers to the ranks of the Army in France doubtless wondered sometimes the purpose of all of this effort—and longed for transfer to Germany or back to the States.

Spoiled by lavish living in Germany, soldiers transferred to France, where they frequently found themselves billeted in tents in muddy fields or forests with little in the way of recreational facilities or even showers, soon became dissatisfied. Boredom tended to turn to dislike of France and of the French people. Eventually the completion of building projects helped to relieve this situation.[32]

But in spite of all discouragements, the line of communication across France was successful by mid-1953. Where trouble had been most expected it had developed little or not at all in many cases. Communist efforts to disrupt activities by strikes had failed completely. Acts of sabotage had been avoided almost altogether. Pilferage, compared to what it had been in 1944, was very minor.[33] In a June 1954 inspection of the line, Lt. Gen. W. B. Palmer found much to praise, although the Army's chief logistics officer still saw a great need for improvement.[34]

Other than the programs of matériel assistance to allies and the Korean War, the establishment of the line of communication across France undoubtedly was the most significant development for U.S. Army logistics and strategy since the end of World War II. The implication was clear that the United States was not holding to the strategy that had characterized much of the postwar thinking—that in the event of war in Europe, American forces would retire behind the Pyrenees to await the liberation of France by bombs. Here was clear testimony that the United States intended to hold Germany and to make a major stand on the Rhine. Nothing could have been more encouraging to the French. At the same time this bound France almost irrevocably to the United States. Any temptation to neutralism was out of the question. If the United States were involved in a European war the French would be in it automatically. But the United States also was bound to France. The French held a trump card that they had used before and could be expected to use again if the situation demanded it: Americans depended upon the French for the security of the line of communication. The French had used the card earlier when, in response to the threat that was developing in the Colmar pocket during the German counteroffensives in January 1945, General Eisenhower had ordered the withdrawal of forces from Strasbourg. The one argument that General Charles de Gaulle found carried enough force to persuade the Supreme Commander to countermand his order was the threat to the Allied lines of communication that the resulting unrest among the French people might create.[35] That argument would continue to carry much weight with American commanders in Europe. But it was the firmest kind of arrangement among allies—mutual dependence.

Relocation of Depots in Germany

In line with the thinking that underlay the establishment of communication across France, it was necessary to reorient logistic support facilities in Germany. Now that tactical considerations had superseded the occupation mission in Germany and dependence upon the Bremerhaven line of communication was minimized, it seemed prudent to move all these installations west of the Rhine where they could receive supplies from France and where they might find protection against attack from the east. But all German territory west of the Rhine was in the French Zone of Occupation (except for the North Rhineland, which was in the British Zone). At the same time Allied planners considered that it would be well to assign to the French responsibility for defending a portion of the battle line if and when an attack should come. This led to the consideration of an exchange of territory by redrawing the boundaries of the occupation zones. But French Foreign Minister Robert Schuman suggested that the objective might be achieved more simply by agreeing to exchange certain facilities and to permit troops to be located without regard to zonal boundaries, while retaining those boundaries for the purpose of administrative responsibilities. This was agreeable to both the British and the Americans. The result was revision of the charter of the Allied High Commission in the fall of 1950 to the effect that troops participating in the defense of Germany could be stationed wherever the High Commissioners and the respective commanders in chief in consultation might determine. Specific arrangements depended upon further agreements that had to be worked out to cover questions of jurisdiction of forces, a revision of budgetary procedures so that one nation could account for the costs of its forces in more than one zone, the acquisition of real estate in various zones, procedures for hiring local labor, local procurement for the forces of one nation in the zone of another, improvement of uniform transportation regulations, and responsibilities for occupation damages.

American and French High Commissioners and military commanders on 2 March 1951 signed an agreement on an exchange of facilities and a transfer of troops between the two zones of occupation. Under the arrangement French troops were to move into a small sector of Hesse in the American zone, south of the line Winterberg-Eschwege, and south of the line Lorch-Friedberg-Butzbach-Bad Hersfeld plus an area south of the autobahn between Karlsruhe and Stuttgart. American forces were to take over installations in the Palatinate—the French northern zone—west of the Rhine and south of the line Bingen-Idar.

In April 1951 French units took over barracks at Marburg and Wetzlar and a hospital at Geissen in the American zone. A kaserne at Pforzheim previously had been turned over to the French in March, and in August they took over installations at Karlsruhe and Fritzlar.

The goal of European Command was to get most of the technical service depots in Germany moved west of the Rhine by 1 July 1951. Theater supply stocks above a thirty-day level were to be moved west of the Rhine, and as soon as facilities were available, rebuild operations also would be transferred to that area. The European Command already had set up the Rhine General Depot at Kaiserslautern, and in September 1950 this depot and its areas and installations were established as a subpost of the Heidelberg Military Post. In March this became the Rhine Military Post with administrative supervision over all U.S. Army activities in the French zone. Establishment of subpost headquarters at various times during the year included those at Baumholder, Bad Kreuznach, Pirmasens, Worms, and Mainz. The commander of the Rhine Military Post stationed a liaison officer at Mainz to deal with the French on all matters pertaining to procurement, requisition, construction, and facilities.[36]

Meanwhile the transfer of depots to areas west of the Rhine was occurring. The relocation program called for the complete phaseout of engineer, medical, and signal, most ordnance, and a major part of quartermaster depot activities over the next two years. This included the transfer of the stocks and functions of the Hanau Engineer Depot and of the Engineer Bridge Depot at Schwetzingen to the Rhine Engineer Depot east of Kaiserslautern. The Rhine General Depot in September 1951 became the Rhine Ordnance Depot, and this, together with the Pirmasens Ordnance Depot, the Mainz Ordnance Depot, the Gemerscheim Ordnance Vehicle Park, and the Rhine Ammunition Depot, assumed most of the functions previously carried out by the Breisheim, Illesheim, and Butzbach Ordnance Depots and the Bamberg Ammunition Depot. A month after the opening of a medical depot at Einsiedlerhof the depot at Fürth in the American Zone was closed out. The signal base depot at Hanau was to be phased out after the activation of a similar installation near Pirmasens. Established in September 1951, the Nahbollenbach Quartermaster Depot had the mission of storing nonperishable food supplies and combat-type clothing and equipment, and of controlling the storage of gasoline and oil in the area. This would permit a reduction in the stocks maintained at Munich and Giessen, but depots there would have to continue important operations until the completion of major construction at Nahbollenbach. Upon its arrival from the United States in September 1951, the Seventh Chemical Depot was located at Kirchheimbolanden in the Rhine Military Post. The chief opposition to the expansion of American military activities in the Palatinate came more from the local German population than from the French. Objecting to the loss of farmland or the marring of historic sites, even though compensated for, farmers were known to have defended their positions with pitchforks. But, on the whole, inhabitants ultimately acquiesced to the changes in their homeland.[37]

A "missing link" still remained in the U.S. Army's supply system connecting forces in Germany with the French ports. That was the Saar. Although the main communication lines between Metz and Nancy in France and Mannheim and Frankfurt in the American Zone of Germany ran through this area, it had been excluded from the agreement on the relocation of American forces and installations in the French Zone. The Saar was a part of the French Zone of Germany, but the French had established a separate administration for it, and French policy frankly sought to gain assurance of economic concessions for France in this rich coal-producing and industrial basin. At the same time the Government of the Federal Republic of Germany was anxious that nothing be done to question the sovereignty of Germany over that area in the eventual peace settlements. The future of the Saar thus was one of the most sensitive questions betweem French and Germans. After World War I the Saar had been set aside under the administration of the League of Nations for a period of fifteen years, after which the people were to vote in a plebiscite whether they wished to continue that arrangement, be joined to France, or return to Germany. During the period the French were to receive the production from the coal mines as compensation for mines in northern France that the Germans had damaged during the war. In the plebiscite, the vote was overwhelmingly in favor of returning to the rule of Germany. Then World War II reopened the question, and once again the French hoped to obtain economic concessions.

Early in 1951 General Handy made overtures to General Guillaume, the French commander in Germany, with a view to obtaining an agreement for the establishment of American facilities in the Saar. Nothing came of these efforts at the time, and in January 1952 the American Embassy in Paris pointed out that some kind of bilateral agreement would be necessary—presumably with the French Foreign Office acting on behalf of the government of the Saar—before military commanders could enter into specific arrangements for locating facilities in the area. The U.S. High Commissioner in Germany, John J. McCloy, also pointed out that German public opinion was particularly sensitive about the Saar, and he recommended that nothing be done that would cause a flareup of anti-French feeling in Germany at the time negotiations for the European Defense Force were being conducted. After the European Command in June 1952 repeated its desire to obtain facilities in the Saar, McCloy indicated that it might be done if the negotiations were handled very carefully. This would be difficult because any agreement signed by the French on behalf of the government of the Saar might imply to the Germans an intention to separate the Saar permanently from Germany. A few days later (7 July 1952) the American Embassy in Paris cabled detailed objections to opening negotiations on such a sensitive subject at that time. Accepting this view, the secretary of state recommended that no action be taken until after ratification of the German contractual agreements and the European Defense Community treaty. The Joint Chiefs of Staff had approved the military requirements given for installations in the Saar, and General Eddy, commander in chief, U.S. Army, Europe, continued to insist at the end of 1952 that the military requirement still existed. He did not recommend opposition to the position of the State Department, but he did recommend that the Department of the Army press for an agreement as soon as the political situation would permit.[38]

Across Italy

The Peace Treaty with Italy that became effective 15 September 1947 provided that all occupation forces should be withdrawn within ninety days. The last ship carrying American troops sailed from Leghorn on 14 December.[39] In Italy, therefore, no American troops remained that could accept logistic missions for forces now being disposed to meet the threat of attack. As in France, it was necessary to make new agreements so that troops could return and installations be set up to carry out a decision for establishing a line of communication. In this case it would be for the purpose of supplying current needs for U.S. forces in Austria and emergency stockpiles for the support of war plans of forces in Trieste as well as those in Austria. The entire operation came under the control of U.S. forces in Austria. The line of communication would extend from the port of Leghorn on the Ligurian Sea northeast some 300 miles through Verona to the Austrian border and thence to the Camp Drum Storage Depot at Innsbruck in the French Zone of Austria.[40]

This program was only a fraction of the size of the one undertaken in the establishment of the line of communication across France, but the diplomatic negotiations were even more drawn out. Communist agitators were more active in Italy than in France, and the government had to move slowly in accepting new foreign commitments. The American Embassy in Rome began negotiations with the Italian government on 25 September 1950; arrangements were not concluded until nine months later, on 29 June 1951. A leak to the press—which seemed to be a trial balloon to test political opposition to the agreement—late in June created some last-minute problems and further delays when members of the Italian parliament demanded a full discussion of the negotiations, but at last an acceptable arrangement in the form of an exchange of notes between the Italian foreign minister and the American ambassador was concluded.[41]

The Italian government authorized the use of necessary equipment for docking, loading, and unloading of ships in the port of Leghorn and for line of communication and depot areas and facilities across the country to the Austrian border. This included facilities for a general depot in Leghorn, a subdepot in Verona, and signal communication facilities. The United States also was permitted to establish a radio system for operation of the line of communication. Movement of personnel and supplies across Italy ordinarily was to be by rail. Any exceptions to that rule were subject to special arrangements by American and Italian military authorities. Priorities and freight rates on the railroads and the use of public utilities were to be equal to those granted to the Italian armed forces. The Italian government would provide railway transportation without charge up to a specific amount, after which the United States would pay the rates charged to the Italian forces. The United States agreed to make improvements and construction costing not less than $1,400,000. At Leghorn the Italian government established a commission for the purpose of coordinating with the U.S. Army in order that such activities as local procurement, the rental of living quarters by members of the American froces and their families, and the hiring of Italian workers would not disrupt the local economy. Insofar as applicable and consistent with domestic legislation, the provisions of the agreement signed by members of the North Atlantic Treaty Organization in London on 19 June 1951, even though not yet in effect as a formal agreement, would govern the questions of juridical status of American troops in Italy, as well as police, monetary, and customs questions.[42]

The arrangement represented a concrete expression of Italian participation in mutual defense, and the Italian government justified it as a measurement in fulfillment of general obligations under the North Atlantic Treaty. The arrangement was to continue in effect as long as the North Atlantic Treaty remained in force unless terminated sooner by mutual consent.

Flexibility was the rule for working out the technical details necessary to making the line of communication effective. Negotiators found it advisable to accept simple and informal Italian forms and procedures where possible instead of urging the acceptance of American or other foreign procedures. The voluminous and detailed railway contract reported by an American officer to have been acceptable to the French Railway System, for example, was completely unnecessary with the Italian Railway Administration.[43] Once the line of communication was in operation, most of the details appeared to work out smoothly.[44]

Notes

1. U.S. Dept. of Army, "Military Government of Germany," monthly report of the military governor, U.S. Zone No. 5, 20 Dec. 45; copy in Army Library, Pentagon, Washington, D.C., 3–4; ibid., no. 19, 1–31 Jan. 47, 6–7; "Establishment of Communications through France, 1950–51," European Command Historical Summary, 1 and Map 1.

2. Dept. of Army G-4 Historical Summary, 1951–52, Tab B, Plans Office, Europe, 12; "Establishment of Communications through France," 122–24.

3. Convention on Relations with the Federal Republic of Germany, Senate Executive Documents Q and R, 82d Cong., 2d sess., 2 June 1952, and the related finance convention, "Rights and Obligations of Foreign Forces and their Members in the Federal Republic of Germany"; and convention, "Settlement of Matters Arising out of the War and the Occupation"; Dept. of Army G-4 Historical Summary, 1951–52, Tab B, Plans Office, Europe, 12–13.

4. "Establishment of Communications through France," 1–2, 5–10; EUCOM Briefing for Mr. Pace and General Collins, 19 Dec. 1950, "Line of Communication Across France," Transcript in G-4 Plans Office, Theaters Branch, French Line of Communications; Brig. Gen. Mason J. Young, CG EUCOM COMZ, "Our New European Supply Line," *Army Information Digest* 6 (Oct. 1951); 56; EUCOM Annual Narrative Report 1950, 22–25, 115; EUCOM Command Report 1951, 210–12.

5. "Establishment of Communications through France," 2–3; James P. O'Donnell, "We're All Fouled Up in France," *The Saturday Evening Post,* April 11, 1953, 40–41.

6. Memo, Colonel C. G. Schenken, 7966 EUCOM Det JA, for Brig. Gen. Mason J. Young, 13 Dec. 50; "Chronology of LOFC Negotiations." Copy in "Establishment of Communications through France," Annex 2; "Establishment of Communications through France," 10–14; O'Donnell, "We're All Fouled Up in France," 41.

7. This remained in effect until the multilateral treaty that had been drawn up within the framework of NATO to govern the juridical status of troops still was pending in the U.S. Senate. The French already had ratified it.

8. Agreement between the United States of America and the Republic of France Regarding the Establishment and Operation of a Line of Communication Across France. Copy in "Establishment of Communications through France, 1950–51," Annex 3. See also Basic Policies of the Dept. of the Army (DA-PB-50A), copy in OCMH, Change No. 8, May 1952, 29.

9. Agreement Relating to the Procurement of Supplies, Services and Facilities from the French Economy for the Operation of the Line of Communication across France. Copy in "Establishment of Communications through France" Annex 4; Operating Procedure for the French-American Fiscal Liaison Office. Copy in "Establishment of Communications through France," Annex 5.

10. "Establishment of Communications through France," 103–4.

11. Ibid., 104–10.

12. Ibid., 107–8.

13. Ibid., 106–7, and Annex 26; Dept. of Army G-3 Historical Summary, 1951–52, Europe and Middle East Branch 5; Message 7650, Secretary/Defense to Acting Secretary/Defense, for Kyes from Wilson, 29 Apr. 53; Dept. of State Message 5811, to American Embassy, Paris, 30 May 53; Message 5882, Paris to Secretary of State, 9 May 53, Tab 20; Report of Critical Problems, G4-6, Augmentation of LOC across France, 26 Mar. 53.

14. Message from Dept. of Army 261027, CINCUSAREUR, to Dept. of Army for G-3, 24 Apr. 53, copy in G-3 Operations Division, Europe–Middle East Branch, Cables LOC France, Tab. 36.

15. Memo, Colonel C. G. Scheken for General Brannon, 19 Sep 52, "Report Covering TDY with MFNG and MFD/SRE, Paris."

16. "Establishment of Communications through France," 35–40.

17. Interview with Colonel Zimmerman, 3 June 53; O'Donnell, "We're All Fouled Up in France," p. 96.

18. Young, "Our New European Supply Line," 57; "Memo of Major Actions," G4/B1 49413, 22 Sept. 50, p. 1.

19. "Establishment of Communications through France," 40–48 and passim.

20. "Establishment of Communications through France," 49–52; Benjamin Welles, *New York Times,* May 26, 1953, 10, and May 27, 1953, 8; O'Donnell, "We're All Fouled Up in France," 41.

21. "Establishment of Communications through France," 114–15; Benjamin Welles, *New York Times,* May 27, 1953, 8.

22. Benjamin Welles, *New York Times,* May 26, 1953, 10; "Establishment of Communications through France," figs. 1–20.

23. Memorandum of Agreement between the Government of the United States of America and the Government of the French Republic Relating to Tax Relief for Expenditures made in France by the Government of the United States in the Interests of the Common Defense, 13 June 52; Dept. of Defense; "Establishment of Communications through France," 115–16; Dept. of Army, DA G-3 Historical Summary 1951–52, Europe and Middle East Branch, 7.

24. "Establishment of Communications through France," 69–78.

25. Message, Department of the Army in 261027, CINCUSAREUR to Department of the Army for G-3, 24 Apr. 53.

26. Dept. of Army, G-4 Historical Summary, 1951–52, Tab B, Plans Office, Europe 10; QM Historical Summary, Global Mission of the Quartermaster Corps, Sep 1951–Dec. 1952, 2:473–75.

27. "Establishment of Communications through France," 79–85.

28. O'Donnell, "We're All Fouled Up in France," 40.

29. "Establishment of Communications through France," 86–90; Office of Chief Signal Officer, Historical Summary, 1951–52, 32; Message OA in 264065, Secretary of Defense from SLIMANE AFE to Acting Secretary of Defense, 3 May 53.

30. "Establishment of Communications through France," maps. 10 and 11.

31. O'Donnell, "We're All Fouled Up in France," 99.

32. Ibid., 100; Benjamin Welles, *New York Times,* May 26, 1953, p. 10.

33. O'Donnell, "We're All Fouled Up in France," 100.

34. Summary of remarks by Lt. Gen. W. B. Palmer at Headquarters USAREUR, Heidelberg, 14 June 1954. Copy in Office of the Chief of Military History.

35. Dwight D. Eisenhower, *Crusade in Europe* (New York, 1948), 362–63; General De Lattre de Tassigny, *Historie de la Première Armée Française, Rhin et Danube* (Paris, 1949), 344–58.

36. This section is based on a 1952 monograph by Joanne M. Lucas, Exchange of Troops and Facilities, United States and French Zones 1950–51, Historical Division, Headquarters USAREUR.

37. Ibid.

38. Memo, Colonel C. G. Schenken, for General Brannon, 19 Sept. 52; Report Covering TDY with MFNG and MFD/SRE, Paris, Exhibit F, U.S. Armed Forces Facilities in the Sarr; Message, Dept. of Army 922816, G-3 to USCINCEUR, 3 Nov. 52. Copy in G-3 Operations Division, European-Middle East Branch, SAAR Base Rights; Message, Department of the Army IN 210686, USCINCEUR to Department of the Army, 24 November 52; Message, Department of the Army IN 221237, CINCUSAREUR to Department of the Army, 24 Dec. 52.

39. U.S. Dept. of Army, "Annual Report of the Secretary of the Army," 1948.

40. U.S. Dept. of Army G-4 Memo of Important Actions, 15 Mar. 51, 1.

41. U.S. Dept. of State, Foreign Service Despatch No. 8, American Embassy Rome to Dept. of State, 2 July 51: "Arrangement for Lines of Communication in Italy Concluded June 29, 1951"; U.S. Dept. of Defense, "Semiannual Report of the Secretary of Defense," Jan. 1–June 30, 1951, 63.

42. U.S. Dept of State, "Exchange of Notes between the Ambassador of the U.S.A. in Rome and the Minister of Foreign Affairs of the Republic of Italy," F.A. No. 7712 and 7713, 29 June 51. See also "Basic Policies of the Dept. of the Army" (DA-PB-50A), Change No. 8, May 1952, 29.

43. U.S. Dept. of State, Foreign Service Despatch No. 8, American Embassy Rome to Dept. of State, 2 July 51.

44. Edmund Stevens, *Christian Science Monitor,* 12 August 1952, 9.

Beginning the U.S. Line of Communication across France, over-the-beach supply operations, near La Rochelle, June 1952. *(U.S. Army Signal Corps photo.)*

Headquarters, U.S. Army Communications Zone, Europe, Coligny Caserne, Orleans, France. *(U.S. Army Signal Corps photo.)*

French workers at a U.S. Army ordnance depot near Bar-le-Duc. *(U.S. Army Signal Corps photo.)*

A trailer transfer point on the Red Ball Express, Toul, France. *(U.S. Army Signal Corps photo.)*

U.S. supply convoy from France proceeding on the German autobahn near Ludwigsha-fen. *(U.S. Army Signal Corps photo.)*

Bags of flour from U.S. Army General Depot at Ingrandes, France, being transferred from U.S. Army trucks to Military Air Transport Service (MATS) aircraft at Chateauroux Air Force Base for shipment to Belgian Congo, July 1962. *(U.S. Army Signal Corps photo.)*

Part 2
NATO Strategy and
Logistic Plans

4
Dilemmas of Strategy and Logistics

Strategy and Logistics

One of the principles underlying the whole NATO military structure is said to be "Logistics is a national responsibility." But to maintain that "logistics is a national responsibility" is to make an artificial distinction in the military process. Logistics can no more be separated from strategy and tactics than the fuel can be separated from a motor vehicle and have it continue to operate.

There is an essential equivalence of strategy, tactics, and logistics. They are different aspects of a military action continuum in which each influences, and is influenced by, the other two. Indeed the major strategic decisions themselves are likely to be based upon the limitations of logistics. If one examines the major strategic decisions of Britain and the United States in World War II, for instance, it quickly becomes evident that those were essentially logistic decisions. There was no purely strategic reason why full-scale offensives should not have been launched simultaneously in Europe and in the Pacific; the decision at the outset to make the major effort first in Europe was the result of the limitation of resources and the estimated capabilities, which is to say logistic positions, of the adversaries. The decision to postpone the invasion of the European continent for a year in favor of an invasion of French North Africa; the decision to put the major effort into a cross-channel attack rather than in the Mediterranean; the postponement of D-day for Normandy; the postponement of the invasion of southern France instead of mounting it simultaneously with the Normandy landings; the timing of the return to the Philippines; the planned invasion of Japan—all these were based upon the relative availability of resources: ocean shipping, landing craft, fuel, ammunition, and so on, or in other words, on logistic assessments. One of the French officers serving in a key staff position of the Allied command in Europe has recalled how he, as a tactical commander, when writing his field orders (divided under the French system into a Part One, "Operations" and Part Two, "Logistics") would do the second part first, since this would tell him what he could do.

85

Since there is an essential equivalence of strategy, tactics, and logistics, it is a serious misconception to suppose, in any long-term sense, that an international agency can determine strategy and tactics while logistics is left to purely national determinations. In his role as commander in chief, U.S. European Command, General Matthew Ridgway recognized that he must have control over his logistics if his unified command were in fact to be effective. This surely was no less true in his role as Supreme Allied Commander, Europe, if his allied command were to be really effective. But in the former case he was able to do something about it, while in the latter there was relatively little that he could do. To the extent that logistics remained a national responsibility, so too did strategy to a considerable degree, for in a very real sense, he who controls the logistics controls the strategy also.

When it came to logistic planning, the first big question was the strategic assumption upon which it should be based. In NATO, where sharp differences of opinion on strategic assumptions prevailed, during recent years at least, one had to contend with a continuing obscurity. Yet, in a certain sense this was not so basic, and may not have been quite the problem that it appeared to be at first glance. The logic of the planning process is that there is an analysis of potential enemy capabilities—how much and what kind of power the potential enemy can bring to bear at given times and places under various conditions; then there follows a calculation of the size and nature of the forces necessary to neutralize an enemy attack at those times and places, and then a calculation of the logistic requirements for supporting those forces. In practice it seldom works out that way, for it is almost impossible for strategic planning to remain sufficiently far ahead of logistic planning to allow for the necessary lead-time in obtaining specific items of matériel to support a particular strategy. The French General, André Beaufre, has observed with much reason that the logistics of war develops in peacetime, and that the interval of realizing basic logistic plans is of the order of five years— so that it is necessary to plan five years in advance for an extremely conjectural future.[1] Consequently, logistics planners are driven to the acceptance of a few broad assumptions and general guidelines, and then to an attempt to provide for the matériel that will permit the greatest possible freedom of choice to the strategic planners.

Still, with the fundamental role that logistics must play in all strategic planning—and with the lip service that nearly everyone is willing to pay to its importance—this aspect of defense policies has received relatively little attention in most of the voluminous discussions over the last thirty years on problems of NATO strategy. As U.S. General James E. Moore put it,

There is a tendency to devote so much attention to the more intriguing nuclear issues that matters such as provision of adequate conventional forces and logistics support, which in the long run are probably more important, have not been and are not being given sufficient consideration. If we seek to achieve political flexibility at the moment of truth, however, we must have the necessary military formations and supplies in being and in proper locations.[2]

With great insight, Rear Admiral Henry E. Eccles (USN, ret.), set down these principles over twenty-five years ago as applying to the NATO situation:

(a) Economic factors limit the combat forces which can be created; logistic factors limit the combat forces which can be employed. (b) Command transforms war potential into combat power by the manner in which it controls and uses the logistic process. . . . We must see it from the point of view of a blend of Politics, of Economics, of Geography, of Strategy, of Logistics, and of Tactics. Then from the Perspective of Command we should try to evaluate the whole without being lost in the fascination of technologies and weapons.[3]

In the continuing discussions about strategy and doctrine, often it has appeared to be the case that a state's preference for one kind of strategy or another is the result of its relative logistic position. It has been suggested that nations rationalize their shortcomings in conventional forces, for instance, by going back to the "trip-wire" and "massive retaliation" concept— that ground forces are in position in Europe simply to provide a *casus belli* if attacked—to act as a "trip-wire" for the immediate release of nuclear weapons against the invader.[4] As Dirk V. Stikker, secretary general of NATO from 1961 to 1964, explained, NATO operates on the principle of the equality of states and of the doctrine of consent—that no one member can impose a course of action on its allies, nor can it be coerced by its allies into some particular action. He then pointed out that NATO strategy had been based de facto on three principles: (1) flexibility—the capability to respond to any kind of attack with appropriate means; (2) forward concept—defense as near to the eastern borders of the NATO countries as possible; and (3) integration of the armed forces of the members. It is noted that the United States agreed with all these principles, but held that the conventional forces of the European members ought to be increased by something like twenty percent; Britain had reservations about too great a degree of "flexibility"; France disagreed with all three principles and favored a trip-wire strategy with immediate nuclear response at critical points; Germany was building up conventional forces but expressed concern about lack of participation in nuclear policy decisions and about possible withdrawal of U.S. forces; Italy desired to improve status by sharing in nuclear decisions but was beset by too many domestic problems to do much more—which was fairly substantial—about increasing conventional forces; and Greece and Turkey, already spending too much on defense, opposed any degree of flexibility in the sense of relying on conventional forces to repel a direct invasion.[5]

Several sets of opposing principles were at work in NATO. Of first importance were the principles of interdependence and national responsibility. While contradictory, these are not mutually exclusive when applied only in degree, as they were applied in NATO. Likewise in the realm of logistics are two principles, often contradictory, usually sought in domestic military policies as well: maximum logistic effectiveness and minimum cost.

The Flexible Response Dispute

Although most of the elements of the current NATO strategy had been present since the early years of the alliance, changing conditions brought different emphasis at different times.[6] In the beginning any effective deterrance as well as effective ground and air counterattack in case of aggression was very largely dependent upon the United States. The United States then enjoyed a monopoly of nuclear weapons, and in the opinion of Sir Winston Churchill, among others, this more than anything else saved Western Europe from a Communist takeover. But to make its nuclear power effective, the United States needed air bases close to the potential enemy, and a number of these it found in the territories of its allies. Furthermore it was expected during this period that European forces themselves could do little more, in case of invasion, than hold a beach head against the day when the Americans could mount a massive reentry. In those circumstances the logistical problem was fairly simple. In effect it was a unified system made so by reliance upon the United States.

The Communist attack in Korea raised concern both in the United States and in Europe about the world situation. As a result the NATO partners accomplished three goals: first, they established the Supreme Headquarters, Allied Powers, Europe, in order to have an Allied headquarters and forces in being to meet any attack. Second, the North Atlantic Council, in its ministerial session at Lisbon in 1952, called upon members to make a two- to threefold increase in military forces, and third, the United States sent reinforcements to Europe. During this time the emphasis was upon "forward strategy"—of defending as far to the east as possible without resorting to a planned delaying action and then liberation. The logistical implications for the European nations simply in creating and providing support for the additional forces were very serious. For the United States it meant providing the support for the additional divisions sent to Europe at a time when it was supporting a major United Nations action in Korea and it was at this time too that the United States sought more secure supply lines for its forces with the establishment of its line of communications across France. Except on a bilateral basis with the United States in certain cases, little was done toward international coordination of logistics—though there was pressure for the members to take their "national responsibilities" seriously. A feeling persisted that this was a time of danger when, with the United States heavily engaged in Korea and France in Indochina, the Soviet Union and its satellites might be tempted to undertake forceful domination of all or a part of West Germany. It was felt too that it ought to be possible to meet small-scale, probing attacks with something other than atomic bombs.

The United States secretary of state, Dean Acheson, in 1951 further emphasized the importance of building up conventional forces.

We have a substantial lead in air power and in atomic weapons. At the present moment, this may be the most powerful deterrent against aggression. But with the passage of time, even though we continue our advances in this field, the value of our lead diminishes. In other words, the best use we can make of our present advantage in retaliatory air power is to move ahead under this protective shield to build the balanced collective forces in Western Europe that will continue to deter aggression after our atomic advantage has diminished.[7]

Having presided over the initial phase of NATO's military buildup as first Supreme Allied Commander, Europe, General Dwight D. Eisenhower, on becoming president of the United States, ushered in a new phase in NATO strategy. Western European nations quickly grasped for the doctrine of "massive retaliation" spelled out principally by Eisenhower's secretary of state, John Foster Dulles. This was a blunt warning to would-be aggressors that Western nations no longer would be content to absorb attacks with conventional means, but calling upon their greatest strength, would respond with nuclear weapons "at times and places of our own choosing." Here was a way for the European nations to escape the heavy burdens of conventional rearmament accepted at Lisbon, for once again the burden would be upon the United States. Moreover the logistic situation was relieved all around, for the United States no longer needed to plan for a massive buildup and support of conventional forces, and since any nuclear effort would have to depend very largely upon United States resources, nagging problems of international logistic coordination could be more or less disregarded.[8]

In 1954 the North Atlantic Council accepted the new doctrine with a momentous decision that nuclear weapons would be used at the outset of any defense against attack in Europe, and it would be assumed that no war in Europe involving NATO would be a limited war. Any war in Europe would be total and it would be nuclear. Field Marshall Bernard L. Montgomery warned, "I want to make it absolutely clear that we at SHAPE are basing all our operational planning on using atomic and thermonuclear weapons in our defense. With us it is no longer: 'They may possibly be used.' It is very definitely: 'They will be used if we are attacked.'"[9]

Now ground forces in Europe were there primarily to serve as a trip-wire for the unleashing of nuclear counterattack. Possibly this had a sobering effect in the Kremlin for a time, but it also provided a rationalization for the neglect of conventional forces. Although some considerable part of the building up of forces in accordance with the Lisbon goals was on paper only, there was a steady decline over the next four years until the number of divisions available to NATO in 1957–58 was less than half the number listed in 1952–53.[10] The nuclear decision had a profound effect on the arms programs in all the NATO countries.

As the Soviet Union began to approach a kind of parity—not necessarily equality, but the capacity to deliver a strong "second strike," in any case—NATO leaders began to feel a growing uneasiness about too great reliance on a deterrent that might be losing its credibility. This led to a fourth stage in NATO's strategy that General Norstad, the Supreme Commander in Europe, called the "sword and shield." The first of the functions of the "shield" (the ground and tactical air forces) he described as being "to 'close a gap in our deterrent' " by removing the risk of a war arising from miscalculation, border incident, or a probing operation invited by weakness in the NATO periphery. An adequate shield confronting the aggressor, he said, makes him stop and think before he would move against us, no matter how limited his objective. For then he would have to use substantial force to breach the shield, an act he knows would bring down upon him the full weight of the deterrent. But this is not the shield's only function—it is also to give NATO an essential military and political function and flexibility. "We must be able to respond to less than ultimate incidents with decisive, but less than ultimate means."[11] Still, even in the so-called shield forces there was emphasis upon (tactical) nuclear weapons. The Heads of Governments, meeting as the North Atlantic Council in December 1957, agreed to provide nuclear capabilities for all NATO forces and to stockpile nuclear warheads in European countries. In April 1958 a conference of defense ministers in Paris confirmed its support of the basic NATO strategy as one "founded on the concept of a strong deterrent, comprising the Shield, with its conventional and nuclear elements, and the nuclear retaliatory forces."[12]

Under the umbrella of what amounted to a de facto nuclear stalemate, in which each of the two major nuclear powers was acknowledged to possess a sufficiently invulnerable nuclear capability to permit the delivery of a devastating second strike against the other, the prospect of conventional war reasserted itself. With a situation in which each side knew that it could not deliver a nuclear strike against the other without receiving such a blow in return, each might be willing to take greater risks on the assumption that the other would not initiate a nuclear attack. It was not inconceivable that the way had been opened for resort to conventional war on a large scale. An updated World War II-type of conflict—general (i.e., involving all or most of the great powers, ranged on opposing sides) and total (i.e., implying an all-out effort, with total mobilization), without being nuclear—was not impossible. This in turn raised the prospect again of a massive logistic effort to support a war effort under such conditions.

President Kennedy and his chief advisers, including Robert McNamara, secretary of defense, and General Maxwell Taylor, who became chairman of the U.S. Joint Chiefs of Staff, were convinced that a large-scale effort was indicated in order to build up conventional forces, which would provide the diplomatic and military flexibility that the situation required. If they were going to rely altogether on nuclear weapons for national security, they were going to be backing up their foreign policy with a kind of force that had lost its credibility. They foresaw conditions in which they would be put in the position of going after a gnat with a sledgehammer. They would find themselves in the awkward position of having to face every diplomatic crisis with only the choice of giving in or throwing the nuclear bomb. The history of international affairs since World War II had been characterized by an almost continuous series of limited and local conflict. Therefore, that was the kind of warfare for which preparation should be made—as well as keeping the nuclear forces viable in order to maintain the stable balance.[13]

President Kennedy, then, changed the emphasis of United States doctrine from massive retaliation to graduated deterrence, and to a response to attack that would not only be flexible, but controlled. This of course meant a renewed emphasis upon conventional forces and their weapon systems.

The new emphasis upon flexible response carried with it the implication that all-out conventional defense of Europe, previously shunned, would now be included among the range of alternatives to be selected. The communiqué released after the Kennedy-Macmillan conference at Nassau reflected the new thinking by reversing the original signification of the sword and shield; it now referred to the nuclear weapons as the "shield." Coupled with the idea of conventional defense was a rejection now of tactical nuclear weapons as carrying too great risks of escalation to total nuclear war to be considered as a substitute for conventional defense. At the same time, it was a part of the American policy to oppose placing national nuclear forces in the hands of any of the other allies. It was said that there should be central control over all nuclear weapons to assure complete coordination. Consequently the European members of the alliance should make major contributions of conventional forces—a minimum of not less than thirty divisions, together with reserves and supporting elements.[14]

Even at the level of general nuclear war, the new American doctrine held to the notion of controlled response. The use of any nuclear weapons at all would be only after the expiration of a "pause" period during which it might be hoped that the enemy would back down, and then the types of weapons used and the targets sought out would depend in each case on the necessities of the situation. Options would be held open to direct attacks against military targets only, against cities only, or against both types of targets, and then either simultaneously or with a delay.[15]

Secretary McNamara explained that the general nuclear war forces of the United States were: "(1) To deter a deliberate nuclear attack upon the United States and its allies by maintaining a clear and convincing capability to inflict unacceptable damage on an attacker, even were that attacker to strike first; (2) In the event such a war should nevertheless occur, to limit damage to our population and industrial capacities."[16]

The capabilities aiming for the first objective were developed under the concept of McNamara called "Assured Destruction; i.e., the capability to destroy the aggressor as a viable society, even after a well planned and executed attack on our forces." This is the aspect of the flexible response emphasizing an overwhelming second-strike capability. The Assured Destruction forces would include a portion of available strategic offensive forces—intercontinental ballistic missiles, submarine-launched ballistic missiles, and manned bombers.

The second of the United States strategic nuclear objectives fell under the concept of the "Damage Limitation; i.e., the capability to reduce the weight of the enemy attack by both offensive and defensive measures and to provide a degree of protection for the population against the effects of nuclear detonations." This comprised what was sometimes referred to as the "counterforce strategy," as well as measures of military and civil defense. Forces and resources with the Damage Limit mission would include the remaining elements of the strategic offensive forces, area defense forces (manned interceptor aircraft and antisubmarine warfare forces), terminal defense forces (antibomber surface-to-air missiles and antiballistic missile missiles), and passive defenses (fallout shelters, warning systems, etc.)

"It is generally agreed," McNamara stated, "that a vital first objective, to be met in full by our strategic nuclear forces, is the capability for Assured Destruction. . . . Once high confidence of an Assured Destruction capability has been provided, any further increase in the strategic offensive forces must be justified on the basis of its contribution to the Damage Limiting objectives."[17]

It was suggested that, with Polaris submarines distributed over the seas and with more than 1,000 hardened and dispersed land-based intercontinental ballistic missiles, the survival potential should be adequate for delivering a knockout blow to the extent of destroying approximately eighty percent of the enemy's total industrial capacity. Damage Limitation was more difficult to calculate, but in order to allow for different methods of enemy attack it was clear that a "balanced" defense was required.

In his statement before the congressional Armed Services Committee in 1965, the secretary of defense went on to say: "Although a deliberate attack upon the United States may seem a highly unlikely contingency in view of our unmistakable Assured Destruction capability, it must receive our urgent attention because of the enormous consequences it would have. In this regard, I should make two points clear. First, in order to preclude any possibility of miscalculation by others, I want to reiterate that although the U.S. would itself suffer severely in the event of a general nuclear war, we are fully committed to the defense of our Allies. Second, we do not view Damage Limitation as a question of concern only to the U.S. Our offensive forces cover strategic enemy capabilities to inflict damage on our allies in Europe just as they cover enemy threats to the continental U.S."[18]

Planning for the programs of military matériel to support operations under these concepts reflected the logistic lag previously mentioned. Programs being established in the 1960s were intended to provide the means to meet a situation as it was expected to be in the early 1970s.

The doctrine of flexible response as spelled out by the American leaders did not win ready acceptance on the part of the NATO allies. Nevertheless there was increasing attention to the buildup of conventional forces and to the idea of flexible response and if it did not become the officially accepted strategy, it came very close to it when the North Atlantic Council in ministerial session in December 1962 adopted a statement to the effect that it was "agreed that it was necessary to increase the effectiveness of conventional forces," and further agreeing "that adequate and balanced forces, both nuclear and conventional," were necessary "to provide the Alliance with the widest possible range of response to whatever threat may be directed against its security."[19] Already a joint session of NATO foreign ministers and defense ministers at Athens in May of 1962 had expressed a conviction that "if the Alliance is to meet the full range of threats to its security, the balance between the conventional and nuclear forces must be the subject of continuous examination."[20] Nevertheless, American leaders had so far oversold the case for massive retaliation and nuclear deterrence that they now were hard pressed to unsell it.

The French, with a good deal of sympathy from the other countries, continued to hold to the doctrine of the trip-wire and nuclear retaliation. The French emphasized deterrence, and they held that for a deterrent to be effective as such, it must rest on the clear threat of the prompt use of nuclear weapons. In their view, preparations for conventional war and indications of a willingness to use conventional means while showing a reluctance to initiate nuclear war would only invite potential enemies to risk small-scale attacks as they choose.[21]

Undoubtedly other factors affecting European reluctance to give up reliance on tactical nuclear weapons in favor of a more general posture in support of an attitude of flexible response were the political and economic implications of heavier burdens for conventional defense. Even while appearing to accept flexible response, the earl of Home, when British foreign secretary in 1963, indicated that these considerations were in the background of British thinking when he said in a public address:

"It is not practical politics—or economics—to plan for Western conventional forces to be brought up to the level of Soviet conventional forces. . . . I believe therefore that the armoury of the enemy being what it is we must certainly be ready to use tactical nuclear weapons in the event of a major assault. But I also think that we must have conventional forces strong enough to be able to identify and hold an aggression. . . . In short we must be able to deter an enemy from aggression at whatever level he chooses to make it."[22]

A similar ambivalence is to be seen in German statements. Sensitive to the devastation that a full-scale conventional war would be likely to bring to Central Europe, and concerned about the likelihood of escalation into nuclear war in any case, Chancellor Konrad Adenauer and Defense Minister Franz-Joseph Strauss opposed reliance upon conventional forces—even though they accepted a long-term goal of 500,000 men for Germany's armed forces at the time of the 1962 Berlin Crisis. The successor to Strauss as defense minister, Kai-Uwe von Hassel, stated that there was no change in German defense policy though he did in fact appear to emphasize conventional forces. But what he expressed as his major concern was the lack of any uniformly accepted strategy for NATO. Since Germany maintained no separate operational commands, it was assumed that its strategy would depend upon NATO strategy. The trouble was that while it might be assumed that Western strategy for the defense of Europe was one of flexible response, this had not been accepted by NATO as a whole, and in the German view it was essential that either this or a different strategy be made binding on all the members. For his part, Von Hassel still held that the nuclear threshold should remain low, and that defense through deterrence should be conducted in a manner that "forces the enemy to give up his idea of aggression by demonstrating that his only alternative will be willfully and deliberately to initiate escalation, which would be equivalent to his own destruction."[23]

Through failure on the part of most European members of the Alliance even to build up conventional forces to the point at which they had accepted commitments, there was no other course but to rely upon tactical nuclear weapons, and willy-nilly, the NATO strategy during the early 1960s remained almost necessarily restricted within a framework of nuclear deterrence and massive retaliation. The major exception to that was the expressed determination of the United States to fight a war, if necessary, with conventional means. The trip-wire theory made no allowance for the accidental, the indirect, the unforeseen initiation of hostilities. This seriously limited the range of choice in responding to a situation.[24] Conceivably it could lead to the same kind of inflexibility by which assumption of no alternatives to full mobilization tied the hands of statesmen with such catastrophic results in 1914 and in the 1930s.[25]

In the United States there was a feeling that the European allies had not fully accepted the strategy of flexible response either because, as Hedley Bull has written, "(a) Europeans do not understand nuclear strategy, or (b) understanding it, they turn a blind eye toward it for budgetary or electoral reasons."[26] But there were other aspects to the matter. At many points serious doubts about reliability and credibility arose. It has been suggested, for instance, that the United States doctrine had serious defects when viewed from the European position. While the United States assumed an indivisibility of security—taking literally the commitment of the North Atlantic Treaty that an attack upon one of its allies would be regarded in the same way as an attack upon its own territory—peoples in other countries could not believe that this was really true. To them there had to be a distinction in the complete action that a state would take to defend territory for which it had sovereign responsibility and its action to defend an area for whose defense it shared responsibility by virtue of treaty obligations.[27] Yet the United States had responded vigorously in Korea, Viet Nam, and other areas where its responsibilities were less clearly defined—and certainly a major purpose of those actions had been to demonstrate the very determination now apparently held in doubt. Further elements of doubt along these lines were to be found in fears that acceptance of flexible response would depend too much upon the maintenance of U.S. forces in Europe that, on account of continuing pressures to curb expenditures abroad in order to reduce the American balance-of-payments problem, might be subject to reduction at any time.[28] But there were two answers to this argument: America continuously made assurances that there would be no withdrawals prior to the agreement of the Allies, and more important, it was at this very point that the American leaders held that the European nations themselves should accept greater responsibility—that the main contribution of the European members should be in providing effective conventional forces.

Possibly more to the point was a consideration that Henry Kissinger expressed this way:

> "Part of the strategic dispute within the Alliance . . . involves jockeying to determine which geographic area will be the theater of war if deterrence fails. . . . A conventional war confined to Europe may appear relatively tolerable to us [the United States]. To Europeans, with their memory of conventional wars, this prospect is not particularly inviting. They may find a nuclear exchange which spares their territory a more attractive strategy and the threat of nuclear retaliation a more effective deterrent.[29]

Further serious questions could be raised about the adequacy of the conventional forces committed to NATO in Europe. There were grave doubts about whether either the thirty divisions urged by the Americans or the twenty-six held to be sufficient by the British could cope with an all-out attack from the east. Fewer than enough troops to do the job might be worse than no troops at all. However, it should not be forgotten that it was assumed that a well-equipped and trained thirty-division force could hold off a Soviet attack of forty divisions for at least a month, and in that time ready reserves could be mobilized in Europe and reinforcements could be flown from America and thrown quickly into the battle—provided adequate stocks of supplies had been stored in Europe ahead of time.[30] Still the French continued to have serious doubts about the role of conventional forces. Pierre Gallois expressed the French view in terms that was difficult to answer:

> What does General Taylor mean by "adequate conventional forces"? If, as he leads us to believe, and as all the other NATO military commanders have declared, nuclear weapons would have to be used at a given time in the conflict (because the opponent is numerically superior and is himself armed with nuclear weapons), it is difficult to see why the Western world should resort to nuclear weapons only after it has sacrificed important conventional forces. The greater these forces and the longer their commitment to a conventional strategy, the more costly and absurd would be their sacrifice and the weaker NATO's capability to stand its ground in Europe when the conflict became nuclear.[31]

The only immediate answers to this, of course, were (a) acceptance of the doctrine of controlled general war without the use of nuclear weapons, and (b) a buildup in the conventional forces of NATO countries—by a Western Europe alone possessing greater population and resources than the Soviet Union—to a point where they no longer would be outnumbered by the forces of the potential enemy. Two contradictory factors regarding what might be assumed as adequate forces need to be noted. In conventional war it usually is not necessary for defending forces to have a numercial parity with those of the attacker. Against well-organized, well-equipped, and well-trained troops in good defensive positions, it ordinarily is necessary for the attacker to have a numerical superiority of 2 or 3 to 1, or even more, in order to break through. On the other hand, if it were assured that tactical nuclear weapons were likely to be used against them, then the defending forces would have to be so dispersed and their mobility would be so impaired that their numbers would become far less effective.

As for the strategic nuclear aspects of the American doctrine of flexible response, some of the most serious criticisms were leveled at the counterforce strategy—that part of the Damage Limitation concept according to which a major objective of the strategic nuclear forces would be to knock out at least a part of the enemy's offensive nuclear systems. Some saw in this an unending nuclear race in which weapons would have to be added for each new such weapon that the potential enemy acquired.[32] This could lead to the absurd situation where enough nuclear weapons would be on hand to destroy the entire economy of the potential enemy several times over, but not enough to neutralize all his nuclear weapons. Still it should be noted that Secretary McNamara recognized an early point of diminishing returns in adding new weapons to counter those of the potential enemy. His contention was that every possible effort should be taken to save even a fraction of the millions of lives and billions of dollars of resources that would be at stake in a nuclear exchange.

One danger was that in its doctrine of flexible response the United States was putting so much emphasis on the counterforce strategy that a kind of new rigidity would arise to replace the old. None of this, however, was persuasive to European powers to give up actual or planned nuclear weapons of their own.[33] As for the situation as a whole, the former Secretary of State Dean Acheson concluded in 1963: "At the present time, NATO knows neither what it is supposed to defend against nor what it should be trying to accomplish. It is not surprising, therefore, that it has neither a strategic military plan nor the forces to execute it."[34]

In a situation where there was apparently a de facto policy of flexible response and an official policy of massive retaliation, where rapid changes were being made in nuclear systems as well as in conventional weapons and equipment, and in which both offensive and defensive measures were based upon a balance of several different systems, the logistical problem was very complex indeed. In the first place, so far as conventional forces were concerned, it made little difference whether there were twenty-five divisions or thirty or fifty, unless ammunition of the right types, repair parts for weapons, fuel, and all the other essential supplies were on hand in sufficient amounts to support sustained combat. There could be no flexible response on the part of the conventional forces themselves without adequate logistic support. As Ferdinand Miksche states, "What is the good of having helicopter units if the ammunition in the dumps will hardly last for 10–15 days of fighting? A military system based too one-sidedly on technology risks defeat, because it lacks the adaptability to meet all situations."[35] In the buildup of conventional forces that the Supreme Allied Commander, Europe, had been urging for years with only partial success, his own case was weakened by the acceptance at SHAPE of the idea that tactical atomic weapons lessened the need for conventional forces.[36]

In the support of strategic nuclear forces there was the vastly complicated matter of maintaining all the repair parts and the different types of fuels necessary to keep operational three completely distinct families of delivery systems—manned aircraft, land-based missiles, and submarines, with yet a fourth family, manned and unmanned spacecraft coming into the picture.[37]

But the most serious complication of all was the attempt to develop, side-by-side, capabilities for both conventional and nuclear war. The two kinds of warfare called for radically different—and often opposing—logistic assumptions. Conventional warfare requires a certain concentration of men and material, for it operates on an assumption that firepower is generally proportional to the forces. It depends upon a fully developed and complex logistical system—one that will provide heavy tonnages of supplies and equipment at the right places and at the right time under variable conditions. In a sustained, full-scale effort this infers further a long-range dependence upon industrial mobilization and production. Such support is essential to provide both the staying power and mobility to sustain a varied and flexible combat power. On the other hand, a strategy depending upon a trip-wire and nuclear retaliation may need little in the way of a traditional logistical system once the nuclear exchange has begun. On the contrary, traditional supply systems in this case would be more likely to invite destruction, and the concentration of men and material would not be practical. Nor is it likely that nuclear warfare would depend upon replenishment from a war industry mobilized after hostilities had begun.

At last in 1967 NATO adopted formally as official policy the strategy of flexible response. Yet it still was difficult to perceive an essential difference in commitments of forces and logistic support to make changes in strategic doctrine meaningful. What had been really unnecessarily large forces for maintaining a trip-wire to effectuate massive retaliation remained too small to give full credibility to flexible response.[38]

Forward Strategy

A special part of NATO's strategic position in Europe was the emphasis on a "forward strategy." Directions to SACEUR from the beginning of NATO's military organization were to defend as far forward as possible. For a time, however, there were doubts about whether the "possible" would be any farther forward than the Rhine. If not other considerations, the adherence of Germany to the North Atlantic Treaty made any such notion as that wholly unacceptable. Then for a time it was assumed that it might be necessary to give ground in the center in case of a major attack from the east, but every effort should be made to hold at the flanks so that strong counteroffensives could be launched against the flanks of the enemy penetration.

Finally, on 1 September 1963, General Lyman Lemnitzer as Supreme Allied Commander, Europe, announced that the forward strategy of his command would embrace a forward defense along the Iron Curtain. This included the establishment of stronger covering forces along the frontier of West Germany and orders for Allied ground forces, in case of attack, to conduct a mobile defense just west of the border. The defensive plan called for the deployment of 30-M day divisions and comparable air forces. It was a policy that the German defense minister called a "matter of life and death for the Federal Republic."

The biggest question in the new defense posture remained the matter of logistic support. In the Central Command, covering what was regarded as the most vital avenue of approach, the question of logistic coordination was most acute. The development of Germany's own logistic system and coordination with the systems of several other nations having forces in Germany— facilitating the rapid movement of forces and supplies from one area to another as called for—had to be constantly taken into consideration in developing an effective forward defense.[39]

Several schemes were put forward to ease the logistical problem in this situation. Probably the ultimate in proposals for forward defense were a suggestion by Ferdinand Miksche for a position defense by conventional forces and a German project for placing tactical nuclear devices at intervals along the border.

Noting in the first place that a hypothetical defense by counterattack in the direction of the Oder River without nuclear weapons would require a minimum of sixty modernly equipped divisions and 3 to 1 superiority in air— forces that simply were not going to be made available, and second, that a mobile defense relying on only twenty to thirty divisions inevitably would have to resort to the use of nuclear weapons, Miksche maintained that the only remaining solution was a defense in place based upon a fortified zone along the Iron Curtain. Militia-type forces would be prepared on short notice to occupy an elaborate system of fortifications resembling in some ways the West Wall, or "Siegfried Line," that the Germans had constructed just before the Second World War. Several advantages were claimed for this plan, not the least of which would be an easing of the burden on the supply system by storing large stocks of ammunition, food, and other essentials in the combat area in advance. The units themselves could be formed, it was suggested, at one-third the cost of mechanized units needed for mobile defense. Furthermore this would minimize the problem of refugees clogging the roads and interfering with the movement of mobile forces, and it would throw upon the enemy the dilemma of having to resort to nuclear weapons and thus invite reprisals or of having to attempt a breakthrough against strong defensive positions.[40] This was a proposal that probably deserved more attention than it received, for it was based upon a realistic appreciation of the logistical situation as few others were.

Miksche wrote, "Such a solution, however rigid it may seem from a purely military viewpoint, would be politically much more flexible than one based essentially on the use of atomic weapons. As things stand at present, this is the only way out of the atomic paralysis to which we shall otherwise succumb politically."[41]

At the end of 1964, press reports were carrying accounts that plans for the installation of a "barrage" or barrier line of nuclear demolition mines along the frontier with East Germany were being carried forward. This pointed to a way to stop or canalize an attack from the east without having to provide the support of a massive logistic buildup.[42] This plan was not necessarily incompatible either with the fortified zone plan or with a mobile defense. It would introduce another formidable element of doubt into Soviet calculations about what kinds of weapons that Allies might employ, and if the mines were in fact used, they could be used to channel an attack toward areas of greatest vulnerability either to mobile counterattacks or toward the strongest positions in a fortified zone.

To the extent that mobile defense would continue to be the policy of SACEUR'S forward strategy, there was something to be said for a suggestion that even if the wide dispersal of defensive forces demanded by nuclear weapons should permit a sizeable penetration by an attacker, logistics would set severe limits to his exploitation. Then in the counterattacking phase, it might be expected that if the enemy threatened the use of nuclear weapons—and this capability always would have to be recognized, whatever the other conditions might be—the ensuing operations would resemble more than anything else the campaigns in the desert in 1941–42 when attacks were launched as much as 120 kilometers from the bases.[43]

Control of Nuclear Weapons

Rapidly changing conditions in the distribution of nuclear power brought differences of opinion among members of the North Atlantic Alliance to critical proportions by the mid-1960s. Where the United States once had enjoyed a monopoly of nuclear weapons, the Soviet Union, as noted above, now had achieved a certain kind of parity, and the perfection of intercontinental ballistic missiles on both sides brought a decline in the credibility of United States guarantees insofar as the use of strategic nuclear weapons— thereby inviting devastating retaliation on American cities—in response to a possible Soviet attack on European allies was concerned. This appeared to be at the crux of the problem of nuclear control in the Alliance. Out of this situation, in the main, grew the pressing questions about the degree of hegemony that the United States should continue to hold over nuclear weapons, the question of the role of other national nuclear forces, the question of a European nuclear deterrent, questions of possible development of an integrated nuclear force.[44]

Solutions proposed for dealing with the problem of nuclear control generally could be grouped under the following headings: (1) a multilateral force of missile-carrying surfaces vessels manned by mixed crews; (2) an "Atlantic Nuclear Force"—an Allied force employing various means; (3) a European nuclear force operated separately from, but in partnership with, the United States; (4) a fully integrated nuclear force, free of any United States veto; (5) United States nuclear trusteeship; and (6) nuclear nationalism and a loosening of the Alliance to something resembling the Entente Cordiale.[45]

As a means of countering the threat against Europe posed by Soviet medium-range ballistic missiles—particularly after the removal of United States intermediate-range missiles from Turkey, Italy, and Great Britain—and at the same time permitting greater European participation in the control of nuclear weapons whole discouraging further development of independent national forces, the United States put forward a proposal for a multilateral force. This had first been proposed for study in 1960, and then President Kennedy and later President Johnson urged acceptance. As finally worked out, the plan called for a force of twenty-five surface ships, each armed with eight Polaris A3 missiles and manned by mixed crews drawn from the participating nations, the whole to be jointly owned, financed, and controlled. The force was to be put on the sea in order to be mobile and in order to avoid the objections of states that the location of MRBM's on their territory would be likely to draw fire. It was to be made up of surface ships largely because of American legal restrictions against the transfer of nuclear submarines. It was to be mixed-manned so that no ship should comprise a national contingent that a captain or a government might withdraw from the force for any reason.

The catch was that the United States would provide the nuclear warheads and would retain a veto over their use. This, then, failed to get at the heart of the problem of political control. On the military side such a force might have been feasible enough, though it offered little in effectiveness beyond the nuclear weapons already at the disposal of SACEUR and available to SACLANT by action of the United States. Technical details for the logistic support of the ships and their crews of many nationalities remained to be worked out. Undoubtedly there would have been complications, but such problems probably would have been easier solved for a sea-borne force of this character than for any such force operating on land.

Of the major European allies, only Germany responded with any enthusiasm toward the MLF proposal—and this in itself posed a problem, for as it turned out, Germany would have been paying about eighty percent of the European share of the cost, and presumably would have had a dominant voice in its control. While a part of the rationale of the plan had been to curb possible German desires for nuclear weapons by granting a means of participation in this kind of force, it was the very fear of German domination and a possibly growing ambition for national nuclear forces that led Denmark and

Norway to decline participation. Far from criticizing the U.S. veto, the Scandinavian members insisted upon it. France rejected the whole project outright, while Britain, though lukewarm, agreed to go along. Other nations participating with the United States, Germany, and Britain in the preliminary studies were Belgium, Greece, Italy, the Netherlands, and Turkey. By 1965 the whole project had become virtually a dead letter.[46]

As an alternative to the multilateral force, the British proposed to extend the idea to embrace national contingents of air forces and land-based missiles, as well as naval forces in what they called an "Atlantic Nuclear Force." As presented by the newly elected Labour Government in December 1964, the Atlantic Nuclear Force (ANF) would include the following elements: (1) the British V-bomber force except for a certain number of aircraft that would be reserved for duties outside the NATO area; (2) the British *Polaris* submarines (armed with missiles—but not warheads—purchased from the United States); (3) at least an equal number of U.S. *Polaris* submarines; (4) some kind of an MLF element (not necessarily seaborne) in which nonnuclear powers might participate; and (5) any nuclear forces that France might contribute. The force would operate under a single collective authority in which each of the participating nuclear powers would have a veto, and each of the other participating powers might have a veto if it desired, or all the others might act together as a group. Prime Minister Harold Wilson strongly opposed any attempt to curtail the American veto over the use of nucelar weapons, and he was strongly opposed to having any additional fingers on the nuclear trigger—of any kind of nuclear proliferation. Once again, in the assessment of the duties of the controlling authority in providing guidance for the commander of the ANF—political guidance, approval of targeting and operational plans, release of nuclear weapons, roles of different strategic and tactical nuclear weapons—no mention was made about logistic support, as, for example, how the participating contingents would be supplied with parts to keep the missiles operational, with fuel for aircraft and ships, with food for crews, and so on.[47] Admittedly these were details that could be worked out, but until then no such force could be effective.

Marshal of the Royal Air Force and Chief of the Air Staff Sir John Slessor urged that the ANF plan be carried a step further to comprise all Allied nuclear units, other than short-range battlefield weapons, on the eastern side of the Atlantic, whether aircraft or missiles, and he would vest command of the force in SACEUR. For the command of the force itself he would set up a headquarters "as international as SHAPE," patterned after the Mediterranean Allied Air Forces of the Second World War.[48]

Several other modifications to the Atlantic Nuclear Force scheme were offered. Perhaps the most significant of these was a plan developed by the Defence Committee of the Assembly of Western European Union. Two particular features characterized the plan. Like Slessor's, this would include virtually all Allied nuclear forces on the eastern side of the Atlantic, tactical as well as strategic, but it would also include a portion of the American

Minute-Man ICBM's based in the United States. Second, and more important, this plan would abolish the formal U.S. veto in the control over nuclear
weapons, though it would preserve most of the substance by a system of
weighted voting in the executive authority to be organized. It was proposed
that the United States be given five votes, Britain and France two each, and
two rotating members drawn from the remaining membership of the Alliance, one each. It would take a majority (i.e., six of eleven votes) for a
decision to use nuclear weapons. By this arrangement the United States plus
one European power, whether large or small, could make the decision. On
the other hand, without the concurrence of the United States, all the European members of the authority theoretically could vote to use the force.
Practically speaking it could be pointed out that the United States would not
be giving up anything substantial, for already it found itself without a veto
over certain nuclear forces in Europe—those of France and, to a lesser
extent, of Britain, and on the other hand if all European members should
vote not to employ the Allied Nuclear Force at a given time, the United
States would retain such an overwhelming nuclear capability outside that
force that it still could exercise its effective initiative in nuclear strikes.[49]

Another proposed voting scheme was for the fifteen nations of the Alliance to assign to the five major powers—i.e., the United States, Britain,
France, Germany, and Italy—responsibility for nuclear control, at which
point any of the remaining ten would have the option of dropping out of the
arrangement of the Five Powers and a vote of any three would be effective in
a decision governing the employment of nuclear weapons, at which point
those voting against the majority would have the option of withdrawing (with
their forces) from the arrangement. However unrealistic such a plan may
appear to be, it was an attempt to get at the fundamental problems underlying all the plans for an integrated force: the individual veto, with fifteen
fingers on the trigger, which made any planned response wholly ineffective;
the matter of assuring the primacy of the political factors, with civilian
control over the military in the ultimate decision to use nuclear weapons;
and the danger of the unauthorized use of a part of the force by one of the
members.[50]

Still it had to be noted that discussions of an Allied Nuclear Force paid
little or no attention to the logistic implications. If there were to be any kind
of real nuclear sharing, then there was in the first instance a need for sharing
in the production and maintenance of weapons. Here was to be found the
key to cooperative participation and control rather than in ingenius voting
formulas. François Duchêne suggested that the most constructive reform
would be in the development of an Atlantic Nuclear Force in which the
European elements were supported by a European joint research and production program for nuclear weapons.[51]

With all of the plans for integrated forces and schemes for collective
control, there still was a feeling—led by the French who, at least since the
return of General de Gaulle to power, showed no enthusiasm for any such
approaches—that too much emphasis was being placed on institutions and

formal agreements and mechanism and structure in dealing with the complex questions of international security.

One view (strictly not French) held that the realities of the situation required frank recognition of American domination of nuclear weapons and that true international participation in the making of strategy was to be found in effective participation in the staff work than in some kind of voting on the final decision that must, in any case, remain with the power possessing the weapons. According to this view, the United States would act as executive agent for the Alliance, and ultimate decisions would remain with the president of the United States, but his decision would be based upon a commonly agreed-upon strategy and on the recommendations of a fully integrated international political staff. The floor leader of the Social Democratic Party in the German Bundestag put it this way: "For years I have urged that the European partners in NATO be given a share in planning, in deciding on common strategy, in preparing future weapons developments and similar matters, leaving the ultimate decisions on the use of nuclear weapons in the hands of the President of the United States, acting as trustee for the alliance, but basing his decision on a commonly agreed strategy."[52]

According to the French interpretation, the realities of the situation argue for independent national nuclear forces—at least to the extent of an independent French force. While American leaders may have regarded efforts at nuclear buildup on the part of the French and British as wasteful, useless, and even dangerous, they saw it as a vital element in their own interests. As Henry Kissinger pointed out, those nuclear forces might be regarded in somewhat the same way as the armies of Switzerland and Sweden. No one assumes that those nations could withstand an all-out attack from a powerful neighbor, but they may be able to exact a price out of all proportion to the gains to be made in the estimates of would-be attackers. Even a few weapons of nuclear power are not to be disregarded by adversaries. Moreover, the possession of nuclear weapons provided a certain bargaining power, not only vis à vis the Soviet Union, but vis à vis the United States. Again, Kissinger suggested that the real reason for the opposition of the United States to (other) national nuclear forces was the fear of the Americans that they may be drawn into a nuclear war against their will as a result of a decision by a European power to use nuclear weapons without seeking the agreement of the United States. This of course was precisely the feeling that Europeans often had about the American control of nuclear weapons.[53]

But the major reason that the French gave for their need of an independent nuclear force was to restore a degree of credibility to the strategic deterrent—and the emphasis always was upon deterrence rather than upon defense per se. The French General André Beaufre, former French representative on the NATO Standing Group in Washington and former deputy chief of staff of SHAPE, probably gave the clearest analysis of this position. He assumed in the first place that the threat of a Soviet invasion of Western Europe had lost its validity because of the success of NATO as a deterrent and because of political and psychological changes within the

Soviet Union. Second, the notion of a nuclear war had become unthinkable because of the recognized capacities for mutual retaliation. But the practical nuclear stalemate that had developed between the United States and the Soviet Union had resulted in a stability that had rendered the nuclear deterrent incredible. The only way that it could be made credible was by restoring a minimum of instability to the situation—by having available different methods that might be used simultaneously to maintain a degree of uncertainty in the enemy's mind, and this required several centers of decision. Deterrence, of course, was a peacetime concept; yet NATO's planning, according to Beaufre, related only to time of war, and there had been no forward planning, except in relation to Berlin, to deal with any crisis that the Alliance might face in peacetime.[54]

Beaufre summarized what he considered to be the guiding principles of deterrence as follows:

(a) Since it is desirable to increase the uncertainty felt by the enemy by more than one method and by basing a strategy of deterrence on more than one center, it is quite useless to create a new force, such as MLF or ANF, if this is dependent directly and openly upon American nuclear strategy, which already possesses a super abundant capacity. To be effective as a deterrent, any new force must, in peacetime, be subject to an antonomous center of decision. On the other hand, a nuclear center of decision cannot be international in character. If it is to be credible, it can only be national.

(b) *The control of deterrent strategy cannot be collective in peacetime.* In such circumstances, only the principle of national independence can be applicable, an independence which naturally applies to nuclear no less than to conventional forces. This principle has not the dangerous implications often associated with it, because the nuclear threshold has become far too stable. . . . A minimum instability must be restored to it if the deterrent is to retain any value.

(c) In these circumstances, *the peacetime problem* of the sharing of nuclear responsibilities no longer lies in the search for an integration of nuclear capabilities—which is, in any case, impossible to achieve— but in *the organization of an effective coordination of national deterrent strategies.* Such coordination must not aim merely at persuading each of the allies to adopt a single method of deterrence. On the contrary, it must aim at promoting a mutual understanding of the needs and fears of each, and at making the best use, by common agreement and in the common interest, of the specific strategies of each of the partners in relation to the interests of the alliance as a whole.

(d) Forward planning for a *war,* however unlikely, remains necessary. This must deal essentially with the organization of a possible system of nuclear command, and with the allocation of responsibilities among the various national forces. Apart from its deterrent value, this forward planning would provide an opportunity to begin the organization of inter-allied consultations in the sphere of nuclear planning, and the preparation of the framework for their European nuclear force which must be established where Europe has eventually taken shape as a political entity.[55]

For at least seven or eight years the French had been calling for a revision of NATO in the direction of a reduction in the integration of military forces. For instance, President de Gaulle stated in a press conference in September 1960 that "it seems to us that the defense of a country, while being of course combined with that of other countries, must have a national character. How indeed in the long run could a Government, a Parliament, a people give their money and their services with all their heart in time of peace, and make their sacrifices in time of war, for a system in which they are not responsible for their own defense?"[56] This was a sentiment eloquently expressed by General Pershing and other American leaders during the First World War. Again, the French foreign minister, Maurice Couve de Murville, said in June 1964 that the NATO military organization had become "more or less outmoded. . . . I think it is in the interest of the United States as well," he said, "to give the European countries—at least the largest European countries—the feeling that they have a big responsibility in this defense. . . . We want more national armies and more national defense, especially in time of peace."[57] The French continued to emphasize these views, with little response from the other Allies, right up to the decision in March 1966 to withdraw from further military cooperation within NATO.

But there also were other expressions of views calling for a European deterrent. Some saw in the American position a one-sided view—insisting upon complete freedom of action for the United States regarding the use of nuclear weapons, but strongly opposing that same freedom for France or anyone else. American attempts to assuage European demands for nuclear sharing by extending opportunities for participation in targeting and tactical dispositions failed to reach the heart of matter—i.e., control over a decision to use the weapons.[58] Franz Josef Strauss had said that it was not for Europe to blame America's not wanting to protect Europe at the risk of its own annihilation (if indeed that were a valid assumption), but that Europe had to develop the defense of its own territory on an independent basis. He saw neither the MLF nor the ANF as providing the proper answer in the circumstances. What was needed, he said, was the creation of a strong European defense system, of which the British and French nuclear forces would form the core, and then to convert the "American protective Alliance" into an American-European alliance of equals. This was a view that would seem to have followed the one outlined by President Kennedy as he foresaw an alliance of equals in what came to be referred to as the "dumb-bell" theory— of two spheres joined solidly together. Yet such suggestions on the part of American leaders never were followed up with any concrete proposals leading toward an independent European deterrent. As Henry Kissinger had put it, "Our [the American's] frequently expressed outrage at the seeming European doubt about the reliability of our nuclear guarantee has blinded us to the fact that we have in effect accused our allies of being too irresponsible to be entrusted with the ultimate means for their protection."[59]

Nor were the French views entirely without sympathy in Great Britain. A study of the Royal Institute of International Affairs suggested that Britain should give up its "special relationship" with the United States at least to the extent of reducing it as an obstacle to closer cooperation with Europe, and it was suggested that some form of nuclear cooperation between the United Kingdom and France was the key to better relationships.[60] Another comment was that Britain never was so popular nor so influential in Europe as when she did accept equality with her continental neighbors—at the time of the Marshall Plan.[61]

On the other hand, many severe and bitter criticisms of the French position arose.[62] Typical of these was a comment by ex-Secretary-General Stikker. Although paying tribute to General de Gaulle for what he had done for France, both in the liberation in the 1940s and in restoring unity in the 1950s and 1960s, Stikker went on to say that "De Gaulle wants a split within NATO, whereby the Six . . . would have their own (he naturally means the French) strategic concept, operational plans and command function—dependent on the French "Force de Frappe" over which De Gaulle as a Roman Emperor or a new Charlemagne would reign and decide for Europe."[63] Elsewhere, describing France as the "Weakest Link in NATO," the former Secretary-General wrote, "This vaunted complete independence of action has created an atmosphere of incompatibility of both aims and methods between France and nearly all of its allies. He who insists on retaining his complete independence of action can never be counted on as a devoted and staunch member of any alliance."[64] Surely the immediate rejoinder on the part of many would be, what about the United States?

French differences with the United States, in particular, on nuclear control grew out of the same differences that lead to divergent views on the doctrine of flexible response. At least in part it was a difference in emphasis on deterrence and defense—on what was needed to make policy effective in peacetime and what was needed to make military efforts effective in wartime.[65]

In a way arguments about the North Atlantic Alliance had come full circle. After analyzing the whole problem of strategy and the sharing of responsibilities for nuclear warfare, Eugene Rostow came to the conclusion that "our goal should be the concord of the Entente Cordiale, the most successful of modern alliances."[66] Seymon Brown suggested a "North Atlantic Concert" of "independent nations, bound together only where, and when, and to the degree there exists a real convergence on ideological goals or concrete interests."[67]

The notions of preserving national identity, independence of action, and even diversity within the alliance was one that found support among the middle and smaller nonnuclear powers as well. Discarding the "dumb-bell" idea as "highly offensive to Canada," a former assistant under secretary of state for external affairs of Canada, John W. Holmes, stated: "While insisting on as much interallied cooperation and consultation as possible, [most members] shy away from the paralysis inherent in proposals for placing all hands on the trigger. . . . They accept, tacitly for the most part, the decisive role of the United States. Dissenters prefer to develop their 'independent' nuclear power rather than hold out for multiple control. Whether or not this is wise and effective, it may be better that dissent take this form than lead us into schemes for tripartite or even multipartite direction of policy which would break down in a crisis."[68] Among other remarks on this theme, the former Canadian official went on to say:

We can be stronger as a team for our diversity. To accept this fact is better for our morale. Some of the problems troubling NATO are psychiatric rather than real. We are driven mad by abstractions, searching for symmetry and unity, making ends out of means, ignoring the virtue of untidiness in an untidy world, seeking to define the undefinable and evoking a mood of despair about the fortunes of the Atlantic world when we might better feel the reasonable confidence which is justified by things as they work out in practice. . . . Orators tend to assume against all evidence that unity means our being united behind policies which, because they are collective, are wise. There are times, however, when members should remain disengaged to do what they can to bail out their foolish partners and avoid the opprobrium they have brought on "the West." . . .

When there is not a consensus of peoples, then a common policy can only be the lowest common denominator and much weaker than the separate but more forthright policies of the component states. . . . To assume that a consensus exists because it ought to exist or that a Council of Ministers could compel it to exist, is to court disaster. . . .

The search for agreement is not helped by pious denunciations of nationalism and sovereignty in the abstract. . . .

Neither the United States nor any other ally could accept North Atlantic institutions in which decisions were made by a simple or even a weighted majority, because the United States, which has a near monopoly on the crucial weapons, could not permit a veto on its freedom of movement, and its allies could not, in such an unequal situation, give up their right to dissent and contract out. In practice, of course, and that is what matters, the United States is unlikely to act in ruthless disregard of the views of its allies; and the latter are unlikely to be so reckless as to put themselves beyond the bounds of Alliance. This is a relationship which can be tacitly recognized but not formally instituted, and there is much to be said for leaving well enough alone.[69]

Perhaps there was a good deal in the contention for recognizing a minimum freedom of action on the part of the North Atlantic allies. But that was precisely the status quo of 1965–66. General de Gaulle's move in withdrawing French military cooperation from NATO—accompanied by protestations of belief in the necessity of the alliance itself if not in its integrated military structure—was something else again. Certainly this was a retreat in the direction of traditional alliances or understandings such as the Entente Cordiale. But if problems of nuclear weapons and the changed security situation in Europe had rendered NATO in its current form obsolete by 1966, whether effective correctives could be found in the direction of the traditional alliances was open to serious question.

This raised the question about the purposes of a defensive alliance. Kissinger had suggested that in the past, three general purposes might be noted: "(1) To provide an accretion of power. . . .(2) To leave no doubt about the alignment of forces. . . .(3) To provide an incentive for mutual assistance beyond that already supplied by an estimate of the national interest."[70] But the greatest value of a military alliance in the modern world is not in the prior commitment to a line of action, but in the prior planning and organization of a command and communications structure and of measures for logistic coordination and preparation that will make action more effective. Whatever commitments a state may have formalized by a treaty of alliance, the treaty as such is likely to have little effect on the policies and actions of that state in a particular situation. If, at a given time, that state's vital interests appear to be in jeopardy, then it is likely to resort to war whether or not it is bound to do so by some treaty; on the other hand, even though a state may be committed by treaty to come to the aid of another, it is not likely to do so if, in the view of its national leaders, its interests lie in the other direction. Just how effective was that "most successful of modern alliances"—the Entente Cordiale? Insofar as bringing Great Britain into the First World War at the side of France is concerned, it should be remembered that German declarations of war against France and Germany did not bring the British immediately into the war. Britain entered the war only after the invasion of Belgium, a circumstance that, in view of British trditional policy, probably would have had the same result if there had been no alliance or understanding. In the 1950s and 1960s alliances made even less difference in the policies of the stronger powers. Neither could tolerate a serious disturbance of the precarious balance of power, and, as Kissinger pointed out, the United States was as concerned about a Chinese attack against neutralist India as against allied Pakistan. This situation, blurring the distinction between neutrals and allies, gave to both a greater freedom of action than they could have enjoyed otherwise. As Kissinger wrote, "Far from doubting America's military commitment to Europe, President de Gaulle is so certain of it that he does not consider political independence a risk. He thus adds American policy to his own in pursuit of his policies."[71]

Again with respect to the Entente Cordiale, the British-French staff conversations prior to the outbreak of the First World War were no substitute for the Supreme War Council, the Supreme command, and measures of logistic cooperation that the crises of war itself later drove the Allies to establish. "The most successful of modern alliances" surely was not the Entente Cordiale, but NATO, and the substance of NATO has been not in the formal commitments of the original treaty—those probably could have been honored for the most part in the absence of any treaty—but in the development of a military command and communications system, together with a number of essential cooperative logistic arrangements, that would permit the alliance to be operative immediately in case of war and thus to make the commitments for mutual support effective. The question was whether that structure now must founder on the rock of the control of nuclear weapons.

NATO and Problems in Other Areas of the World

One of the major stumbling blocks to high-level strategic and logistic planning in NATO has been the lack of coordination of policies respecting problems in regions outside the NATO area. With the exception of a short-lived flareup or two over Berlin, all of the major international crises since 1949—including Korea, Suez, Lebanon, Quemoy, Indochina, Malaysia, Congo, Cuba, Angola, Iran, Falkland Islands, Central America and Afghanistan—have been outside the NATO area, and frequently have found the NATO partners divided.[72]

This was one of the main points of contention of President de Gaulle throughout the period of his leadership in France. Shortly after returning to power, de Gaulle in September 1958 sent a memorandum to London and Washington that, though never made public, has been reported authoritatively to have called for the division of the areas outside NATO into clearly defined and well-organized theaters of operations, and for the coordination of the policies of the powers having worldwide responsibilities—i.e., France, Great Britain, and the United States—in each of the major areas of the world.[73] This proposal was widely criticized as an attempt to set up a Western "troika," as an attempt to have a few powers rule the world, or simply as an apparent French effort to break down the peculiar relationship that Great Britain enjoyed with the United States.

It might have been seen as an attempt to find a way to deal with the complete world situation in which policies might have the benefit of some prior coordination. Instead the United States paid repeated lip service to the idea of political consultation,[74] and then went ahead making unilateral decisions on the war in Viet Nam, and then called upon its allies for support. Likewise, the British made unilateral decisions about Malaysia that could affect their NATO commitments.

Two years later de Gaulle stated that one of the essential points on which NATO must be revised was "the limitation of the alliance to the single area of Europe. We feel that, at least among the world powers of the West, there must be something organized—where the Alliance is concerned—as to their political conduct and, should the occasion arise, their strategic conduct outside Europe, especially in the Middle East, and in Africa, where these three powers are constantly involved."[75] But neither this nor other statements over the next six years had any greater results than the original memorandum.

With the Chinese explosion of a nuclear device, the problem of control of nuclear weapons leaped outside the European area, and the potentially critical problem of the proliferation of nuclear weapons loomed as one of those that although of very serious concern to all members of NATO, would be beyond the scope of the alliance. This development itself would add to the significance of Asia in the policies of the United States and its allies. It was difficult to see how strategic and logistic planning for NATO could be made effective without taking into account in some way demands for other parts of the world.[76]

Notes

1. André Beaufre, *Introduction à lá Stratégie* (Paris, 1963), 90.
2. James E. Moore, "NATO Today," *Army,* August 1964, 31.
3. Henry E. Eccles, *European Logistics, 1956.* The George Washington University Logistics Research Project, ONR 41904 (Washington, D.C., 1956), 31 and 85.
4. See Moore, "NATO Today," 31.
5. Dirk V. Stikker, "NATO—The Shifting Western Alliance," *The Atlantic Community Quarterly* (Spring 1965): 11.
6. See James E. King, "NATO: Genesis, Progress, Problems," in *National Security in the Nuclear Age,* ed. Gordon E. Turner and Richard D. Challener (New York, 1960), 143–72.
7. U.S. Senate, Hearings, Committee on Foreign Relations and Committee on Armed Services, 82d Cong., 1st sess., 1951, 79, quoted in ibid., 153–54.
8. George E. Lowe, *The Age of Deterrence* (Boston, 1964), 50–92.
9. B. H. Liddell Hart, *Deterrent or Defense* (New York, 1960), 56.
10. See B. H. Liddell Hart, "NATO—Sword or Shield," *Ordnance* 47 (July–Aug. 1962): 43–46; Lincoln Gordon, "NATO in the Nuclear Age," *The Yale Review* 48 (March 1959): 321–35.
11. Quoted in King, "NATO: Genesis, Progress, Problems," 164.
12. Final Communiqué, Conference of Defense Ministers of NATO-Member countries, 17 April 1958.
13. See Maxwell Taylor, *The Uncertain Trumpet* (New York, 1960), 1–10.
14. Lowe, *The Age of Deterrence,* 225–53; Henry A. Kissinger, "NATO's Nuclear Dilemma," *The Reporter,* 28 March 1963, 22–23; Kai-Uwe von Hassel, "The Search for Consensus: Organizing Western Defense," *Foreign Affairs* 43 (January 1965): 209–16; Ferdinand Otto Miksche, "Tactical Nuclear Weapons and the Defense of Western Europe," *Military Review* 44 (June 1965): 35–42; Taylor, *The Uncertain Trumpet,* 130–64; Henry A. Kissinger, *The Troubled Partnership: A Reappraisal of The Western Alliance* (New York, 1965); Timothy W. Stanley, *"NATO in Transition,"* (London, 1965); Hedley Bull, *Strategy and the Atlantic Alliance: A Critique of U.S. Doctrine,* Center of International Studies, Policy Memorandum no. 29 (Princeton, N.J., 1964); Robert R. Bowie, "Strategy and the Western Alliance," *International Organization* 17 (Summer 1963): 709–19; Pierre M. Gallois, "U.S. Strategy and the Defense of Western Europe," *Orbis* 7 (Summer 1963): 226–34; T. D. White, "New Era in NATO," *Newsweek,* 29 October 1962, 27–28; Charles V. Murphy, "NATO at a Nuclear Crossroads," *Fortune,* December 1962, 84–87; D. Healey, "Turning Point for NATO," *The New Republic,* 24 April 1961, 144–47; Robert Strauss-Hupe and William R. Kintner, *Building the Atlantic World* (New York, 1963): 75–78; Livingston T. Merchant, "Evolving United States Relations with the Atlantic Community," in *The Atlantic Community: Progress and Prospects,* ed. Francis O. Wilcox and H. Field Haviland, Jr. (New York, 1963), 92 109.
15. See Robert S. McNamara, "McNamara on BDM," Extract from Defense Statement, *Survival* (April 1967): 108–14, 121.
16. Robert S. McNamara, "American Strategy Now," *Survival* 7 (May–June 1965): 98.
17. Ibid, 99.
18. Ibid, 103.
19. Final Communiqué, Ministerial Session of North Atlantic Council, Paris, 13–15 December 1962.
20. Ibid., Athens, 4–6 May 1962.
21. See Pierre Gallois, *Stratégie de l'Age Nucleaire* (Paris, 1960); Besislav Badurina, "France's Military Policy," *Review of International Affairs* 15 (Oct. 20, 1964): 17–19; Badurina, "NATO's Nuclear Policy," *Review of International Affairs* 15 (Dec. 5, 1964): 8–10; Raymond Aron, *The Great Debate: Theories of Nuclear Strategy* (Garden City, N.Y., 1965).
22. Release of Speech by the Earl of Home, Secretary of State for Foreign Affairs, at Wilton Park, 18 February 1963. Copy in Institute for Strategic Studies, London. See also Anthony Hartley, "The British Bomb," *Encounter* 12 (May 1964): 22–34.
23. Hassel, "The Search for Consensus," 209–16. See also Wallace C. Magathan, "West German Defense Policy," *Orbis* 8 (Summer 1964): 292–315; Statement of Chancellor Erhard to Fifth Bundestag, 10 November 1965, *NATO Letter,* January 1966, 24.
24. See Alan S. Nanes, "NATO's Strategic Dilemmas," *Current History* 39 (September 1960): 133–38; Anthony Verrier, "British Defense Policy under Labor," *Foreign Affairs* 42 (January 1964): 291.
25. Henry Owen, "NATO Strategy: What is Past is Prologue," *Foreign Affairs* 43 (July 1965): 682–90.

26. Bull, *Strategy and the Atlantic Alliance.*
27. Ibid.
28. Alastair Buchan, "NATO and the American-European Strategic Relationship," address given at RAND Corporation, 15 November 1963. Copy of text in files of Institute for Strategic Studies, London.
29. Henry A. Kissinger, "Coalition Diplomacy in the Nuclear Age," *Foreign Affairs* 42 (July 1964): 528.
30. See Otto Heilbrunn, "NATO and the Flexible Response," *Military Review* 45 (May 1965): 22–26.
31. Gallois, "U.S. Strategy and the Defense of Europe," 235.
32. See Verrier, "British Defense Policy under Labor," 288–89.
33. See Kissinger, "NATO's Nuclear Dilemma," 23–26. Cf. Thomas C. Schelling, "Wie neu ist die 'neue Stratequie' der Vereington Staaten?" *Europ-Archiv,* 15 February 1963, 551–64.
34. Address by Dean Acheson, Institute of Strategic Studies, Adelphi Papers no. 5 (London, 1963), 16.
35. Ferdinand O. Miksche, *Failure of Atomic Strategy* (New York, 1958), 137. See also W. A. Smallman, "Mobility and Logistics," *Revue Militaire Générale,* March 1960, 392–409.
36. See Hart, "NATO—Sword or Shield," 43–46.
37. See Samuel E. Anderson, "Aerospace Power and Logistics," *NATO's Fifteen Nations* 5 (Winter 1960): 9–19.
38. See Timothy W. Stanley, "NATO's Strategic Doctrine," *Survival* 11 (November 1969): 344–45.
39. Hassel, "The Search for Consensus," 210–11; Moore, "NATO Today," 32; Horst v. Zitzewitz, "Vorwärtsverteidigung am Eisernen Vorhang," *Wehrkunde,* February 1964, 63–68.
40. Ferdinand O. Miksche, "The European Shield," *NATO's Fifteen Nations* 7 (August–September, 1962): 15–22; Malcom Hoag, "Rationalizing NATO Strategy," *World Politics* 17 (October 1964): 121–42.
41. Ibid., 22.
42. *Army,* January 1965, p. 63; Moore, "NATO Today," 32–33.
43. Suire, "Logistique et Stratéqie en Climat Nucleaire," *Revue Militaire d'Information,* May 1963, 15–23.
44. See series of essays by Klaus Knorr, James E. Moore, Friedrich Ruqe, André Beaufre, Stefan T. Possony, Sir John Slessor, and Philip Mosely in *NATO in Quest of Cohesion,* ed. Karl H. Cerny and Henry W. Briefs (New York, 1965), 149–256; Kissinger, "Coalition Diplomacy in the Nuclear Age," 525–45; Alastair Buchan, "The Changed Setting of the Atlantic Debate," *Foreign Affairs* 43 (July 1965): 574–86; J. R. Schaetzel, "Tides of Change," *Department of State Bulletin,* 4 March 1963, 322–28; Alastair Buchan, *NATO in the 1960s,* rev. ed. (New York, 1963), 42–58; Stanley Hoffmann, "Discord in the Community," in *The Atlantic Community,* ed. Francis O. Wilcox and H. Field Haviland, Jr. (New York, 1963), 21–29; Alastair Buchan, "NATO After Nassau," *Air Force College Journal* (Canada) (1963): 45–49; Robert R. Bowie, "Strategy and the Atlantic Alliance," *International Organization* (Summer 1963): 719–20; 730–31. For an excellent general survey of the problems of NATO as they appeared to the secretary general at the end of 1965, see Manlio Brosio, "The Substance and Spirit of the Alliance" (speech given at the 11th Annual NATO Parliamentarian's Conference in New York), *NATO Letter,* December 1965, 2–10, and Henry A. Kissinger, *Nuclear Weapons and Foreign Policy* (New York, 1957), 269–315.
45. See Elliott R. Goodman, "Five Nuclear Options for the West," *The Atlantic Community Quarterly* 2 (Winter 1964–65): 571–87; Bowie, "Strategy and the Atlantic Alliance," 721–22; Lord Kennet (Rapporteur), "The State of European Security (Navies in the Nuclear Age)," Western European Union Doc. 269, 1963 (draft), 2–48.
46. Alastair Buchan, "The Multilaterial Force," *International Affairs* 60 (October 1964): 628–37; Kissinger, "NATO's Nuclear Dilemma," 29–36; Moore, "NATO Today," 27–29; Nils Orvik and Niels J. Haagerup, *The Scandinavian Members of NATO,* Institute of Strategic Studies, Adelphi Papers no. 23 (London 1965), 6–7; Drew Middleton, "Britain Backs Land Force over NATO's Mixed Fleet, *New York Times* (Int. ed.), 23 June 1964, 1, 2; Robert R. Brunn, "NATO's Next Step," *Christian Science Monitor,* 27 May 1963, 1; Kai-Uwe von Hassel, "Detente through Firmness," *Foreign Affairs* 42 (January 1964): 189; Frederick W. Mulley, "NATO's Nuclear Problems: Control or Consultation," *Orbis* 8 (Spring 1964): 21–35; George Ball, "The Nuclear Deterrent and the Atlantic Alliance," *Department of State Bulletin* 49 (May 13 1963): 736–39; Wayland Young, "MLF—A West European View," *Bulletin of the Atomic Scientists* (20 November 1964): 19–21; L. L. Doty, "NATO Working Group Supports U.S. Plan

for Mixed Nuclear Fleet," *Aviation Week and Space Technology,* 21 September 1964, 25; Edmond Taylor, "What Price MLF," *The Reporter,* 3 December 1964, 12–14; Denis Healey, "Britain under Labor," *NATO's Fifteen Nations* 9 (June–July 1964): 31; Wallace C. Magathan, "West German Defense Policy," *Orbis* 8 (Summer 1964): 292–315; Guido Colonna, "The State of the Alliance," *Atlantic Community Quarterly* 2 (Fall 1964): 397–407; Henry Owen, "What the Multilateral Force Could Achieve," *European Review* 4 (Autumn 1964): 12–14; K. Regelin, "Multilateral Confusion," *Interavia* 19 (1964): 1461; John Silard, "The Case against the MLF," *Bulletin of The Atomic Scientists* 20 (September 1964): 18–20; André Fontaine, "The ABC of MLF," *The Reporter,* 31 December 1964, 10–14; Wilfrid L. Kohl, "Nuclear Sharing in NATO and the Multilateral Force," *Political Science Quarterly* 80 (March 1965): 88–109; Carl H. Amme, "Nuclear Control and the Multilateral Force," *Proceedings of the United States Naval Institute* 91 (April 1965): 24–35.

47. Harold Wilson, "Britain and the ANF" (extracts from statement in the House of Commons, 16 December 1964, *Hansard*), *Survival* 7 (March–April 1965): 52–54; Blair Fraser, "Can We Succeed in NATO without Really Trying?" *Atlantic Community Quarterly* 3 (Spring 1965): 50–55.

48. Sir John Slessor, *Command and Control of Allied Nuclear Forces: A British View,* Institute for Strategic Studies, Adelphi Papers no. 22, (London, 1965); Slessor, "Control of NATO Nuclear Capacity," *Atlantic Community Quarterly* 2 (Fall 1964): 469–71; and 3 (Spring 1965): 56–63.

49. Elliott R. Goodman, "The Duynstee Plan," *NATO Letter,* July–August 1965, 2–9; Assembly of Western European Union, "Recommendation on the State of European Security Aspects of Western Strategy," rapporteur: Anthony Duynstee, *Atlantic Community Quarterly* 2 (Winter 1964–65): 683–84. Cf. Sir Edward Beddington-Behrens, "Using the Multi-national Idea," *European Review* 15 (Spring 1964): 7–9; Kurt Birrenbach, *The Future of the Atlantic Community; Toward European-American Partnership* (New York, 1963), 8–20; Paul Stehlin, "French Thoughts on the Alliance," *Military Review* 44 (January 1965): 28–34.

50. Klaus Knorr, *A NATO Nuclear Force: The Problem of Management* (Princeton, N.J., 1963).

51. Francois Duchêne, *Beyond Alliance* (Boulogne-sur-Seine, 1965), 53–59.

52. Fritz Erler, "The Alliance and the Future of Germany," *Foreign Affairs* 43 (April 1965): 442. Cf. Altiero Spineili, "Europe and the Nuclear Monopoly," *Atlantic Community Quarterly* 2 (Winter 1964–65): 595; Mulley, "NATO's Nuclear Problems," 21–35; Eugene Rostow and Edgar S. Furniss, *The Western Alliance: Its Status and Prospects* (Columbus, Ohio, 1965).

53. Kissinger, "NATO's Nuclear Dilemma," 26–28.

54. André Beaufre, "The Sharing of Nuclear Responsibilities—A Problem in Need of a Solution," *International Affairs* 61 (July 1965): 411–19.

55. Ibid., 417–18.

56. Senate Committee on Government Operations, Subcommittee on National Security and International Operations, *The Atlantic Alliance: Allied Comment,* 89th Cong., 2d sess., 1966, Committee Print, 36.

57. International television interview with Maurice Couve de Murville, reported in *New York Herald Tribune* (European ed.), 30 June 1964, 3.

58. See Josef I. Coffe, "A NATO Nuclear Deterrent?" *Orbis* 8 (Fall 1964): 584–94; Fred Luchsinger, "France's A-Force," *Swiss Review of World Affairs* 14 (January 1965): 304; David Thomson, "General de Gaulle and the Anglo-Saxons," *International Affairs* 61 (January 1965): 11–21.

59. Kissinger, "NATO's Nuclear Dilemma," 27.

60. Kenneth Younger, *Changing Perspectives in British Foreign Policy* (London, 1965), 110.

61. Review by Thomas Barman, *International Affairs* 61 (April 1965): 317.

62. See, for example, J. H. Huizinga, "Which Way Europe?" *Foreign Affairs* 43 (April 1965): 486–500.

63. Dirk V. Stikker, "NATO—The Shifting Western Alliance," *Atlantic Community Quarterly* 3 (Spring 1965): 7–17.

64. Dirk V. Stikker, "Weakest Link in NATO," *Life International,* 20 December 1965, reprinted in *The Atlantic Alliance: Allied Comment,* 78.

65. See also (anon.), "Must We Reform NATO?" *Politique Etrangère,* reprinted in *Survival* 8 (January 1966): 2–8; Roger Massip, "An Atlantic Europe—Where Do We Stand?" *NATO Letter* (July–August 1964): 2–8; Alfred Grossner, "France and Germany in the Atlantic Community," *The Atlantic Community,* 46–50; Moore, "NATO Today," 27.

66. Eugene V. Rostow "Prospects for the Alliance," *Atlantic Community Quarterly* (Spring 1965): 34–42.

67. Seyom Brown, "An Alternative to the Grand Design," *World Politics* 17 (January 1965): 232–42.

68. John W. Holmes, "The Atlantic Community—Unity and Reality," address to the Atlantic Treaty Association, Ottawa, 15 September 1964, printed in *The Atlantic Alliance: Allied Comment,* 13–15.

69. Ibid., 15–17.

70. Kissinger, "Coalition Diplomacy in a Nuclear Age," 526.

71. Ibid., 530. Cf. Edwin H. Fedder, "The Concept of Alliance," *International Studies Quarterly* 12 (March 1968): 65–86.

72. See René Pleven, "France in the Atlantic Community," *Foreign Affairs* 39 (October 1959): 29–30.

73. Ibid., 21–26.

74. See, for example, Dean Rusk, "The State of the North Atlantic Alliance," *Department of State Bulletin* 49 (5 August 1963): 190–98; also his address to Cleveland Council of World Affairs, 6 March 1965.

75. President Charles de Gaulle, Third Press Conference 5 September, 1960, French embassy, Service de Presse et d'Information, New York.

76. See Buchan, "The Changed Setting of the Atlantic Debate," 576–77.

5
General Logistic Planning

Civil Emergency Planning

What potentially may have been one of the most significant of NATO's planning efforts was that relating to civil emergency planning.[1] In the early days of NATO various committees sprang up in response to perceived needs for some particular planning to relate certain civil aspects to other problems of war planning. At first these never were looked upon as comprising any kind of systematic structure. Then an official was appointed as head of civil emergency planning to bring together the various committees that already had been at work and to initiate additional efforts to fill in gaps in the planning. However, the emphasis during this phase of the organization was largely on civil defense—measures of passive defense against nuclear attack, protection from fallout, first aid, and emergency measures to restore essential services of an area when disrupted by nuclear attack. Later, with some change in organization and leadership, the emphasis shifted to economic planning. The rationale for planning continued to be the requirements for meeting nuclear attack—steps to be taken by way of stockpiling, dispersing, and planning for the use of resources in advance of an attack, and then measures to be taken to make up losses, to restore devastated areas, and so on. The assumption was that a NATO deterrent gained credibility if the enemy could see that civil defense measures had been taken that might indicate a willingness to accept the risk of a nuclear exchange. But what could be by far the greatest significance of civil emergency planning was the possible entering wedge that this could provide for the coordination of general economic mobilization within the Alliance. Thus anticipating the Allied committees, boards, and executives of the First and Second World Wars, civil emergency planning could form the very basis for effective coordination of the whole Allied logistic effort.

Yet for several years planning in this area remained rudimentary and incomplete. That this was so was due in large part to a dichotomy between military and civilian requirements. Military authorities showed little interest in plans aimed at keeping segments of the civilian economy operating, and they were concerned about steps that might draw resources away from direct military operations. This is a problem that nearly always appears in any national war effort of significant proportions, and its bearing on the logistic feasibility of strategic plans can weigh just as heavily as the seemingly more immediate problems of military transportation and supply.

Technical committees were organized to provide for planning in each of several segments of civil emergency planning, and they operated under the direction of the Senior Civil Emergency Planning Committee. Composed of the civil emergency planning heads of each of the member countries, the Senior Committee met once a year to consider the annual progress reports of the subordinate committees, to discuss an annual review of civil emergency plans and projects of the individual countries, and to develop policy guidance for future planning. This was the only committee, other than the North Atlantic Council, of which the Secretary-General served as chairman. A Civil Emergency Coordinating Committee served as a kind of standing committee for the Senior Committee to give continuous direction and coordination to civil emergency planning.

A segment of NATO's permanent international staff was organized to serve the various committees engaged in civil emergency planning. Under the general supervision of an executive secretary, who also served as deputy chairman of the Senior Committee, the Civil Emergency Planning Bureau and a small secretariat provided expert guidance and administrative services. The bureau was composed of a group of technical advisers representing the major areas of civil emergency planning and was headed by an official who also served as chairman of the Coordinating Committee. The head of the secretariat acted as secretary both to the Senior Committee and the Coordinating Committee, and the other members of his staff served as permanent secretaries to the various subordinate planning committees.

Three of the principal technical committees operated in the field of transportation planning. The Planning Board for Ocean Shipping, in addition to its primary task of preparing plans for a wartime NATO Ocean Shipping Pool,[2] made such special studies as the redirection of Europe-bound ships in case of outbreak of war, the evacuation of ports, naval control of shipping outside the NATO area (in cooperation with SACLANT), problems of resupplying Europe in the initial phase of war, relationships between wartime control of shipping and control of supplies, and the organization of coastal shipping in time of war. The Planning Board for European Inland Surface Transport also was concerned mainly with the organization of wartime agencies for the coordination of transport and in the constitution of a central Europe Wagon Pool for the control of railway cars. The Civil Aviation Planning Committee gave its attention mainly to the preparation of plans for the evacuation of civil aircraft—including evacuation across the Atlantic—in time of emergency and in plans for the organization of a wartime board for the coordination of civil aircraft.

In the field of supply planning, three additional committees went to work. A considerable part of their efforts, as indeed was much of the work of the coordinating committees, was in the development of plans for a wartime Central Supplies Agency together with its component organizations for food and agricultural supplies, petroleum, and industrial goods.[3] In conformity with the earlier emphasis, the Food and Agriculture Planning Committee also continued to study the problem of protecting food against nuclear fallout and continued to encourage household stocking of food, as well as the establishment of an agreed-upon policy that all member nations should maintain a minimum thirty-day supply of foodstuffs stored in protected places. The Petroleum Planning Committee aimed at achieving a thirty-day supply of petroleum products in all countries, and it further served as a forum where country representatives were able to exchange information on national planning for petroleum supply. The Industrial Planning Committee aside from its role in planning for wartime agencies, had to be content mostly with exchanging information on national planning.

As for other areas of civil emergency planning, the Civil Communications Planning Committee has found itself squarely up against military demands for priority. Yet it had to be recognized that communications for shipping, civil aviation, and railways were as vital for military operations as were strictly military communications systems. Moreover, the normal FTT networks of the member countries carried the relays of the vast military warning system. The Civil Defense Committee, beginning in 1954, continued to make studies through special working groups that dealt with planning for such problems as public information, civil warning against attack, evacuation and dispersal of populations, design and location of fallout shelters, wartime firefighting, civil defense in industry, and scientific problems regarding the effects of and possible means of protection from thermonuclear explosions. The Manpower Planning Committee provided guidance and an exchange of information in national planning for the control and allocation of labor to meet the disruptions of attack and the requirements of war. A special NATO Medical Committee, working closely with the supreme military headquarters, studied the problems of coordinating civil and military use of hospitals in wartime.

Civil logistical exercises sponsored by the civil emergency planning organization provided valuable experience in developing various plans for wartime organization, in testing the feasibility of plans, and in providing experience in this kind of activity for the individuals involved.

Probably in no other aspect of planning were the difficulties of strategic assumptions and national priorities more apparent than in civil planning for war emergencies. Yet the fact that a great deal of study, thought, and planning had been applied to the various problem areas would in any case provide a fund of experience to draw upon in meeting emergency situations, whether or not any of the specific plans previously drawn found direct applicability.

Coordination of Economic Mobilization Planning

Taking leaves mainly from the lessons of the Allies in the First and Second World Wars, the North Atlantic Allies of the 1960s prepared detailed plans for wartime organizations and procedures intended to coordinate their economic resources for a sustained military effort. As indicated above, this planning went forward mainly under the aegis of the Senior Civil Emergency Planning Committee, the Coordinating Committee and several special planning committees that operated under it and the section of the International Staff that served it.

Here as in other aspects of NATO logistic plans and preparations, the whole process was caught up in the dilemma of strategy. Planning for cooperation in the mobilization of economic resources appeared then to be based upon an assumption of a "broken-back war"—accepting the notion that there would be a nuclear exchange in the early phase of a war in Europe, but thereafter, all concerned would somehow pick up the broken pieces and strike back by whatever means still might be at hand. However unlikely, this assumption at least had the merit, if it could be called that, of supporting preparations for both nuclear and conventional war, however opposed those two might be to each other.

The North Atlantic Council agreed that for the purpose of coordinating the supply programs of the member countries in wartime there should be a Central Supplies Agency (sometimes referred to as the International Wartime Supply Agency), comprising major divisions or organizations for industrial raw materials and equipment, for food and agricultural products, and for petroleum.

According to those plans, the headquarters for this agency would be in the United States. However, in order to facilitate the movement of resources from one European country to another during the early stages before the Ocean Shipping Pool would become fully operative, and so before resupply from North America could be depended upon, it was intended that a smaller counterpart of the Central Supplies Agency, to be known as the European Supplies Agency should be set up on the European continent—preferably in France. This agency would maintain data on the status of such items as food, medical supplies, and clothing that might be made available for civil emergency relief. Then at times of crisis, it would undertake to direct the shipment of those critical items in accordance with a program hastily worked out on the basis of information on requirements received from affected European NATO countries.

The more general operation to be centered under the Central Supplies Agency would be mainly matters of the coordination of various national programs into an international supply program. Essentially this would mean matching supplies and shipping. Each nation, within its own wartime organizations for industry, food, and fuel, would prepare long-range supply programs. The appropriate divisions of the Central Supplies Agency in each case would review those falling within its area of primary responsibility. If supplies and shipping could be found to meet stated requirements, then the proposed program would become an agreed-upon program. Otherwise recommendations would have to be made before agreement could be effected.

Concurrent planning for the Industrial Division of the Central Supplies Agency was in the hands of the Industrial Planning Committee. The Industrial Division presumably would function through a series of commodity committees or boards similar to the various international executives and boards of the two world wars. Meanwhile the Division assisted member countries in developing their own wartime industries boards. Similarly the Food and Agriculture Planning Committee prepared plans for the Food and Agriculture Division in wartime and for the protection and sharing of foodstocks. Finally, the Petroleum Planning Committee prepared the organization of the NATO Wartime Oil Organization. While a part of the machinery of the Central Supplies Agency, the Oil Organization probably would function autonomously, with the right of direct appeal to higher political authority. An Oil Authority would be constituted as the executive of the Oil Organization, and it would act under the direction of an executive board having an eastern branch in the United Kingdom and a western branch in the United States. It would have a joint operational staff to work national civil and military requirements into an overall NATO program. Meanwhile the Petroleum Planning Committee acted as a forum where country representatives compared their respective programs and searched for ways to develop national organizations and national programs—and for ways of bringing coordination among them and for meeting the challenge of other nations.

Although most emphasis heretofore in planning for international supply had related to civil emergency relief, the basic structure was fairly complete—at least equal to what the Allies developed during the two world wars—if there were the need and the will to use it. Actually, nominations already had been made of people to be on call to fill out the skeleton staff in case of a war emergency. The hope was that much of the lost motion of the early phases of coalition efforts could be avoided in prompt acceptance of measures for close cooperation in the mobilization of economic resources. Already the planners had the benefit of testing the organization and functioning of the organization for international wartime supply in exercises such as NATO's CIVLOGEX (Civilian Logistics Exercise) so that it was possible to make refinements on the basis of a certain kind of experience, and key leaders had a chance to become practiced, even if in a limited way, in their anticipated wartime duties.

Continuing Problems

Difficulties in NATO's planning process, though heightened by the French withdrawal from active participation in 1966, had in fact persisted for years. In a way, military planning had to proceed in a vacuum. Political direction remained vague and uncertain while the formulation of military policy was confined largely to military channels. A further deficiency was the lack of full discussion in the international staffs of the possible use of strategic nuclear weapons by the United States, but this too went back to the underlying problem of finding a way for effective political consultation.[4] At least since General de Gaulle's memorandum of September 1958 when he proposed a three-power directorate for coordinating policies of the West worldwide, the Atlantic Alliance had been troubled by dissatisfaction and ineffectiveness in political consultation.[5]

Advocates of improved political consultation among the North Atlantic Allies still pointed to the need for coordination of policies outside Europe and for the coordination of assistance to underdeveloped countries, as well as to the need for common policies and political direction in the defense of Western Europe itself. Again support was growing for the idea that NATO should become an instrument for improving relations between Eastern and Western Europe.[6]

However, such a leader as Paul-Henri Spaak announced himself as "opposed absolutely to a political directorate for NATO," though he would not hesitate to accept the idea of a nuclear directorate.[7] Others pointed to a "dangerous bilateralism" in attempting to deal with the political problems facing the NATO countries.[8]

The United States as well as France had come in for a good deal of criticism for the failure of political consultation. Henry Kissinger explained the attitude of the United States in this way: "The tendency of the United States to confine consultation to elaborating its own blueprint reflects less a quest for hegemony . . . than a desire to avoid complicating still further its own decision-making process."[9] On the more general problem he went on to say: "The emphasis on a unitary strategic system for the alliance has reversed the proper priorities. The real challenge to the consultative process is less in the field of strategy than in diplomacy. The ability to fight a centrally controlled general war is useful; but the ability to devise common policies in the face of a whole spectrum of eventualities is much more important."[10] He then suggested that "the time seems ripe to create a political body at the highest level—composed perhaps of the United States, the United Kingdom, France, Germany, and Italy—for concerting the policies of the nations bordering the North Atlantic."[11] In a similar vein, Alastair Buchan warned that reform of the machinery of NATO could not be long delayed "if the strange divorce between political reality and military planning is to be avoided." "There is a clear need for a multilateral system of crisis management," he wrote, "applicable not just to the more remote contingencies of direct nuclear war, but also to the many lesser or less clear-cut situations which a more diversified Communist strategy makes possible." He recommended steps for "pre-decision coordination of policy in Washington" where he suggested forming a series of overlapping regional councils or long-term planning centers covering the major areas of the world and bringing into consultation the nations particularly concerned in each area.[12] Sir Anthony Eden on several occasions advocated the formation of a "political general staff, made up of representatives of the United States, the United Kingdom, France, Italy, Germany, and perhaps one or two others, to function in the political arena as the combined Chiefs of Staff did in the military during World War II."[13]

Already in the mid-1960s three significant steps had been taken toward the improvement of planning and consultation. The first was adoption of special procedures for relating strategy to logistics (1963–66). The second was the reorganization of the planning staff of the standing group (June 1964). The third was the formation of a special ten-nation committee of defense ministers to study ways of coordinating policies with respect to nuclear weapons (November 1965).

Although at least since 1951 the North Atlantic Council had been concerned with the problem of reconciling military requirements with the economic and financial resources of the member countries with the appointment of the Committee of Three to make a special study, and although this problem had been the subject of annual and triennial reviews since that time, the difficulty had persisted. Indeed this was a problem always faced in any general military planning, but in NATO, differences over national defense efforts in terms of what was being done as against what could or what ought to be done led to underlying dissension. Seeking broader coverage of information, the NATO Ministerial Council meeting at Ottawa in May 1963 approved projects for making two special studies, the first on the inter-related questions of strategy, force requirements, and the resources available to meet them, and the second, an analysis of national force programs and defense budgets. Probably the most important immediate result of the studies was the introduction of new procedures of review on the basis of overlapping five-year plans—i.e., a regular triennial review that in each case would project force goals and requirements five years ahead. For their part the Americans had hopes that the additional information might result in a further revision of the cost-sharing formula to lessen to some degree the burden on the United States.[14]

The reorganization of the planning staff of the Standing Group was intended to "internationalize" the staff, since members now would serve in an international capacity. After 1 July 1964 the staff would be headed by a director holding the military rank of major general or the equivalent and chosen from a country not represented on the Standing Group itself. Of four deputy directors to assist the director, two were to be chosen from Standing Group Nations and two from other nations. One of the deputies from a non-Standing Group country would be designated vice director.

Largely at the suggestion of Secretary McNamara of the United States, a special committee of the defense ministers of all the NATO members except Norway, Iceland, Portugal, France, and Luxemburg met in November 1965 to review nuclear capabilities and arrangements and to consider ways of improving allied participation in nuclear policy and planning. The committee established three working groups—on communications, data exchange, and nuclear planning—to operate under a steering committee composed of the permanent NATO representatives of the ten participating countries. The full committee of ministers would meet again from time to time to review progress and take up special problems.[15] This effort was regarded as a means of consultation rather than as a substitute for ANF or other plans for controlling nuclear weapons. Others would have moved more directly to the control of weapons. General Lauris Norstad, immediately after his retirement as SACEUR in January 1963 after a little over six years in that post, recommended that authority over nuclear weapons intended for the support of NATO defense plans be vested in the alliance itself. He proposed that an executive body made up of representatives of the powers contributing nuclear weapons, perhaps with an additional representative from Germany and one or two other countries on a rotating basis, be empowered to act for the council in deciding on the use of nuclear weapons in an emergency. In addition he would have sold France missiles and nuclear warheads both as a means of gaining more economical target coverage and as an aid to the U.S. balance of payments.[16] Spaak suggested that it ought to be possible to find a way for nations to assign or earmark nuclear forces to NATO, with the right to withdraw them at any time to meet national necessities, just as was done with conventional forces.

The major bar to any such steps for cooperative planning and control over nuclear weapons remained the American policy of attempting to retain a monopoly over nuclear power in the West. Even if he were disposed to do so, it must be remembered, it was impossible for the president of the United States to move to full cooperation in exchanging atomic information so long as his hands remained tied by the MacMahon Law of 1946. Although as president he had done little to change the law, former President Eisenhower in May 1966 sent a letter to the chairman of the U.S. Senate subcommittee studying problems of NATO in which he recommended "radical modification" of the law in the interest of nuclear sharing.[17] However, this had little more immediate effect than had similar suggestions made by various people over the last twenty years.

Pierre Gallois would have had NATO, at least insofar as its military aspects were concerned, exclusively an agency for sharing nuclear weapons development. With neither the fear of nuclear proliferation nor the hope in conventional weapons of the United States and other Allies, Gallois contended that the principal use of NATO should be in setting up technological and financial cooperation to enable all members of the alliance to obtain the most advanced weapons, which they might use as they saw fit. Powers that failed to develop their own nuclear weapons would have to depend upon bilateral arrangements with a "guardian power," and in doing so probably would have to accept the presence of troops of that foreign power on their territory—"more for stage dressing than for fighting." However, Gallois would reject Secretary McNamara's suggestion for a "common market of arms," for in his view this simply would extend the reliance of the other members on the United States for advanced technology, and would lead to the scientific and industrial impoverishment of Western Europe.[18]

Possibly the most serious danger of the French position for strategic and logistic planning was the rigidity that it introduced into the situation. In denying the relevance of the flexible response and the effectiveness of conventional defense, the French would "put all their eggs in one basket." In doing so they ran the risk of returning to a rigidity that had led the European powers to the extravagance of 1914 and that in 1936 had left the French paralyzed as the Germans reoccupied the Rhineland. In both instances general staffs had rejected the flexibility of partial mobilization in favor of a policy according to which no crisis could be met except by total mobilization. In both instances they paved the way for total war.[19] Furthermore, the rigid posture of fixed nuclear weapons robs diplomacy of the flexibility of force supporting it, which often gives it its effect. As Kissinger asked, with solid-fuel missiles all ready to go in hardened sites, what serves as a warning in a crisis situation that preparations are being stepped up for possible conflict—dispersing aircraft of the Strategic Air Command (as at the time of the Cuban crisis of 1962), or moving divisions forward, or calling up the reserves, or dispatching a fleet to critical waters?[20]

Notes

1. For a brief description of the organization and procedure for civil emergency planning, see *NATO: Facts About the North Atlantic Treaty Organization* (Paris, 1966), 163–73; *Aspects of NATO: The Importance of Civil Emergency Planning* (Paris, n.d.).

2. See chap. 13.

3. See chap. 12.

4. See Alastair Buchan, "The Reform of NATO," *Foreign Affairs* 41 (January 1962): 165–82; James E. Moore, "NATO Today," *Army*, August 1964, 29; J. M. A. H. Luns, "Independence or Interdependence," *International Affairs* 18 (January 1964): 10–20.

5. See Herbert Luthey, "DeGaulle: Pose and Policy," *Foreign Affairs* 43 (July 1965): 571; Robert Strausz-Hupé, "The Crisis in Political Leadership," in *NATO in Quest of Cohesion*, ed. Karl H. Cerny and Henry W. Briefs (New York, 1965), 138–43; Hans J. Morgenthau, "The Crisis of the Alliance," in ibid., 125–27.

6. See U.S. Senate, *Hearings before the Subcommittee on National Security and International Operations of the Committee on Government Operations, The Atlantic Alliance* 89th Cong. 2d sess., 27 April 1966, 1:27.

7. Paul-Henri Spaak, "A New Effort to Build Europe," *Foreign Affairs* 43 (January 1965): 208.

8. See "NATO and the Defense of Europe" from *Il Giornale d'Italia*, 9 June 1965, reprinted in *Survival* 7 (Oct. 1965): 266–67.

9. Henry A. Kissinger, "Coalition Diplomacy in a Nuclear Age," *Foreign Affairs* 42 (July 1964): 539.

10. Ibid., 540–41.

11. Ibid., 544.

12. Alastair Buchan, "The Changed Setting of the Atlantic Debate," *Foreign Affairs* 43 (July 1965): 585–86.

13. Interview with Sir Anthony Eden on CBS television, 27 December 1964; also in *Freedom and Union*, October 1961, 3–5.

14. NATO Press Communique M3 (65)2, 16 December 1965; Robert R. Brunn, "NATO to Assess Strength," *Christian Science Monitor*, 27 May 1963; Clare Hollingsworth, "U.S. Puts Pressure on NATO Partners; Five-Year Package Deal Urged," *Manchester Guardian*, 5 June 1963; Don Cook "Strategy and Sentiment," *New York Herald Tribune* (European ed.), 13 July 1963; Don Cook, "French to Veto Plan for NATO Strategic Study," ibid., 24 July 1963; "M. Seydoux Informe l'O.T.A.N. de l'Opposition de la France," *Le Monde*, 26 July 1963; "Plan to

Study N.A.T.O. Resources and Aims," *Financial Times* (London), 31 July 1963; Dirk V. Stikker, "Britain's Role in NATO," *Financial Times,* Defense Supplement, 23 March 1964, 29. See also Lawrence C. McQuade, "NATO's Non-nuclear Needs," *International Affairs* 18 (January 1964): 11–21.

15. NATO Press Release (65) 19, 27 November 1965; *The Atlantic Alliance* hearings, 1:21–22.

16. Moore, "NATO Today," 32–33.

17. *Le Monde,* 24 May 1966, 3.

18. Pierre Gallois, "The Case for France," *Diplomat,* April 1966.

19. Henry Owen, "What's Past is Prologue," *Foreign Affairs* 43 (July 1965): 682–90.

20. Kissinger, "Coalition Diplomacy in a Nuclear Age," 532.

6
Military Logistic Planning

Allied Command Europe

With responsibility for preparing defenses and controlling Allied military activities in a sector extending all the way from North Cape to the Black Sea, Allied Command Europe faced a considerable logistic task simply in keeping track of its forces and installations. But concern for the problems of building and maintaining an organization made effective by advanced communications systems and other facilities could only be secondary to the much greater concern for the measures that would make the defense posture effective in deterring attack and the defense plans effective in meeting an attack.

Logistic planning at SHAPE was made difficult not only by the international aspects of the problem, but also by a general assumption that plans must assume both conventional and nuclear warfare.

Although it always had been assumed that ground defense in Europe should be as "far to the east as possible," logistic limitations and the availability of forces set the limits to "the possible." It was not a question of conflicting ideas about strategy, which in the early days of NATO led to a general assumption that any defensive stand would have to be made deep in Western Europe, or, a little later, that a stand might be made in the vicinity of the Rhine. It simply was a question of judging what could be done with the means at hand. As soon as he could be satisfied that forces and equipment had been built up sufficiently to permit it, General Lemnitzer was glad to announce in 1963 the adoption of a "forward strategy," according to which a mobile defense would be maintained, with outposts near the Iron Curtain, to cover all the territory of the Allies.[1] But in adopting such a policy, the supreme commander was well aware of the greater logistic efforts needed. "Forward defense calls for greater firepower and cross-country mobility," he said, "so we are urging the equipping of army forces with more personnel carriers, self-propelled artillery, fast-moving light and medium tanks, helicopters, and so on."[2] The irony of this statement was that the supreme commander had to say "we are urging" rather than "we are ordering" or "we are directing."

The second strategic factor complicating SHAPE logistic planning was the assumed use of nuclear weapons. Following up its 1954 decision to use atomic weapons against any attack, the North Atlantic Council in a meeting of heads of governments and ministers in December 1957 decided to establish stocks of nuclear warheads that would be readily available in case of attack (though remaining under the control of the United States) and to put IRBMs at the disposal of SACEUR.[3] In 1963 the North Atlantic foreign and defense ministers, meeting at Ottawa, approved several more steps to reinforce the hand of supreme commander in Europe. These included the assignment of three U.S. Polaris submarines as well as elements of the British V-bomber force to SACEUR, arrangements for broader participation of officers from the NATO countries in nuclear warfare planning at SHAPE and in the coordination of operational planning at the headquarters of the U.S. Strategic Air Command in Omaha, Nebraska, and establishment of a deputy for nuclear affairs on the staff of SACEUR.[4] Of significance is the fact that the ministers at this same meeting directed the Council in Permanent Session "to undertake, with the advice of the NATO military authorities, further studies of the inter-related questions of strategy, force requirements and the resources available to meet them."[5]

Actually, SACEUR had had representatives at Omaha since the establishment of SAC Headquarters there, and the U.S. Strategic Air Command always had had a liaison team at SHAPE. This practice now had the official encouragement of the ministers, and it now would be the practice to include more non-U.S. officers in these exchanges. As for participation in the planning for nuclear warfare, General Lemnitzer estimated that over 1,000 Allied officers were participating in these activities at various levels. There was some question as to whether the nuclear deputy would serve a useful purpose. A recent reorganization of the Supreme Headquarters had brought together planning and operations, including planning for nuclear warfare, and had included a readjustment of national representation. Now there was a possible danger that the regular organization and planning procedures might be disrupted, though that would depend largely upon the personalities involved and upon informal arrangements for coordination.[6]

About the same time, work had begun on a NATO Missile Firing Installation, to be operational in 1965. Located on the island of Crete, in the vicinity of Sauda Bay, this would be a firing range for training and annual service firing practice by NATO units equipped with NIKE, HAWK, and SERGEANT missiles. Ten of the NATO member countries (all except Great Britain, Canada, Portugal, Iceland, and Luxembourg) were participating in this program.

As SHAPE logistics staff officers pointed out, atomic warfare would appear in a way to lighten the logistics problem. Its effect presumably would be to bring a change from the logistics of the First World War, when artillery ammunition was a heavy item in the supply of all the warring powers, and the Second World War, when motor and aircraft fuel and bombs were added to artillery ammunition as the major items, to a lighter logistics to support rocket and nuclear forces. But in fact this new dimension of war added more doubt about the kind of war that might be waged and so the kind of equipment and ammunition that might be needed. Having to be ready for both conventional and nuclear warfare further complicated an already complicated problem.

The staff organization of SHAPE gave a prominent place to logistics. Of two deputy chiefs of staff, one was for Logistics and Administration and the other for Plans and Operations. A very able lieutenant general of the French army was serving as Deputy Chief of Staff for Logistics and Administration during the period 1964–65. Of the eight divisions into which the staff was divided, at least five touched on some aspect of logistics. The Plans and Policy Division included sections for force plans, weapons requirements, and infrastructure plans—as well as a special projects branch. The Programs Division included a branch for force programs, which of course depended very directly upon availability of material resources, and a branch for infrastructure program that was a major element of logistics. The Communications and Electronics Division was very much concerned with the maintenance of key installations and with the supply of highly specialized parts to keep technical equipment in operation. The Budget and Finance Division of course had a key role in the financial arrangements for the various cooperative logistical efforts falling within the preview of SHAPE. Finally the Logistics Division itself (headed in 1964–65 by a major general of the Italian army) included policy, plans, and movement and transportation sections, an infrastructure branch and a medical branch. The great gaps in the logistical staff organization that were apparent immediately in a way pointed up the special problem that the entire NATO military program was up against. There were no staff sections dealing with supply nor specifically with maintenance of matériel or with related services. These were functions generally considered at the heart of any logistic support effort.

In the makeup of the staff itself, its international character, involving officers from so many different nations in such a large-scale organization, presented a unique problem of coordination of effort. Officers from countries that lately were bitter enemies now found themselves working side by side. Undoubtedly some of the older officers were still resentful. They accepted the logic and the necessity of the arrangement intellectually, but they could not feel emotionally bound to it. Yet they were able to share fully in the staff work, and resentment was generally abstract and seldom if ever directed against individuals. The care with which the governments selected officers of the highest caliber for assignment to this duty assured a smoothly working staff in which good personal relationships contributed to a general sense of achievement. This was accomplished in spite of the difficulties of personal feelings, problems of language and usage, different habits of work and procedure brought from the different nations, and differences in particular national interests and policies.

Of course the biggest problem for SHAPE when it came to logistic planning, which in turn affected strategic and tactical planning, was the dictum that logistics is a national responsibility. This difficulty resulted from the fact, as one logistics staff officer put it, that "nations are much more willing to pool blood than resources." But it was a principle that the responsible military commanders would contend that, carried all the way through, made no logistic sense. General Lemnitzer agreed that logistic support of NATO forces by the nations concerned worked well in peacetime, but he maintained, "I'm sure that anyone with military experience would understand that this system would result in some complications in time of emergency."[7] And, putting his views mildly, he stated further, "In many respects it would be [better if supply were an international responsibility]. There are many areas in which a national logistic-support system is satisfactory, but in a war of movement with logistic lines of communication constantly shifting, it should be quite obvious that the maintenance of purely national lines of communication presents serious problems."[8]

The immediate reason for naming a supreme allied commander during the First World War was to permit the prompt shifting of reserve forces from the sector of one nation to that of another. Whenever this is done, it immediately raises service problems of supply. The nation into whose sector the other forces move must accept responsibility for supplying them, or all the forces must draw their essential supplies from a common pool, or the nation to whom the forces belong must maintain a separate supply system and line of communication, in whole or in part, intertwined with the lines of the other nation. In the Second World War this problem for the Allied forces remained relatively simple. Even in Italy, where the number of national contingents participating was greatest, there were only two lines of communication, the American and the British. When a new unit went into the line, it was sent to the U.S. Fifth Army or the British Eighth Army, according to whether it was equipped with American or British equipment, and the battle zones were adjusted accordingly. Thus, for example, the Brazilian contingent, with U.S. equipment, went to the Fifth Army, and the Polish Brigade, with British equipment, went to the Eighth Army. But even this arrangement had the drawback of making it difficult for the forces from one army to be shifted to reinforce those of the other. In practice some such system is what might develop in case of a war involving NATO forces in Europe. But in a situation such as that in the area of Allied Forces Central Europe, where forces of nine nations were deployed on the territory of five of them, the pattern of interlaced lines of supply soon become chaotic.

Two sectors of logistics in which SHAPE exercised a very considerable degree of control as well as in determination of requirements—the infrastructure program[9] and the petroleum pipeline system[10]—illustrate what might be done in the way of international logistic support. But for the most part, the major military commands had to be content with establishing supply policies, calculating requirements, and negotiating to see that nations were prepared to support their forces in the way necessary for them to carry out their planned tactical and strategic missions.

On the basis of its operational plans, SHAPE determined the required supply levels that were to be maintained in each country. Beyond this it was a question of persuasion and national will. In practice nations tend to permit logistic support to lag behind the raising of troops. Through some apparent psychological conditioning, people tend to see more immediate steps for defense in the mobilization of men than in the mobilization of matériel. Yet if one must suffer, plans for defense and large-scale mobilization usually will be better served by a prior emphasis on matériel preparations.

The main considerations in determining supply requirements—beyond the initial supply of forces—are the supply level that has been established for the maintenance of reserve stocks, consumption rates, and the nature, intensity, and scope of operations. The consumption rates and scope of operations in turn affect the level of supply. The level of supply is expressed in terms of a number of days of supply fixed by the supply policy of the commander. But what constitutes a day of supply—i.e., the quantity of stated items needed for a certain number of men under certain operational conditions—depends upon the rates of consumption under those assumed conditions, and these must be very tentative judgments indeed when the nature of the war cannot be foreseen. In any case, the Supreme Allied Commander Europe established a supply policy calling for a ninety-day level of supply to be stocked in the various countries for the support of war in the theater. Furthermore SHAPE prepared a series of logistical standards—i.e., consumption and replacement factors for certain essential items including various types of ammunition, vehicles, and petroleum products—for distribution to the countries. These factors were based on experience of various kinds for various types and conditions of combat. They did not correspond necessarily to the factors developed in the United States or any other country on the basis of their own experience. The individual countries could accept or reject the SHAPE planning factors. In practice they tended to pick and choose those that seemed most suitable to them.[11]

The Allied commanders, including the commanders of the major subordinate commands, were empowered to make known their logistic requirements directly to the governments of the nations within their respective areas, and in peacetime these commanders might call for reports on the strength and effectiveness of the forces assigned to them including their arms, equipment, and supplies and arrangements for logistic support. Current policy called for reports on the status of supply and equipment of all assigned matériel contingents twice yearly for land forces and more frequently for air forces. Moreover, the commanders might make field inspections of assigned forces, including the logistic resources made available for them. This provided leverage in persuading the nations to build up their supplies to prescribed levels and to provide for adequate logistic support generally. But results were very spotty. It was estimated in 1959 that it would cost Great Britain, France, Belgium, and the Netherlands alone a total of half a billion dollars to bring their supply levels up to the ninety-day goal—an amount equal to six percent of all the defense expenditures of those countries for the entire year.[12] When U. S. Secretary of Defense McNamara accompanied the supreme commander on a visit to the various European Allies at the time of the Berlin Crisis in late 1961, they found most serious imbalances in the various stocks of supplies. One country would have far too much of one item and hardly any of another, while another country would have serious overages and shortages in other items. Proper balance is difficult enough to maintain in the best organized and supported of military establishments. For a group of a dozen nations at various stages of readiness, this was bound to be a continuous problem. Only slight improvement in this general situation could be seen after years of prodding and persuasion.

Even when supplies might be more or less adequate, the military commanders had no control over them in rear of army areas. There were no army group troops or line of communication units assigned to NATO commanders. For handling supplies or transportation, the commanders had to reply on separate logistic support organizations for the forces of each nation.

The nature of the key problems relating to the logistic support of NATO's field forces were brought into sharp focus with the organization and maneuvers of the Allied Command Europe Mobile Forces.

During a time of serious deterioration in the international situation—the Berlin Crisis in 1961—the Supreme Allied Commander established, with approval of the North Atlantic Council, a Europe Mobile Forces command that would be prepared to deploy combat units on short notice wherever a sudden emergency might require it. But as might have been expected, a serious weakness in keeping forces ready for rapid and effective intervention was the logistics. In a series of exercises conducted during the next several years—including one in Sardinia, an airlift to Greece, and two exercises in northern Norway,[13] among others—logistical arrangements seemed to be improvised, tentative, and ad hoc. For one of the exercises held in Norway, for instance, it was necessary to make special arrangements for flying up Italian rations; when U.S. trucks broke down they had to wait for repair parts to be flown from an American depot in France; parts for British equipment had to be flown from Great Britain. In a ten-day exercise involving the land mobile force, even the logistics of keeping the exercise going was difficult. Such a system would be unthinkable in wartime.

Aside from the general imperfections arising from deficiencies in national support and the ever-present problems of coordinating efforts among nations, the most pressing immediate problems of matériel for NATO forces were modernization and standardization. In a way these two problems go together and are serious problems for all national military programs. The expense of keeping modern weapon systems and equipment up-to-date with the latest technical equipment is a greater burden than many nations are willing or able to bear.

After a long-range program, perhaps with assistance from other nations, a given nation may at last equip their divisions, but as soon as this is done, the equipment so laboriously gathered is obsolete. But obsolesence is judged not only by what latest refinements or new devices have been designed, but also by the kinds of weapons and equipment that a potential enemy may have. There also arises the great dilemma of production logistics—quantity versus quality. Is it better to have large quantities of a certain model of obsolete equipment or too few of a later and better model?

Many of the logistic undertaking of the Alliance effected steps for modernization of weapons and equipment. These included the various combined development and production programs[14] of mutual defense assistance, and other measures. In particular, the work of such groups as the SHAPE Air Defense Technical Center, which was operated under contract by a Dutch research institution, the Advisory Group for Aeronautical Research and Development (AGARD), which advised the Standing Group on matters of research for improvements in aviation and space, and the NATO Science Committee, whose chairman acted as scientific adviser to the Secretary-General, aimed at cooperative efforts that might result in common advances in defense.

SHAPE above all was interested in obtaining standardization agreements, yet when they called for modifications or additions to SHAPE's own standing operating procedures (SOPs), the agreements were slow in coming. SHAPE was reluctant to alter its SOP until each nation had given its assent to the implementation of each standardization agreement involved. Undoubtedly this grew from an understandable desire to avoid international friction, but it generally had been assumed that a military headquarters such as SHAPE could develop its own standing operating procedures without reference to individual nations.

One of the more promising steps aimed at improvement of supply planning was the establishment of a Logistics Coordination Center (LCC) at SHAPE for the purposes of studying the details of logistic support problems and providing an informal exchange for the communication of information and the coordination of activities with the various nations.[15] Activated in November 1964, the Logistic Coordination Center (LCC) comprised two major elements: a small nucleus of officers, operating as a branch of the Logistics Division of SHAPE, that provided continuity and permanent staff direction, and, second, representatives from each of the nations. In addition, a representative of the NATO international staff and a representative from each of the major subordinate commands attended the meetings as observers. After the manner of many other agencies, specific problems were assigned for detailed study to special working groups appointed for the purpose.

For peacetime full-session meetings, the SHAPE staff prepared an agenda and circulated to each nation a "SHAPE position" on each item sixty days before the meetings. National officials might prepare their own positions, also to be distributed in advance, or, as was more likely, the national representatives would present their views during discussion of the item at the meeting. Certain problems would be referred to working groups for special study and recommendations.

Early full-session meetings of the LCC agreed upon an SOP for peacetime operations, discussed the necessity of developing a complete list of all multilateral and bilateral agreements that the nations made that affected the logistic support of forces assigned or earmarked for SACEUR, discussed the practical problems of moving supplies in connection with SACEUR's authority to reallocate resources among the major subordinate commands, and considered generally the coordination of movement and transport throughout the command. By informal inquiry, with rapid reaction and quick information, much was gained in solving basic logistic questions before going through all the red tape of formal negotiations.

If its logistic planning was to bear any relation to reality, SHAPE badly needed an accounting of each nation's store of supplies for all of its own forces, as well as for those assigned or earmarked for SHAPE. Although, with great effort, the SHAPE logistics staff was able to work out more nearly balanced supplies for assigned and earmarked forces than was possible previously, it remained difficult to get any precise notion about the reserve supplies in each nation to back up those forces.

Recognizing the resupply difficulties of forces drawn from many nations, SHAPE logistics officers sympathized with the Miksche strategy of position defense—with large stocks of prepositioned supplies. Some of them noted with envy the Swiss system where prepositioned supplies were locked in fortified storehouses underground, for which the local commander had the key. These storehouses were distributed all through the critical approaches and the key mountain passes, and in case of emergency, the local commander could simply go to the storehouse in the vicinity, draw out what he needed, and leave a receipt covering the withdrawals.[16] in any case, the threat of nuclear warfare, as well as the need to cover great areas, indicated the desirability of implementing the small general depot concept. A large number of relatively small depots, each carrying all or several different types and classes of supply needed by a given kind of unit, offered greater flexibility in support and far greater protection against attack than the theoretically more efficient system of maintaining only a few large general depots with smaller depots, each specialized in a particular type or class of supplies.

Altogether the logistic problems that SHAPE had to face were formidable. On their solution depended very largely the real effectiveness of the Allied military effort.

Each of the major subordinate commands of Allied Command Europe had to deal with the problems of logistic support in its own area, and the policy was to encourage direct contact between the military commanders and the governments concerned in each area on logistic matters.

Allied Forces Central Europe

The keystone in the arch of European defense was in the area covered by Allied Forces Central Europe with headquarters at Fontainebleau (AFCENT). Its area included all of Germany south of Schleswig-Holstein, the Low Countries, and France. Here the problem of logistic planning under the principle that each nation retains total responsibility for the support of its own forces came into sharpest focus. Clearly operational integration had to be related to logistic requirements and capabilities. In later years subordinate regional commanders were given more authority to develop logistic requirements for their forces. It was then up to the logistics staff of AFCENT to consolidate and analyze requirements, and, in cooperation with SHAPE and national officials, to determine the national capabilities for meeting the requirements. A general supply plan then would be prepared for approval by SHAPE and each nation concerned. This gave to the Allied commander in chief the authority to state where supplies should be delivered and the authority to reallocate resources from one region of his command to another. Territorial service forces, of course, would remain under national control, but they would provide logistic services according to agreements drawn between host and user nations. Some of these agreements included very minute plans, but in many cases plans for continued support over a period of time appeared to be rudimentary indeed. AFCENT received annual reports on the status of supplies in each nation in its area.[17]

All of this divided authority called for a dual system of liaison. First, there were delegates from each nation concerned at headquarters AFCENT, each maintaining contact with its own defense staff and representatives at the army group level. In fact, in 1965–66 AFCENT had what amounted to a little Logistic Coordination Committee, functioning much as did the LCC at SHAPE, though its activities were strictly limited to matters of matériel. Second, liaison had to be maintained with SHAPE and with the National Military Representatives in Paris on matters of high policy, finance, and general coordination.

The AFCENT headquarters organization followed in general that to be found at SHAPE. A French army general served as commander in chief, and another as chief of staff. The deputy chief of staff for logistics and organization was an officer of the U.S. Army, while a French air force officer headed the Logistics Division. The Logistics Division included a Plan Branch, Medical, Maintenance, and Supply Branch, Infrastructure Branch, Petrol, Oil and Lubricants Branch, Movements Branch, and the secretariat for the Central European Pipeline Office. The subordinate headquarters for Allied Land Forces Central Europe, embracing two army groups and Allied Air Forces Central Europe, had structures roughly paralleling this. In addition there was a naval staff organized under a naval deputy and one of the major sections was for shipping and naval logistics and organization, though the command had no separate naval forces as such.

AFCENT logistics officers anticipated the problems involved in maintaining logistic support of forces shifted from one area to another in response to tactical requirements. There could be cross-servicing—i.e., the forces of one nation could, by agreement, draw on the resources of another in obtaining rations, transport, petroleum products, and some types of ammunition, but when it came to repair parts for weapons and equipment, the great problem was lack of standardization. This was especially the case with respect to the older equipment already on hand; as newer equipment was developed, more could be done toward improving standardization.

Cross-servicing was especially important for the Allied air force in the central area. Special efforts for the standardization of services were necessary where German, Belgian, and Netherlands air contingents were being reequipped with European-built F-104G aircraft; Canadians had a Canadian version of this airplane; the French were flying *Mirage III Cs* and *III Rs;* the Americans had the F-105 *Thunderchief;* and the British were contemplating a changeover to the *Lightning.* But by 1964 and 1965 a fairly large number of the air bases were able to refuel and service several of the different types of aircraft. This provided an essential element of flexibility for the more than 2,000 aircraft assigned to AFCENT.[18]

The most serious situation in strategic and logistic planning for this key defense area arose in March 1966 with the French announcement of intentions to withdraw from NATO military bodies. This threatened to leave a gaping hole in the very center of Western defense, to undo what logistic arrangements had been made for mutual logistic support in the area, and to pose serious questions about any of the logistic planning and coordination that had been undertaken.

Allied Forces Southern Europe

Allied Forces South, including within its area Italy, Greece, and Turkey, faced the particular problem of planning for the support of military operations in a tripeninsular command having no land connections between any of the three countries and with relatively sparse inland transportation facilities in two of them. On the other hand, as long as the NATO Allies could maintain air and naval superiority in the area, the arms of the Mediterranean, serving as essential connecting links, remained an important logistic advantage.[19]

Planning in the southern area was complicated somewhat by what amounted to a divided command. The security of the Mediterranean itself—keeping open the vital sea lanes—was the responsibility of a separate command, Allied Forces Mediterranean, with headquarters on Malta. This was essentially an Allied naval command, but the powerful U.S. Sixth Fleet, operating in the Mediterranean, was earmarked not for AFMED, but for AFSOUTH. Its wartime mission would be mainly to provide carrier-based air support for land operations throughout the area and to launch strikes against enemy territory.[20] It had been alleged that the main reason for having a separate Mediterranean command had been the insistence of the British on having a major command in this area,[21] while for their part the French had maintained that this was an area of vital French interests and therefore ought to be under French command. Failing in that, the French in 1959 withdrew elements of the French fleet earmarked for the command, which further complicated the problems of planning.

AFSOUTH itself comprised Allied Land Forces Southeastern Europe (Izmir, Turkey), Allied Land Forces Southern Europe (Verona), Allied Air Forces Southern Europe (Naples), and Naval Striking and Support Forces Southern Europe (Naples). Spain, not being a member of NATO, could not of course be included in any of the area commands, but by virtue of bilateral agreements the United States maintained important naval and air bases in Spain that in practice provided substantial support for any NATO effort in the Mediterranean region in which the United States might participate.

The headquarters organization of AFSOUTH at Naples was similar to that of the other commands except that there was much stronger emphasis on the naval elements, and American officers held most of the key positions. The commander in chief was an American admiral; the chief of staff was a major general of the U.S. Army, and both the deputy chief of staff for logistics and administration and the assistant chief of staff for logistics (chief of the Logistics Division) were rear admirals of the U.S. Navy.

Probably the greatest continuing problem for the preparation of effective logistic arrangements in the South was the development of the national economies of Greece and Turkey. Both countries depended to a very large extent on United States aid programmed under bilateral agreements. Here there was an especially great need for the modernization of equipment and for the buildup of reserves of ammunition and other battle supplies.[22] Yet steps in that direction, even with outside assistance, had been gravely affected over a period of several years by the explosive Cyprus situation.

Greece and Turkey were at the low end of the scale in per capita gross national product among the NATO nations, yet they were above the NATO average in their military efforts. In the interest of developing a certain degree of independence in the supply of some items as insurance against the cutting of supply lines, and with the encouragement of AFSOUTH and the United States, both Greece and Turkey took steps to set up local military industry for the production of some ammunition, petroleum products, and other general-use items. With grants of surplus weapons and equipment on a "where is, as is" basis, they set up plants to rebuild the items into usable supplies.

As suggested above, the greatest problem of wartime logistics in the Southern Europe command undoubtedly would be transportation. This may be the case generally, but to logistics officers of AFSOUTH it seemed especially acute. For this reason the work of the Committee on Inland Transportation Southern Europe (COMINTSE) in Rome, the regional committee of the Planning Board of European Inland Surface Transport (PBEIST), was, if anything, regarded here as more important than its central European counterpart. AFSOUTH had a permanent military representative on the committee, and the committee had a PBEIST liaison officer in the Transportation Branch of the AFSOUTH Logistics Division. The committee functioned through four working groups—on rail transport, road transport, inland waterways, and ports and beaches.

As in other commands, the Commander in Chief, Allied Forces South had completed reallocation agreements with each country to enable him to shift supplies from one area to another in wartime, and in addition the headquarters attempted to promote the conclusion of bilateral agreements between nations so that the forces of one might draw upon the resources of another for logistic support to the extent that it was practical.

Impressed by what they had seen in the discussion of common logistic problems at the SHAPE Logistics Coordination Center, logistics officers of AFSOUTH decided to hold a logistics conference for the southern region in March 1966. Some forty logisticians and guests assembled in Naples for the three-day meeting. Items discussed included plans for the logistics play in the fall exercises scheduled for 1966; the gauging of logistic requirements to intensity and character of operations factors, including time phasing; the AFSOUTH program for the XVIIIth infrastructure slice;[23] logistic support capabilities; presentations by representatives of the ministries of defense of the three countries on national capabilities and plans to meet wartime logistic requirements; planning for nonorganic support forces (service troops); simplification of logistics reporting systems; and POL supply, including the operation of oil pipelines in the region, and the buildup and maintenance of operational reserves in Greece, Turkey, and Italy. Thus the first of what likely was to be a series of logistics conferences ranged over pretty nearly the full spectrum of the logistic problems that were bound to be of continuing concern to Allied Forces Southern Europe.

These problems were linked to the more specific ones of preparing for logistic support of combat operations under a wide range of contingencies such as defense against attacks on the Turkish straits or attacks against northern Greece that aimed at footholds in the Aegean and Adriatic seas.

Allied Forces Northern Europe

If French attitudes and policies complicated Allied cooperation in Central Europe and the Mediterranean, Norway and Denmark's reservations on foreign bases and nuclear warfare created similar problems in the North. And if political antagonism between Greece and Turkey was an obstacle in the South, the continuing Scandinavian wartime animosity toward Germany likewise was a hindrance in the North.

Except for the effects of the rigorous northern climate, the tactical problem was somewhat similar to that in the South. Again it was a question of controlling the straits against possible Soviet attempts to break through, in this case to the North Sea, or to win bases in Norway to support submarine operations in the North Atlantic. Similar too was the question of protecting a flank of the NATO area where an enemy might gain a foothold to support a major thrust into the central area.[24]

A peculiar situation existed in the northern area because of the policies of Norway and Denmark respecting the basing of foreign troops and nuclear weapons on their territory. To some extent both countries, but mainly Norway, had been under heavy Soviet pressure to deny their territory to foreign forces, and in fact to minimize their roles in NATO altogether. In February 1949, before signing the North Atlantic Treaty, the Norwegians pledged in a note to the Soviet Union that Norwegian territory would not be used for bases for foreign forces. This policy had continued, though not to the exclusion of NATO forces for the purpose of maneuvers, of facilities for wartime use, and for communications constructed under the infrastructure program, nor of headquarters for NATO commands, although the Soviet Union strongly protested the presence of these as well. Although under no direct pledge to the Soviet Union, Denmark followed a policy similar to Norway's in excluding the basing of foreign forces on its soil (except for American bases in Greenland). Foreign forces never even participated in exercises on Bornholm—an island in the Baltic a considerable distance (some 100 miles) to the east of the main Danish islands, about which the Soviet Union were especially sensitive. In addition, both Norway and Denmark held to a policy prohibiting nuclear weapons on their soil. Both went along with the North Atlantic Council's decision of 1954 authorizing SACEUR to plan on the use of nuclear weapons in his defensive plans, and they agreed to the council decision in 1957 for the establishment of nuclear stockpiles in Europe under American control, but none of these was to be for their own territory. Both accepted U.S. HONEST JOHN and NIKE missiles, but never with nuclear warheads.[25]

At first the structure of Allied Forces Northern Europe comprised simply a staff for Land Forces Northern Europe working directly under the commander in chief and separate headquarters for air forces and naval forces. Then in July 1962 a subordinate unified command for the Baltic approaches was established, and at the end of that year the whole command was reorganized. Headquarters, AFNORTH, remained at Kolsaas (near Oslo), Norway, with an officer from the British Army as commander in chief. In addition, then, to Allied Forces Baltic Approaches (BALTAP) (Kolvrå, Denmark), there was Allied Land Forces Norway (Oslo), Allied Naval Forces Scandinavian approaches (Jattanutan, Norway), Allied Tactical Air Forces Southern Norway (Voksenllo), and Allied Task Forces Northern Norway (Bodo)—essentially an organization "on paper."

Local logistic problems and preparations become clearer by a closer look at the principal subordinate command, Allied Forces Baltic Approaches (AFBALTAP), which, including all of Denmark and Schleswig-Holstein within its area, stood guard over the Danish straits and so was in effect the linchpin of the northern flank defenses. This in itself was a unified command, and while subordinate to AFNORTH, it had in fact a considerable degree of independence. A Danish officer served as commander with a German vice admiral as deputy, and it had four subordinate commands. The policy was to maintain an international balance in the staff, so that one-third of the officers were Danish, one-third were German, and one-third altogether came from Norway, the United Kingdom, and the United States.

Being in a subordinate command, the AFBALTAP staff did not have direct access to the Danish and German ministries of defense, but it did have direct access to the chief logistics officials in the two countries. While the territorial jurisdiction of the command was limited to Denmark and Schleswig-Holstein, Germany itself had bases in Norway and Scotland as well as on the north German islands, and undoubtedly in time of emergency these would be called upon for logistic support. The North Sea, an important communications area for this support, remained under the Supreme Allied Commander Atlantic, and it was referred to here as the "SACLANT Pocket."

In planning for logistic support, the BALTAP logistics staff emphasized flexibility. Recognizing that they could not make specific, detailed plans for unknown future situations, the staff made studies and conducted map exercises and conferences to establish general concepts and procedures, and prepared general directives, on what should be done in certain circumstances. Officers assigned to this duty learned to operate by the rule of patience. They saw difficult political, economic, and technical problems, but they knew that they had to learn to live with them, confident that in time of emergency local political difficulties and national feelings would be subordinated to action against a common danger. While Danish and German officers worked together on operational and logistic problems in April 1966, for instance, the Danish people were observing with appropriate exercises the twenty-sixth anniversary of the German occupation of Denmark, and a few days later the Danish Government rejected plans for a Danish-German exercise that called for the participation of about 800 German infantrymen on Danish territory.[26] Earlier combined maneuvers had been held, always in the face of local protests and demonstrations since a small contingent of engineers in 1965 became the first German soldiers to enter Denmark since the Second World War.

Actually some degree of integration in logistic support for forces of the two countries was achieved. It was possible to pool certain common-use items, for instance, for the one German division and the one Danish division committed to Land Forces Jutland, though separate lines had to be maintained for their distinctive weapons and equipment. As elsewhere, differences in weapons and equipment were the usual source of major problems of local logistic support. Danish equipment was mostly British, while the Germans used mostly American types. In the naval forces, the Danish vessels were mostly World War II types requiring black oil, while the Germans had newer vessels requiring a different grade of fuel.

Thus in the Baltic area a subordinate command faced the complications both of interservice—army, navy, air—and of international coordination in a difficult political climate but in an essential area for defense of the West. Many would contend with Liddell Hart that, aside from Berlin, the Marburg-Copenhagen area was "the most precarious spot" in the whole NATO defensive scheme. Here Hamburg was only twenty to thirty miles from the East German border, and Bremen only seventy-five miles—both essential ports for allied logistics—and the Danish straits were the keys to the Baltic. Yet only small Danish and German forces were deployed there. He urged moving the British Army of the Rhine to cover this gap, and then shifting the U.S. Seventh Army northward to cover the approaches to the Ruhr and Frankfurt. But he acknowledged that this probably would not be done because of the expense involved in moving elaborate installations and supply systems. If this were so, it would indeed appear to be a case of the "logistic tail wagging the strategic dog." Why was the Seventh Army, acknowledged to be one of the best fighting units in the whole NATO area, deployed in Bavaria? Was it because of a strategic estimate that this was a most likely and dangerous avenue of enemy approach? No, it was purely a result of the logistics of the occupation. Placed there because this was the United States zone of occupation, the Seventh Army had been allowed to become cemented there with apparently little attention to the more general requirements for the defense of Western Europe.[27]

Allied Command Atlantic

The North Atlantic Alliance is perforce a maritime alliance, and the mutual support of the major members depends to a very large degree upon maintaining the security of the north Atlantic Ocean and adjoining seas, whose waters furthermore provide avenues for carrying military power to the homeland of a potential aggressor.

A potentially grave threat to the security of the countries of the North Atlantic appeared in the Soviet Union's development of the largest peace time submarine force ever seen up to this time. Two major area commands under the Supreme Allied Commander Atlantic (SACLANT), the Western Atlantic Command, and the Eastern Atlantic Command had the principal missions of keeping open the oceanic trading routes between North America and Europe and defending coastal and island areas within those areas. Meanwhile a separate Striking Fleet Atlantic was charged with offensive operations and submarines were grouped under a Submarines Allied Command Atlantic. The major emphasis was on antisubmarine warfare, organized around antisubmarine warfare groups, while the Striking Fleet would be prepared to strike enemy bases and to provide naval support for land and air elements of the command and of other commands. Territorial jurisdiction of Allied Command Atlantic extended from the North Pole to the Tropic of Cancer, and from the eastern shores of North America to the shores of Europe including Portugal and the islands except for the British Isles.[28]

Security of the English Channel and southern North Sea was the responsibility of a separate Allied Command Channel organized under a Channel Committee made up of naval chiefs or their representatives of Belgium, the Netherlands, and the United Kingdom. However, in 1966 this command was merged with Allied Command Eastern Atlantic, and the British commander was made commander in chief of the channel command as well.[29]

In a good deal of popular thinking and general comment about Allied Command Europe, the magnitude of forces assigned to SACEUR and the extent of his control over them in peacetime frequently have been exaggerated. When it comes to SACLANT, it must be kept in mind that except for the temporary attachment of certain units for brief periods of combined exercises, in peacetime the commander had no forces assigned to him at all. Some American, British, and Dutch vessels had been earmarked for assignment in time of emergency, but so far as forces were concerned, Allied Command Atlantic consisted only of commanders and staffs with fleets, as well as air and ground elements only on paper. Thus the earlier French withdrawal from Allied Command Atlantic, though accompanied by considerable furor, was quite different from the withdrawal of the two French divisions and air force units in Germany from SACEUR's command. In the former case, it was a simple matter of eliminating the current earmarking on the French Atlantic squadron of some sixteen destroyers and frigates. Since the Atlantic Command, like the European Command, had been from the start under an American supreme commander who also was commander of U.S. forces in his area, the position of American forces appeared to be somewhat different. Thus when American naval units were earmarked for SACLANT, they simply were marked to be transferred in time of war from the command of the American admiral in his capacity as Commander in Chief Atlantic Fleet (U.S.) to the command of the same admiral in his capacity as Supreme Allied Commander Atlantic.[30]

Having some forces at his command, SACEUR was able to inspect them, to detect shortcomings in logistic support, and to seek corrective action. SACLANT, on the other hand, had to work more in the dark. Moreover (and here the situation was similar to that found in Allied Command Europe) those forces that had been earmarked comprised only combat elements. Supporting elements remained under separate national command. At the same time, the principle "logistics is a national responsibility" was more practical when applied to naval units. Ships were able to carry considerable quantities of supplies, and when necessary they could return to home ports for supplies and repairs. Cooperative arrangements for cross-servicing between national elements were made, and it was to be expected that extensive arrangements of this kind would be found in wartime. But generally speaking this was arranged by bilateral agreements between the nations concerned rather than by NATO instruments as such, so that it was still up to the nation concerned to make its own arrangements by agreement with other nations for support as needed. Even during NATO training exercises, SACLANT, again as was the case with SACEUR, had little or no opportunity to test logistical support, for ships arrived full and returned to home ports before replenishment was necessary.

Since large national staffs were at work to develop logistic support for elements from their respective nations, whether by their own resources or by bilateral arrangement with another nation, SACLANT maintained only a small logistics staff. This staff developed logistic planning factors for use in general and national planning, developed guidance for the logistic elements of operational plans, screened requirements and proposals from major subordinate commands for infrastructure projects,[31] prepared proposals for the Military Agency for Standardization[32] such as for a port logistics handbook (to show the availability of resources such as fuel, military supplies, and repair facilities at ports throughout the NATO area), and sought other measures of general cooperation and coordination. On the last point, the problem reduced itself mainly to one of communication among all the nations and staffs concerned.[33]

The greatest need for making cross-servicing and mutual support among various nations effective was for the standardization of equipment and procedures. For mobility and endurance, a fleet has to have means for replenishment at sea. The first essential is fuel, and for a vessel of one nation to take on oil from a tanker of another nation, for instance, fuel fittings must be standardized. After considerable effort, the nations concerned were able to accept a standardization agreement to make interchangeable hose connections and rigs in order to transfer fuel, water, and solid packaged stores from one ship to another among all the participating nations. At first this applied only to vessels earmarked for Allied command, but a further major step in logistical cooperation came with extension of this agreement to apply to all vessels.[34] In addition the nations concerned were able to arrive at standard procedures transferring supplies and providing services in port.[35]

Already cooperation in the support of naval aviation had reached the point where American aircraft, jet as well as piston types could operate from British and Canadian aircraft carriers, and vice-versa.[36]

Although the infrastructure projects developed under SACLANT represented perhaps not more than ten percent of the magnitude of those prepared under SACEUR, still their relative importance loomed especially large in what was essentially a naval command. Probably the most important projects were: (a) airfields for maritime patrol aircraft; (2) facilities for handling petroleum products; and (3) communications facilities. An antisubmarine research center was established under Allied Command Atlantic at La Spezzia, Italy. Other specific projects included such items as an antisubmarine boom across the Clyde at Fairlie, Scotland, oil storage depots, and headquarters buildings.

To a great extent the effectiveness of Allied Command Atlantic depended upon the completion of the infrastructure program and upon specific arrangements for the transfer of adequate forces to the command in time of emergency. Unfortunately the command suffered from deficiencies on both counts.[37]

Notes

1. Tom Margerison, Interview with General Lyman Lemnitzer, *The Sunday Times* (London), 6 October 1963; interview with General Lemnitzer "Facing the Iron Curtain: How Good is Western Defense?" *U.S. News and World Report*, 30 December 1963, 54–60; Jean Vailuy, "Danger de Mort," *Revue Militaire Générale*, January 1961, 3–12.

2. General Lyman Lemnitzer, Interview in *The Sunday Times* (London), 6 October 1963.

3. North Atlantic Council, Communiqué, Ministerial Meeting, Ottawa, Canada, 16–19 December 1957, Press Release M2 (57) 2.

4. Ibid., Final Communiqué, Ministerial Session, Ottawa, Canada, 24 May 1963, NATO Press Communiqué MI (63) 4.

5. Ibid.

6. James E. Moore, "NATO Today," *Army*, August 1964, 28.

7. General Lemnitzer, "Facing the Iron Curtain, 56.

8. Ibid.

9. See chap. 8.

10. See chap. 11.

11. See Frank S. Besson, "Logistics and Transportation in the Defense of Western Europe," *National Defense Transportation Journal* 12 (March–April 1956): 54–57.

12. See Western European Union Doc. 180, 25 October 1960, appendix; Henry E. Eccles, *European Logistics, 1956*. The George Washington University Logistics Research Project, ONR 41904 (Washington, D.C., 1956), 31.

13. *NATO Letter*, June 1964, 25; John S. Hodder, "NATO's Mobile Force in Action," *NATO Letter*, September 1964, 11–19.

14. See chap. 9.

15. This section is based on personal interviews at Supreme Headquarters, Allied Powers Europe, Casteau, Belgium, July 1967.

16. Cf. Liddell Hart's suggestion for a system of militia-type forces for local operations in Europe, "NATO—Sword or Shield," *Ordnance* (July–August 1962): 65.

17. Personal interviews at Headquarters, Allied Forces Central Europe, Fontainebleau, France, June 1964, Brunnsum, The Netherlands, April 1967.

18. Dominique Berretty, "Aircent—Seven Nations, One Command," *NATO Letter*, June 1964, 14–18; Humphrey Wynn, "AAFCE: Europe's Air Defense," *Flight International*, 15 March 1962, 397–402, 418.

19. Personal interview at Headquarters, Allied Forces Southern Europe, Naples, Italy, March 1966.

20. "Southern Shield," *NATO's Fifteen Nations* (February–March 1963): 72–80; E. Hinterhoff, "Protecting the Flanks of the Alliance," *NATO Letter*, January 1965, 16–17.

21. See Western European Union, Doc. 269 (1963); draft, "The State of European Security (Navies in the Nuclear Age)."

22. Norman Locksley, "NATO's Southern Exposure," *U.S. Naval Institute Proceedings* (November 1962): 41–53.

23. See chap. 8.

24. Personal interviews at Headquarters, Allied Forces Baltic Approaches, Kølvrå, Denmark, April 1966; see Hinterhoff, "Protecting the Flanks of the Alliance," 10–13; Sidney B. Whipple, "AFNORTH: NATO's Left Flank," *NATO's Fifteen Nations* (April–May 1964): 60–68.

25. Nils Orvik and Niels J. Haagerup, *The Scandinavian Members of Nato*, Institute for Strategic Studies, Adelphi Papers no. 23, London, 1965.

26. *New York Hearld Tribune* (European ed.), 16–17 April 1966, 2.

27. B. H. Liddell Hart, "The Defense of West Germany and the Baltic," *The Marine Corps Gazette*, February 1964, 18–22.

28. Jerauld Wright "NATO's Naval Forces: The Future," *NATO's Fifteen Nations*, 7 (Spring 1959): 114–21; Sir Michael M. Denny, "The Atlantic in a World War—What Does It Mean," *Journal of the Royal United Service Institution* (August 1956): 351–63; H. T. Deutermann, "International Navy; A Decade of Unity," *NATO's Fifteen Nations* 10 (April 1962): 32–34.

29. "A Look at Allied Command Channel," *NATO Letter*, January 1966, 17–21; "Focus on NATO," *Nato Letter*, March 1966, 29.

30. See Jean Planchais, "Le Retrait de l'Esadre Française de l'Atlantique a des Raisons Politique et Technique," *Le Monde*, 18 July 1963. Cf. Raymond H. Dawson, "What Kind of

NATO Nuclear Force?" *Annals of the American Academy of Political and Social Sciences* 304 (Jan. 1964): 30–31.

    31. See chap. 8.

    32. See chap. 10.

    33. See A. P. Zavald, "SACLANT Communications," *NATO's Fifteen Nations* 8 (February–March 1963): 62–66.

    34. Wright, "NATO's Naval Forces," 117.

    35. Draft, STANAG 1062 (Edition 2).

    36. Deutermann, "International Navy," 32.

    37. See R. M. Smeeton "Oceans to Defend," *NATO Letter,* March 1963, 7–11.

7

The French Disconnection

When French President Charles de Gaulle tossed his "NATO bombshell" with the announcement at his press conference on 21 February 1966 that the French would withdraw from participation in the Allied commands, he at once put a different light both upon the procedure and the substance of NATO strategic and logistic planning. The impact of the changed situation would be felt most, of course, in Allied Command Europe.

Although the French attitude had been known for years and although the French move to disassociate from Allied military organiztions had been anticipated, it still was greeted with consternation in Washington, London, Bonn, and other Allied capitals.

The French contended that conditions had changed in the seventeen years since the signature of the North Atlantic Treaty in 1949 and held that if the treaty were to live, the institutions developed under it must adapt to new conditions. "For it is quite clear," de Gaulle said at his press conference, "that owing to the internal and external evolution of the countries of the East, the Western world is no longer threatened today as it was at the time when the American protectorate was set up in Europe under the cover of NATO." Then he went on to say:

> But, at the same time as the alarms were dying down, there was also a reduction in the guarantee of security—one might say absolute—that the possession of the nuclear weapon by America alone gave to the Old Continent, and in the certainty that America would employ it, without reservation, in the event of aggression. For Soviet Russia has since that time equipped itself with a nuclear power capable of striking the United States directly, which has made the decisions of the Americans as to the eventual use of their bombs at least indeterminate, and which has, by the same token, stripped of justification—I speak for France—not the Alliance, of course, but indeed integration.
>
> . . . .
> Consequently, without going back on her adherence to the Atlantic Alliance, France is going, between now and the final date set for her obligations, which is April 4, 1969, to continue to modify successively the measures currently practiced, insofar as they concern her. . . . She will hold herself ready to arrange with one or another of them, and in the same

143

manner in which she has already proceeded on other points, the practical relations for cooperation that will appear useful on both sides, either in the immediate present or in the eventuality of a conflict. This naturally holds for allied cooperation in Germany. In sum, it means re-establishing a normal situation of sovereignty, in which that which is French as regards soil, sky, sea and forces, and any foreign element that would be in France, will in the future be under French command alone. This is to say that it in no way means a rupture, but a necessary adaptation.[1]

General de Gaulle made the further point that current international crises no longer were centered in Europe, but mainly were in Asia, where not all the members of NATO were involved.

In a series of notes to the Allied governments the French made it clear that they intended to move swiftly to liquidate French participation in the integrated military commands and to "restore French sovereignty" over all forces and installations remaining on French territory. They indicated that French personnel assigned to integrated Allied commands would be withdrawn on 1 July 1966 and that French ground and air forces in Germany would be withdrawn from Allied command on the same date. They proposed that the Supreme Command Allied Forces Europe and Allied Forces Central Europe be transferred from French territory by 1 April 1966, and they further suggested that the transfer of command or the closing of U.S. and Canadian installations in France should be accomplished by that same date. They suggested that liaison should be established between the French forces and the various Allied headquarters in order to determine the conditions under which the French would participate in common military efforts in time of war or emergency.[2]

At the root of the differences between France and the other Allies—particularly the United States—was the basic difference in strategic assumptions discussed above: the French notion of deterrence based upon the threat of nuclear retaliation, and the American theory of defense based upon flexible response.[3] In the debate in the French National Assembly, Premier Pompidou replied to critics of the French policy: "You think in terms of war of yesterday; we think in terms of deterrence, that is to say, of peace."[4] In a similar vein, Foreign Minister Couve de Murville said,

As for saying that under conditions of modern war it serves no purpose to form an alliance if you do not organize defense in common in advance and if you do not maintain a corresponding organization permanently, perhaps for generations, allow me to say that I do not understand this view of those who see the future of the French army as a conventional contingent in an Atlantic "Grand Army," a contingent that would have been stripped of any right ever to possess its own atomic weapons. But, militarily speaking, this is again the method that consists of preparing each time for "la guerre de papa." No one, obviously, can predict the form that a world war between the major powers would take if, by misfortune, one were to break out. What is known, however, is that its essential element would be the atomic weapon, and that this weapon is not and can never be integrated.[5]

Significantly, the rationale for the French position, as developed by Pierre

Gallois, for instance, emphasized the reduced importance of traditional logistic factors for modern nuclear war. He maintained that in atomic war "nobody needs a supply base" and debated that thirty-day or sixty-day or ninety-day supply levels were irrelevant in an age when a major war "must be fought with the weapons in hands," in a matter of hours. Moreover, he held, instead of heavy industry, only advanced technology and small-scale industry was needed; population was no longer so important as previously, and the size of the country and the length of supply lines "have little meaning." In his view, old rules of diplomacy and balance of power make little sense in the nuclear age: "The great powers opened Pandora's box, and out sprang the end of their hegemony." In East as well as West, he went on, the destructive power of the atom, combined with the present invulnerability of nuclear forces "has terminated the military alliance as an instrument of diplomacy." Clausewitz's famous diction that war is the continuation of diplomacy by other means "is now nonsense." Focusing on the differences in strategic assumptions and the question of credibility, Gallois asked, "Who believes that the United States would risk thermonuclear attack for any but a vital United States interest?" and "Who doubts that France, with limited nuclear power, can give even a mighty enemy pause when a vital French interest is at stake?" The American doctrine of flexible response, he says, was the result of the American loss of geographic invulnerability, but it ignored "the total incompatibility of planning for conventional war and planning for atomic war. . . . NATO's deployment still resembles 1944 more than 1966."[6]

In appraising the French position, several facts need to be kept in mind. First of all, it never was assumed that U.S. forces would remain in Europe "forever." In the beginning the general expectation was that American occupation forces would remain in Germany for four or five years. Second, under the protection of NATO and the United States, the European nations had been able to devote most of their effort to economic expansion without carrying their share of the defense burden; some loosening of the U.S. umbrella might have resulted in a greater total defense effort. So far as the posture of the West was concerned, surely it was better to have a number of relatively independent but strong allies than to have an integrated system of weak puppets. When the voice of a relatively strong power, known to be independent of outside domination, is raised in support even of a more powerful ally, as was the case of France during the Cuban crisis of October 1962, surely that carries far more weight in foreign circles than would any suppliant words of a weak client government. At the same time, there may have been some hope that a loosening of the bonds of NATO would pave the way for a reduction of Soviet domination over the countries of Eastern Europe. It should be remembered too that, in spite of a show of solidarity on the part of the other fourteen NATO members, France was not altogether alone in its attitude: Britain enjoyed a somewhat favored position insofar as the maintenance of U.S. bases was concerned, and Denmark and Norway, although cooperating fully in the integrated Allied commands, would not permit the stationing of foreign forces or bases on their territory. Some attention should be given too to the French contention that "multiple centers of decision" increase the credibility of the nuclear deterrent.

On the other hand, the weakness of the French position was in ruling out the prospect of conventional war in Europe. If nations are prepared to wage only nuclear war and a major war does break out in Europe, then assuredly it will be nuclear. But if plans and preparations have been carried out to develop a capability for flexible response, then that does not necessarily have to be so. Moreover, the French view does nothing to overcome the dilemma of nuclear diplomacy where a nation allows itself to be put into the position of meeting any threat, however slight, only with nuclear retaliation or with nothing at all—which, if the nuclear threat has been neutralized by the relative invulnerability of the opposing forces, opens the way for limited aggression without fear of retaliation.

Reaction to the French initiative within the United States government revealed considerable differences of opinion. One view was that the main objective of the United States ought to be to retain access to facilities in France by whatever means might be necessary. A contrary view was that the United States should insist upon a written, ironclad guarantee of access at any time. The second view was the one that prevailed.

Ironically the United States was pleased to maintain bases in Spain—not as U.S. bases, but as "guests" on Spanish bases, where the Spanish flag flew—under the kind of conditions that would have satisfied the French. The supreme irony was that the Americans moved many of their supplies from France to Great Britain without the kind of guarantee that they demanded of France.

But there was further irony with respect to Germany. Several years earlier the Germans had created a furor throughout the Alliance when it was discovered that they were seeking bases in Spain. This looked too much like a revival of a World War II-type of Axis alliance. In meetings with the North Atlantic Council and various committees the Germans insisted that they needed further space for their military supplies and equipment. They were so overcrowded with Americans, British, and French, that they had no place for their own impedimenta. But then, admitting that overtures to Spain had been a gross mistake, they raised the possibility of gaining supply bases in various Allied countries. This made more political sense since it would demonstrate a deep commitment to the Alliance itself. After negotiations with the Dutch, the Belgians, and the Norwegians, German leaders obtained base rights on some offshore islands, but most important, they turned to France. After a year or so of negotiations they came up with an agreement with the French that gave them a certain number of supply depots in France and several air bases, including some near Marseilles, one on Corsica, and elsewhere. In addition, they made agreements for the training of German soldiers in France on French bases.

Now the Germans received the same kind of notes as did the Americans. While the United States pulled out everything except the pipelines (which, incidentally, continued to function quite well under French supervision), the Germans made no move to leave—they were content to accept the French conditions. Consequently here was the strange situation where one of France's oldest allies pulled out in a lack of trust, while France's oldest enemy remained, with continued access to supply bases and training facilities.

While there was no question that SHAPE was going to move out of France, by De Gaulle's directive, the French did not insist that the political headquarters should leave. But again, largely at U.S. initiative, the North Atlantic Council decided that its headquarters should leave Paris at the same time.

Most official American responses carried an evident note of pique. Immediate comments were to the effect that the Alliance could get along without France if necessary, though the door must be kept open for the French to return. American officials announced that nuclear warheads previously made available to France would be withdrawn. Already, since 1964, the United States had been refusing to make further shipments to France of enriched uranium (needed for fuel for nuclear-powered submarines) as had been agreed to in 1959. The French were accused in effect of ignoring their solemn treaty obligations in spite of the fact that the agreement on the establishment of a U.S. line of communication across France, for instance, permitted either party to abrogate it on six months' notice after it had been in effect for five years. Both London and Washington insisted that any negotiations would have to be conducted within NATO and with the consultation of all interested Allies, and not simply as a series of bilateral discussions.[7]

Within the United States, however, a number of leaders and commentators expressed concern about an attitude that they feared might lead to a serious break. Edmond Taylor wrote critically:

> Washington's failure, both now and on numerous occasions in the past, to practice effectively "the arts of consultation and negotiation" in dealing with our European allies . . . seems to be no less important a factor in bringing about the present dangerous impasse within the alliance than de Gaulle's stubbornness or "old-fashioned" nationalism.[8]

He warned further that European attitudes were colored by a "Yalta complex"—a fear that the United States would move to settle European affairs by bilateral negotiations with Moscow without consulting the Allies.

The respected dean of American columnists on public affairs, Walter Lippman, commented, "If our object is to preserve the Western alliance, a rein should be put on the zealots in the State Department who are indulging in an all-out quarrel with General de Gaulle."[9] Holding that it was essential to obtain a "patched-up compromise on NATO," Lippman suggested that a sufficient purpose of NATO was not to be found in the integration of military forces since the principal instrument for defense was the unintegrated U.S. nuclear forces. The importance of NATO now was mainly political—to give weight and authority to the diplomatic positions of the Western nations. He would define a new purpose for NATO in aiming for a settlement of the European cold war—in healing the division between Eastern and Western Europe.[10]

Possibly the most serious consequence of the French withdrawal from military cooperation was in relations with Germany. Aware of fears of a revival of dangerous nationalism, the French foreign minister replied:

> With regard to Germany, the formula is almost a stereotype. General de Gaulle's France is practicing a nationalistic policy, and that French nationalism will by contagion reawaken German nationalism. Then what is this famous French nationalism? Is our country lodging national revindications against any one of its neighbors? Is it in any way demonstrating, inside or outside Europe, the slightest desire for adventure or domination? Does anyone think that France is a risk, however minimum, to the general peace?[11]

This was an important point, but the French spokesman overlooked another. This was the fact that the revival of German armed forces had been carried out entirely within the framework of NATO, and relying upon the integrated NATO staffs, the Germans had made no move to constitute an independent German general staff. Now if the French attitude were to prevail generally, and the NATO military staffs were to be dissolved, the Germans might be driven to reorganize a national general staff—a step dreaded by most of the nations of Europe.[12] For his part, Chancellor Erhard stated categorically that "Germany regards military integration as absolutely essential."[13] The French did wish to keep their two divisions and air elements (65,000 to 70,000 men) in Germany, and the Germans indicated a willingness to have them remain, but only if satisfactory arrangements could be made to bring them under NATO command in time of emergency.

But whatever justification might be found for the French position, it would seem that the French had lightly thrown away their bargaining position in NATO. If a nation would wish its voice to be heard among allies, including those more powerful, surely one of the best ways to assure this is to make itself logistically indispensable. By its central location; by the presence of American, German, and Canadian facilities on its soil; by the location of pipelines and NATO headquarters as well as the NATO Supply Center and various agencies of the Alliance, France virtually was in that position. Now the voice of France, previously strengthened by the mere prospect of doing what now had been done, would be reduced to a whisper in NATO military planning.

The move from France led to a reorganization of certain of the NATO political and military structures. The French emphasized that they were not proposing to leave the Alliance and that they would continue to cooperate as appropriate, but they would not continue to participate formally in the military planning.

Thus when the North Atlantic Council had specific military items to discuss, it became the Defense Planning Committee, meeting without France.

France withdrew its member from the Military Committee but continued to be represented by the head of the French Military Mission to the Military Committee. The Standing Group that, with representatives of the chiefs of staff of the United States, Great Britain, and France, had functioned as a kind of executive committee, now had lost its meaning and was abolished. The Military Committee and its international staff moved from Washington to be located with the political headquarters in Brussels. The French also maintained missions at SHAPE and other military headquarters and actually continued to cooperate in various international exercises and maneuvers.

On the broad question of the impact of the French withdrawal on strategic and logistic planning, it remained to be seen whether the liaison officers that the French proposed to maintain at the various Allied command headquarters really could be an effective substitute for full staff participation. As for the substance of planning, staff officers now would be concerned about whether it was valid to assume that French territory might be used in time of war, whether tactical dispositions should be modified, whether combined training exercises in the central area could be meaningful without the French, or whether France could be counted upon for major logistic support—even by bilateral agreements—for its allies.[14]

At the heart of the absence of coordinated logistic policy and planning was the absence of a single strategic concept among the nations of NATO. Somehow a way had to be found to resolve the strategic dilemma. On the one hand, as Hanson Baldwin wrote, "It is time to recognize that President de Gaulle has a point, to shift our emphasis to coordination rather than integration, and to attempt to influence, rather than to control, Europe's nuclear future."[15] On the other hand, prudence seemed to indicate the maintenance of flexibility and, with some kind of compromise in planning and control for nuclear warfare, the American doctrine of flexible response, with an attitude neither assuming that nuclear weapons would be nor would not be used and attempting to gear both strategy and logistics, however difficult it might be, to preparations for either or both. While it is true that logistic plans and preparations for nuclear and nonnuclear war are in many respects contradictory, it does not mean that an exclusive choice must be made between them. In life, many great truths are found to stand in apparent contradiction to each other, but that does not mean one must be rejected. On the contrary, each must be grasped in its own sphere and in its own time.

Henry Kissinger pointed up the dilemma in this way:

Exclusive U.S. control of nuclear strategy is politically and psychologically incompatible with a strategy of multiple choices or flexible response. The European refusal to assign a meaningful military mission to conventional forces in Europe is incompatible with the indefinite retention of large U.S. forces there. If the United States prizes a conventional response sufficiently, it will have to concede Europe autonomy in nuclear control. If the Europeans want to insist on an automatic nuclear response, a reconsideration of our conventional deployment on the Continent will become incompatible. Refusal to face these facts will guarantee a perpetuation of present disputes and increasing disarray within NATO.[16]

Looking to a resolution of this dilemma, several political leaders and writers for a number of years had been urging the creation of an effective political executive authority and fuller participation of the Allies in nuclear planning. Robert R. Bowie, for instance, recommended the appointment of "a high official who could act as a sort of NATO defense minister" and "expansion of participation in the existing system of planning and targeting through the SHAPE nuclear planning and liaison at the Strategic Air Command in Omaha."[17]

A study by the U.S. Senate Subcommittee on National Security and International Operations arrived at conclusions that seemed to fit the situation:

Clearly, since the United States has 95 percent or more of total Western nuclear capabilities, it necessarily and unavoidably has the decisive power, positive and negative, with respect to the use of these nuclear weapons. And that power is and will be located in Washington; no President can delegate it to anyone else.

However it may be accomplished, therefore, Canada and the European allies need greater access to the policy counsels of the United States—and vice versa—not just regarding the more remote contingencies of nuclear war, but also the ambiguous challenges that a flexible communist strategy makes probable. What the allies, including West Gremany, need is confidence that they are, in fact, involved in major issues of strategic and political planning in such ways as to influence the actions of the United States government in a crisis. And again, vice versa.

Here is where organizational imaginativeness is needed, rather than a managerial pseudo-science which formally locates power in bodies to which no member government will in fact delegate real authority.

For example, there is every good reason why the allied capitals in Europe and North America should be linked by the most effective communications arrangements that modern technology has made possible. There is still much to be done to update present arrangements.

For another example, we should be able to find ways of involving allied military officers more deeply in strategic planning that will receive a President's attention—without altering in any essential way the powers of decision. SHAPE and SACLANT now participate in the Joint Strategic Planning System, based on the U.S. Strategic Air Command at Omaha, Nebraska, and allied officers are stationed at the headquarters of U.S. Strategic Air Command. In addition, since 1963, the United States has committed three POLARIS submarines to the planning control of SHAPE. The United Kingdom has similarly committed RAF Bomber Command. Such arrangements are a good start.

The steps now being taken to develop a special nuclear committee may also be useful, especially if such a committee can be located in Washington where it could involve key men in the central and most worrisome problems of strategy and give them access to each other on matters high on the agenda of national governments.

What is required is access of key men to key men—at the North Atlantic

Council and by new consultative arrangements close to, or closely linked with, the centers of national decision-making.[18]

More specifically, recommendations adopted by the Assembly of Western European Union in December 1963 bore directly upon strategic and logistic planning:

Recommendation 98. . . .

(1) That NATO Defense planning ensure that within the limits of resources the forces available to meet any aggression shall provide the political authority with the widest possible choice of courses of action;

(2) That continuing political decision and control govern any use of nuclear weapons, ensuring that these weapons shall not be used in the case of an attack by conventional forces when such attack can be repelled by NATO conventional forces:

(3) That there be developed within NATO a unified strategic planning system aimed at the development of a common strategy and of common rules for the use of both nuclear and non-nuclear forces;

(4) That to this end NATO governments undertake consultations toward the elevation of the NATO Council into a high level allied forum for unified strategic planning with appropriate military advisory staff, the membership of such a revised NATO Council to be drawn from the highest levels of government:

(5) That such a revised NATO Council should engage in strategic planning in the broadest sense; political as well as military planning on questions affecting war and peace.

Recommendation 99. . . .

(1) To instruct their Ministers for Foreign Affairs and of Defence to seek unanimous agreement between the WEU and NATO countries on an overall strategy for the central front, with particular regard to forward defence and weapons for the land forces;

(2) To agree, in the event of the forward defence policy being retained, to take all steps to strengthen the land forces in this front so as to make the policy applicable and in particular to increase the number of men and improve their armament so that the ratio of nuclear weapons to conventional weapons is identical in all units having similar tasks.[19]

Although there appeared to be little prospect of change, defense ministers as well as officers at SHAPE were persuaded that operational control and logistics control were inseparable. Rear Admiral Henry E. Eccles wrote some conclusions in 1956 that remained no less valid a decade later. After noting the distinction in the types of operations with which SACEUR and SACLANT had to be concerned, he went on to say:

Since both SACEUR and SACLANT must operate under the same general NATO policies, necessary compromises between the military principle that a commander should control his own logistic support and the NATO policy that logistics is a national responsibility pose many dilemmas.

Some persons who recognize the need for more command control in logistics in cases of actual combat are reluctant to grant this control to the NATO commanders until the need is actually demonstrated by events. This attitude fails to take into account the realities of logistic planning and coordination. . . .

Senior commanders . . . must have up-to-date logistic information and planning factors immediately at hand. Their headquarters, facilities, and their staffs must be prepared in advance to process and manipulate these data with great speed.[20]

While no one would deny the difficulty of predicting the future, he would also assume that at least to some degree influence can be exerted upon it. It is not enough to say with resignation that no one can foresee the nature of warfare. The assumptions that planning staffs make about it and the kind of planning and preparation that they make against it will indeed affect its nature. If the design of war is not to be left completely to the enemy and to chance, then the means as well as the objectives must be the subject of thorough planning with this clearly in mind. Strategic planning will contribute little if it must proceed in a political vacuum. Neither can it be effective without logistic planning as its constant companion.

Notes

1. See Full Text of President de Gaulle's Press Conference Held in Paris at the Elysée Palace on February 21, 1966," Speeches and Press Conferences no. 239, Ambassade de France, Service de Presse et d'Information, New York, 8–9. See also *The Times* (London), 22 February 1966; *New York Herald Tribune* (European ed.), 29–30 January 1966, 1; "NATO-Reform," *Der Spiegel,* 28 February 1966; *The Times* (London), 22 February 1966. Public satisfaction with the French position was expressed only in Moscow and Peking (*Le Monde,* 11 March 1966, 3).

2. Texts of the Two French Memorandums on NATO delivered on March 8 and 10 and March 29 and 30, 1966, French Affairs No. 192, and Text of the Third French Memorandum on NATO handed to the Ambassador of the United States on April 22, 1966, French Affairs No. 192A, Ambassade de France, Service de Presse et d'Information, New York.

3. See *Le Monde,* 11 March 1966 and Raymond Aron in *Le Figaro,* 22 April 1966, Premier Pompidou put it this way before the National Assembly: "Within NATO itself, we have seen the replacement, gradual and without our agreement, of the initial strategy that was based on deterrence and, consequently, on the immediate use of atomic reprisals, by a strategy called 'flexible' which, under the pretext of lessening the risk of total war, actually consists in enabling the United States to limit the field of the initial operations by sparing the territory of the main potential agressor. . . . Such a strategy risks dooming us to atomic bombardment first, to invasion next. It occupies the general staffs with planning operations of the most superannuated type, in which we would indeed risk being defeated." See "Full Texts of the Statements on Foreign Policy by Premier Georges Pompidou before the French National Assembly on April 13 and 20, 1966," Speeches and Press Conferences nos. 243A & 245A, Ambassade de France, Service de Presse et d'Information, New York, 4. For 22 April 1966, see French Affairs no. 192A.

4. *Le Monde,* 21 April 1966, 1; *Le Figaro,* 21 April 1966, 1.

5. "Full Text of Speech Delivered by French Foreign Minister Maurice Couve de Murville before the French National Assembly on April 14, 1966," Speeches and Press Conferences no. 244A, Ambassade de France, Service de Press et d'Information, New York.

6. Pierra Gallois, "The Case for France," *Diplomat,* April 1966. Cf. Michel Eyraud, L'Alliance Atlantique: Court Terme et Moyen Term," *Stratégie,* January–February–March 1966, 103–29. For a fascinating exchange of views between two high French officers, see the dialogue

between General Gallois and General Paul Stehlin, "Aprèa la Rupture, seron-nous plus en danger qu'aujourd'hui?" *Paris-Match,* 16 April 1966, 56–69.

7. See "Dean Rusk Répond à 20 Questions de Paris-Match," *Paris-Match,* 16 April 1966, 42–45 (the official English text of the Rusk-*Paris-Match* interview was published by U.S. Information Service, American Embassy, London, 13 April, 1966); *New York Herald Tribune* (European ed.), 29–30 January 1966, 1 (already anticipating de Gaulle's statement of 21 February); *New York Times,* 18 April 1966, 1; *Manchester Guardian,* 11 March 1966; *Le Monde,* 9 March 1966, 1; *Le Monde,* 24 May 1966, 3.

8. Edmond Taylor, "This Long NATO Crisis," *The Reporter,* 21 April 1966.

9. *New York Herald Tribune,* 20 April 1966.

10. Ibid., 22 April 1966.

11. "Full Text of the Speech Delivered by French Foreign Minister Maurice Couve de Murville Before the French National Assembly on April 14, 1966," Speeches and Press Conferences no. 244A, Ambassade de France, Service de Presse et d'Information, New York, 6. Cf. Herbert Luthy, "De Gaulle: Pose and Policy," *Foreign Affairs* 43 (July 1965): 572.

12. *Times* (London), 11 March 1966.

13. *New York Herald Tribune* (European ed.), 11 March 1966.

14. See U.S. Senate, *The Atlantic Alliance, Basic Issues, A Study Submitted by the Subcommittee on National Security and International Operations to the Committee on Government Operations,* 89th Cong., 2d sess., 1966; *Manchester Guardian,* 11 March 1966; James Reston in *New York Times,* 10 March 1966.

15. Hanson Baldwin, "Taking Stock of Europe's Nuclear Defenses," *The Reporter,* 25 April 1963.

16. Henry A. Kissinger, "Coalition Diplomacy in a Nuclear Age," *Foreign Affairs* 42 (July 1964): 535.

17. Robert R. Bowie, "Strategy and the Atlantic Alliance," *International Organization* 17 (Summer 1963): 731.

18. *The Atlantic Alliance, Basic Issues,* 12.

19. *NATO Letter,* February 1964, 23.

20. Henry E. Eccles, *European Logistics, 1956,* (Washington, D.C., 1956) 30–31.

Part 3
NATO Logistics Programs

8
The Infrastructure Program

Everywhere in NATO one encounters continuous reiteration and emphasis of the "basic principle"—"Logistics is a national responsibility." One might suppose that would be the end of it. But clearly if combined military planning is to be taken at all seriously, some serious attention must be given to the logistic ingredients that make military operations possible. True, NATO as such had none of the basic resources for logistic support, and ultimately reliance had to be upon national contributions. However, all kinds of international logistic efforts occurred within NATO. The very fact that there was an assistant secretary general for production, logistics, and infrastructure indicated the serious concern for logistics. Many types of committees of the council functioned in this area. One finds elaborate projects for the standardization of supply and service, a number of programs in cooperative development and production, extensive plans for pooling and coordinating transportation, and even a rudimentary international supply system under the NATO Maintenance and Supply Organization, which operates international depots. But probably most striking of all in international logistic achievement has been NATO's common infrastructure.

The Origin

Borrowing the word *infrastructure* from the French railways, where it refers to the work of filling, cutting, grading, bridging, and tunneling that must be done before track can be laid, NATO has applied the term to the basic fixed installations such as airfields, communications systems, missile sites, naval shore facilities, petroleum pipeline and storage facilities, and air defense radar systems that are necessary for effective military operations. The use of the term in this sense and the system of international programming for these kinds of installations in Western Europe actually predates the NATO programs as such. Before the North Atlantic Treaty Organization had yet really begun to assume form, the five Brussels Treaty powers (organized as "Western Union," forerunner of "Western European

157

Union") already had begun work on an integrated program of military construction that they referred to generally as "infrastructure." That original
program, approved in 1950, called for the completion by 1951 of thirty-five
airfields in France and the Netherlands, with certain communications, at a
cost of about $92.7 million.

With the development of NATO, the common infrastructure program was
expanded to include the broader membership and the requirements of the
combined Allied commands—at first the European, and later the Atlantic as
well. Thereafter the original program was referred to as the "first slice," and
the various projects approved for subsequent years became parts of second,
third, and fourth slices. In May 1951 SHAPE submitted a survey of initial
minimum requirements for additional airfields and communication facilities
in the central European area. At the Ottawa meeting of the North Atlantic
Council in September, the governments agreed on the division of costs for
the resulting $223 million second slice. The third slice, approved at the
Lisbon meeting of the council in February 1952, provided for additional
facilities to cost about $425.6 million (later increased to about $478 million
because of rising prices for 1952). The fourth slice comprised two parts, the
first for $219 million approved at a ministerial meeting of the council in Paris
in December 1952, and the second for $187 million, approved at a ministerial
meeting in Paris the following April. Construction projects financed in the
fourth slice were intended to provide the common infrastructure needed for
the support of forces expected to exist through December 1954.

In their April 1953 meeting the ministers went further. Looking beyond
the annual slice program, they adopted a longer-term three-year program
that would provide commanders and staffs with a more firm basis for planning. Approval of specific projects still would be on a year-to-year basis, but
they would be viewed within the framework of the broader plan. The agreement on this long-term program provided that projects should be approved
for construction by the North Atlantic Council not later than 30 June 1955.
The hope was that the funds to be made available under the three-year program would be enough to provide basic installations needed for common
defense through December 1956.

All this, it should be emphasized, was in addition to the "national infrastructure" that the nations continued to build out of national budgets solely
for the use of their own forces, including those built under bilateral arrangements such as American line-of-communication facilities in Germany,
France, and Italy.[1]

The System

Procedures for initiating, screening, approving, financing, implementing,
and accepting common infrastructure projects were in general similar to
those for government projects in any of the member countries, but with the

considerable added complications growing out of their international charac-ter.[2]

PROCESSING OF NATO COMMON INFRASTRUCTURE PROGRAMMES & PROJECTS

From *NATO; Facts about the North Atlantic Treaty Organization* (Paris: NATO Information Service, 1965), 139.

Specific procedural steps varied over the years according to the nature of the project, the countries concerned, and NATO's own policies and organizational structure prevailing at the time. In general, proposals would go up through military channels. As a rule in later years the major military commands, i.e., SACEUR or SACLANT, provided planning guidance to their major subordinate commanders with target dates for submitting proposals for the coming infrastructure slice. In exceptional cases major subordinate commanders might initiate a proposal, but ordinarily this had to be done by the prospective host nation—i.e., by the nation on whose territory the facility was to be located. On the basis of his guidance from higher headquarters the major subordinate commander consulted with his own subordinate and with national agencies in the area of his command. Obviously the subordinate commander saw his duty to point out needs, but it was up to the government concerned to make the request. The subordinate regional commander (e.g., AFCENT or AFSOUTH) then might accept or reject proposals, or assign priorities as between nations or between types of projects within his region. Major subordinate commanders had to submit their proposal projects by a given date, say 1 November, to the supreme commanders for consideration in the slice schedules to be approved some fourteen to eighteen months later. In some cases the national defense ministry of a prospective host nation or the military headquarters of a prospective user nation might submit a proposal directly. Usually the proposals were for projects upon which construction could proceed immediately on approval, but for especially elaborate items of long lead-time, planning funds, at two percent of the estimated cost, might be programmed.

The supreme commanders reviewed the proposals for installations or facilities within their respective areas to see how they could be coordinated in a general program and to see that they represented essential military requirements attuned to operational plans, that they were required to support the forces agreed to by the nations in the annual or triennial review, and that they were eligible for common funding. The supreme commanders, or members of their staffs, would consult with the infrastructure section of the NATO International Staff to make sure that cost estimates submitted with project proposals were reasonable, that military requirements were being met at lowest possible cost, and that the proposals were sound technically.

By about June in the following year, the supreme commanders were ready to submit preliminary programs for the slice to the NATO Military Committee and to the Infrastructure Committee of the North Atlantic Council (with copies to all interested agencies, including national ministries of defense). The former considered the proposed program from the viewpoint of military necessity, while the latter considered it from the technical and financial angles. Then members of the Military Committee, the Infrastructure Committee, and national representatives would discuss the programs.

Taking into account the various comments, the supreme commanders revised their programs and again submitted them to the Military Committee and the Infrastructure Committee. Meanwhile, the host nation was preparing plans and detailed cost estimates for each particular project. These had to have the approval of the Infrastructure Committee before funds could be committed. The supreme commanders and the user nations reviewed the preliminary plans before making them a part of the final recommended program. Approval by the Military Committee might be expected by December, and by the Infrastructure Committee by February. The North Atlantic Council considered the reports of the two groups simultaneously, and within another few months gave its approval for the next slice of NATO's Common Infrastructure. Approval by the council automatically committed member countries to financial contributions according to agreed-upon percentages.

And here in a way was one of the most complicated and sensitive steps in the whole infrastructure program—finance. But it was NATO's ability in finding a financial formula that made the program successful.

The cost-sharing formula was based essentially upon three criteria: (1) the capacity of each country to pay—as determined by its gross national product; (2) the advantage to be gained by the user countries; and (3) the economic benefit for the host country. Common financing covered only construction and installation. Host countries still had to cover the cost of the land, public utilities, and maintenance except in special cases where some assistance might be given a host country when these expenses were unusually high relative to the country's economic capacity.

Percentages of the total common cost assigned to each country varied considerably. For Slices II, III, and IV-A (remembering that Slice I was developed under the auspices of Western Union), the North Atlantic Council negotiated the cost-sharing percentages in each instance at the time that it gave its approval for the slice. But this was such an exhausting and time-consuming procedure that the members sought a way to make their agreements last longer. This indeed provided much of the impetus for adopting general long-range programs into which the annual slices would be fitted. After Slice IV-A, the council agreed to approve funds up to a set ceiling to cover general programs three or four years in advance. The agreed-upon cost-sharing percentages then applied for that entire period regardless of specific modifications in annual slices.

Changes in NATO membership and participation, aside from the other factors at work, brought changes in the proportionate share that each had to bear. Thus Iceland, having no military forces, never participated in the infrastructure program. Greece and Turkey acceded to the North Atlantic Treaty in 1952, and their first contribution to common infrastructure was for Slice IV-A. Although Italy was an original member of NATO, it did not begin participation in the infrastructure program until Slice III (i.e., the second year of the strictly NATO program). Germany's acceptance of membership in 1955 brought very significant additional resources as well as additional requirements for infrastructure. As a beginning, and for projects to be located in Germany, the Federal Republic agreed to pay half the cost of Slice VII-B, while the other half would be funded under the cost-sharing formula, and then for the other slices in the 1957–60 program, the German share was 13.72 percent. For the next period, 1961–64, the German share went up to 20 percent. At the outset the United States was bearing nearly half (48.1 percent) of the cost. Gradually the U.S. contribution was scaled down until it was equal to 25.767 percent for the 1965–69 program. Finally, the French withdrawal from general participation brought profound changes. The French share of 21.52 percent of the cost for Slice II and later shares of from 11.87 percent to 13.76 percent would be very much missed. In effect the French carried no part in the general program for 1965–69, though they did continue to pay their share on earlier slices. With the French withdrawal, it was left to the others to make up the difference. This was done by applying to the French quota a proportionate share on the same basis as for the original amount for each nation. At the same time, the program was cut back by the amount that had been planned for installations in France so that the share of each nation in terms of percent of the total amount went up, but since the total amount had been proportionately lowered, the actual monetary commitment for each nation remained essentially the same.

Once the council had approved the projects comprising a particular slice and had allocated its funds, the host nations assumed full responsibility for the construction. Still, while the responsibility was theirs, it was not without conditions or limitations. The host government developed detailed engineering designs, which they submitted together with refined cost estimates to the supreme commander concerned and to the user nations for their further review. After this review, the host government developed contract designs and specifications and requested approval of funds. Then in consultation with the military authorities it selected the exact site and acquired the necessary land at its own expense. About the same time the host government advertised the project internationally for construction bids.[3]

Again, while the host government was responsible for design and construction of common infrastructure installations, it had to be governed by limiting criteria that had been agreed upon for certain specialized facilities such as airfields and missile sites, or user nations and military commands would share in the development of certain things such as unique naval facilities. Meetings of experts in various fields of infrastructure were held to exchange technical information on methods of construction, to discuss methods of improving construction work, of effecting economies, of coordinating activities. One meeting might consider airfield construction, another pipelines, and another communication facilities. One meeting, for example, called by the controller for Infrastructure with the approval of the Infrastructure Committee and presided over by the head of the naval section of the Infrastructure Branch of the International Staff, brought together over fifty experts from interested countries to discuss the construction of naval facilities.[4] Such discussions had direct influence on construction projects whatever the ultimate responsibility of the host.

Moreover, after a contract had been let and construction was underway, performance was subject to international inspection at every stage. A team of technicians representing the International Staff, SACEUR or SACLANT, interested subordinate commanders, user nations, and the host nation inspected the work in progress and submitted reports. Upon completion of a project, a similar team, with a representative of the International Staff as chairman, made a final inspection. The report of this team formed the basis for consideration of NATO acceptance by the Infrastructure Committee. If acceptance were given, the International Board of Auditors for Infrastructure Accounts checked accounts to see that all charges were justified for NATO payment. If all was in order, the board issued a certificate to the host government authorizing reimbursement. The NATO Infrastructure Committee itself might visit various countries from time to time at the invitation of the governments concerned, to spend a week or more in inspecting infrastructure installations.

The International Staff actually handled no funds. Allocation of funds, approval of expenditures, and assessment of shares all were on an international basis. But each nation paid its net share directly to the host nation. Since work would be going on in several countries simultaneously, certain payments would cancel each other, and it was only necessary to make actual payments for the net difference in each case. A system had been worked out for the clearing of accounts and transfers of funds on a quarterly basis.

Common infrastructure procedures were fraught with difficulties at every step of the way. Undoubtedly the key to the whole program was in arriving at agreements to establish a financial ceiling for a general program extending over a three- or four-year period, and then agreeing upon a cost-sharing formula to cover the whole period. Thus far this had been outstandingly successful. Still, when national representatives came to bargain on these points they often were paralyzed by such secondary considerations as international balance of payments and the flow of gold. Actually the United States, the financial giant among the partners, led the way to certain restrictive attitudes by insisting that an amount equal to its contribution be spent in the United States. Other countries were quick to follow suit until this had become almost an unwritten policy. Unfortunately such a policy did not always square with military requirements—not to mention the general policy of obtaining goods and services at the most economical rates possible. On the other hand such an informal arrangement (there was, in general, no formal guarantee) might be an essential element for the participation of each country. As will be seen, this was and was intended to be one of the key features of the NATO Air Defense System and of the cooperative production programs. In this way, international cooperation could proceed while avoiding international balance of payments complications.

National and local complications inevitably hampered expeditious completion of projects. Allowance had to be made for different administrative machinery and procedures in the different countries. In Norway and Portugal, for instance, a division of the Defense Ministry handled military construction. In France the PTT supervised the installation of communications facilities, Ponts et Chaussees the overseas airfield construction, and Travaux Maritimes was charged with construction of naval facilities. Most complicated of all was the German system. Here not only was it necessary to deal through the several federal ministries and agencies at Bonn, but much of the work had to be done through the Länder offices. The Länder governments in Germany selected the sites, acquired the land, prepared plans and specifications, and awarded contracts. Moreover, the Länder governments were jealous of their prerogatives and compliance was not automatic.

Sometimes a decision in any country to choose a certain site for an installation might be greeted by a chorus of opposition from local inhabitants who wanted to prevent the destruction of a scenic spot or who feared having their homes become a military target or who were anxious to avoid noise and other nuisances. On the other hand, there might be lively competition among areas anxious to gain employment opportunities and the economic side effects of having a military construction project nearby.

Again local conditions were likely to affect the nature of the construction itself. Members of the International Staff might have thought it a simple matter, for instance, to order uniform, prefabricated housing for certain outposts. But in Greece the housing had to be built of stone in order to employ Greek stone cutters and masons; in Norway the houses had to be of wood in order to use the Norwegian lumber industry and carpenters. In a great many cases it was difficult to induce the nations to bring building standards *down* to minimum requirements in order to save costs. Whether out of habit or in order to give a further advantage in profits to local builders, the nations nearly always tended to overbuild and to make the system far more elaborate than necessary. When, on the basis of military estimates, an eight-year standard, for example, was set for certain buildings, the host country still was more likely to settle for structures built to last fifty or a hundred years.

In the construction of some facilities the question of national civilian as well as military use arose. This was especially true in the case of oil pipeline and communications facilities. When it would not interfere with the military mission, would not increase the cost to NATO, and was otherwise feasible, the policy was to permit such multiple use and to include such an assumption in the construction plans. In one case when NATO required a certain number of radio relay circuits, the host nation countered with a proposal to build several times that number in order to use the facility for national television. NATO then calculated the cost for a facility to meet its own minimum requirements and paid this amount in a lump sum to the host nation, which then built the much-bigger facility with a guarantee of the required number of circuits for NATO's use.

Language was a problem, not only in the relatively simple mechanics of making translations, but in making sure that technical concepts were clear to all concerned, and particularly in developing international agreements that were clear enough for all to understand, but general (or obscure) enough for all to accept.

There was a problem—potentially a serious one—regarding completion dates of projects and the acceptability of the work. There were no sanctions in the system to apply against a nation if the final inspectors and auditors were not satisfied, except perhaps withholding of approval, which could delay payment. But if there were differences about successful completion of a project, this was a matter for negotiation. If agreement was not possible, then the matter might be put to a board of arbitration—and if necessary carried to the council. But negotiation generally was successful.

With the intrusion of local politics, local economic consideration, and red tape arising out of the efforts at coordination internationally as well as meeting national regulations and customs, delays in completion of some projects were inevitable. Generally, the International Staff or the Military Commands had not assumed an expediting or progress management role, but in later years a trend emerged in this direction, at least in special instances.

Maintenance of installations, once they were in place, was not a matter for infrastructure. The infrastructure and other construction programs covered only construction. Maintenance was the responsibility of the users or of the host nation (which might also be the principal user) or of special common funding under a military command. Finally there was the problem of liquidation, or of renewal, and of the restoration of real property, but this will be discussed later.

The Projects

Perhaps seventy-five percent or more of the total NATO infrastructure effort during this period went into various aspects of air defense, including airfields, missile sites, communications, warning and intercept systems, and a significant share of fuel pipelines and storage facilities. The work of infrastructure was an unending process. When one series of projects had been completed, inevitably there would be requirements for as many more in the constant race to keep pace with new strategic concepts, new weapons and communications systems, and shifting political conditions. It was not enough just to keep adding more. It was necessary to look to needs for renovation of previously completed facilities in order to keep up with new requirements.

Airfields

For the first several years half of the annual infrastructure slices was for airfield construction. Since NATO took over completion of the airfields first programmed by the Brussels Treaty Powers, more than 220 airfields had been constructed (and several *re*constructed) in eleven of the European member countries up to 1966. All had to conform to standards established by the NATO military authorities. Each new airfield cost between $5 and $6 million, depending on geographical location, local construction conditions, and accompanying installations. The total outlay in airfields, then, had been well over $1.2 billion.

In terms of current operations, the airfield construction was considerably over half completed by 1956. Then, with the beginning of Germany's participation and with greater emphasis upon a "forward strategy," the special Slice VIIb added to the 1956 program was essentially a program of $106 million for construction of airfields in Germany.[5]

One major airfield, at Suda Bay in Crete, went through three transformations in the first ten years after work first began on it in 1954. In this case an American company began to work on the runways, but shortly an Athens firm took over. Originally, Suda Bay was intended as a base for naval aviation when it was programmed under Infrastructure Slice IV, but its role later was broadened for tactical support. The field became operational in 1960, but had to have modifications and improvements to meet revised NATO criteria, which reflected changes in strategic assumptions and aircraft design. Much of the area had to be blasted out of solid rock or cleared of loose boulders, and if inspectors were startled to find marble being used for doorsteps and expansion joints in the barracks, they had to be reassured that marble, quarried close at hand, was the cheapest material available. A lower grade of marble was even used in the concrete for the runways. In the case of the latest renovation and expansion, construction kept up with or at times was ahead of all the schedules. Workers recruited locally, with supervisors from Athens, worked in double shifts through the winter of 1963–64 with dynamite charges, pneumatic drills, and the various implements for moving earth (mostly rock), laying concrete, and erecting buildings. Roads and runways were completed in six months. A Greek Air Force squadron continued to operate from one part of the field while construction crews were at work on another. The local population was not altogether enthusiastic about having a NATO air base near their homes and they became especially resentful when they saw cherished ancient olive trees fall victim to dynamite and bulldozers. Still the economic benefits could not escape them, and in the long run they probably outweighed the earlier uneasiness.[6]

The construction of each NATO airfield was a special story of overcoming obstacles, of working to measure up to standards, and of dealing with attitudes and ways of local people. But taken altogether, the network of airfields built under the NATO infrastructure program stood as a monumental achievement in international cooperation.[7]

In fitting into strategic requirements and retaining utility for wartime operations, the complex of airfields fell into the dilemma which troubled all NATO logistic efforts, that of conventional versus nuclear war. The biggest problem for the airfields was their vulnerability. Their own aircraft and the highly developed NATO air defense system could provide reasonably adequate protection against conventional air attack. But what about attacks by missiles carrying nuclear warheads? Some saw the only way out of this dilemma to be, first, in putting full emphasis on vertical and short take-off and landing aircraft, and eventually for missiles to replace aircraft for most strategic and tactical air attack roles. Some suggested curtailment of expenditures for long runways and conventional airfields because within twenty years vertical take-off and landing (VTOL) surely would have replaced virtually all military aircraft of the conventional types. If this came to pass, then infrastructure would have to be reduced and modified drastically to meet the changed requirements for large numbers of small installations where planes would be dispersed.[8]

Missile Sites

While the basic need in building airfields was to find big tracts of ground at the right places, missile sites required a very large number of relatively small tracts located in all kinds of terrain in such a way as to be mutually supporting. Sites for NIKE, HAWK, and MACE missiles were spread all across Europe from Denmark to Greece under the infrastructure program. Again, the infrastructure program and staffs had no responsibility for either operation or maintenance of the weapons or for the maintenance of buildings and equipment on the sites. Infrastructure covered preparation of the ground, buildings for control centers and administrative needs, launching platforms, radar hardstands, revetments, frequency converters, and communications.

The NIKE, a two-stage surface-to-air missile for use against aircraft at high altitudes, required two or three separate areas for each site—a control area, a launch area, and an administrative area (which might be joined to one of the other two). A further complication in the selection and preparation of sites arose from the fact that the tracking radar had to be able to pick up the missile before it left the launcher. In addition to the spherical radome for tracking the missile itself, each NIKE control area contained a second radome for tracking the target, an acquisition radar, and an integrated fire control unit. The latter, ordinarily built into trailers, included the quarters of the battery control officer and the computer, which translated information from the target-tracking and missile-tracking radars into guidance instructions. The launching area was divided into several sections, each with protected launchers on which the missiles rested. The four batteries making up each battalion were tied to battalion headquarters not only by ordinary communications, but by an Automatic Data Link, which could select a certain battery of the battalion according to the availability and readiness of its missiles to take on a specific target. Both the older NIKE-AJAX, and the improved NIKE-HERCULES were on site in Europe, though the former was being phased out.

The HAWK, a surface-to-air missile designed for protection against low-flying aircraft, made simpler demands for sites in that its radars, launchers, and battery control centers could be located within a single area. However, for HAWK to be effective against the low-flying targets for which it was designed, its close-range radars had to have a clear field of vision at low angles. This meant they had to be located away from hills, buildings, and other obstructions. Sometimes a choice had to be made between felling trees and clearing other obstacles over an area of up to thirty hectares, and of going to the expense of elevating the radars on high towers.

A third missile assigned to NATO forces and depending upon sites built under the infrastructure program was the MACE surface-to-surface missile. The control system for this weapon differed in that each was programmed for a specific target, and the necessary data already was stored in the computer to permit accurate launching at a moment's notice.

Owing to the size and strategic position of Germany, a very large number of the missile sites went into that country. There in northern marshlands, it was necessary at times to put installations on pilings (where the sites were on as much as ten meters of peat), to skirt valuable industrial areas, and then in the south to cut and fill in leveling-off sites in the hills, and then to build additional access roads. In the mountains of Greece and Turkey, and in some parts of Italy, of course, this was even more of a problem. A special factor in arranging for the selection of all those sites and acquiring all the parcels of land in Germany was the previously noted fact that there this was left to the Länder governments, and no agency of the Federal government exercised central control or direction over these procedures. At times differences between NATO's infrastructure authorities and local officials have come to near impasse, but eventually agreement in all cases was reached. In spite of the cumbersome procedures it was possible on occasion to speed them up considerably. At the time of the Berlin Crisis of 1962–63, the North Atlantic Council agreed to modify the regular procedures of budgetary control, and the federal and Länder governments of Germany agreed to waive certain regulations in the interest of expediting the program. As a result, a substantial increase in missile sites was achieved within little more than one year from programming to completion. Understandably, costs for missile sites varied a great deal from time to time and place to place, but in general it may be said that the cost to the infrastructure budget for a NIKE site had been approximately $1.4 million, with an increase to about $2.25 in especially difficult terrain.[9]

NADGE

The linchpin in NATO's air defense and by far the greatest single project undertaken under the infrastructure program up to that time was NADGE (NATO Air Defense Ground Environment). This was a program intended to supplement and modernize the Early Warning radar system that already had been installed in the 1950s as an infrastructure project, and to link the various national systems (and a tripartite system, of Great Britain, France and Germany) into a single integrated system. Key features of the new system were the addition of much-improved radar equipment and computerized response to guide either manned interceptor aircraft or surface-to-air missiles against intruder aircraft of the most modern types (though of course it was not intended as a defense against missiles). In its operation, the system would disregard international boundaries, for the truth of General Norstad's observation in the 1950s, "Except as part of the whole, there is no air defense of any one nation,"[10] by now was clear to nearly everyone.

As early as 1957 planning began toward an advance NATO air defense system. In that year SHAPE and the national defense ministries appointed a fact-finding mission to assist in obtaining information for working out general European requirements. A major contribution came from the United Kingdom where considerable work had been done on advanced radar and data-processing techniques relating to air defense. But three years of negotiations with national defense ministries ensued before SHAPE could present an agreed plan, even in general terms, to the Military Committee and the Infrastructure Committee and get a decision from the council. This came, at least in preliminary form, in 1960 with the council's recognition of the requirement. It still was necessary to develop a detailed plan and to take the necessary steps to bring such a system into being.

This process took another four years of prolonged negotiations, preliminary plans, and revisions. At one point, in 1963, when it appeared that costs were going to spiral far beyond any previous estimate, it seemed that the whole project might blow up. According to one report, the United States had agreed to accept its thirty percent share under infrastructure of financing the program, but when it was said that cost estimates had tripled over the $300 million originally estimated, the United States was refusing to go along. At the same time, it was pointed out that the 1,000 F-104-G interceptors that would be depending upon the system for their effectiveness already had cost about $2 billion, and without NADGE they would be relatively useless. European countries that had taken the F-104-G as their principal fighter aircraft were said to be "up in arms" over the situation, and one report said, this "crisis may make the Skybolt affair look like an apple-bobbing party."[11]

Feverish efforts during the next eighteen months succeeded somehow in revising plans sufficiently to push estimated costs back down to the original figure. The International Ground Environment Subcommittee, a technical subsidiary of the Infrastructure Committee, and the Ground Environmental Team of the International Staff evolved respectively into the NADGE Policy Board and the NADGE Management Office (NADGEMO) to give guidance and supervision and direction. By the autumn of 1964 plans had been completed to the point that it was possible to invite bids for the construction.

The conditions for the bids were in a peculiar form. First of all, it was laid down that the contractor must be an international consortium, for unlike most infrastructure projects in which only one host country was involved, in this case there would be *nine* host countries (Norway, Denmark, Germany, the Netherlands, Belgium, France, Italy, Greece, and Turkey.) There would, therefore, be a general contract between NADGEMO and the consortium, and then nine individual contracts between the consortium and the host countries. Moreover, the formation of the consortia would be up to the interested companies, and the proposed consortia would be formed *before* the bidding. Another special condition formalized an arrangement that had tended to be followed only as an informal guide in infrastructure programs—and even that had not been without criticism: each country was to receive orders for work or equipment roughly equivalent to its financial contribution to the project. In other words, each country's contribution would be spent, as nearly as possible, in that country. This of course included not only the host countries, but all the fourteen participants in infrastructure. It would be up to the consortium to parcel out its work through subcontracts and orders to meet this condition. Ideally the consortium would be made up of companies in each country prepared to handle its share of the work. Finally, bids were to be within an overall ceiling of about $310 million. The award was to go to the low bidder who could demonstrate capacity to perform and to meet all the conditions.

A lively competition followed in choosing up sides and preparing bids. Four consortia were able to form and to prepare bids. However, one dropped out almost immediately, and a second, headed by International Telephone and Telegraph, dropped out in the final phase of bidding. This left two, one headed by the Westinghouse Company and designated "Westinghouse NADGE Associates," and the other headed by the Hughes Aircraft Company under the designation "Hughes NADGE Consortium" (HUCO).

But now a difficulty arose over the financial ceiling. Neither group was willing to quote a price, for both maintained that it would not be possible to complete the project under the stated ceiling. Now the question was whether the ceiling should be raised or requirements cut. After further discussions among NADGEMO, SHAPE, and the defense ministers, it was decided to trim requirements by about ten percent and retain the ceiling. The two consortia then submitted their bids. The Hughes group, being about seven to eight percent lower, received the award.

The successful consortium, soon redesignated NADGECO, Ltd., included a number of veterans of infrastructure and cooperative production work. Those mainly concerned with building technical equipment in addition to Hughes of the United States were Thompson-Houston of France, Marconi of the United Kingdom, Telefunken of Germany, Selenia of Italy, Hollandse Signaal Apparaten of the Netherlands, and Northern Electric of Canada. Other firms in other countries would handle most of the construction work on the sites.

When completed, the modern air defense ground environment would provide a solid screen of interlocking sectors from the northern tip of Norway to the eastern frontier of Turkey, where computer-guided missiles or computer-directed piloted aircraft could respond within split seconds against an unidentified plane. Some saw in NADGE not only the most expensive, but also the most important project of the infrastructure program.[12]

ACE High

An infrastructure project closely related to NADGE, and in many ways setting precedents for it, was the ACE High (Allied Command Europe) signal communication system that was just being completed as invitations for bids were going out for NADGE. While ACE High comprised many conventional installations and connections that had been developed over the years under the aegis of SHAPE, its unique technical feature was the "Forward Scatter" system of radio communication.

The scatter system depended upon a phenomenon long known but not put to practical use until 1954: a certain portion of high frequency radio signals are reflected against the tropospheric and ionospheric layers of the earth's upper atmosphere, and are scattered back to earth. Although a very small portion—only one ten-millionth part—the random scattering is such that a small portion *always* is present, and with powerful transmission and sensitive reception amplified adequately, it will yield a signal not only as clear as that of the ordinary telephone, but 99.9 percent reliable, secure, and jamproof. Here was a way of overcoming the strict limitation on high-frequency transmission imposed by the fact that its signals ordinarily can be received only in direct line-of-sight—that they can be received neither over the curvature nor through the earth.

Coming to the conclusion that a military emergency would require a completely reliable communications system, one that was independent of civil and national systems, officers at SHAPE recommended that a complete system be built, based upon the forward scatter principle. The United States released its technical information on the subject to SHAPE in 1955, and SACEUR began to develop a plan for the new communications system as an infrastructure project proposal. An early technical decision was to choose the tropospheric (at 15,000 feet) rather than the ionospheric layer as requiring less power and giving more channels, though having a short range (200 miles).[13]

As a single system cutting across many nations, ACE high was another program where it was necessary to alter standard procedures. In this case SHAPE in effect served as the host nation and principal user. It was for SHAPE to arrange with each nation concerned for the necessary land, and then at NATO expense to prepare the sites for erecting buildings, bringing in electrical power, preparing antenna foundations, and sometimes building towers. Further, it was up to SHAPE to determine the equipment needed and to arrange for its procurement on the international market and to prescribe the construction and technical installation.

Central coordination for the project was provided by an ACE High project manager, who also served as chief of the Forward Scatter Branch organized in the SHAPE Signal Division. With some forty-six military and civilian experts, it became the largest branch in the division. One section coordinated all the planning and phasing of the work, including construction by host nations, delivery of equipment, and scheduling of the installation teams. Another group let and administered the contracts for electronic equipment, while a third consulted closely with the prime contractor and with scientific experts from the SHAPE Air Defense Technical Center at The Hague in monitoring technical aspects of the general contract. An Operations and Maintenance Section took care of the system once it was completed. Forward Scatter branches at each of the four major subordinate headquarters maintained direct liaison with the military authorities and government agencies in the various host countries.

In the Budget and Financial Division of SHAPE a Forward Scatter Financial Branch was established for the financial management of what turned out to be a $75 million project.

SHAPE awarded the prime contract for design and construction of the system to the International Telephone and Telegraph Company, which organized a subsidiary, International Standard Engineering, to act as executive agency. Many subcontractors, working closely with SHAPE staff representatives and with local government officials, participated in the construction, and over one hundred manufacturers provided equipment. Marshalling points were established at Oslo, Hamburg, London, Paris, Livono, Piraus, and Izmir to receive and safeguard all of the items of equipment and thousands of accessories until they could be sent to the respective sites for uninterrupted installation.

Careful plans had to be laid for a number of special problems of coordination and preparation. First, electric power was provided by nine different countries and had to be uniform. Radio frequencies had to be coordinated in each nation, and to achieve this the SHAPE officers worked through the European Military Communications Coordinating Committee and the European Radio Frequency Agency. There remained a sore point in the matter of coordinating civil and military communications in NATO. SHAPE still would have to depend upon the regular PTT networks for much of its local communications, including the effective local transmission of signals from its early warning system. On the other hand the NATO civil planners—in particular the Civil Communications Planning Committee—were anxious to have access to reliable long-range communications, and they thought it a mistake to look upon many of the civil emergency requirements as having a lower priority than many of the military requirements. They were quick to point out, for instance, that communications needed for shipping, civil aviation, and inland surface transport—not to mention fallout warnings—were just as vital to the military as to the civil segments of defense.

In order to train operators for the system, SHAPE established a Tropospheric Forward Scatter Communications School at an Italian Air Force technical training center at Latina, south of Rome.

As a matter of priority, in order to fill a serious gap in the existing communications, an ionosphere system first was installed in the South, while the first link in the tropospheric system itself, to serve as a pilot model for the whole system, was completed in the North in 1958. Because of climate and terrain this was in some ways the most difficult part of all. Called the "Hot Line," it covered the region all the way from Oslo to the North Cape.

Each locale had its special construction problems. What otherwise would have been routine construction tasks when it came to the actual on-site construction acquired a difficult and sometimes hazardous character from the desirability often of putting the installations on mountain tops. A helicopter had to brave the thin air and tricky currents of high altitudes to deliver lumber to a barren mountain top in Norway. In Germany workers who were preparing a foundation for a giant antenna paused when they struck what appeared to be a rich vein of coal, but the order came back: forget about the coal and keep working on the foundation. In the winter of 1961 two stations in France had been half finished when snowfalls nearly buried them and work had to be suspended for weeks. Near Athens the buildings for a station rose in gleaming marble. In Turkey an engineer asked simply for quantities of soil to be sent in, for the site had only rock and sand.

In 1963 the ACE High system, covering 13,360 kilometers from northern Norway to eastern Turkey, with 82 stations providing 250 telephone and 180 telegraph circuits, was finished. It was the largest communications system ever completed under a single internationally funded project and the largest integrated system under a single field headquarters ever built.

Now the second phase of logistic support began. In order to assure continuous operation, five two-man teams were assigned to each ACE High station. Thus over a thousand people were employed in the system. The problem was to keep them supplied and to provide the parts necessary to keep the complex equipment in operation over all kinds of terrain, in all kinds of weather, and under all kinds of conditions.[14]

SATCOM

What promised to be an even more spectacular communications system was the satellite communications system, known as NATO SATCOM, which began in an experimental stage in June 1967 with plans for the beginning of a fully operational stage to be in effect before the end of 1969. This project began with an offer by the United States in September 1966 for NATO to share in that country's Initial Defense Communications Satellite Program. The council accepted the offer and it fell to the Forward Scatter Branch of SHAPE to develop a plan. Turning for assistance to the SHAPE Technical Centre at The Hague, where studies for such a system had been going on since 1961, the Forward Scatter Branch within three weeks prepared a preliminary plan for the research and development phase of the program, which was concerned mainly with experimentation, familiarization, and training. With earth terminals obtained from the Philco Company of the United States, one installed at SHAPE in Belgium and the other at AFSOUTH Headquarters in Naples, it became possible for the NATO staffs to have access to American communications satellites several hours a day.

Meanwhile, the project for the construction of physical facilities—mainly a chain of terminals—went forward. Each one of the participating countries other than the United States was guaranteed that ninety percent of its contributions for construction of terminals would come back in production contracts.

The space segment of the project—the manufacture, launching, and initial control of the satellites—remained the responsibility of the United States. The cost was about $20 million, and most of it was borne by the United States as its contribution to the program. European companies could compete with American firms for contracts for satellite components.

When completed, the NATO system was tied in with the American system and with the one being developed by the United Kingdom. This program gave to the secretary general and his staff, to the North Atlantic Council and its agencies, and to the military authorities and major commands the most reliable and effective communications system ever known on such a scale. It was one of the most effective steps undertaken to make NATO coordination operational.[15]

Pipelines

In a sense, the construction of pipeline systems to supply fuel for the air and land forces of NATO in Europe was an example par excellence of the working of the Infrastructure program. When petroleum products made up more than half of the total supply requirements of modern forces, the building of pipelines was bound to be high priority if there was to be any international logistic effort at all among the nations of the North Atlantic Alliance. Success in the construction and operation of an adequate pipeline system would alone nearly justify all the efforts at international cooperative logistics.

Conceived originally to provide fuel for the Allied air forces, the plan was quickly revised to meet demands for serving the land forces as well. The North Atlantic Council gave its approval for the first phase of the project in December 1952, and work began early the next year.

Since military considerations prevailed in making decisions, the location of terminal facilities and storage capacities depended upon military estimates. These estimates were the basis, too, for the selection of sizes of pipe, from twelve-inch to four-inch diameter (with over seventy-five percent being eight inches or greater). Again because of military needs, the pipe was laid in a telescopic pattern, beginning with the largest-sized pipe at the ports of entry and becoming progressively smaller toward farthest inland terminals. The four-inch pipe was mainly for direct connections to airfields.

Since approval of the first phase in 1952, the pipeline system accounted for a substantial part of each infrastructure slice, amounting to about one-sixth of the common funds. The letting of contracts for the construction work followed more or less usual procedures, but the method was different for equipment. Here there was greater opportunity for international competition, and particularly in Central Europe where certain requirements of performance had to be met. In the interest of obtaining the pricing advantage of large-scale procurement as well as the simplicity for maintenance and supply of spare parts by uniformity of design, it was desirable to obtain all the pumps and engines for the Central European System for a single source. To accomplish this, the participants, with staff coordination from SHAPE, resorted to an ingenious method of bidding. First they agreed upon minimum characteristics and then invited potential suppliers to submit bids in two envelopes. The first was to contain a technical description of the equipment that the bidder proposed to furnish to meet the requirement. The second was to contain prices. As the envelopes were opened the staff decided which supplier met the performance specifications and which were technically qualified. Then the second envelope revealed the lowest prices. The contracts were awarded to the lowest bidders among the qualifiers.

Many companies shared in the vast enterprise of pipeline construction. In Turkey alone, for example, American, French, German, and Italian, as well as Turkish companies, participated in the designing, supplying of equipment, and construction.

By its very nature the pipeline program encountered a series of special problems. Inevitable delays arose early on account of the lack of laws and regulations to govern pipeline construction in a number of countries. Decisions and policies had to be worked out to deal with the legal as well as the physical complexities of crossing railroads, roads, canals, streams, and international boundaries. Then there were delays in the acquisition of land, especially in the long negotiations and costly settlements in the populous areas of Belgium, the Netherlands, and Germany. Few European companies had the kind of equipment needed for a major task of pipe-laying. Usually some bulldozers could be found, but there were few if any tractors with side booms, and usually no pipe-bending machines, coating machines, road-boring machines, or line-up clamps. Improvisation was the order of the day. At one place, where no skids were available, metal chairs were used to support the pipe for welding. At another, where there were no line-up clamps, each section was aligned and braced and all other operations were halted until the joint was welded. Since coating machines were not available, mill-coated pipe had to be used, and since there were no bending machines, bends in the pipe had to be made in the factory from measurements taken in the field. The ultimate in the immobility of labor was reached in an area where government regulations forbade the moving by a contractor of a worker out of his home district; this meant that labor crews had to be discharged and others hired about every ten kilometers. Most pipe handling was by hand. At one place where the contractor was able to use proper equipment, he discovered it was cheaper to use hand labor anyway. However, in Germany and certain other areas where regular pipe line construction equipment and methods were used, the rate of progress was three to four times faster than that achieved elsewhere, though the slower hand methods proved to be generally satisfactory so far as quality of work was concerned.

By the end of 1965 it could be said that the NATO pipeline system was substantially complete. It included 9,000 kilometers of pipeline, storage facilities for about two million cubic meters of fuel, together with all the necessary pumping stations, tanker discharge facilities, and terminal facilities.

The Central Europe System was the most intricate and the most extensive integrated pipeline system in the world.[16] This system alone included over 5,000 kilometers of pipelines, approximately one million cubic meters of storage, and about one hundred pumping stations, and it had direct connections to a large number of airfields. It cost about $220 million.

Actually, the NATO pipeline system comprised a number of individual systems within the geographic regions of Allied Command Europe. In addition to the Central System, which ran through the territory of five nations (France, Germany, Belgium, Luxembourg, and the Netherlands), the Southern Region had separate systems in Italy and Greece and two systems in Turkey. In the Northern Region there were small separate systems in Denmark and Norway.

The NATO pipeline system was another remarkable achievement of the infrastructure program that could also be called one of the most significant accomplishments of NATO, and for purely logistic considerations it undoubtedly was most important of all.[17]

Other Projects

The most important category of infrastructure projects from the standpoint of total expenditures was the construction of airfields. Signal communications were second in total outlay, the pipeline systems third, and missile sites fourth. Next and approximately equal to the missile sites came naval facilities. Here the Atlantic Command as well as the European Command entered the picture, though still a major share came under the purview of SHAPE.

One example of a naval facilities project was the Norwegian naval base at Haakonsvern, near Bergen. In this case the Norwegian government already had decided to shift its navy's principal base from the Oslo Fjord to Haakonsvern when NATO authorities proposed to expand the project in order to accommodate vesssels of the Allied navies whenever emergency might require it. The original Norwegian plan, estimated to cost about $15 million, was expanded to a $28-million project to include the NATO requirements. Now the NATO infrastructure budget would cover seventy-five percent of the cost, while Norway, for facilities for the use of its own forces, would bear the remaining twenty-five percent. Here the infrastructure program provided docks, slipways, quays, sheds, and underground storage and repair facilities. Millions of tons of rock were blasted out of a mountainside to prepare the way for the dock and the underground facilities. In protected shelters deep in the rock was a dry dock and maintenance and repair shops for torpedos, guns, electronic equipment, engines, and navigational equipment. Long stretches of underground storage space were reserved for Allied naval forces. Similarly, the infrastructure budget financed the construction of base facilities, again carved deep into rock, near the fishing town of Trom, while again the Norwegian government picked up the bill for the chiefly administrative facilities built in the open.[18] Other types of naval facilities included piers, breakwaters, storage for fuel oil, and storage for naval ammunition at various sites among the NATO nations.

Remaining categories of infrastructure projects include the construction of war headquarters for the military commands, training installations such as the missile firing range in Crete and SACLANT's antisubmarine warfare training center in Italy, and navigation aids, sometimes considered in the same category as the early warning and air defense systems.

Related Projects: Headquarters Installations

It must be remembered that NATO's infrastructure per se related only to the fixed installations needed for the wartime operations of the Allied military forces, though of course the pipeline and the NADGE were in operation in peacetime as well. But the headquarters and related facilities needed for NATO's civil staff and activities came under a separate budget, and the military headquarters facilities, which were essentially for the peacetime use of the military commands, came under yet another military budget. For these, formulae for cost-sharing had to be agreed upon for each case. The award and supervision of contracts came under the aegis of different agencies and different elements of the International Staff, though they did make use of the infrastructure experience and at times borrowed members of the infrastructure staff to assist in various aspects of the work.

The outstanding examples of construction projects of these kinds were in the major military and political headquarters of the organization. These came prominently into focus in 1966–67 with the construction and preparation of new headquarters for the removal of NATO Headquarters and SHAPE from France to Belgium, and the removal of AFCENT to the Netherlands.

During the first several months of its existence, SHAPE occupied quarters in the Hotel Astoria in Paris, until in July 1951 it was able to move into hastily erected prefabricated buildings at Rocquencourt just outside Paris. For that first construction there was a great deal of doubt about how it should be financed and supervised and about what the common costs should cover. It was reported, for instance, that the French government required compensation for the pheasants that had disappeared with the forest during construction. A little later "SHAPE Village" for family housing was added at Saint Germain, and "Camp Voluceau" was built across the road from the main headquarters for quartering soldiers assigned to SHAPE.[19]

Then, after nearly fifteen years in the Paris area, SHAPE received the word that it must move. In suggesting that 1 April 1967 would be an appropriate time to complete the move, the French government was allowing barely a year for the search for a new site, for the involved diplomatic negotiations, and then for the complex task of construction of a new headquarters. Many said that in no way could it be done in that time. Others said that it could be done only in a haphazard way, and it seemed a great pity that there was not the time for proper planning so that all the experience of the previous fifteen years might be used in designing a really ideal headquarters. General Lemnitzer said that it would be done—in the allotted time and properly.

It was not until its ministerial session in Brussels on 7 and 8 June that the North Atlantic Council agreed to ask the Benelux countries to provide the new site for SHAPE. The Belgian government immediately consulted with the Netherlands and Luxembourg governments and laid the problem before its parliament. Anticipating that Belgium should make the offer, the government already on the 9th had set up an "Interministerial Committee for the Installation of SHAPE" (CISMISH), and with the conclusion of parliamentary discussion on 22 June, the committee began its work. Four weeks later, the Belgian government proposed a choice of two sites, at Chièvres or at Casteau. After several weeks SACEUR indicated that the Casteau site was the more desirable of the two. Between 30 August and 9 September a NATO committee of experts drafted a report on the relocation and SHAPE prepared a report showing its requirements and a program for the construction. The North Atlantic Council, meeting as the "Group of Fourteen," (i.e., without France) gave its approval on 14 September. Quickly the Interministerial Committee for the Relocation of SHAPE (CIRSH), as it was now called, the technical services of the Belgian government, the SHAPE Relocation Team, an engineer colonel of the U.S. Army as project officer, and a group of American, Belgian, British, and Danish experts organized as the "consortium of SHAPE Engineers and Architects" went to work on the planning and execution. They drew up technical specifications for the first phase in just over a week (15–23 September), and by the 27th Belgian authorities began negotiations with construction contractors. Invitations for bids went out to 47 firms. First offers were approved in only three days, and work began on 10 October.

The "Casteau Camp," a 500-acre tract three miles from Mons, already was state property, so there was no problem of land acquisition. It had been a military installation, and a number of barracks and sheds could be converted to the use of SHAPE. A small airfield, used in recent years by a flying club, also was on the tract. But most of the ground was rolling and covered with forest and would require a great deal of clearing and leveling in order to put in streets, sewers, and utilities. The first phase included the headquarters building itself, together with the communications, kitchens, and service areas needed to make it operational.

By 19 October the first prefabricated components were being put into place. In five weeks workmen completed the erection of all prefabricated framework, beams, and partitions for the 405 × 66' building. On 15 December, forty-three days after work on it began, this first major building was completed. The others followed closely according to the tight schedule that had been drawn up.

The first construction phase included 270,000 square feet of headquarters offices, 54,000 square feet for the operations center, and 67,000 square feet for a general support building. Also constructed at this time was a communications building with towers and telephone, telegraph, and radio facilities; a superior command building, men's barracks and women's quarters; an administrative building, kitchens; bachelor officers quarters; maintenance and service areas; and a reserved area. This phase represented an outlay of $14 million.

The second phase, completed in October 1967, comprised another 220,000 square feet of construction costing $7 million. It included clubs for officers, noncommissioned officers, and other ranks, a cinema, chapels, nursery, primary, and secondary schools, and a gymnasium and indoor swimming pool. The third phase, costing $4 million, was completed in December 1967 and included a hospital, supermarket, shopping center, youth building, bowling alley, and athletic field. To all this was added the new SHAPE Village of 600 family housing units on the site. These were financed privately under a Belgian government scheme of guaranteed rentals. Under similar arrangements another 1,100 such units were built on various sites in the surrounding communities of Mons, Obourg, Soignies and Braine-le-Comte.

The huge SHAPE relocation project soon was being referred to as "the miracle of Casteau," since it was remarkable for both the speed and quality of the construction. Officials of NATO, SHAPE, and the Belgian government worked ceaselessly to make quick decisions, overcome difficulties on the spot, and get on with the work. The weekly progress reports prepared by the Consortium of SHAPE Architects and Engineers showed a consistency in adhering to detailed schedules that was little short of amazing.[20]

The move of AFCENT Headquarters from Fontainebleau to Brunssum, Holland, did not involve a major construction program, though it did have problems of its own. As in Belgium, protracted negotiations were necessary to settle upon a site and to agree upon the terms under which that NATO headquarters would move into Holland. The closing of a coal mine—the Hendrik National Colliery—in December 1966 provided an opportunity. Plans made in anticipation of the availability of the buildings at the coal mine quickly were put in effect so that here, as at SHAPE, the headquarters could become operational in its new location by 1 April 1967. The buildings were not altogether suitable for military purposes, but they could be adapted. The most serious immediate difficulty was the installation of communications equipment. Then the biggest problem was to provide some 1,500 housing units in or near a town of only 26,000 inhabitants. As a military post, the coal mine lacked some of the attractions of a SHAPE built almost from scratch, but it had the advantage of early availability at low cost, and it appeared to be adequate for the needs.[21]

A project of similar magnitude to that of SHAPE, though of a different nature, was the move of NATO's political headquarters to Brussels, and while work progressed rapidly on the SHAPE complex, so too was it proceeding on the NATO headquarters. At its ministerial meeting in December 1966, the North Atlantic Council agreed to move the political headquarters to Belgium. Determined to leave Paris before the end of 1967 but recognizing that this would not give the time needed for the building of a new headquarters building as desired, the Council accepted the added expense of construction and moving and decided to go first into temporary buildings, and then to build a permanent headquarters building at a second site. It chose the Brussels suburb of Evere, near the Brussels airport, for the temporary headquarters and Lacken Park, the grounds of the 1958 Brussels World's Fair (on the site of the French pavilion!) in the Heysel quarter, for the permanent building. After an international call for bids for the construction of the temporary headquarters, the Belgian government chose two consortia with the council's approval. Work began on 20 March 1967 to erect fifteen prefabricated buildings. The project was scheduled to be completed within six months at a cost of about $7 million so that the NATO staff and national delegations could carry out their phased move during the month of October.[22] The temporary buildings worked out so well that the council then decided to remain at that site for the permanent structure. Though some doubted it ever would come to pass, the new permanent building was ready in 1970–71. It allowed bringing together agencies previously located in Washington and London with those from Paris. The estimated cost was put at $20 million.

Summary of Achievements

The Infrastructure Program by the end of 1968 had constructed 220 airfields; fuel pipeline systems comprising 8,500 kilometers of pipelines, 25 tanker terminal points on the Atlantic and the Mediterranean, 250 bomb-proof pumping stations, and 160 underground depots with capacity for storing 2 million cubic meters of fuel; a communications network of 44,000 kilometers of landlines, submarine cables and radio relays, as well as the extensive Early Warning radar system and Air Defense Ground Environment, special ammunition sites, missile sites, naval facilities and other projects. The total expenditures for these facilities up to that time was $3.125 billion. Slices approved for the next three-year period would run the total outlay up to $3.446 billion. Airfields were still the greatest expense, while communications facilities were second and the pipeline system third. By far the greatest share of expenditures (well over $750 million) had gone into France, with Germany second, Turkey a close third, and Italy and Norway fourth and fifth respectively. Lowest as recipient countries were Iceland, which did not share in the program, and the United States, which contributed thirty to forty percent of the funds.[23]

By any terms the accomplishments of the Infrastructure Program was impressive. The experience of the participating nations in developing a workable cost-sharing formula, in overcoming balance-of-payment problems, in collective supervision of major construction projects, and in combined or coordinated contracting provided a fundamental guide to future international collaboration in logistics.

The Problem of Liquidation

Now that all these facilities were being built with international financing under the infrastructure program, what was to become of them in the long run? This problem was long recognized but never settled. No general policy covered either the liquidation of facilities when they were no longer needed or their renewal if they were needed for a longer period than was originally intended. Each situation had to be dealt with as it arose.

Even the question of ownership of facilities really was never settled. The Netherlands, for instance, never could agree to having installations on Dutch soil technically "owned" by NATO.

Ordinarily when a facility was built, its usefulness was assumed to be, say, fifteen years. Part of the original agreement stated that the host nation was responsible for maintenance during this period. But left open was the question of restoration for a period beyond the original fifteen years when ordinary maintenance no longer would keep it usable. Then it became necessary to add this to a further infrastructure program.

Still more difficult was the problem of liquidation. If the facility had served for the period originally planned and could no longer be kept in operation without major restoration, then it might be simple enough to let the facility go to the host nation for whatever disposition it wished to make of it. Then the host nation would be entitled to whatever residual value might remain, for presumably its worth was taken into account in the calculation of the formula for sharing in the original financing. But this did not cover two other aspects of the situation. The first was the case where the facility was to be given up while several years remained of its usefulness. Then how could fair residual value be calculated, and how could the host country be persuaded to make a fair payment? The second problem was the other side of the coin. What if the host nation insisted upon restoration of the site or the payment of damages? It might well be the case that the host government saw no need for its own airfield at a particular place. Therefore, when abandoned by NATO, the hangars, runways, and other facilities, while still usable for their intended purpose, had no value for the host government. On the contrary, the government desired above all to return the site to agricultural production, but this could not be done before an expensive removal of concrete runways and buildings. Now what would be a fair settlement in this situation? So far most serious problems of this nature had been avoided, but NATO's international staff lived in constant dread of having them come up.

The French initiative that resulted in the removal of NATO military and political installations from France gave rise to what might have been most serious problems of this nature. But to the surprise of many of those involved in the negotiations, settlements with the French went very smoothly. In each instance teams of negotiators met to work out a settlement. They agreed upon a fair price for the French to pay to cover the additional residual value of facilities that had continuing utility, and the French made payment on the spot.[24]

In September 1966 France's permanent representative to the North Atlantic Council announced to the council that from January 1967, France no longer would participate as a full partner in the infrastructure and other programs. This meant that the French share, twelve percent of the total, would have to be divided proportionately among the remaining participants. Still the French indicated that they would like to continue to participate in certain specific projects such as Early Warning and AGARD. This raised the sensitive question as to whether one member of the Alliance should be able to pick and choose specific projects while the others shared in support of the program as a whole. It appeared that this would be permitted for the time being, not only on account of the importance of French cooperation for these to be effective for the Alliance as a whole, but also in the hope that one day French cooperation might return to a more general and normal pattern. For infrastructure, as for other aspects of logistics, the French move posed an acid test for effectiveness, significance, and survival of the enterprise.

NATO Logistics Programs

Notes

1. *NATO: Facts About the North Atlantic Treaty Organization* (Paris, 1965), 135–36; Lord Ismay, *NATO's First Five Years* (Paris, 1955), 114–24; Maj. Gen. T. W. Parker, "NATO Military Development, 1949–1959," *NATO Letter*, April 1959, 7; (U.S.) *Dept. of Defense Operations under MDAP*, December 1952, xi–xii, and May 1953, xii–xvii; Second Annual Report, SACEUR, 30 May 53, p. 17; *NATO Infrastructure*, Fact Sheet, Dept. of Defense Office of Public Information, No. 243–52, 29 December 1952.

2. See Johnson Garrett, "An Alliance Goes into the Construction Business," *NATO Letter*, February 1965, 2–10; F. W. Mulley, *The Politics of Western Defense* (New York, 1962), 188–92; Otto Pick, "The 'O' in NATO," *NATO Letter*, December 1965, 17; H. George Franks, "The Great Achievement of Infrastructure," *NATO's Fifteen Nations* 4 (April 1959): 130–42; *NATO's Fifteen Nations* 5 (1960): 24–33; Ernest H. Meili, "Defense Production and Infrastructure," *NATO Letter*, April 1959, 25–28; Col. Stanley W. Dziuban, "NATO Infrastructure: Marvel of Military Construction Achievement, Part 1," *NATO Journal* (April 1962): 18–22, and Part 2 (May–June 1962): 26–32; Wing Comdr. P. G. M. Ridsdale, "Military Infrastructure—The Backbone of NATO," *NATO's Fifteen Nations* 7 (August–September 1962): 38–47; Parker, "NATO Military Development," 5–9; *NATO Facts*, 136–43; *Aspects of NATO: Defense Production and Infrastructure* (Paris, 1963), 11–19; Ernest H. Meili, "Nations United for Peace—NATO Infrastructure," *Signal*, December 1959, 12–13.

3. Dziuban, "NATO Infrastructure," 26–28; Ridsdale, "Military Infrastructure," 43–47; Meili, "Defense Production and Infrastructure," 27–28.

4. NATO Press Release no. 16, 8 November 1957.

5. NATO Press Release no. 10, 12 June 1956.

6. Anne Sington, "A NATO Airfield in Greece," *NATO Letter*, March 1965, 16–19.

7. Cf. Lord Ismay, "The Story of an Airfield" in his *NATO's First Five Years*, 120–22.

8. Frank S. Besson, Jr., "Logistics and Transportation in the Defense of Western Europe," *National Defense Transportation Journal* 12 (March–April 1956): 64–65; M. Carpenter, "Current Comment," *General Military Review* (July 1963): 287.

9. Anne Sington, "NATO Missile Sites in Germany," *NATO Letter*, June 1965, 14–20.

10. Quoted in Anne Sington, "NATO's Air Defense—A Child's Guide to NADGE," *NATO Letter*, April 1967, 10.

11. *Daily Telegraph* (London), 6 May 1963. Cf. *Le Figaro*, 2 May 1963; C. L. Sulzberger, "Let Us Not Try to Cadge on NADGE," *New York Times*, Int. ed., 10 April 1963; "Pentagon hits NATO Air Plan Europe," *New York Herald-Tribune*, Paris ed., 17 April 1963.

12. Sington, "NATO's Air Defense," 8–16; NATO Press Release no. (66)7, 20 June 1966; NATO Press Release no. (66)16, 28 December 1966; Robert Rhodes James, *Standardization and Common Production of Weapons in NATO*, Institute for Strategic Studies, Defense, Technology and the Western Alliance no. 3 (London, 1967), 21.

13. See R. B. Dyott, "Radio Communication by Tropospheric Scatter," *The New Scientist*, 16 July 1959, 72–73.

14. Frank Willoughby, "Communications and Electronics in Allied Command Europe," *NATO's Fifteen Nations* (January 1961): 41–46, and (March 1961): 53–56; Dziuban, "NATO Infrastructure," 22; Anne Sington, "French Link in a NATO Communications System," *NATO Letter*, April 1965, 10–17; idem, "NATO Defensive Installations in Norway," *NATO Letter*, January 1966, 2–9; idem, "NATO Communications Net Completed," *Military Review* (February 1964), also in *Le Figaro*, 18 November 1963.

15. Anne Sington, "NATO 'SATCOM,'" *NATO Letter*, March 1968, 14–21.

16. For operation of the system, see chap. 11.

17. Besson, "Logistics and Transportation in the Defense of Western Europe," 65; Dziuban, "NATO Infrastructure," 28; *Aspects of NATO: Pipelines for NATO* (Paris, 1960), 1–3, 8–9, and (1965) 1–4 and 11–12; "Pipelines for NATO," *The Review* 45 (September–October 1965): 41, 106, 109; Anne Sington, "NATO Pipelines in Turkey," *NATO Letter*, July–August 1965, 18–22; James H. Winchester, "NATO's Fuel Pipeline Almost Complete; Invaluable Logistic Support System," *NATO's Fifteen Nations* (August–September 1962): 83–86.

18. Sington, "NATO Defensive Installations in Norway."

19. Jean de Madre, "SHAPE's Fifteen Years at Rocquencourt," *NATO Letter*, April 1967, 17–23.

20. Fremont Felix and S. B. Newan, "The New Shape of SHAPE," *The Military Engineer* (July–August 1967): 258–60; "The Transfer of SHAPE to Belgium," *NATO Letter*, December

1966, 12–13; "Building a New SHAPE at Casteau," *NATO Letter,* January 1967, 14–17; "Shaping SHAPE," *The Bulletin, the Belgian Weekly in English,* 16 December 1966, 17–19; brief prepared by SHAPE Office of Public Information, Consortium of SHAPE Architects and Engineers, Group Alpha, SOBEMAP, ELECTROBEL, Gibbs & Hill Inc., "Scheduling Progress Report No. 34," 14 July 1967.

21. "AFCENT Leaves France for The Netherlands": Richard Sunder, "Goodbye to Fontainebleau," and Els van Rossum, "Welcome to Brunssum," *NATO Letter,* March 1967, 12–19.

22. NATO Press Release M3(66)3, 16 December 1966, 5; NATO Press Communiqué, 13 March 67. See Anne Sington, "NATO Settles Down To Work in Brussels," *NATO Letter,* December 1967, 14–23. Inauguration ceremonies for the new temporary buildings were held on 16 October 1967.

23. *NATO Facts,* 143; Garrett, "An Alliance Goes into the Construction Business," 10; Winchester, "NATO's Fuel Pipeline," 83; Dziuban, "NATO Infrastructure," 18–20; Meili, "Defense Production and Infrastructure," 27; Ridsdale, "Military Infrastructure," 39; "NATO Infrastructure," U.S. Information Service Press Feature, London, 4 April 1956.

24. Although the original cost of the NATO political headquarters building in Paris had been about $10 million, NATO officials asked France for $20 million on the ground that market prices had doubled in the seven years (and this would be the estimated cost of the new permanent structure in Brussels); finally the French agreed to $17.5 million, and this was accepted as a generous settlement. The French agreed to pay about $51.5 million for surplus material left by U.S. forces; this amounted to about 25 cents on the dollar of original cost, which also seemed generous enough (*Atlantic Community News,* March 1968, 4.).

Airfield construction in Holland under the NATO Common Infrastructure Program. *(NATO photo.)*

NATO air force installation in Norway. *(NATO photo.)*

A NATO airfield in Norway. *(NATO photo.)*

NADGE radar site under construction in Norway. *(NATO photo.)*

Civilian and military construction engineers from five countries inspecting a NADGE installation under construction in Greece. *(NATO photo.)*

NADGE Height Finder radar antenna in eastern Turkey. *(NATO photo.)*

NADGE site in Turkey. *(NATO photo.)*

Forward Scatter (ACE High) antennas in Norway. *(SHAPE photo.)*

SATCOM ground terminal that serves both the NATO Headquarters in Brussels and SHAPE, near Mons (Casteau), Belgium. *(NATO photo.)*

Inside a SATCOM terminal control and switching center. *(NATO photo.)*

NATO pipeline under construction. *(NATO photo.)*

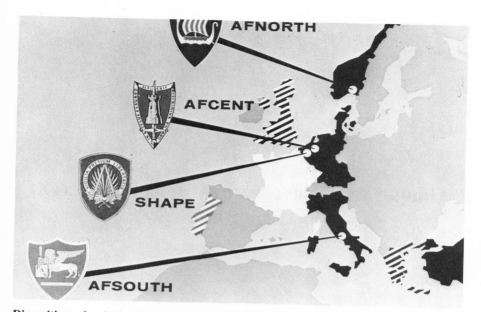

Disposition of principal headquarters of Allied Command Europe and subordinate commands after move of NATO installations out of France. *(NATO photo.)*

Disposition of installations of the NATO Air Defense Ground Environment (NADGE). *(NATO photo.)*

9
Cooperative Development and Production Programs

In modern times perhaps the most significant gauge of military strength is the nature and magnitude of the industrial production supporting it. In these terms, Europe, once the seat of greatest military power, remained weak during the latter 1940s from the destruction of World War II. During this time the balance of military and industrial power had shifted from Central and Western Europe to the Soviet Union. While countries in the former region gave priority to meeting the demands for civilian goods in industrial recovery, the Russians retained a high degree of military mobilization and continued to devote a relatively large segment of industrial production to meeting military requirements. As already noted, a Europe without economic aid and military arms and equipment from the United States appeared at that time to lay at the mercy of the Russians.

In those circumstances military strength and economic efficiency would have been served best by rebuilding according to a coordinated plan among all the countries concerned, and indeed this was the course being urged by a number of leaders. Actually, European economic integration and unity were stated objectives of the Marshall Plan. Similarly the Mutual Defense Assistance Program called for a correlation of requirements of the members of the newly formed North Atlantic Treaty Organization.

Very soon after it began to function, the North Atlantic Council in November 1949 set up the Military Production and Supply Board. This board almost immediately initiated studies on means of increasing defense production. With specific tasks of increasing production and promoting the joint use of the industrial installations of member countries, the Defense Production Board, established in December 1950 in order to continue and expand the functions of the Military Production and Supply Board that it replaced, drew up several proposals that it referred to the Financial and Economic Board. Noting the financial implications of the proposals, the latter board concluded that these could be considered only in relation to all the other requirements for building up NATO military forces. This triggered the setting up of the Temporary Council Committee in September 1951 with the major task of reconciling military requirements, including arms and equipment, with available means. This resulted in the annual review of defense plans, budgets, and plans for production or purchase of arms and equipment.

With the far-reaching overhaul of the NATO structure after the Lisbon meeting of 1952, the Defense Production Board was dissolved, but the Production and Logistics Division, renamed Production, Logistics, and Infrastructure Division, in 1960 took over the studies being prepared by the Defense Production Board on material requirements and industrial capacity to meet them. It developed plans for correlated production programs for such items as aircraft, artillery, small arms, radar and radios, motor vehicles, ships, and ammunition of various types. The staff continued to prepare studies on such proposals for the Defense Production Committee organized by the council in the spring of 1954. (This committee was renamed the Armanents Committee in 1958, with broadened responsibilities for cooperative production.)[1]

Already in 1949 Belgium and the Netherlands had entered into a cooperative program for the joint production of aircraft and engines under British license. This served as precedent for later combined production programs for aircraft by NATO partners, though multinational production did not really begin until 1954.

A decisive influence in this direction came from policies of the United States with respect to its foreign military assistance. With the exhaustion of World War II surplus stocks in the support of operations in Korea, the United States turned to an emphasis on off-shore procurement and defense production assistance for military aid to Europe. In contracting for the production of U.S.-type equipment in Europe for use in U.S. military aid programs, the United States was not only building up current equipment for reconstructed European forces, but was helping to build up the military production base in those countries. Now the United States entered into a number of agreements for cooperative production of equipment in which the United States provided the designs, bore the development costs and a share of the production costs, and provided guidance in getting the programs started.

The U.S. Congress, in approving the Foreign Assistance Acts, expressed its intention to support combined production. Sponsors of the weapons production program saw in it a means for promoting standardization, for reducing costs for other countries in getting advanced weapons by eliminating duplicate research and development costs and by taking advantage of lower costs of production; for reducing costs to the United States of providing grant aid while at the same time contributing to local economic growth; for improving the general military strength of NATO; for gaining the advantages for industrial mobilization by broadening the production base; and, as an outgrowth of the close collaboration required, for contributing to the economic, military, and political unity of the North Atlantic Community. The

Mutual Security Act of 1954 as amended in 1959, continued to carry this statement of policy:

> The Congress believes it essential that this Act should be so administered as to support concrete measures to promote greater political federation, military integration, and economic unification in Europe, including coordinated production and procurement programs participated in by the members of the North Atlantic Treaty Organization to the greatest extent possible with respect to military equipment and materials to be utilized for the defense of the North Atlantic areas.[2]

Later the United States participation took the form of coordinated production without the use of American appropriated funds, and then, as American officials became concerned with a growing balance-of-payments deficit, emphasis shifted to a quest for substantial purchases of military equipment in the United States, especially on the part of Germany, in order to offset to a degree the costs of maintaining forces there. To the extent that this effort succeeded in inducing European governments to substitute purchases in the United States for local production, it of course reduced the potential production in Europe, whether cooperative or otherwise, by that much. At the same time, by encouraging the use of American types of equipment, this extended the standardization of military equipment among the countries concerned, and to the extent that local facilities were used for the production of repair parts and replacements, it encouraged the growth of cooperative production efforts.[3]

Without the initial stimulus of American offshore procurement orders, efforts at cooperative production probably would have not gone very far. Nevertheless, after the orders had been largely removed, those efforts continued. But in all cases the obstacles to such cooperation remained formidable. Predictably national authorities continued to favor home industries at the expense of parceling out resources to finance multinational projects. Differing economic policies and stages of economic growth and industrial efficiency made it difficult for several countries to cooperate effectively. There was mutual suspicion when it came to sharing industrial methods and military secrets. Furthermore, there was resistance to any large-scale program of military production, whether cooperative or not, on the grounds that it might interfere with needs for the domestic economy and threaten to smother incentive and private competition in some countries.[4]

Aircraft Production

G-91 Lightweight Reconnaissance Aircraft

About 1954 SHAPE began seeking a "simple, inexpensive, robust," very light jet aircraft for close support of ground troops, reconnaissance, and certain interdiction and counter air missions. At the time there were no established procedures within NATO for developing such a project, but SHAPE took the initiative in pushing ahead.

The staff of Allied Air Forces Central Europe at Fontainebleau developed a statement of characteristics and specifications required for the proposed aircraft. This formed the basis upon which the aircraft industries of NATO countries were invited to submit design proposals. Ten designs, from France, Germany, and Great Britain, were submitted. A committee appointed by the chairman of NATO's Advisory Group for aeronautical Research and Development (AGARD) evaluated the proposals. It chose three—the Bréguet 1001, the Dassault Etenard VI, and the Fiat G91—to prepare prototypes for testing. After flight test trials held in the autumn of 1957, the Italian Fiat G-91, powered with a British Bristol Orpheus engine, was selected for production.

Although the French models could claim a certain technical superiority, the Italian plane—essentially a scaled-down version of the U.S. Sabrejet—had advantages of simplicity of production and an ongoing production line. The French were told that their projects were too sophisticated for immediate requirements but they could expect favorable consideration when it came to choosing a second-generation aircraft to replace the G-91. (Yet, when that time came the French were informed that their models were not sophisticated enough!) As so often seems to be the case in international competition, disappointment led to disengagement. The French, expected to be a major customer for the new aircraft, refused to buy any. Only the agreement of the U.S. to purchase fifty G-91's for its Allies and acceptance by Italy and Germany saved the project.

Production began in Italy, and a little later, under license, in Germany. A French undercarriage and Dutch electronic equipment were used with the Italian airframe and the British engine. In the summer of 1958 an experimental international squadron equipped with these planes carried out tactical tests in Italy. In later trials in the Central European area, the squadron trained with Allied Land Forces Central Europe.[5]

The Bréguet Atlantique

During NATO's 1956 annual review, the question arose about the need for finding a successor to the maritime reconnaissance and antisubmarine aircraft that the United States had supplied to several European countries as a part of its military assistance program. The approaching need for a modern maritime patrol aircraft came to the attention of the North Atlantic Council at its ministerial meeting in December of that year.

After further discussion of the problem, the Defence Production Committee early in 1957 invited interested governments to name a Group of Experts to study how an aircraft of the type desired could be developed and produced on a multilateral basis. After consideration of several designs, the Experts recommended acceptance of the Bréguet 1150 submitted by the Société Anonyme des Ateliers d'Aviation Louis Bréguet of France. After further consultation, four countries—Belgium, France, Germany, and the Netherlands—with the support of the United States under its mutual weapons development program, agreed to finance jointly the research and development phase of the project, including the production of prototypes. Bréguet built a new assembly shop at Toulouse-Colomiers, and there representatives from the other participating companies joined in the building of two prototypes. After flight testing, the production design of the aircraft was adopted in February 1962, and production-sharing procedures were completed the following month. British Rolls Royce engines went into the first planes, but then another consortium made up of Rolls Royce, Hispana Suiza of France, MAN turbo of Germany, and Fabrique Nationale of Belgium manufactured Tyne turboprop engines for the production model. The propellers, by de Havilland of the United Kingdom, were made in France under license; the center section of the fuselage was built by Fokker of the Netherlands; the rear section and tires by Dornier of Germany; the undercarriage by Hispana Suiza, and the wings by Sud Aviation. Could such a conglomeration possibly get off the ground?

Perhaps surprisingly it did, and although by no means an advanced aircraft, it did fly well and met the stated requirements. Perhaps even more remarkably, the complicated supervisory organization worked well enough too. The NATO Maritime Patrol Aircraft Steering Committee, set up to manage the project, operated under a rotating chairmanship and under a rule of unanimity for decisions. Technical supervision was entrusted to the French agency, Direction Technique et Industrielle de l'Aeronautique Française.

Remarkably, the whole program kept within the financial ceiling and consistently remained ahead of schedule. In spite of a delay when the second prototype crashed and it had to be determined that the accident was not the result of a weakness in design or manufacture, the production prototype flew three weeks ahead of schedule, in September 1964. The Steering Committee accepted the aircraft in December 1964 after the first prototype had completed 867 hours in the air.

But again the big disappointment was in the form of orders. At the outset provisional requirements had been set at 126 to 144 aircraft for six nations. But national requirements were withdrawn or cut down until only France and Germany were left, with combined orders for forty. Clearly a project of this kind needed firmer commitments than the expression of some vague hope. Surely at the outset, participating countries should be called upon to accept commitments for certain minimum orders sufficient to make the effort worthwhile.[6]

For the production of two simulators to be used for training pilots for the *Atlantique* aircraft, the French Government, acting as agent for the NATO Steering Committee, awarded a contract in September 1963 to General Precision, Inc., of the United States. The simulators would be built by General Precision's Link Division, with the Electronics Division of the American Car and Foundry Company given responsibility for supplying the tactical portion of the trainer. Again European companies would participate, but in this case as subcontractors. These would include the Société d'Electronique et d'Automatisme of France; Precitronic of Germany, and Audium N.V. and Handelscompagnie N.V. of the Netherlands.[7]

The F-104 Starfighter

After a year's study of the technical problems, production plans, and other aspects, the defense ministers of Belgium, Germany, Italy, the Netherlands, and the United States in December 1960 signed an agreement for production in Europe of the American fighter aircraft, the Lockheed F-104G Starfighter. The nations formed a production organization for general supervision and a consortium coordinated production that began in the four participating European countries within the next few months. The United States contributed certain basic parts to Belgium, the Netherlands, and Italy to enable those countries to supplement their numbers of the aircraft. Canada, which was producing a similar version of the Starfighter, contributed to the development work. Plans called for a four-year program to produce a total of approximately 1,200 planes. A high-performance jet aircraft capable of a speed of 1,500 miles an hour and useful as a fighter bomber and a reconnaissance plane as well as an interceptor, the Starfighter was expected to become the backbone of several of the NATO air forces in Europe.

In June 1961 the North Atlantic Council approved the project as a NATO program, and the production organization became a NATO subsidiary body.[8]

Soon more than one hundred firms employing several thousand workers were engaged in the program. For the J79-11A jet engine designed by General Electric Belgian workers in Liège were assembling turbines, an Italian auto company in Turin was making compressors, and a German factory in Munich was producing gear-box assemblies. Each nation sent parts to the other countries and each assembled and tested complete engines.[9]

Unfortunately, almost as soon as the Starfighter squadrons became operational in the German Air Force, a series of accidents plagued the aircraft in Germany. Although other European countries in the cooperative production program appeared to be having no such trouble, nor were other countries among the total of fourteen using similar models,[10] by the end of November 1966, sixty-five of the Luftwaffe's 700 Starfighters had crashed, killing thirty-seven pilots. This situation had led to controversy within the German defense ministry, and, in September 1966, to a "revolt of the generals" when several high officers, including the inspector general (chief) of the Luftwaffe resigned. A week after a crash on 28 November, the new inspector general, Lt. Gen. Johannes Steinhoff, ordered the entire fleet of Germany's F-104Gs grounded indefinitely until the difficulty had been found and corrected.

It was not at all clear whether the problem was in maintenance, in pilot training, or in some defect in design or construction. No common cause was apparent; however, the F-104G carrried some 320 pounds of extra electronic equipment and sometimes was described as the most complicated one-place aircraft in operation. A team of experts from the Lockheed Company (United States), designers of the aircraft, went to Germany to assist in the setting up of an improved system of maintenance. But for the time being no German F-104G was allowed into the air unless there was an outbreak of war. During this period Germany's most powerful weapon system remained immobilized.[11]

While doubts nagged the German determination to continue with the F-104G as well as the search for possible alternatives for a follow-on aircraft, the Italians, in cooperation with the United States, were proceeding with the production of a more advanced version, the F-104S "Super Starfighter."

The new program was the result of an agreement between the United States and Italy for the production of 165 of these new aircraft for the Italian Air Force. In general, the development work was done in the United States, while production was accomplished in Italy. Of the total cost, estimated initially at $400 million, about one-third was spent in the United States and two-thirds in Italy.

As in the earlier version, the F-104S was powered by General Electric jet engines of a new, more powerful design, the J79-J1Q. General Electric's plant in Evendale, Ohio, built about five of these engines, and again, production shifted to Italy. International General Electric signed an agreement with the Italian Air Force for the production, under license, of about 250 of these engines by Fiat, Alfa Romeo, Saca, and Piaggio.

With the advanced engines, the F-104S required a twenty-six percent shorter takeoff distance, had a thirty-seven percent improvement in transonic acceleration, had a four percent higher combat ceiling, had a capacity for rate of climb that was twice as great as the earlier aircraft and was able to reduce interception time by forty-six percent in comparison with the older F-104G.

Similar arrangements to those for the airframe and the engines governed the other components going into the 104S weapon system. The Autonetics Division of North American Aviation received a $2.9 million contract to develop the radar for the new aircraft. With the completion of development and flight testing in the United States in 1967, Fabbrica Italiana Apparecchi Radio in Milan, as licensee, began production. Litton-Italia, Italian subsidiary of Litton Industries of the United States, shifted from the production of inertial navigation systems for the F-104G to a new LN-3-13 system for the F-104S. Selenia, as the Italian subsidiary and licensee of Raytheon, received a contract for the production of Sparrow guided missiles to be carried by the F-104S.[12]

UH-ID Helicopter

With the F-104G production program nearing completion, German officials expressed interest in entering into a coproduction program for helicopters. This would add to the German forces a valuable aircraft of a different kind, would stimulate the development of additional technology in a field so far undeveloped in Germany, and, at the same time would keep alive the skills and industrial capacity already developed under earlier programs. For the United States there would be the same advantages as in other, earlier programs—further standardization of military equipment, expansion of cooperative logistics and maintenance agreements, and further assistance for the U.S. balance of payments.

The two governments entered into an agreement for the production in Germany, through intercompany licensing and support arrangements, of 406 helicopters, UH-ID, over a five-year period. The Bell Aircraft Corporation agreed to build three prototype versions of the UH-ID, modified respectively to meet the requirements of the German army and the U.S. Air Force and Navy.[13]

Other Cooperative Aircraft Production Ventures

Several other agreements had been concluded by various combinations of NATO countries (though not necessarily as NATO projects) for the cooperative production of various types of aircraft and for preliminary studies looking to future production. A consortium of British, French, German, and Belgian companies entered into the production of the Transall C-160 military transport.

In addition, the British and French cooperated on several other joint programs of special significance. The first was for an advanced trainer and lightweight, high-performance tactical support aircraft, the *Jaguar*. The SEPECAT company, recently formed by Avions Louis Bréguet and the British Aircraft Corporation, developed this aircraft. The second was for a variable geometry (swing-wing) fighter-bomber that was under development by Avions Marcel Dassault and the British Aircraft Corporation. Its sponsors hoped that this might be a significant step in reducing the dependence of European air forces on U.S. aircraft. The British hoped that by the mid-1970s this Anglo-French model would replace both the Canberra and the fifty U.S.-built F-111's (swing-wing) that the R.A.F. had purchased, and presumably would fill the place of retiring V-bombers.[14] These hopes were dashed, however, with an announcement in July 1967 that the French were abandoning the project on "purely financial grounds." The French had been reluctant negotiators for the past year and a half because of the high costs involved, but in January 1967 it was announced that agreement had been reached and the project would go forward. At that time the estimated cost was given at $600 million. It had been indicated that West Germany and perhaps other countries would be offered a chance to share in the project, either as coproducers or as purchasers. Then it was reported that in April Germany had declined, and from that point the French moved to drop it. When the decision to do so was announced in July, the estimated cost was given at $800 million. This left Great Britain in an awkward situation. Some suggested that the best course would be to rely upon additional purchases of

F-111's from the United States, but this would add to foreign exchange difficulties and would lend further credence to an impression of American dominance at a time when Britain was seeking entrance into the European Common Market. Others urged another attempt at cooperative production with the Netherlands, Germany, and Italy as partners. For their part, the French found some hope for a much less costly swing-wing aircraft in a prototype developed by Dassault, builder of the Mystère fighter. Presumably other Anglo-French aviation projects, including the Jaguar jet trainer, three types of helicopters, and an "airbus," as well as the commercial supersonic liner, Concorde, would continue.[15]

These were the kinds of programs likely to continue, in many directions, for a long time in the future. Some observers saw a need for a vastly increased emphasis on integration if the aircraft industry of Europe were to survive in a significant way at all. The cost of research and development had become so great that European countries, acting singly, could no longer hope to compete with the United States. While looking to continued cooperation with American companies in the production of aircraft, a feeling persisted that this would be a much healthier arrangement if the European industry could first be integrated with a pooling of resources for research and development, in order to maintain a truly competitive position.[16] On the assumption that NATO would be strongest if it rested on a fully developed European as well as North American industrial base, this kind of development could also be in the long-range security interest of the United States.

Production of Missiles

The HAWK

The first instance of a program for cooperative weapons production with U.S. assistance was for the HAWK ground-to-air (antiaircraft) missile. This program was the first concrete result of the policy approved by the North Atlantic Council in the chiefs-of-government meeting of December 1957 when the United States offered to provide such assistance.

After preliminary studies were made by representatives of interested nations on various questions relating to cooperative weapons production, NATO's assistant secretary-general for production, logistics and infrastructure in July 1958 submitted to the council a report recommending production in Europe of the HAWK. It took another year for the details of organization and procedure to be worked out. Each government nominated a leading electronics firm to participate in the studies, and in each case the designated company became the "national prime contractor" in the new organization.

The missile, said to be especially effective against very low-flying aircraft but also effective at altitudes as high as 18,000 meters, had been developed by the Raytheon Company in the United States. This company and its prin-

NATO HAWK PRODUCTION ORGANIZATION

Adapted from Annex III to AC 74-WP/19, NATO HAWK Production Organization.

cipal subcontractors, Northrop Aircraft and General Aerojet Corporation, would work directly with the European companies. The initial program was estimated to cost about $600 million. Of this the United States agreed to provide $140 million—$47 million as grant aid and $93 million as reimbursable—as purchases for battalions of equipment that would be transferred to Allies receiving U.S. grant aid, mainly Greece, Turkey, and Denmark.

To coordinate the effort the five European companies formed a new international company, Société Européenne de Teleguidage (SETEL), under French law. For overall supervision and coordination, the five governments set up the NATO HAWK Production Organization. With an administrative budget of its own, the HAWK Production Organization operated independently of the NATO International Staff or other NATO subsidiary agency. The general manager prepared the budget and submitted it through the Budget Committee to the Board of Directors for approval. After approval it was binding upon him. However, the general manager had no operational budget since operational costs were handled through SETEL as European prime contractor.[17]

In the preliminary planning it had been expected that the NATO Mainte-nance and Supply Organization (NAMSO)[18] would take over support of the HAWK, but as the time approached in 1963 when it would be necessary to establish a support system, NAMSO did not yet have the capacity to handle it. Although NAMSO would probably be able to take over by 1967 or 1968, in the meantime it was necessary to set up a separate system. France agreed to operate a common depot for the HAWK program at Chateaurault. In the production program itself, spare parts for two years were to be included. The intention was to distribute two months' worth of those parts to the using battalions and to store those for the other 22 months' at the common depot. In addition, each nation would maintain about three months' supply of parts in a national depot.

During the first two years the HAWK organization gave particular atten-tion to the establishment of industrial facilities and the procurement of ma-chinery, tooling, factory test equipment, and to industrial training. During this period parts and components were being obtained from the United States. By the time the support phase of the HAWK program was beginning in 1964, it was clear that parts were not going to be wholly interchangeable with those from the United States, for the United States had continued to introduce changes in its system since the standardization of the 1960 model for European production.

Air-to-Surface Missiles

The structure of the NATO Production Organization set up for the coor-dinated production of the U.S. air-to-surface missile, BULLPUP, was al-most identical to the HAWK organization. But there was an important difference in the industrial organization that, rather than the HAWK organi-zation, became the model for subsequent NATO production organizations. In this case, rather than organizing a new international company to act as prime contractor, the participating governments agreed to designate a well-established company in one of the countries to act as the prime contractor for the whole program. This assignment went to a Norwegian firm, Kongsberg Vapenfabrikk. This company then let subcontracts to companies in the participating countries according to the proportion of the total output each government had agreed to accept.

The production plan was developed in three stages. In the first stage the European assembly plants began putting together missiles from U.S. subas-semblies; in the second stage they used European-produced parts, together with some U.S.-made critical components, and in the third they depended wholly on European parts with the exception of a few special items that were not economical to manufacture. The United States provided technical assist-ance only in the beginning of production. The Martin Company provided experts in such fields as engineering, procurement, programming, and qual-ity control and gave management assistance to the prime contractor and subcontractors in electronics engineering, quality control, procurement, and manufacturing. Direct U.S. government assistance was provided through the Department of the Navy's Bureau of Weapons in the form of the delivery of long-lead time items, electronic components, and training in the United States of management personnel and government inspection representatives.[19]

About the same time that the cooperative production organization for BULLPUP was being set up, the North Atlantic Council also approved (June 1962) the creation of a steering committee for the production of the French air-to-surface missile, the AS-30. The United Kingdom and Germany shared with France in this program. But the BULLPUP was the one that retained the advantage in the approved cooperative production program.

SIDEWINDER

Another of the early cooperative projects was for the production of the U.S. air-to-air missile, the SIDEWINDER. Again with the benefit of U.S. technical assistance, six members entered into a coproduction arrangement late in 1958, and the North Atlantic Council approved the organization a year later. In this case a German firm, Fluggerätewerk Bodensee GMBH, served as prime contractor, with subcontractors in each of the participating countries—Denmark, the Netherlands, Norway, Greece, and Turkey, in addition to Germany, and later Belgium and Portugal as well. Deliveries under the program began in November 1961, and while problems inevitably arose, the whole arrangement worked out well. A firing range in France was made available for flight testing of the missiles. France, although not a member of the organization, purchased several hundred of the European-produced SIDEWINDERS.[20]

Other Projects of Cooperative Production

A number of items in addition to aircraft and missiles were brought into cooperative production programs. After an earlier arrangement for production of the U.S. Mark 44 torpedo in the United Kingdom and Canada, France and Italy in late 1960 entered into an arrangement for the production of this antisubmarine weapon. The United States made a small grant of funds to help get the program started, handed over sets of drawings (which, as with all the others, had to be converted to the metric system), and through "reimbursable aid," provided materials, training, and technical assistance. The NATO Armaments Committee established a Group of Experts to facilitate full exchange of information among all those involved, but France and Italy each maintained its own production and proving facilities, funded its own projects, and made its own contracts.[21]

In a purely bilateral arrangement the United States agreed to an Italian proposal for the coproduction in Italy of the M-113 armored personnel carrier. Under conditions laid down in an agreement between the United States and Italian governments, the FMC Company of San José, California, entered into an agreement with Oto-Melare of La Spezia, Italy. With the technical assistance of the American company and with half the machine tools and equipment purchased in the United States, the Italian company converted an empty building in La Spezia into a modern plant for production of the personnel carrier. Beginning by assembling components obtained entirely from the United States for the first 100 vehicles, the Italian company turned to Italian suppliers for certain components for the next 400 carriers, and then the remaining 2,500 scheduled for the program were to be assembled from the most economical combination of Italian-and U.S.-made components.

With the benefit of the experience gained in producing the armored personnel carrier, the next step, which occurred by 1966, was to move into a similar program for the Italian production of the American-designed M-60 A-1 tank.[22]

The United States entered into an agreement in August 1963 for the cooperative production in Germany of a main battle tank. It took nearly another year before the U.S. Department of Defense chose the General Motors Corporation from among three companies submitting proposals to carry out the American part of the program. The development contracts involved an outlay by the United States of about $750,000 for the initial phase and an estiamted $20 million all together. Germany would bear an equal share of the total expenses. The new tank was not in operation until the 1970s.[23]

In May 1964 Canada and Norway began a joint program for the production of the M-72 light antitank missile—a hand weapon weighing only five pounds and costing about $50 each. Like the British-French projects, this program had the complication of bringing together two different systems of measurement in the drawings. The United States provided only the basic drawings without charge. Later drawings would be paid for. The United States had a seat in the directing organization where it retained a right of veto only on questions regarding security and standardization. Norway acted as prime contractor, produced certain components, and was responsible for final assembly. Canadian firms contributed certain components as subcontractors.

Meanwhile, with the encouragement of NATO agencies, other programs were being developed. In the spring of 1960 the defense ministers asked the Armaments Committee to extend its efforts in promoting multilateral cooperation in research and development as well as in production. The committee then developed what came to be known as "The Twenty Projects Program," which covered a wide variety of aircraft, missiles, and combat vehicles such as those discussed above, and various electronic devices. Results were uneven. Several notable successes occurred but so did many delays and disappointments.[24]

Yet the promise remained of large-scale cooperative efforts, although not necessarily under the aegis of NATO. Significant cooperation among European nations in nonmilitary space research began in 1960. Early in that year ten countries (seven European members of NATO, together with Spain,

Sweden, and Switzerland) formed the European Space Research Organization. Operating for its initial eight-year program on a budget of $300 million that was supported by the participants in proportion to national income, the organization established its headquarters in Paris, a research institute in Italy, a data center at Darmstadt, and a technology center at Delft.[25]

In 1962 six European members of NATO (Belgium, France, Germany, Italy, the Netherlands, and the United Kingdom) and Australia formed the European Launcher Development Organization. The first project for launching a satellite reflected the international character of the operation. Britain provided the first-stage rocket (based on Blue Streak), France the second stage, and Germany the third. Italy was responsible for building the satellite, Belgium for installing control stations around the world, and the Netherlands for the long-range telemetry. Australia was to set up the launching site at Woomera.[26]

For military missiles, suggestions were being made in the spring of 1967 for a joint British-French project to develop and produce a successor to the U.S. POLARIS. If such a project could be worked out it would have the advantage of keeping those two nations up to date in missiles without having to bear the foreign-exchange outlay that would be required for purchasing U.S. POSEIDONS (scheduled to replace the POLARIS on sixteen American submarines by the end of 1972). At the same time, it would give to Britain an important link with France at a time when admission into the European Economic Community was being sought. This would be in sharp contrast to the Nassau agreement of December 1962 that tied Britain to the United States for POLARIS missiles at the time when the previous bid for entry into the Common Market was being considered, and which may have been significant in the French rejection of the British application.[27]

Since 1951 exchange of scientific and technical information had been a matter of continuing concern for the NATO military agency known as AGARD (the Advisory Group for Aerospace Research and Development). Its principal aims were to stimulate progress in aerospace sciences and technology and to advise the NATO military authorities on the state of developments in this field having potential significance for defense. Its panels of experts operated in specific areas, and by a program of studies, surveys, publications, and meetings it sought to keep the scientific and technological communities of participating countries informed on developments, plans, and needs.[28]

The Impact of Cooperative Production

Undoubtedly the cooperative production program contributed significantly to European defense in particular, and to the European economy in general. One student concluded:

> Western European co-production of weapons of U.S. origin has stimulated and caused a fantastic international movement of all of the

factors of production considered (in this study)—labor, capital and technology, including designs, processes and other knowledge. Perhaps it can be said that in view of all the encompassing effects of co-production, this method of foreign aid has had more impact on the movements of the factors of production than any other form of military aid. . . .

Co-production's greatest impact, it is felt, has been its stimulus and support of the unprecedented movement of technology to and among the nations of Western Europe.[29]

At the same time the European countries felt that the whole cooperative production effort was too much of a one-way street. It was mostly a matter of accepting U.S. designs for production in Europe. Certainly this often represented a substantial contribution on the part of the United States, and many did recognize that the United States held a substantial technological advantage. On the other hand, the United States was little inclined to accept European designs for cooperative production in the United States. In the competition of designs for NATO cooperative production, the U.S. F-104G Starfighter was chosen over the British de Havilland Firestreak and the French Mirage III. Although the French air-to-surface missile, AS-30, won a certain degree of acceptance in Britain and Germany, it lost out to the U.S. BULLPUP. For a surface-to-air missile, the U.S. HAWK was chosen over the British BLOODHOUND, and for air-to-air, the American SIDEWINDER was selected over its French competitior. Again, the French Alouette helicopter, even though the Alouette 3 was in use by eight countries and the Alouette 2 by twenty-eight, lost out to the American UH-1D. The British considered their BLUE WATER missile the best of its type, but it was scrapped when the United States backed its own SERGEANT. The British also were disappointed when they could not get their Centurion tank accepted by NATO.

According to one view at the time, this situation was the natural result of American technological superiority and Yankee salesmanship.[30] Another opinion was that it resulted at least in part because of pressure by the U.S. government, which in turn had been lobbied by its own defense industries.[31]

Nevertheless cooperative production provided an alternative to reliance upon direct purchases of weapons from the United States in cases where a nation desired American weapons and equipment to keep its forces modern. At least to some extent it kept alive elements of European defense industries, it provided a means for gaining technological information as a beneficiary of the very large American investment in weapons research and development that no European nation could be expected to match, and European nations gained a stimulus to their general economic activity that was altogether lacking under a program of direct purchase. But the question remained, was this the most effective way to do it?

The McNamara Proposal for a "Common Market" in Armaments

When it came to simple cost-effectiveness, there was little doubt that cooperative production, as carried out under the NATO and related programs, rated poorly. In nearly every case, weapons produced jointly by several countries could have been obtained more cheaply by direct purchase from the United States or by concentrating production in a single European country.

Now while contributing assistance in various forms to cooperative production projects—mainly in the form of the benefits of very costly and time-consuming research and development—the United States was pushing vigorously a program of direct sales of military weapons and equipment. Aside from the natural interests of the defense industries involved, the major impetus for this program came from a desire to offset the costs of maintaining forces abroad, an important factor in the balance-of-payments problem in the United States. Other objectives given for the sales program were: (1) To promote the defensive strength of Allies of the United States, consistent with U.S. political and economic objectives, and, (2) to promote the concept of cooperative logistics with U.S. Allies.[32] In 1965 officials of the U.S. Department of Defense announced that in the preceding four years the United States had received orders, commitments, and options for over $9 billion in military equipment that would yield cash receipts of nearly $5 billion. Further, McNamara was saying that it was expected that the United States could maintain the current level of military exports, about $2 billion a year, for the next ten years. This was a jump from U.S. military exports in the 1950s of about $300 million a year. Now these exports were offsetting about forty-five percent of the cost of keeping all U.S. forces overseas except those in Southeast Asia.[33]

Frequently the United States had been accused of applying "pressure tactics" to promote military sales in its preoccupation with the gold outflow problem and in order to benefit its own defense industries.[34] This tendency seemed to be especially strong upon Germany, where a certain level of arms purchases from the United States appeared to be a price for maintaining a certain level of U.S. forces in Germany. The position of the United States was not unreasonable in principle. Clearly the United States was contributing substantially to German security, and Germany's own defense expenditures were proportionately lower than those of the other major Allies. Nevertheless, the American selling efforts were bound to create reaction and resistance. These tactics, more than the cooperative production program, threatened to make American dominance even more pronounced and to make European countries military dependencies of the United States— not to mention the fact that European nations were as sensitive to the loss of foreign exchange as was the United States.

Military armaments had become a victim of international finance. Looming larger in the calculation of troop strength and logistic requirements than assessments of the relative capabilities and vulnerabilities of the Allies and their potential enemies was the ever-present question of cost and foreign exchange. Largely on this basis it appeared in the autumn of 1966 that Britain and the United States would make substantial reductions in their forces stationed in Germany. Another round of perennial negotiations resulted in an arrangement between the United States and the Federal Republic in which it was agreed that the German Central Bank would purchase about $500 million in medium-term United States securities. Added to an anticipated $300 million in German arms purchases from the United States, this purchase would almost offset the dollar cost of maintaining the 225,000 U.S. troops in Germany. After long negotiations with the British, the West German government agreed to increase military and commercial purchases in Britain to $126 million. But since this would offset only about fifty-five percent of the cost of maintaining the British Army of the Rhine, the United States agreed to purchase $35 million worth of arms in Britain. In addition the United States would be spending about $56 million in Britain for forces already stationed there or being redeployed to Britain from France. This still left a gap of about $48 million in Britain's costs in Germany. In April 1967, yielding to urgent appeals from both Germany and Britain, the United States "reluctantly" agreed to pruchase an additional $20 million worth of arms in Britain. Now it was expected that reductions in troop strength in Germany during the coming year could be limited to a loss of 30,000 men for the United States and to one of the five brigades in the British Army of the Rhine.[35]

But then it was Germany's turn. In July 1967 the German cabinet created some consternation across the Atlantic with an announcement that defense expenditures would be cut by $2.3 billion for the period 1968–71. This was expected to involve a reduction in the strength of the armed forces to 400,000 men from the 461,000 currently maintained, and it was expected to entail sharp cuts in armaments purchase in Allied countries.[36]

Recognizing what was appearing to many as the growth of an unhealthy situation, Secretary of Defense McNamara earlier had suggested a "common market" for armaments within the NATO alliance that would encourage trade among all the Allies on the basis of economy and quality, including better opportunities for the European nations to sell to the United States. As former Assistant Secretary of Defense for International Affairs Mansfield Sprague put it, "How long will this trend [high-volume U.S. sales to the European allies] be allowed by foreign governments to continue without some compensating inducement to them to sell less expensive but essential equipment to us?"[37]

In developing a "common defense market" McNamara sought an accommodation among the NATO Allies that would reduce to a minimum barriers to the movement of capital, technology, skilled labor, and materials for defense industries; would develop an effective specialization so that each country would emphasize the manufacture of products for which it had the greatest capability and efficiency; would lead to application of the "economy of scale" as practicable, and would develop a network of industry-to-industry relationships through technical association. He hoped that this arrangment would lead to the development of Allied defense industries on a low-cost, high-quality basis.[38]

This hope appeared to be reasonable enough, but unless it was accompanied by specific positive action on the part of the United States, it was unlikely to lead to very much. The problem was not essentially trade barriers. Tariffs already had been virtually eliminated among the six NATO members belonging to the European Economic Community; among four others who were members of the European Free Trade Association, they were very substantially reduced by the Geneva negotiations under the General Agreement on Tariffs and Trade and special agreements among various members, as, for example, between Britain and the European Economic Community and in the acceptance of Greece as an associate. Purely on the basis of economy and efficiency, the ideal solution might have been to encourage the free development of defense industries in each country according to the principle of comparative advantage. But the impediment to this scheme was to be found, not mainly in trade barriers, but in government procurement policies.

A potentially serious blow to anything approaching the kind of "common market" that Secretary McNamara envisaged came in the fall of 1967 with a nationalistic restriction that the U.S. imposed on the defense appropriation act. In March 1966 the United States and the United Kingdom entered into an offset agreement wherein the British were to purchase $2.6 billion worth of military equipment from the United States, including fifty of the new F-111 "swing-wing" aircraft, and for the United States to place orders for military equipment with Britain over a ten-year period amounting to $325 million, plus another $400 million in sales to other countries with U.S. support. Then in September 1967, the U.S. House of Representatives added to the defense appropriation bill an amendment forbidding the construction of U.S. Navy vessels in foreign shipyards. Immediately at stake was a possible contract for the construction of seven minesweepers at a total cost of about $60.7 million. American officials already had invited British firms to bid on these and other minesweepers. There had appeared to be good prospects for the British to get the order, but now Congress had stepped in to nullify an executive commitment. There was an immediate outcry in Britain for cancellation of the F-111 order. Several American senators saw this action as a "doublecross," a going-back on a commitment. The action itself was not so serious as what it might foreshadow—a rising sentiment of protectionism in the United States that could cripple all efforts at international cooperative production and unhampered trade in arms. Actually British leaders felt that this move on the part of the United States should not be taken too seriously, since it applied to only one category, naval vessels, and only for a single year. Thus far British firms had done very well in obtaining U.S. defense contracts, for in only a year and a half they had received orders amounting to $136,780,000 (of which $100 million were for Rolls Royce-Spey aircraft engines), or nearly half of the total anticipated for ten years. In addition they had sold $275 million worth of military goods (mostly to Saudi Arabia) of the $400 million anticipated in sales to other countries. Still, the incident was one more indication of the obstacles in the way of an effective common market in arms. In this instance the congressmen who offered the restrictive amendment evidently were interested mainly in eliminating foreign competition for shipbuilding industries in their home districts. But the vote in support was so large that it seemed likely that other congressmen might be seeking similar protection for other kinds of goods later—in spite of the fact that the British were committed to buying eight times as much equipment from the United States as vice-versa.[39]

It was not to be expected that a nation, when it finds quality and price even close, will favor foreign arms over those produced in its own industries. Nor was it to be expected that the United States would give up its self-sufficiency in arms manufacture in the interest of the economy of comparative advantage. But what could be done was for the United States to help strengthen European defense industries by participating in the cooperative production of a good number of European-designed items as well as by continuing to make U.S. technology available in the European production of American items.

Conclusions

If nothing else, programs of cooperative development and production launched under the auspices of NATO opened up important possibilities that promised to have continued significance whether formally under NATO organizations or carried on under outside arrangements. These programs had shown what could be done in international cooperation even in the most complex and technical fields. But their real impact on NATO logistics remained problematical.

It was probably true that the cooperative production programs had added modern weapons to the inventories of the participating nations that otherwise would have been beyond their reach. They had contributed a measure of standardization among the nations concerned, and so had eased by just that much their common logistic problems. Perhaps too they had provided a basis for future expansion of international production, which could be the most significant achievement of all.

It has been suggested that cooperative production in Europe had been a very significant stimulus to the movement among the nations of the major factors of production—captial and labor.[40] But this theory is very questionable. Was not the entire impulse of the NATO cooperative production programs *against* the movement of capital and labor? Indeed one of the greatest claims for the advantage of the system was that all the goals mentioned above had been achieved without aggravating balance-of-payments problems. The idea had been in each case to so divide up the work that the production effort in each country would be equal to that country's orders for the finished product. Surely it was not necessarily the most efficient way to have the nose of an airplane made in Italy, the tail in Germany, and the middle in Holland. The most efficient way, economically, would result if each nation would buy at the best advantage and let industrial specialization develop according to resources, technology, and labor. But this method came up against the competition of the advanced technology of the United States. Here possibly could be a greater contribution of NATO: technological cooperation. The emphasis needed to be not so much on a "common market" with the United States as upon a true common market in armaments among the European partners. The greater emphasis needed to be upon integration and rationalization of the European defense industry so that NATO might then rest upon two great, mutually supporting, but fairly self-sufficient industrial bases, one in Europe and one in North America.

But the development of such a system would require major steps of self-denial on the part of all concerned, and it was doubtful if any of the nations were equal to it. Yet the success of the European Economic Community suggested that it was possible. What was needed was a certain deemphasis on national arms industries in the interest of a vastly improved arms industry that could serve all the Allies.

For the United States this system would mean a deemphasis in the sale of American arms, and yet greater efforts to encourage the integration of the European arms industry and to provide technological assistance toward this improvement. This plan might appear to run contrary to American industrial interests, and it would mean giving up arms sales as a major instrument in reversing the gold flow. But even greater interests might be at stake. Surely this would be no more contrary to American long-term interests than was the general economic recovery of Europe, which the Americans did encourage with the far-reaching Marshall Plan. What was needed was an American-backed European Defense Community, the like of which modern Europe never had seen.

In 1966 and 1967 the trend was in the opposite direction. In order to modernize forces in a way to be prepared to meet conditions anticipated for the 1970s, force-level studies were undertaken to develop more specific requirements for a five-year modernization program. But the indication was that there would be a further shift away from NATO-sponsored projects in favor of national defense production.[41]

Emphasis upon national production was not just a simple matter either of national pride or of immediate financial selfishness. In a way it was nationalism itself and the continuing reliance on the nation, in the final analysis, for security. Each nation was anxious to maintain its own industrial establishment—especially its defense industry. If it lost out on all military procurements, in the long run it would also lose its own capacity to produce. The question here was whether ultimately some kind of European Defense Community—one comprising arms production as well as military units—could better satisfy the demand for security of European peoples than could their nation states acting individually.

Notes

1. *Facts about the North Atlantic Treaty Organization* (Paris, 1965), 119–21.
2. Mutual Security Act of 1954 as amended (1959), Sec. 105.b.1.
3. M. Domenic Palumbo, "An Analysis of Western European Co-production of Weapons of United States Origin," Industrial College of the Armed Forces, Washington, D.C., 1966, 8–12.
4. NATO *Facts*, 120.
5. Robert Rhodes James, *Standardization and Common Production of Weapons in NATO,* Institute for Strategic Studies, Defense, Technology and the Western Alliance no. 3 (London, 1967), 11; NATO Press Release (58) 21, 19 December 1958; NATO *Facts*, 126.
6. NATO Press Release (60), 21 January 1960; NATO Press Release (61) 2, 24 January 1962; NATO Statement, 15 November 1962; *NATO Facts*, 126–27; W. T. Gill, "European Cooperation in Britain's Aerospace Industry," *NATO's Fifteen Nations* 11 (August–September 1966): 30–31; James, *Standardization and Common Production of Weapons in NATO*, 12ff; "Dutch ASW Aircraft Selection Seen Critical in NATO Plans," *Aviation Week and Space Technology,* 11 March 1968, 17; J. C. Stone, "NATO Cooperation in Research, Development, and Production," *NATO Letter,* October 1969, 22–25; Walter Schütze, *European Defence Cooperation and NATO* (Paris, The Atlantic Institute, 1969), 43–48.
7. NATO Press Release (63) 5, 16 September 1963.
8. NATO Press Release M2 (60) 2, 17 December 1960; Press Release (61) 14, 12 June 1961.
9. Philip Shabecoff, "Europeans Join in Jet Venture," *New York Times* (Int. ed.), 10 July 1964, 7; Otto Pick, "The 'O' in NATO," *NATO Letter,* December 1965, 17–20.
10. NATO countries using the F-104 included Germany, Belgium, Italy, the Netherlands, Canada, Denmark, Greece, Norway, and Turkey.
11. Philip Shabecoff, "All F-104 Flights Halted by Bonn," *New York Times,* 7 December 1966, 15.
12. Col. Barney Oldfield, "The F-104S salutes Leonardo da Vinci," *NATO's Fifteen Nations* (August–September 1966): 78–84.
13. Palumbo, "An Analysis of Western European Co-production of Weapons of United States Origin," 30–31.
14. Gill, "European Cooperation in Britain's Aerospace Industry," 27–31; John W. R. Taylor, "European Fighters: 1966," *Nato's Fifteen Nations* (August–September 1966): 38–44 idem, "European Bombers: 1966," ibid., 47–48; L. Perret, "Coopération Industrielle Aéronautique en Europe," *Revue Militaire d'Information* (May 1963): 62; UPI Dispatch, *Marion Chronicle-Tribune,* 14 April 1965, 2.
15. Richard E. Mooney, "Paris and London Will Build a Swing-Wing Jet," *New York Times,* 17 January 1967, 3; "France Abandons Joint Air Project," ibid., 6 July 1967, 1, 2.
16. See A. E. M. Duynstee, "The European Aircraft Industry Must Be Integrated," *NATO's Fifteen Nations* (August–September 1966): 23–24.
17. North Atlantic Council Armaments Committee, Basic Agreements, "Methods of the NATO HAWK Production Organization," Working Paper AC/74-WP/19, 12 December 1963; NATO Press Release (59)1, 17 January 1959; NATO Press Release (59)8, 18 June 1959; Pick, "The 'O' is NATO," 17–20.
18. See chap. 12.
19. North Atlantic Council Armaments Committee, Basic Agreements, "Methods of the NATO BULLPUP Production Organization," NATO Working Paper AC/784-WP/22, 17 December 1963; NATO Press Release (62) 14, 10 August 1962.
20. NATO Press Communiqué (59) 12, 12 August 1959; NATO Press Communiqué (61) 23, 25 November 1961; *NATO Facts,* 128.
21. *NATO Facts,* 128–29.
22. Palumbo, "An Analysis of Western European Co-production," 28–30, 31–32.
23. "GM Chosen to Help Make New Tank," *New York Herald Tribune* (Paris ed.), 24 July 1964, 1.
24. *Aspects of NATO: Defense Production and Infrastructure* (Paris, 1963), 7–8; NATO Press Communiqué MD (60) 1, 1 April 1960.
25. *France Air and Space* (New York, 1963), 52–53.
26. Ibid.
27. Karl E. Meyer, "Joint Missile Program with France is under Consideration by Britain," *Washington Post,* 11 May 1967, A28.
28. *Aspects of NATO: AGARD.*

29. Palumbo, "An Analysis of Western European Co-production," 33–34.

30. Ibid., 57.

31. See Tom Margerison, "Lemnitzer's Awkward Army," *Sunday Times Colour Magazine* (London), 9 June 1963, 7–9. L. L. Doty, in "U.S. Pressure Delays NATO Target Buy," *Aviation Week and Space Technology,* 2 November 1964, 23, referred to a "growing concern [in the United States] that French industry is penetrating deeply into areas once considered primarily U.S. markets." This concern was given as a major reason for "American political pressure," which had delayed the purchase of Nord CT 20 target missiles for the training of NATO ground crews. See also Perret, "Coopération industrielle aeronautique en Europe," 57–63.

32. U.S. Dept. of Defense, Military Assistance and Foreign Military Sales Facts, May 1967, 25.

33. Claude Witze, "The Case for a Common Defense Market," *Air Force/Space Digest International,* January 1966, 4–5; John Maffre, "Military Deals Balance Trade," *Washington Post,* 26 March 1967, 33; Military Assistance and Foreign Military Sales Facts, 35; *New York Times,* 5 January 1968, 1.

34. See Walter Goldstein, *The Dilemma of British Defense,* Mershon Pamphlet Series no. 3 (Columbus, Ohio, 1966), 90.

35. John W. Finney, "ULSL to Aid Britain on German Costs," *New York Times,* 27 April 1967, 1, 28.

36. "Bonn to Review Defense Policy," *New York Times,* 8 July 1967, 1, 6.

37. Quoted in Witze, "The Case for a Common Defense Market," 5.

38. Ibid., 4–5.

39. "Senate Votes Defense Bill; Curb on British Accepted," *New York Times,* 14 September 1967, 1; Dana Adams Schmidt, "F-111 Deal in Jeopardy," ibid., 20; Kenneth Owen, "Still Hope for F-111 Offset Deals," *The Times* (London), 15 September 1967, 1.

40. Palumbo, "An Analysis of Western European Co-production," 33–34.

41. "NATO Shifts Procuring Plans to meet Military Needs," *Aviation Week and Space Technology,* 6 March 1967, 94.

10
Standardization of Supplies and Services

International cooperation in logistic support of almost any kind calls for at least some degree of standardization in matériel and procedures. Whether it be cooperative production programs or the sale of military equipment among nations or cooperation and mutual support in supplying forces in the field, standardization is almost *sine qua non* for achievement of results.

Indeed standardization always has been a major concern for logisticians even within the national forces of a single country. Undoubtedly a part of the traditional resistance to the introduction of new types of weapons and equipment has been a concern about the complications of supplying many different types of ammunition, different kinds of spare parts, different kinds of fuels and lubricants. In spite of an impulse for standardization within the armed forces of a nation that may extend back over decades, this remains a problem to some degree in most countries.

What measure of international standardization has come into effect heretofore has been the result largely of dependence upon one nation within an alliance or coalition for particular items of military equipment. Some standardization appeared among the Western Allies during World War I as a result of the dependence of the American Expeditionary Force on purchases, mostly from France, for most of its artillery, tanks, and airplanes, and for a third of its automatic weapons, and from Great Britain for its trench mortars. The Allies of that time did arrive at a certain de facto standardization in programs for the cooperative production of tanks. Although the war ended before production had become fully effective, the United States had entered into a cooperative arrangement with France and Great Britain wherein the United States undertook the production of a light tank modeled after the French six-ton Renault. In addition the United States and Great Britain entered into a treaty for the cooperative production of a heavy tank, known as the Anglo-American Mark VIII, to be assembled in France from armored hulls and guns supplied by the British, and with engines, traction mechanisms, and electrical equipment from the United States. This program was proceeding with great success, though only one tank had been completed when the armistice was signed.

During World War II, Allied forces in Italy comprised units from many nations. Nevertheless they were able to have the benefit of international logistic support and to share common equipment and procedures. But this support was possible largely because those forces operating on the northeast side of the peninsula were attached to the British Eighth Army and used British equipment and supplies. Similarly forces on the opposite side, attached usually to the U.S. Fifth Army, had the benefit of standardization imposed by dependence upon United States equipment and supply lines.

This method is one way to have some measure of international standardization. Another way is to develop measures by international agreement. Without some kind of standardization, there can be very little international logistics. The irony here was that many words of agreement on this point came from the leaders of NATO countries and from NATO agencies, but performance on the part of the governments did not match the words—or the need. As Alastair Buchan noted, "It is very much easier to talk about standardization of weapons and specialization on the part of different countries than it is to achieve them, despite the fact that the advantages of interdependence are most obvious in this field."[1]

In one of a long series of statements expressing similar sentiments, the ministerial meeting of the North Atlantic Council of December 1957 announced in its communiqué: "Better use of the resources of the Alliance and greater efficiency for its forces will be obtained through as high a degree of standardization and integration as possible in all fields, particularly in certain aspects of air and naval defense, of logistic support and of the composition and equipment of forces." It further stated that a military conference at the ministerial level should be held early in 1958 to discuss progress in these fields.

But in November 1959 Secretary-General Paul Henri Spaak reported: "We have still not managed to obtain any worthwhile standardization of our equipment in NATO. With one or two minor exceptions, we have not succeeded in properly apportioning armament production tasks among the Allies. We repeat experiments in one country which have already been concluded in another; we insist on re-inventing what has already been invented; and we refuse to trust our friends with secrets which have been known to the enemy for a long time."[2] A year later, with still greater feeling, Spaak said in a speech at Tufts University in Massachusetts:

As Secretary General of NATO, I find that, after eleven years, we have still not achieved real standardization of our armaments. Each one wants to keep his rifle, his machine gun and his tanks and his shells. Each one, above all, wants his air force, his own national aircraft, which can only be used under restricted conditions. Each one wants to be free to build aircraft which are neither better nor worse than those of his neighbor and which, at least in the European countries, are produced under ridiculous economic conditions, because they come from firms which can only survive with the help of the taxpayer's money.[3]

And a year after that General Le Compte told the rapporteurs of the Western

European Union's Committee on Defense Questions and Armaments, "Our armies employ 14 different types of small arms ammunition, while Russia and all the satellite countries have only one type of round for small arms. . . . In spite of all the attempts at standardization, we have today three times the number of types of rifles and machine-guns that we had then (1956) and nearly five times more different types of vehicles."[4]

The need for standardization of matériel and logistic procedures was most apparent to those most concerned about logistic support. General Lyman Lemnitzer, Supreme Allied Commander Europe, said that for all the members of the Alliance to use the same weapons and ammunition "would be the millenium." While noting the great value of standardization in reducing logistic problems, the Supreme Allied Commander put his finger on the main difficulties in achieving the desired standardization when he observed that "national pride, commercial interests, local requirements, industrial capabilities and, of course, economic considerations, all affect the situation."[5]

Even if the major barriers against international standardization—the questions of pride and political differences and competing economic interests—could be resolved completely, the remaining technical problems would continue to be formidable indeed. As already noted, individual nations frequently had difficulty in promoting standardization of equipment among elements of their own armed forces. But the problem went deeper than that. Increasingly as the pace of technical improvement quickened, the problem of maintaining standardization of almost any item of equipment, whether in the hands of troops or only in the production line, became more pronounced.

Always one of the most difficult questions of production logistics is the timing of the standardization of a given item of equipment for production. If the design is standardized too soon, then the result may be a large quantity of the item, but of obsolete design. If standardization for production comes too late, then the design may be the most advanced to be found, but not of sufficient quantity to be effective. Even when production on an item has begun, design changes may be so frequent as to interrupt the whole process. Again the dilemma is always whether one should disrupt production in order to incorporate improvements, or ignore improvements in the interest of maintaining production. At times during wartime production, governments found it necessary to declare a moratorium on design changes in order to meet requirements at all—even when it could be shown that proposed changes would be highly desirable. How much more complex this could become when independent nations are striving for improvements!

Even when NATO partners entered into cooperative production arrangements, the standardization implicit in such an agreement did not necessarily last, since individual nations added their own improvements or sought other equipment that quickly made the cooperative item obsolete. When the United States made the design of the F-104G aircraft available to NATO partners, the United States continued to improve the aircraft. Not only did this cancel out a certain degree of standardization between the United States and European nations that would have been an advantage in wartime servicing of aircraft, but it also set up complications in providing spare parts from the United States for U.S.-design aircraft in the hands of its allies. No commander wants to hear that he must be content with an inferior item of equipment in the interest of maintaining international standardization.

In its original directive on standardization in February 1951, the Standing Group of the Military Committee took a broad view. It stated that standardization was essential "when the implementation of operational plans depends on it," desirable "whenever it facilitates the implementation of those plans," and undesirable "when no benefits accrue from it or when it hinders research." Standardization itself might consist of common, compatible, or "interchangeable supplies, weapons or equipment." The Standing Group laid down two aims for matériel standardization: one, a short-term aim, was "to achieve the greatest possible use of existing equipment or equipment at present being manufactured by nations"; the second was "a long-term aim, which consists in achieving a greater degree of standardization in order to arrive at the maximum efficiency of the NATO combined forces; from the military point of view, it is not necessary to achieve full standardization, but it is necessary to reach agreement on the characteristics of the equipment and to arrive at an interchangeability of spare parts and short-life components."[6]

An analyst of the problem at that time drew a distinction between what he called "standardization from the top" and "standardization from the bottom." The former was based on a United States statement that said,

> Maximum standardization and economy of resources can be achieved only if agreement can be reached in the concept stage. Under this approach the member nations would agree to basic military requirements for NATO as a whole, and then participating nations in a project would share in research, development, and production so that each would receive a share of the work in proportion to its commitment. The second approach would concentrate upon procedures and specific items, even though minor, as being much more realistic.[7]

Here matériel standardization would put more emphasis upon "interoperability" and "battlefield compatibility." The members would agree upon minimum specifications, and each would produce or purchase its own accordingly.

Actually the emphasis in NATO went mainly from the first to the second of these approaches, though some effort at the first has continued in the various cooperative production programs, although these have been limited to only a few cooperating nations in each project. Convinced of the clear desirability of standardization as the very key to international logistic support, NATO officials and military authorities in the beginning sought to standardize practically everything throughout the Alliance. Quickly, however, it became evident to them that this would not work. In effect, they "reached for the stars and fell on their faces." Then they backed away and took a more modest approach. They would make their main efforts toward a relatively few key items that seemed to be within reach and that in themselves had an important impact upon logistics.

Early Efforts at Standardization Among NATO Countries

Based to some extent on the experience of cooperative efforts during World War II, the United Kingdom, Canada, and the United States soon after that war began a program of standardization. The program was referred to as "Standardization of Operations and Procedures," and the resulting agreements came to be known as "SOLOG Agreements," or simply as "SOLOGs." These agreements ranged over a wide selection of subjects from adoption of a common weapon component to agreement on procedures to be used in the relief of troops of one of the nations by a unit of another of the nations in a combat situation. The SOLOGs became the basis for U.S. proposals for NATO standardization agreements. NATO efforts thus did not supersede the earlier U.S.-Canada-U.K. programs, but they were related. While many SOLOGs became NATO Standardization Agreements (referred to as "STANAGs"), a number of STANAGs also later became SOLOGs. In 1963 Australia joined the SOLOG arrangements.

The first, and in some respects the most successful, efforts at matériel standardization was with respect to small-arms ammunition. This too was based upon efforts antedating NATO itself. In 1945 each of the major Western powers had a good degree of standardization for rifles and machine guns within its own forces, but all systems differed from each other. The principal French round was 7.5 mm; the American was caliber .30; and the British .303. The principal German small-arms ammunition was 7.92 mm. Military staffs in France, the United Kingdom, and the United States, and in Belgium made studies during 1947 and 1948 on an uncoordinated, national basis.

Everyone knew that the problem of ammunition supply was a logistic consideration of major proportions, and anything that could be done in that way of standardization would be a significant contribution to logistic cooperation within the Alliance. Ideally, the nations concerned would have standardized their weapons as well as their ammunition, but here the difficulties appeared to be too great to overcome. Nevertheless, Britain, Canada, France, and the United States had come to the conclusion by 1951 that standardization at least of small-arms ammunition was within reach and would be of advantage to all. In a sense it was more difficult to achieve standardization of small-arms ammunition than of such modern devices as guided missiles because all of these nations for many years had been engaged in the manufacture of the former. In September 1951 these nations, together with Belgium, agreed on the basic military characteristics for a common small-arms round of ammunition, and then individually they began studies on which they exchanged information. At last they agreed upon a 7.62 mm round for common acceptance. This was the same as caliber .30, the caliber of U.S. ammunition, but this round was different in other respects such as being of shorter length. The five nations then proposed that this be made the NATO Common Round. After approval by the North Atlantic Council in December 1953, representatives met in Ottawa in January 1954 for technical discussions. Later in the year the STANAG was issued to give effect to the agreement, and most of the NATO members subsequently ratified it.[8]

But conclusion of an agreement is only the beginning of standardization. There still was the question of maintaining minimum standards in production so that the ammunition would in fact be acceptable and interchangeable, whatever the country of its manufacture, among all the participating nations. The matter of maintaining quality standards was not left to chance. Rather it called for constant monitoring and testing.

NATO's Small Arms Ammunition Panel, made up of one technical representative from each participating country, prescribed tests for the ammunition and supervised the maintenance of the set standards. Meeting in plenary session once a year, the panel had two regional divisions, one each for North America and Europe, each operating a NATO Test Center, with an executive committee for continuing coordination. Whenever a firm or armory in one of the participating countries prepared to begin the manufacture of the NATO Standard Round, the regional panel for the area conducted preliminary tests and thereafter tested production samples. Under the supervision of the regional panels, national authorities conducted surveillance tests on ammunition that had been put in storage. Each cartridge head and outer package of the approved ammunition bore a special symbol so that it might be used interchangeably with confidance among the allied nations.[9]

During the next several years after NATO adoption of the standard 7.62 mm cartridge, steadily increasing quantities of this ammunition were being produced throughout the Alliance.[10] Still, this round could not immediately become, nor remain, the only small-arms ammunition for participating countries. An announcement in a French military journal in May 1964 that the French government was making additional procurements of its old 7.5 mm rifle in what appeared to be obvious disregard of the whole spirit of standardization and cooperation created a furor in the Alliance and brought sharp criticisms of the French, particularly in the United States. Then the French Ministry of the Armies explained quite simply that it had large quantities of the old ammunition on hand that would be wasted if enough weapons were not provided to make use of it in training and other missions.[11]

Then the news spread that not only was the United States continuing to use its M-1 rifle, partly for the same reason, but after developing a new rifle, the M-14, which took the NATO 7.62 mm, it had proceeded to adopt the newer M-16, which took 5.56 (caliber .223) ammunition.[12] The latter rifle became the principal individual firearm for U.S. forces in Southeast Asia. A major reason for its use there was logistical. A man could carry nearly twice as much of the smaller ammunition that this rifle used than of the NATO round (which in turn was lighter than the old M-2 ammunition). At the same time, the problem of standardization with forces of other NATO nations did not arise in Viet Nam. On the other hand U.S. forces in Europe continued to be armed with the M-14 and the standard NATO ammunition. Actually U.S. stocks and production of this ammunition were much greater than of the 5.56 mm, even though the latter was being used in an active combat theater.

Meanwhile, by 1957 NATO countries had agreed on the basic characteristics for a common 9 mm round for pistols and machine carbines. NATO land forces in Central Europe in the 1960s still were using at least three kinds of ammunition for rifles and machine guns, at least two for similar kinds of artillery, and five for tank guns.[13]

Standardization of the NATO round was a significant contribution to logistic cooperation, though small-arms ammunition was not the really difficult item, either in manufacture or in transportation. Artillery ammunition, of incomparably greater complexity and tonnage, remained outside the standards of interchangeability among the weapons of the various nations.

Other early efforts at standardization were in the direction of achieving compatibility of certain components of motor vehicles so that vehicles of the different nations could be mutually supporting on the battlefield. A few of the interested nations began this work in 1949, and then NATO took over its direction in 1952. The result was agreement on basic characteristics, which would provide a minimum of interchangeability and compatibility of such components as braking systems, towing bars, and batteries.[14]

The Military Agency for Standardization

During most of the first twenty years of NATO's existence, three agencies had primary responsibility for questions and projects of standardization. The Armaments Committee in Paris was concerned mainly with standardized production of future equipment, the Communications-Electronics Committee in Washington had responsibility for standardization projects in communications equipment and procedures, and the Military Agency for Standardization in London was made responsible for projects in the standardization of procedures and existing equipment and for the promulgation and publication of all Standardization Agreements.

Upon abolition of the Armaments Committee in June 1966, a conference of armaments directors was formed to take over the functions of that committee. The conference was scheduled to meet twice a year and representatives of the national directors would be available to meet under the chairmanship of the assistant secretary-general for production, logistics and infrastructure. With the abolition of the Standing Group at the same time, the work of the Military Agency for Standardization came directly under the Military Committee and the International Military Staff.

The major elements of the agency were an international chairman (a position filled during the 1964 period by a Greek lieutenant general) and an advisory committee to assist him; a terminology coordinator, three service boards (i.e., the Army, Naval, and Air Boards); an international staff comprising a secretariat for the chairman, administrative staff, and secretariat for each of the service boards; and various working parties, panels of experts, and custodians as needed for the various projects under consideration at a given time. The Advisory Committee was made up of the MAS chairman, the deputy chairman, and the chairman of each of the service boards. Each service board, the Army Board, for example, was made up of an Army member from each of the member nations (Canada, France, the United Kingdom, and the United States), and an accredited representative from each of the other NATO nations (excepting Luxembourg, represented through Belgium, and Iceland, which had no armed forces). The board in turn was served by a corresponding committee made up of members of their deputies and as many accredited representatives as might be able to attend. The committee handled preliminary coordination of draft STANAGs and routine matters involving no change in policy.[15]

The Military Agency for Standardization maintained close liaison with the Production, Logistics, and Infrastructure Division of NATO's International Staff, which sought to obtain national ratifications of standardization agreements—and which had a standing invitation to be represented at meetings of working parties and panels of experts. SHAPE also had a standing invitation to be represented at such meetings, and MAS maintained liaison with major subordinate command headquarters as well as with this and the other supreme headquarters. As indicated earlier, the MAS also received copies of regional agreements in the area of standardization and took action where warranted to incorporate these into NATO agreements. Regional groupings in this area included, in addition to Britain, Canada, and the United States (ABC), France, Italy, the Netherlands, Germany, and Belgium (FINABEL), and Western European Union.

The working heart of MAS was in the service boards. From here came proposals for standardization. Such a proposal might originate with one of the nations and be referred by its representative to the board; or it might come directly from one of the Supreme Commanders, from the Military Committee, or from the working parties and panels of experts associated with the service board itself. The board decided whether the proposal merited further study, and if so, decided whether to refer it to a working party, a panel of experts, or a "custodian." Working Parties as used in the MAS were more or less continuous bodies assigned a certain area of interest in making studies and developing standardization agreements. They were composed of members from all the nations, NATO agencies, and commands wishing to participate. They met according to their workloads.[16]

A panel of experts was constituted in a similar way, but it was convened to deal with a single proposal for a single standardization agreement, or to prepare agreements in a very restricted field. It might operate under a working party or it might operate directly under the board. The Army Board and the Air Board used working parties most frequently for their studies. Air Board working parties, as did those of the Army Board, operated over a wide range of subjects. The Naval Board used about five working parties, but it relied a great deal on the custodial method of doing its work.[17]

Standardization Agreements

Procedures for the preparation of a formal Standardization Agreement (STANAG) would vary from one case to another, but the procedures laid down for the Army Board were generally applicable. On the basis of a proposal or study, the board invited a working party (or panel of experts or custodian) to prepare a STANAG, and provided general direction as to scope, service applicability, and security classification. To take the case of a working party, some member, subcommittee, or panel of experts designated by the working party would prepare the basis for an agreement, and then in a formal meeting, the working party agreed to a preliminary draft of the STANAG. The secretary of the working party then issued a copy of the preliminary draft to all members of the party, who referred it usually within three months to their national authorities with a request for comments. On receipt of the comments, the working party again met to reconcile differences. It might be possible to find agreement immediately, or it might be necessary to prepare another preliminary draft. In any case, when the working party had agreed on the preliminary draft it then became simply a draft and was forwarded to the Army Committee for approval and issued to the nations and the military commands for ratification or further comments. In its preliminary draft the working party confirmed or recommended modifications of the board's original directive with respect to service applicability. STANAGs coming from the Army Board, for example, might fall within any of four categories of applicability—NATO Armed Forces, NATO Army and Naval Forces, NATO Army and Air Forces, NATO Army Forces. On receipt of a draft STANAG, a nation might ratify it, ratify it with reservations, ratify it with comments that did not affect the ratification, or refuse ratification, giving the earlier reasons. At the same time the Supreme Commanders were asked to comment on whether the STANAG would meet their operational requirements and what their desired date might be for putting it into effect. It might be necessary to return the draft to the working party for reconciliation of comments, and then for the working party to produce a second draft. When the working party had dealt with all the comments and when a majority of the nations had ratified the final draft, the proposed STANAG was forwarded to the Army Board for its decision on a recommendation of promulgation by the chairman of the MAS. Naturally, the hope was that all the nations would ratify, but at times it clearly was to the advantage of nations most directly concerned to put the agreement into effect among those nations having ratified it without waiting for the others. When the service board finally approved a draft STANAG, the MAS chairman promulgated and issued to ratifying nations for implementation. Copies also went to the nonratifying nations, to operational commanders, and to other interested agencies of NATO. Subsequently amendments might be proposed to the STANAG, and they were processed as was the original agreement. It was the policy of MAS for each working party to review each of its STANAGs every two years in order to keep it up to date.[18]

By the summer of 1966 the Military Agency for Standardization had published some 240 agreements on procedure of which over 140 had been implemented by all or a majority of the NATO members. It had published about 170 STANAGs for the standardization of matériel, and about 80 of them had been implemented. Most of these STANAGs had dealt with relatively minor items, yet each was a gain for logistic cooperation and they pointed the way for future achievement.[19]

A few examples suggest the nature and significance of the STANAGs that had been put into effect. One dealt with the format for adminstrative and logistic orders for NATO Army and Air forces. It consisted of a single page and a one-page annex. It simply spelled out the sequence of subject matter for an administrative/logistic annex to an operation order or for a separate administrative/logistic order. Now the commander of any NATO force, whether from his own nation or another, would know that he could look in the second paragraph of such an order for instructions on matériel and services.[20]

Another agreement dealt with one of the most basic elements of battlefield logistics—procedures for ammunition supply. This recognized different national units of measure but regularized procedures in prescribing command responsibilities for defining basic loads of ammunition for combat units, for prescribing the required supply rate (expressed in rounds per weapon per day), and for defining the rate of consumption of ammunition that could be allocated for a given period, expressed as the available supply rate. The agreement further established forms and procedures for ammunition status reports, for requisitions, and for transfer requests and orders for calling forward ammunition from a designated depot or transferring it from one supply installation to another.[21] Closely related to procedures for ammunition supply was a further agreement on the marking of dumps,[22] which was correlated to an earlier agreement on military symbols,[23] and a draft on interchangeability of demolition accessories.[24] Several projects related to highway transportation. There was an agreement on military route marking,[25] one on military road traffic lighting regulations,[26] and one road tunnels, ferries, and fords.[27] All of these projects were under the Army Board's Movements and Transport Working Party, which also had undertaken studies on transportation documentation, classification and marking of bridges, weight and dimension cards for vehicles, and restrictions on traffic. All the tasks of this working party were in close liaison with the Planning-Board for European Inland Surface Transport (PBEIST) in Paris, which usually had an observer at meetings of the working party and received all MAS papers relating to its area of planning.

The Naval Board and the Air Board each had prepared an interchangeability chart of NATO standardized fuels, lubricants, and Allied products.

These charts showed the wide range of standard fuels in use by naval and air forces of the NATO nations and that country's own designation for the same product, if available, with acceptable substitutes for emergency use. The Air Board standardizations were included in a single STANAG,[28] while each of some thirty naval fuels was standardized by a different STANAG, and then the information was brought together in a chart issued as an annex to a Naval Board memorandum.[29] A conversion chart showed the equivalents of liters in gallons and imperial gallons.

Another seemingly minor item receving the attention of the Naval Board in order to make the standardization of fuels effective was the matter of standardizing couplings so that ships of one nation might be refueled by a tanker of another nation.

Projects occupying the attention of the Army Board's Medical Working Party included procedures for the exchange of medical and dental property,[30] the medical employment of helicopters in ground warfare,[31] the training of nonmedical personnel in basic hygiene and first aid; standardization of medical kits; protection against chemical attack; blood transfusion equipment; agreement upon common dimensions for stretchers so that those of one nation will fit the ambulances of another nation; hypodermic needles; the development of adapters so that tubes for oxygen cylinders could be made interchangeable; medical documentation to include common patient evacuation tags, field medical cards, classification of wounds, injuries, and diseases that could be used in three-figure-code radio messages; procedures for disposing of patients from one nation evacuated to a hospital of another; and the color-coding of medical equipment for ease of identification when packed in boxes or crates. In addition to the Army Medical Working Party, a similar working party worked under the Air Board on the special problems of treating air casualties and of air (other than helicopter) evacuation, though there was no overlap between the two groups. Both worked in close liaison with the NATO Medical Committee, and all the STANAGs of both were tri-service.

An especially useful project of the Army and Air Equipment Working Parties was the preparation of books of equipment comprising a dozen or more "Broadfields," each of which covered a broad category of matériel. The NATO Book of Army Equipment, for instance, included twelve Broadfields that covered such categories as field artillery, combat vehicles, small-arms and infantry weapons, and engineer equipment. The purpose was to make available to all NATO nations, agencies, and commands a list of equipment currently in use by the forces of the various NATO nations and to give a list of equipment in an advanced state of development. The book was further intended to make known to all the status of equipment in each Allied nation so that availability of the equipment and of spare parts and ammunition might be known. The Broadfields also gave the minimum characteristics of each item of equipment so that nations might be assisted in selecting major items when needed and in providing such information to military commands and national headquarters to assist their cooperation. Finally, these publications gave information on the interchangeability of ammunition where applicable.[32]

In a number of fields such as those mentioned, most of the basic work had been done. Now, in addition to keeping the agreements current, the major effort was toward codification of existing agreements in order to combine many of the smaller agreements into a smaller number of larger agreements. This and other work might also provide the information needed for developing logistic planning data. Some of it also came from national efforts. Germany, for example, prepared data on fuel consumption, which they then submitted to MAS for distribution to the other nations. Each nation prepared information on its own roads, inland waterways, railroads, and urban areas—virtually an economic atlas—that the Geographic Documentation Working Party distributed.

Complex as it was, the development and ratification of a STANAG was only half the battle. Not infrequently the gaining of implementation that was more than mere lip-service was far more difficult.

When the NATO standard 7.62 mm cartridge was adopted, there was no accompanying agreement governing link belts for the ammunition for machine guns. Each country went ahead on its own. Soon it was apparent that even though the cartridges were the same, there was no standardization of machine gun ammunition so long as the belts could not be used in different machine guns and could not be folded into the different ammunition boxes of the different countries. Soon stockpiles had been built up and immediate, complete standardization was out of the question. But no agreement was forthcoming, even to be effective years later when current stocks might have been reduced. The problem seemed to grow at least in part out of competition among the countries—especially among Belgium, France, and Germany—for the business of manufacturing the links.

The Air Board prepared and obtained ratification of a series of STANAGs on the cross-servicing of aircraft at Allied airfields. But it became clear to visitors that these were not being implemented. In this case it was largely a question of finance. It was too expensive for each airfield to carry all supplies for servicing all the different aircraft of the Allied nations. The question then was, which ones should be selected? Then should some extra supplies for other aircraft be carried for possible emergency use? Here it was up to AFCENT to prepare a list of aircraft for which cross-servicing arrangements should be maintained.[33]

More serious was the appearance of a certain inertia in the military headquarters. International standardization had been slow to catch on in the field commands. Some local commanders would admit that they never had heard of a STANAG. Teams from MAS had gone out to field headquarters to brief all interested officers on standardization, only to find that they had more people in the visitors' party than had turned out to hear the presentation. Sometimes staff members who had spent months bringing about the successful conclusion of a STANAG had the feeling that they were engaging in only a paper exercise when they visited the field. But military commanders hesitated to implement agreements until word also had come down to them from the interested national authorities. In effect this was a requirement for a second ratification. The Supreme Headquarters and the major subordinate headquarters had had from the beginning various Standing Operating Procedures (SOPs) for their staff and command procedures. The STANAGs coming to them for implementation generally required a modification of an SOP. The same authority that put the SOP into effect, the commander, should also have had the authority to change it. But somehow this seemed to be different. In a way it was more difficult to implement an informal agreement, such as an SOP, than a formal one such as a STANAG. It was the same situation with disarmament agreements. A nation or a people quite willing to see its armed forces reduced—for economic or other reasons—may balk completely at entering into a formal disarmament treaty calling for a similar reduction.

Aside from inertia and reluctance on the part of commanders to invite criticism from some of the nations, other factors were also at work against the effectiveness of standardization. One of these was the need for certain nations, in particular the United States, the United Kingdom, and to some extent France and Portugal, to maintain forces in Asia or Africa or the Pacific, where equipment standardized on the basis of European requirements might not be appropriate. A second factor involved the expanding arms industries of the various nations. NATO long had encouraged increased armaments production on the part of its members, but the fact was that the stimulation of various individual industries and national production resulted in a greater diversity of weapons and equipment throughout the Alliance. It was another of those Alice-in-Wonderland situations where it was necessary to "run as fast as you can" in developing standardization agreements just to "stand still" in relation to the total production. But the very term *NATO logistics* probably is related more to standardization as the basis for international cooperation in combat support than to any other aspect.[34]

Notes

1. Alastair Buchan *NATO in the 1960s* (London, 1964), 144.
2. Quoted in Robert Rhodes James, *Standardization and Common Production of Weapons in NATO: Defense, Technology, and the Western Alliance,* Institute of Strategic Studies no. 3 (London, 1967), 2.
3. Ibid., 4n.
4. Ibid., 4.
5. "Facing the Iron Curtain: How Good is Western Defense?" *U.S. News and World Report,* 30 December 1963, 56.
6. James, *Standardization and Common Production of Weapons in NATO,* 2, 25. For definitions, see *NATO Glossary of Military Terms and Definitions,* AAP-6D, 15 November 1963, 1-117–1-118.
7. James, *Standardization and Common Production of Weapons in NATO,* p. 4.
8. L. W. C. S. Barnes, "The NATO Small-Arms Ammunition Panel," *NATO Letter,* November 1963, 22–24; James, *Standardization and Common Production of Weapons in NATO,* 6–7.

9. Barnes, "The NATO Small Arms Ammunition Panel," 22–24.

10. Ibid.

11. *L'Armée,* May 1964; *New York Times,* ed., 10 June 1964; *The Evening Star* (Washington), 15 June 1964, A-14 (editorial); *Le Figaro,* 19 June 1964.

12. "A Guide to U.S. Army Equipment in Operational Use or Development," *Army,* October 1967, 130–31.

13. WEU DOC 180, 25 October 1960.

14. James, *Standardization and Common Production of Weapons in NATO,* 7.

15. "Organization and Method of Work of the Army Board," Military Agency for Standardization, MAS (Army) (63) 339, 16 July 1963, 1–12; James, *Standardization and Common Production of Weapons in NATO,* 25–26.

16. See for example Enclosure I to Navy 10/5, June 1964: "Naval Fuels and Lubricants Working Party Report."

17. MAS (Army) (63) 339, 13–19.

18. Ibid., 23–27.

19. James, *Standardization and Common Production of Weapons in NATO,* 6.

20. STANAG no. 2032 (edition no. 3), 27 January 1964.

21. STANAG no. 2034, MAS (Army) (56)96, 8 August 1965.

22. STANAG no. 2035 (edition no. 2).

23. STANAG no. 2019 (edition no. 2).

24. STANAG no. 2818 (draft), MAS (Army).

25. STANAG no. 2012, MAS (Army) (63)2, 12 February 1963.

26. STANAG no. 2024, MAS (Army) (62)402, August 1962.

27. STANAG no. 2274, MAS (Army) (62)536, 15 October 1962.

28. No. 3437 and Annex A, MAS (Air) (64)195, 16 June 1964.

29. Navy/0/5, 6 July 1964; Annex A to Terms of Agreement of STANAG 1135, 11 August 1964.

30. STANAG no. 2064, MAS (Army) (58)138, 22 September 1958.

31. STANAG no. 2087, MAS (Army) (63)175, 15 March 1963.

32. MAS (Army)(63) 339, 28–29.

33. Cf. Dominique Beretty, "AIRCENT—Seven Nations, One Command," *NATO Letter,* June 1964, 14–18.

34. Cf. George C. Dyer, *Naval Logistics* (Annapolis, Md.: U.S. Naval Institute, 1960), 260.

11
Transportation

In any situation involving the support of conventional war operations, the critical factor of logistic limitation will probably be some aspect of transportation. Therefore, Allied coordination of transportation is likely to be the key to the coordination of Allied logistics generally. Moreover, the direction of transportation is bound to carry with it a measure of direction over supply as well. If NATO, then, were to be an effective instrument of Allied planning and possible action for collective self defense, the coordination of transportation was an area demanding a high priority of attention. To a certain extent this has been so. Very early in the history of the North Atlantic Alliance, NATO statemen and officials turned to laying plans for wartime control and coordination of transportation. The establishment and continuation of planning boards for transportation indicated, as did the Alliance itself and then the organization of Allied military headquarters, an assumption of the possible need for conventional defense—for something less than nuclear retaliation, whatever the threat, and something more than nothing, whatever the provocation[1]—in a word, the steps taken for Allied transportation planning already implied a posture that, a decade later, would be rediscovered as a "strategy of flexible response."

Ocean Shipping

Hardly more than a year after the signing of the North Atlantic Treaty, and more than a year and a half before the organization of SHAPE, the North Atlantic Council in May 1950 established the Planning Board for Ocean Shipping (PBOS), with the first meeting to be held in June in London. In succeeding meetings in Washington and London during the next year, the board agreed upon procedures for forming a pool of Allied shipping in the event of a war emergency.[2] The board based its plans directly upon the experience of the London-Washington shipping pool in World War II, and certainly the Allied Maritime Transport Council of World War I provided a further precedent.

During World War II the British took six months to bring their shipping under government control, but by 1942 most of the world's shipping had come under the central direction of the United States and Britain. This arrangement evolved into a common pool in which a London committee coordinated the use of shipping in the Eastern Hemisphere, while a Washington committee directed that in the Western Hemisphere and the Far East. Ultimately representatives of other Allied governments joined the committees.

Now again, the NATO representatives agreed upon a two-headed organization with an executive board having coordinating headquarters both in Washington and London, which could come into operation to control shipping immediately in case of war. Again this was based upon an assumption that control of shipping should be entrusted to an agency that itself, unlike a ministry of supply, would have no interest in shipping for purposes of its own.

Under the plan, the Planning Board for Ocean Shipping would give way to a Defense Shipping Authority, which had as its objective the organization of shipping in order "to achieve the greatest possible economy in its employment and to render it effectively and readily available to meet the needs, both military and civil, of the cooperating nations according to approved priorities."[3] Participating nations would place all ocean-going merchant ships flying their flags in the common pool for allocation by the Defense Shipping Authority. Financial arrangements between governments and shipowners would be the domestic concern of each government, but would be such that owners would have no direct financial interest in the use to which their ships happened to be allocated. All participating governments would have the right to be represented both in the London and the Washington branches.

The planned wartime organization would coordinate shipping both for sustaining the civil needs of the several nations and for supporting direct military operations. Competing requirements between those two categories made it clear in the view of the planners that neither a civil agency of the government responsible for the former nor a military agency interested primarily in the latter would be satisfactory. Instead, the Defense Shipping Authority should be an independent international agency, functioning directly under NATO and should be charged with satisfying needs in both categories because support for both would be essential for the common defense effort.

Two committees organized under the Planning Board would continue to make studies in their particular spheres. One was the Shipping Availabilities Committee, while the other was the Civil Demands Committee. Presumably SACEUR and SACLANT would develop the military requirements for merchant shipping.

In the two decades after the Planning Board for Ocean Shipping was set up, it continued its detailed planning for a war emergency situation, and the basic assumptions under which it was organized remained essentially unchanged—mainly because the board was based foremost upon an assumption of nonnuclear general war in Europe. For a number of years it may have appeared that the PBOS was completely out of tune with strategic plans of the military authorities. Many insisted that plans for ocean shipping were based upon the very least likely contingency, for the idea of a nonnuclear general war in Europe seemed out of the question. At any rate, the shipping planners held to planning for the one contingency in which their work would be essential for the security of the nations that they represented, and over the years they worked diligently to perfect those plans. In the mid-1960s, the board included representatives from all NATO nations except Iceland and Luxembourg, with observers from SACLANT, SACEUR, AFCENT, and other major subordinate military commands. During this period, items on its agenda included the discussion of questions bound to pose problems in a war situation. In considering the question of war losses of merchant shipping, members of the board discussed the matter of war risk insurance and proposals for international pooling of risks that might be called for under circumstances where the ships of one nation happened to be sent into war zones more frequently than those of another. They discussed the matter of cooperating with naval authorities so that plans for merchant shipping would complement those for naval operations. Similarly they cooperated closely with the Military Agency for Standardization in projects for standardizing equipment and procedures to make more efficient the use of shipping in serving all the participating nations, and they were anxious to make sure that merchant shipping plans conformed to planning in other areas—particularly in supply. In its annual work the board, while mindful that, as in all other areas of logistics, "civil emergency planning is a *national* responsibility," maintained a close interest in the national planning of each NATO nation and made an annual review of national progress. Toward the perfecting of its own organization, the board convened a working group in London to develop procedures for activating the executive board of the Defense Shipping Authority. Other matters discussed during this period included the problem of oil bunkering for ships and the question of warning ships about fallout in the event of nuclear attack. Finally the board considered the reports of exercises conducted to test the effectiveness of the organization.

The importance, or even the desirability, of such planning for the wartime pooling of Allied shipping as PBOS had been able to accomplish was subject to continuing differences of opinion. Some experienced shipping men— including some of those directly involved in the planning—harbored serious reservations about the value of such definitive plans as PBOS had attempted. According to this view it was too difficult to envisage the conditions under which a future war might be fought for such plans to be effective. The prospect of nuclear attack in any all-out war, it was held, would render much of this planning useless. On the other hand, for anything less than an all-out effort, it would not be needed. Normal national procedures would be sufficient, it was said, for a limited-war situation.

Others held that the PBOS plans were very desirable. Admittedly they were based upon World War II experience, but that very experience had revealed the desirability of prior planning for ocean shipping. Then it had taken a considerable time to develop an effective system. Now the thought was that there would be a great advantage in having an organization ready to function at the outbreak of a war emergency.

In World War II the Allied shipping situation never was altogether satisfactory until 1945 in meeting either military or essential civilian requirements. And this situation was not attributable only to direct enemy action. Such factors as congestion at ports, slow handling of cargo, the holding of ships by theater commanders as floating warehouses, and the convoy system all contributed to the shortage of shipping.[4]

In a way, an assumption of nonnuclear general war in Europe, however improbable, underlay NATO itself and its military commands. Whether as deterrence against conventional attack or preparation for defense against an actual attack, the posture had to be essentially the same. If credible deterrence depended upon availability and disposition of forces and an apparent ability and willingness to use them, not the least part of that stance had to be an apparent ability and willingness to support the forces. Surely it could not be assumed that large-scale conventional war was any more out of the question than any other kind of war, and if that were the only kind of war for which a wartime shipping pool would be needed and effective, that was no less reason for planning for it.

European Inland Surface Transport

As stated earlier, in any given war requiring long-term logistic support, transportation is likely to be the limiting factor of that support. Within the transportation chain itself, the weakest links are likely to be in the capacities of the ports and local transportation at the destination in any major operation depending upon oversea supplies. At least that was the story of Allied oversea support in World War II and in the Korean War. The effectiveness of NATO logistics is likely to be measured in the ability of European ports and beaches to clear incoming ships, and in the ability of local transportation to move supplies out of the port and beach areas.

Probably no other aspect of NATO logistics was the subject of such thorough going planning as that concerned with European inland surface transport. The approach was similar to that for ocean shipping. In this case, as noted previously the organizing body was the Planning Board for European Inland Surface Transport (PBEIST). The two major committees under the board, the Central Europe Committee and the Southern Europe Committee, developed detailed plans through working groups for ports and beaches, railways, highways, inland waterways, and, for the Central Europe Committee, a working group for the movement of petroleum products. In addition there was a Northern Europe Committee with a much less structured organization where planning was in the hands of planning boards for Denmark and Norway, rather than in functional working groups.

Again, as for ocean shipping, the plans entailed blueprints for a wartime organization that, as operational agencies, would supersede the Planning Board's committees. In central Europe the Authority for the Coordination of Inland Transportation in Central Europe (ACITCE) would take over the coordinating function, while in the south the corresponding agency would be the Authority for the Coordination of Inland Transportation in Southern Europe (ACTISUD). No comparable organization was foreseen for northern Europe, though its essential role would be filled by the North Europe Transshipment Organization (NETSO), set up by Norway, Denmark, and Germany with representation for both civil and military transport interests.

For several years the Planning Board for European Inland Transport held plenary sessions twice a year. Between these sessions, a steering group carried on the work of the board in coordinating the work of the regional groups. In the magnitude and completeness of its plans, PBEIST soon gained a reputation for being one of the most prolific of the NATO agencies. Its planned wartime machinery included the nomination of persons to fill certain key positions, and it made careful analyses of anticipated wartime requirements. Planning was probably most complete in railway transportation. In wartime a Central European Wagon Pool (CEWP) would come under the operational direction of ACTICE, for instance. Again, in cooperation with the Military Agency for Standardization, steps were taken for uniformity of shipping documents, the development of a uniform weight and dimension card for motor vehicles, and a standard travel order for individual travel across international boundaries.

Among studies completed in one recent year by PBEIST was a consideration of problems relating to evacuation of the Rhine River, a study on the use of prefabricated sectional bridges both for railways and highways, and a review of a series of exercises in which the planned wartime machinery was tested. Further, the board encouraged bilateral negotiations between nations directly concerned for emergency use of port facilities and the clearing of port areas.

Some knowledgeable people said that PBEIST had gone as far as it could—that its planning had been so complete that there was nothing more for it to do apart from keeping up with changes. And once again some questioned whether all this effort in making very detailed plans for an unknown situation in the future could be worthwhile.

Others, however, emphasized the value of planning such as PBEIST was able to accomplish.[5] In a sense it was this planning as much as anything else that gave meaning to the military planning of SHAPE and its subordinate commands, since the limiting factor on military movements is likely to be transport capacity, and careful planning could extend the limits of that capacity. The Planning Board for European Inland Surface Transport maintained close liaison with SHAPE, and its regional committees worked closely with the respective subordinate military commands. The logistics staffs in those headquarters were quick to pay tribute to the planning of

PBEIST and to acknowledge how much their own plans for logistic support depended upon that planning and upon effective operation of a coordinated system in time of emergency.

The NATO Pipeline System

In the conduct of modern war no category of supply, after ammunition, looms greater in bulk or importance than petroleum products—POL (petrol, oil, and lubricants)—and for the peacetime support of military forces in their training and maneuvers, POL becomes most important. It was the largest supply item for the U.S. Army's Communications Zone in Europe throughout the post-World War II period. This being the case, and transportation being a key element in logistics as a whole, the transportation of POL must always be a matter of major concern for any defense organization.[6]

In Europe, railways, highways, and waterways all provide important means for transporting motor fuels, but by far the most efficient means is a pipeline system whenever available. The U.S. Army Petroleum Distribution Command there found that fuel could be transported by pipeline at one-twelfth the cost of transporting it by rail, and one-third the cost by water. It estimated that the use of pipelines in Central Europe in the early 1960s was saving the United States $2 million a year in storage and transportation costs.[7]

The building of the NATO pipeline system as a major part of the common infrastructure program already has been related.[8] As far as plans and operations were concerned, the pipeline agencies sharply contrasted to those related to ocean shipping and inland surface transport. Whereas the activities of boards and committees in those areas were confined almost altogether to planning, the pipeline organizations had to be concerned with current operations as well as with planning for wartime contingencies.

As will be recalled, the NATO Infrastructure pipeline project had resulted in the construction of pipelines organized in several individual systems within broad regional groupings corresponding to the regional military commands. The Northern Region included small independent systems in Denmark and Norway. In the Southern Region were separate systems in Italy, Greece, and Turkey, of which the last was of considerable size. The Central Region, in contrast with the others, comprised a very extensive, complex, integrated system covering the territory of five nations (France, West Germany, Belgium, the Netherlands, and Luxembourg). A NATO Pipeline Committee acted on behalf of the North Atlantic Council in maintaining liaison with the military authorities for supervising the operation and maintenance of the system as a whole. User nations or host nations had primary responsibility, but SACEUR had a special supervisory function, since the system existed for the support of allied military forces. The subordinate commands acted for SACEUR in their respective regions.[9]

Central European Pipeline Systems

Operating on the territory of five nations and serving the forces of eight (those of Canada, the United Kingdom, and the United States, in addition to those of the host nations), the Central European Pipeline System was an example par excellence of NATO logistics in operation. Its organization was the first of its kind in the NATO structure.

The system, highly interconnected and integrated so that products could be sent by different routings to avoid breaks in the lines or local congestion, connected points on the Mediterranean, the Atlantic, and Channel coasts of France, North Sea ports in the Low Countries and Germany with military areas in Germany and at intervening points. The main West–East line began with twenty-inch pipe at LeHavre and ran northeast to Cambrai, eastward to Aachen, and thence on to various points in Germany. An eight-inch line ran from a huge terminal and tank farm near Dunkerque to Chalôns-sur-Marne, and then southeast to Chaumont, where it connected with the main line running north from Lavera, in the Marseilles area, up the Rhone valley to Lyons, thence to Strasbourg and to Oldenburg in southwestern Germany. Other main lines connected to the system from Zeebrugge and The Hague. In addition, the pipeline that the United States built from Donges to Metz and thence to Zweibrücken and Huttenheim for support of its own forces was intended to be incorporated into the NATO system in time of war.[10] It was likely that the French LeHavre–Paris line might be incorporated for emergencies as well.

The Central Europe Operating Agency, with headquarters at Versailles, was responsible for the overall operation and provided technical and operating centralization for the system. It was charged with general planning for movement and storage and for the general accounting for equipment and spare parts of all kinds, as well as for funds and products. In carrying out its duties the Operating Agency was responsible to two masters: the Central Europe Pipeline Policy Committee (CEPPC) and the Central Europe Pipeline Office (CEPO). The former, made up of civilian government officials from each of the eight user nations, developed general policies relating to finance, petroleum traffic, distribution and tariffs, relation of pipeline activities to other transportation systems, and so forth. The Central Europe Pipeline Office brought together officers representing Allied Command Central Europe and those representing the nations whose forces were being supported. This committee developed policy relating to operation and maintenance.[11] the two supervisory groups, of course, had to work in close liaison. They held joint meetings from time to time and they shared in the selection of a general manager for the Operating Agency.

While the Central Europe Operating Agency planned and controlled centrally the movement of fuel, the seven divisions (each manned by local nationals) into which the system was divided were responsible for day-to-day operations. Of the seven divisions, three were French—and France further emphasized its national character by organizing a French national agency to supervise their activities; two were German, and a head office in Germany exercised a degree of supervision there. Single divisions operated in Belgium and the Netherlands. (Lines running through Luxembourg came under one of the French divisions.)

Each of the divisions maintained close contact by teleprinter with the Central Europe Operating Agency, with its neighboring divisions, and with every pump and filling station in its area. The agency could pass an order down to any operator within minutes. It kept up-to-date reports of the status of fuel in each of the countries or commands served, and it was in frequent communication with the military headquarters at Brunssum, Holland.

One of the most perplexing questions of current pipeline operations had to do with civilian use of the system. The matter came up in 1959 and 1960. Some NATO officials urged that the system be made available for commercial use for two reasons: (1) to earn revenue to reduce the operating deficit, and (2) to gain experience in operations and improve technical efficiency. At the same time this might be a practical way of demonstrating the peacetime effectiveness of NATO. On the other side was the argument that reliance by certain companies on the NATO system might lead to their becoming dependent and to cutting back on railway tankers and barges, all of which would be needed in wartime. However, the pipeline could provide only a small fraction of needed commercial capacity, while it never would be used to capacity for military purposes in peacetime. Moreover, civilian demand would be less than might have been expected, because, designed for military support, it avoided the commercial centers where civilian demand would be greatest.

In 1959 the North Atlantic Council adopted the principle that, under proper safeguards for the primacy of military requirements, civilian use might be allowed. It was decided to permit two alternative procedures, always providing for military priority in time of emergency. Under the first, CEPO would continue to control the lines and companies would be charged stated fees for using the system. Contrary to military agencies, private companies sometimes had objections to having their products lose identity in the system. Under the second procedure, a given section of line would be leased for a given time and under agreed conditions to an outside body—a governmental agency of the host country or even a private company. The leasing agency then would be responsible, except in emergency, for operating the sector for military as well as commercial use. The French insisted strongly on the latter arrangement. In particular they were anxious for the French national agency to lease and operate the Rhone valley line.[12]

Commercialization of the Central Europe system handicapped military control to some extent since regulations to cover the agencies brought other operations under the same rules. The general manager thus found his freedom of action restricted, and political considerations became more prominent in the undertaking. Nevertheless the system did operate very efficiently. Indeed, one authority wrote, "As a military supply line—for which it was designed—this NATO system is one of the best logistic support systems for fuels ever constructed."[13]

Independent Systems

As mentioned above, the NATO pipelines in Norway, Denmark, Italy, Greece, and Turkey operated essentially as national units without the complex integration that characterized the Central Europe system. The largest of these, the Turkish, actually consisted of two systems or divisions. One of these was in the western part of the country, running northward from the Mediterranean with a spur to the east. The other covered the eastern section of the country.

The question of civilian use seldom arose with respect to the independent lines of the northern and southern regions. Running across sparsely settled regions, paticularly in a country like Turkey, these lines could contribute little to the more populous regions, which were far from the areas of defense installations and frontier outposts. The United States made some use of the Turkish lines, but ordinarily in peacetime the only users were the Turks themselves. For this the Turkish government had to bear almost the entire cost of operation and maintenance.[14]

Although pipeline operations generally went smoothly and satisfactorily, a number of problems persisted. These difficulties related to such matters as security against sabotage or attack, fire protection, insurance, damage claims, equipment, spare parts, maintenance (especially in Italy and Turkey), and funding, including the question of civilian use.

Air Transportation

Planning and organization for air transportation on a cooperative basis were much less advanced than for the other forms of transportation. A Civil Aviation Planning Committee (CAPC) was responsible for the planning for a wartime Board for the Coordination of Civil Aircraft (BOCCA). But nations that had been willing to agree to the pooling of ocean shipping and of railway cars in wartime were not willing to accept the pooling of commercial aircraft. Persistence of this attitude left BOCCA at best as an agency for coordinating requests and then for seeking from the countries individually some allotment of airlift as required.

A second kind of study being carried on by the Civil Aviation Planning Committee was for the evacuation of civil aircraft in case of emergency. These studies generally assumed flight from east to west, and they were made in cooperation with the military authorities in Europe and North America. Surely such cooperation in studies for flights from west to east, and for reinforcement as well as for evacuation, should have been in order.

One of the most serious potential weaknesses in NATO's military posture in terms of an ability to wage modern conventional warfare and an ability to respond quickly to a critical situation was a lack of the air transport that would permit rapid moves to isolated places.[15]

A serious drawback to any significant reliance upon air transportation for the buildup of a tactical force was the inability of available aircraft to lift heavy equipment. Something could always be said for a policy of prepositioning supplies and equipment and then simply flying the men to those sites if the situation required it. However, such a policy was expensive—though not as costly as airlifting of equipment—and lacked flexibility.

Now aircraft had been designed and built that would permit the airlift of entire divisions and their heavy equipment. The C-141, in service for the U.S. Air Force during the mid-1960s, could lift over half of the various items of equipment of an infantry division. In other words, half of the equipment of a division was air-transportable. With the aircraft previously available, it took thirty days to move a force of 41,000 men and its 34,000 tons of equipment across the Atlantic. With a full complement of 250 C-141s, that time would be reduced appreciably, but when the huge new C-5s came into service in 1968–69, that force could be moved from North America to Europe in seven days. One C-5 could carry 30 jeeps, or it could carry a 74-ton mobile bridge—the biggest single item in a U.S. infantry division.[16] In thirteen hours, forty-two of the new C-5s could have moved the 15,000 troops from the United States to Europe in Exercise Big Lift, which took 243 aircraft of other types 63 hours. This big new transport of the U.S.A.F. weighed nearly 350 tons gross. It could carry 125 tons 3,000 miles. Twelve C-5s could have handled the entire Berlin airlift, which required 300 C-54s.[17]

The availability of such aircraft brought a new dimension to logistics. These aircraft were still no match for sealift in large-scale support, but when it was possible to airlift whole divisions with all their heavy equipment, then the need for forward bases needed to be reassessed (though the need for secure bases for airlanding operations could not be overlooked). Furthermore, this raised serious questions about the number of American and other foreign troops that really needed to be stationed in Europe.

Trends and Conclusions

One of the hallmarks of modern times is the continuing revolution in transportation. Since automation was being used in scheduling and in actual operation of terminal facilities, railways, and other aspects of transportation service, NATO planning had to be kept up to date.

In the United States developments in loading and unloading of ships promised to reduce what always had been a major bottleneck in ocean shipping. With new equipment introduced in U.S. Pacific ports in the 1960s, a ten-man gang could load a ship in just two shifts, whereas a few years before, a fourteen-man gang needed twelve shifts to do the same job; six longshoremen could unload the cargo from a Liberty ship in nine days, whereas earlier it would have taken eighteen men fourteen days; and where previously it had taken six days to transfer a load of passenger cars, a ship now could discharge the automobiles and be back at sea within seven hours.[18]

The British Railways had developed a cellular container ship connected with freightliner rail services and highway transportation to move freight rapidly between points in Great Britain and on the Continent. A manufacturer in Manchester could load one of the standardized thirty-foot containers with eighteen tons of finished goods and have it delivered in Düsseldorf within thirty-six hours at twenty percent less cost than by ordinary shipping procedures. A British agent could ship out a container on a Monday afternoon through an east coast port of England to Zeebrugge and be assured of its arrival in Metz or Belfort by Tuesday morning. In addition to gaining a great deal of time, the container system reduced time and costs of packing, cut down damage, and practically eliminated pilferage.[19]

To speed up the unloading of military cargo, the U.S. Army developed a continuous circuit trainway system, and for moving cargo inland from beaches it developed an overland conveyor system. Another new kind of equipment for cross-country transportation off the beaches was the logistical cargo carrier, a car with a capacity of fifteen tons and equipped with huge tires for cross-country movement, which could be linked with other cars to form a tractor-drawn overland train needing neither tracks nor roads.

NATO planners needed to be alert to every opportunity for possible improvement in transportation resources and procedures for supporting NATO military plans and contingencies. Not only should innovations such as these be under constant consideration, but the planners themselves should take the initiative in proposing others.

As we have seen, there was a great deal of planning for the pooling of ocean shipping, and even more for the coordination of European railway transportation. However, there was less on the effective employment of airlift, little on motor transportation, and less still on coordination among various modes of transportation, including division of labor with respect to certain tasks according to needs and priorities and on continuous shipments of containerized cargo. Too much of the planning appeared to have been content to deal with what was rather than with what could or ought to have been, to rely upon what the nations could and would provide in their individual responsibilities rather than in looking to international machinery for improvement.

The question of mobility needed constant study. The use of floating warehouses and machine shops could be considered; mobile supply points with supplies kept on railway cars and highway trailers deserved more attention. Plans for the pooling of motor transport according to the plans of the Military Board of Allied Supply in the First World War should have been taken into account.

Ultimately what was needed was some kind of NATO Transport Board, a large transportation agency that could function across the board for all elements of transportation as the Allied Maritime Transport Council and Executive did for sea transport in the First World War. It would be charged not only with coordinating the planned use of existing transportation facilities, but would sponsor projects for the improvement of transportation systems and would function as a rudimentary international ministry of transport to develop the fullest possible assistance in meeting NATO.

The impact of modern transportation upon relations among nations and upon the very nature of war, as well as determination of the side of the greater advantage could hardly be calculated. Clearly transportation, just as war itself, had to be closely related to political purpose and to the political authority. Too little attention had been given in general to the political and military implications of transportation. Here it was not only a matter of technique and economics, but the broader concern of a total relationship.[20] In this way transportation was at the center of concern for the purpose and dispositions of NATO itself.

Notes

1. Cf. Henry E. Eccles, *European Logistics, 1956*. George Washington University Logistics Research Project no. ONR 41904 (Washington, D.C., 1956), 32.

2. *Lloyds Daily List*, 29 June 1950; *Journal of Commerce* (London), 29 June 1950 and 26 May 1951; Adm. Sir Michael M. Denny, "The Atlantic in a World War—What Does it Mean?" *Journal of the Royal United Services Institution* 100 (August 1956): 356.

3. Quoted in *Journal of Commerce*, 26 May 1951.

4. Denny, "The Atlantic in a World War,", 356.

5. See Frank S. Besson, Jr. "Logistics and Transportation in the Defense of Western Europe," *National Defense Transportation Journal*, 12 (March–April 1956): 55–57, 64.

6. Henry R. Westphalinger, "U.S. Army Communications Zone, Europe," *Army Information Digest*, December 1962, 13–14.

7. Ibid.

8. See chap. 8

9. "Pipelines for NATO," *The Review* 45 (September–October 1965): 106, 109.

10. James H. Winchester, "NATO's Fuel Pipelines Almost Complete," *NATO's Fifteen Nations* 7 (August–September 1962): 83; "Civilian Uses for the NATO Pipelines," *Financial Times* (London), 8 August 1963.

11. "Pipelines for NATO," 109–10.

12. "Civilian Uses for the NATO Pipelines"; Winchester, "NATO's Fuel Pipeline," 86.

13. Winchester, "NATO's Fuel Pipeline," 86.

14. Anne Sington, "NATO Pipelines in Turkey," *NATO Letter*, July–August 1965, 19, 22.

15. See "Air Transport and Cargo Facilities Within the NATO Countries," *Fifteen Nations* 6 (January 1961): 84–85.

16. *The Times* (London), 20 October 1966; *NATO Background Information Notes*, 3, December 1966, 21–22.

17. Statement of Secretary of Defense Robert S. McNamara before Committee on Armed Services and Subcommittee on Dept. of Defense Committee Appropriations, 28 February 1966, *Department of Defense Appropriations for Fiscal Year 1967, Hearings on H.R. 15941, part 1*, 89th Congress, 2d sess., 1966, 341. See also John A. Hoefling, "The Army and the C-54," *Army*, January 1968, 67–71.

18. *Time*, 27 December 1963, 19.

19. R. A. Etherington, "The Container Ship Revolution," *European Review* 7 (Summer 1967): 30–32.

20. See Roy I. Wolfe, *Transportation and Politics* (New York, 1963).

12
International Supply and Maintenance

In spite of the continuous reemphasis on the old saying "Logistics is a national responsibility," the North Atlantic Allies made impressive strides toward cooperative arrangements for wartime logistics. Some of these plans remain only for wartime implementation. Others include specific measures for common logistic support even in peacetime. A fundamental and unanswered question is whether the principle of national responsibility can or should be eroded away to the point of acceptance of a truly integrated system of international logistics. On the other hand, if that does not appear to be within reach, certain procedures and organizational structures, even if only half measures, may contribute sufficiently to military effectiveness.

In a way it may be that international logistical preparations can go far toward restoring the credibility of the Alliance. For what could be more impressive to an adversary than the common purpose exhibited by pooling economic resources for effective logistic support? This combined effort, well done, could carry more weight than all the declarations, public accords, and strategic staff planning to be found anywhere.[1]

NATO Maintenance and Supply Organization

Though only a faltering first step, the NATO Maintenance and Supply Organization represented perhaps the most far-reaching attempt so far in international logistics management.

Mission and Organization

Proposed by the U.S. delegate at a meeting of the North Atlantic Council on 21 November 1957, the NATO Maintenance Supply Services System (as it was then called) was approved by the council the following April.[2] Apparently the leaders of the American Department of Defense hoped that a common NATO system for the acquisition and distribution of spare parts for certain major weapons might result in a reduction of U.S. military expenditures in Europe and at the same time might ease the burden of such expenditures on the part of the European Allies.[3]

In its resolution of approval, the council gave the purpose of the new organization in these terms:

In order to make the best use of NATO resources and to sustain the common defense, the nations recognize the need to solve the logistics problems connected with maintaining military equipment in operational condition, which requires adequate availability of spare parts needed for maintenance and overhaul.

In view of the fact that a fully satisfactory solution to these logistics problems so far has not been achieved by all individual nations, and of the fact that several countries operate the same type of equipment, it is considered that an effective solution has to be sought in the establishment of a common NATO Maintenance Supply Services System. Such a System would carry out the functions of management that are most difficult for individual countries and that promise substantial savings to the member countries.

To achieve the objective of maintaining the effectiveness of military forces at minimum cost, such a System should operate through an Agency working under multi-national control. It should assume such maintenance spares supply functions as are considered most suitable for efficient operation on a collective basis.

The mission was further defined in the charter as facilitating "the supply of maintenance materials among NATO nations with the objective of maximizing the effectiveness of logistic support to NATO armed forces and minimizing the cost to NATO nations individually and collectively." To carry out this goal the organization would have important functions in supply management, maintenance management, procurement, and technical assistance.[4]

The impression is that the North Atlantic Council did not regard the NMSS as a really essential element in the NATO defense arrangements. The council more or less set it adrift and left it to prove itself. If the Organization turned out to make certain aspects of logistic support a little more convenient or a little less expensive, then all well and good. If it failed, however, the loss presumably would not be serious. According to the charter, the NMSSS was to be an autonomous entity and a subsidiary body under the terms of the "Agreement on the Status of the North Atlantic Treaty Organization, National Representatives, and International Staff," signed at Ottawa on 20 September 1951. And the charter went on to say:

Its continued existence will depend on its ability to perform, more effectively than can individual countries, certain spare parts supply management functions. The system should be so established that it is free to operate in accordance with its charter and the logistics policy determined by the Board of Directors.

The System shall endeavour to be self-supporting as soon as practicable. All costs incurred during the initial establishment of the System shall be borne by the participating countries until a Management Fund is established. Thereafter all costs will be borne by that Fund, by means of suitable surcharges included in the prices of spare parts and services charged by the Agency.

Program objectives as worked out over the next several years followed closely the original ideas of the ad hoc working group that drafted the charter. As spelled out in 1963, these objectives in the field of supply included: (1) Planning and operation of a supply system; (2) performance of the tasks associated with and required for (a) receiving, processing, and controlling demands for, (b) computing requirements for, (c) receiving, storing, and issuing, (d) receiving and transshipping, and (e) redistributing, spare parts; (3) maintaining and improving the supply methods and procedures needed (a) to operate and control separately managed and funded support programs, (b) for processing demands for nonstocked matériel (brokerage), and (c) for common administrative support for those programs; (4) maintaining a review program to insure economic use of and to determine requirements for designated weapons or equipment; (5) provision of technical assistance to countries as required. At the same time emphasis would be given to the continued preparation of a master file of spare parts information, increasing the scope and effectiveness of annual order programs, improving the redistribution program with special attention to "cross support," maintenance of Priced Weapons Stock Lists containing listings of items approved for stockage, and stock status reporting.

Amendments to the charter in 1960 and 1962 affected the basic mission only to the extent of defining more precisely responsibility for providing maintenance support for advanced weapons in Allied Command Europe. The revised charter, adopted in 1964, recognized that the basic mission might be broadened by specific action of the board of directors and approval by the North Atlantic Council.

As Air Commodore E. J. Smith, then NAMSA director of logistics, explained in 1964, "The basic philosophy of the system is that by providing centralized maintenance and supply management, it is possible to consolidate nations' requirements, make bulk procurement, provide services, maintenance and parts more cheaply and quickly than is possible when a number of individual nations make their own arrangements, sometimes in competition with each other."[5]

All NATO members except Canada and Iceland joined the NATO Maintenance and Supply Organization. The organizational structure followed more or less closely what had become common for specialized international organizations: an assembly or general authority to which it had overall responsibility (a role in this case taken by the North Atlantic Council), a council to form general policy (in this case a board of directors) and an executive agency (here the NATO Maintenance and Supply Agency—NAMSA—with its general manager and international staff) charged with day-to-day operations, and with the direction of subordinate institutions including in NAMSO the NATO Supply Center at Chateauroux and the NATO Procurement Center at Koblenz.[6]

Made up of one member from each of the thirteen participating nations, the NAMSO board of directors was responsible for making the policy decisions and framing the directives necessary to enable the agency to carry out its mission; it provided guidance for the operations and administration of the agency; approved the organization of the agency, and approved its budget. It had a permanent chairman and secretariat and was served by two committees—a Logistics Committee and a Finance Committee—made up of experts drawn from the participating countries. Although the board was answerable directly to the North Atlantic Council, NAMSO had a special relationship with the Supreme Allied Commander, Europe. During peacetime, SHAPE, as an entity, was treated in effect as a fourteenth participating nation. The Supreme Headquarters did not have a full member on the board of directors, but SACEUR did nominate a representative who served as the board's military adviser. Thus a relationship of coordination rather than of subordination was established for the activities of NAMSO extended somewhat beyond the interests of SHAPE. However, in time of war or imminent war, SACEUR was to be prepared, when approved by the North Atlantic Council, to bring NAMSO under his direction. It then would be up to him to form the necessary operational directives for the agency. The board of directors was supposed to work with SACEUR to develop procedures for the execution of these directives.[7]

The general manager headed the NATO Maintenance and Supply Agency, the executive body of the organization with headquarters at Paris. He was responsible to the board for implementing its decisions and converting general policies into operating policies, for preparing plans for organization and operation, and for preparing budgets and financial reports for submission to the board. He had an international staff of sixty to seventy persons organized into four directorates: administration, finance, logistics, and procurement.

From this point the organizational waters became a little muddy, for relationships and responsibilities of the commandant and staff of the NATO Supply Center, described as the "principal operating arm" of NAMSO, were not always clear with respect to the general manager and his staff. Presumably the latter were supposed to be concerned with broad policy and direction, while the former executed the directives and engaged in actual supply operations. But at least for the time, the general manager and the staff of the agency appeared in some respects to be an unnecessary "layering" between the board of directors, or its committees, and the commandant and staff of the Supply Center. With reorganization of the Supply Center staff on the basis of assigning full responsibility for the support of a certain weapon system to a single "weapon system manager" or "program manager," it still was not always clear how far this responsibility extended into areas of immediate interest to the headquarters staff in Paris. To the extent that the two permanent committees organized under the board of directors dealt directly with the NATO Supply Center Commandant, the general manager's authority and responsibility for management were diluted, and the supervisory and policy-making functions of the board itself declined. On the other hand, when each element played its full role and respected carefully the channels of the chain of command (program managers—commandant—General Manager—Logistics and Finance committees—Board of Directors), there appeared to be unnecessary layering and red tape inasmuch as each higher echelon represented no broadened span of control, but simply single-unit supervision of a single unit in successive steps. Except for the Procurement Center, which began operations later and whose activities were limited, the NATO Supply Center was the only subordinate unit under the general manager.[8]

Policies and Procedures

Decisions of the NAMSO board of directors were by simple majority vote on all matters concerning the functions of supply, maintenance, procurement, and technical assistance, though it was understood that no nation could be bound without its consent by any decision requiring financial responsibility on its part. Any nation had the right to appeal any decision to the North Atlantic Council where the general rule of unanimity did prevail.

Frequently considerations of peculiar national interest animated the board's deliberations. Keen competition among countries was evident in discussions affecting choices of sources of supply and the distribution of facilities. Political factors might weigh as heavily as military in these decisions, and sometimes a compromise, necessary as it might appear to be, would result in almost hopeless complications for common military procurement and for the storage and distribution of military supplies.

Since none of the member nations used the same weapons, different groupings of nations formed according to their interest in the supply or services of the various weapons in the system. Thus policy decisions for the support of the different weapons, as well as for the financial arrangements involved, were the responsibility of separate groupings of states rather than of the total membership. In a particular case the governments concerned might choose any level of common support through NAMSO from a request that the Organization stock the comlete range of spare parts needed for the given weapon to a very limited number of parts, or to the brokerage function (purchasing agent) only. Thus the member states coming together would form what was referred to as a "Weapon System Partnership" for specifying in common the kind and means of logistic support that they wished to arrange through NAMSO for this particular weapon.

Principal sources of supply available to NAMSO included redistribution among nations in the system, repaired items, U.S. military sources, and procurement on the open market. Redistribution of stocks among the partners simplified the financial arrangements. Books were kept on debits and credits in these exchanges, and then, with procurement programs developed on the basis of requirements beyond the exchanges, procurement funds could be kept in the system without being returned to the ministries of defense for reallocation on an individual nation basis. This system operated as an informal clearing house where funds could be applied to making up common deficiencies.[9]

A number of approaches were developed in financing the various projects under NAMSO. Contributions of the United States and Germany amounting to some $40 million in matériel, cash, or credit provided the general working fund for the system. The first step in this arrangement was a loan of $25 million made in the form of a sales agreement between the United States and the agency in June 1959.[10] Special projects such as Forward Scatter and Early Warning (discussed below) were financed through SHAPE and the nations. The rockets and missiles inventory was financed mainly by the United States and Germany to the extent of some $30 million. On brokerage transactions—that is, common procurement through NAMSO—the nations paid a five percent fee. Objections were raised on the ground that the nations were not going to pay a premium for going through NAMSO, but the hope was that by pooling the requirements of several nations, lower prices might be obtained. Moreover, those favoring this arrangement suggested that a nation would probably save far more than the five percent in warehousing and other handling costs.

The operation referred to as brokerage was the processing and filling of demands placed by member nations on NAMSO for items that the Organization did not stock. What this amounted to, then, was a pooling of requirements for common procurement. Here each nation met its share of the procurement cost, plus the five percent service charge. The programs or "weapon partnerships" were arrangements by which certain member nations agreed to have supply and/or maintenance services furnished by NAMSO on a collective participation basis. In most cases these partnerships involved collective investments in spare parts inventories. Since member nations might participate in a particular program to the degree they chose, items of supply in any given program might be considered brokerage for some members while not for others who were participating in a common stocking program. In either case, a major function of NAMSO was contract administration.[11]

At the outset it was assumed that NAMSO (then NMSSS) should become the channel for a major part of U.S. military aid to NATO countries, and might in fact take over a good deal of the coordinating function of the Foreign Aid Division of U.S. European Command. In practice, however, this did not turn out to be the case.

NATO Supply Center, Chateauroux

In the beginning the NATO Maintenance Supply Services System was not intended to operate a depot. The expectation was that the agency might arrange as needed for storage of a few seldom-demanded items in certain national depots, but regular depot operations would be beyond its scope. At Chateauroux, in central France, the U.S. Air Force had been maintaining a

NATO SUPPLY CENTER ORGANIZATIONAL CHART (1963)

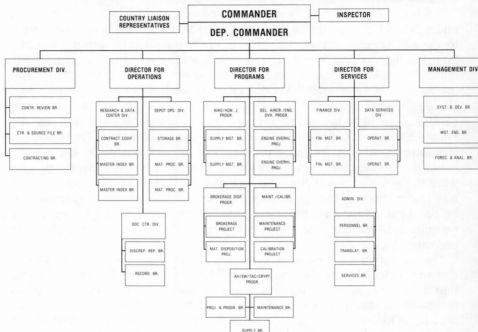

Adapted from NATO Supply Center Organizational Directory Chart 1963, Ref. NMCAP August 1963.

supply base for several years, and in September 1959 the U.S. Army established a MAP (Military Assistance Program) Inventory Control Point, Europe, as a tenant at the Air Station providing support for U.S. rocket missile systems that had been furnished NATO nations under MAP. Then American officials suggested that a NATO international depot might be established there to support certain common weapon systems. Thus began operations in January 1960 under U.S. Air Force management. To get the project underway, the United States and France agreed to advance the estimated cost of the first year's operation, estimated at $2.5 million (the French put a ceiling of $500,000 on their contribution), and the United States and Germany agreed to provide a spare parts inventory package to the amount of about $40 million, of which the German share was set initially at $12.2 million, though later this was reduced to $11.2 million. The organization remained provisional while the United States and France negotiated a new agreement on the use of the Chateauroux facilities, and a further agreement between France and NMSSA was concluded to govern the new center. This done, the depot became permanent in March 1960, though the United States entered into an agreement to retain responsibility for management until 1 July 1961. On that date the U.S. Air Force transferred full management and control of the Supply Center to NAMSSA. Still, a large share of the staff remained American. A new organization went into effect in January 1962, but only 88 out of 183 authorized spaces were filled by persons from countries other than the United States.[12]

Problems of organizing and coordinating an international staff at a time of sweeping procedural changes and inconsistency on the part of nations in using the depot proved to be almost too much for the new supply center during the first two years of its operation. Many doubted whether it could or should continue. But it managed to survive, to gain respect for effective operations in its very limited fields, and to build backlogs of valuable experience in international logistics.[13]

The mission of the NATO Supply Center, the operating arm under the NATO Maintenance Supply Services Agency of the NATO Maintenance Supply Services System, was to manage supplies of designated items of military equipment, including the calculation of combined requirements, inventory management, and distribution; procurement for combined needs; maintenance management at the depot or contractor level, and technical assistance. The center would develop backup stocks for certain items at Chateauroux, though apparently it was not expected at this time to develop central repair or overhaul shops. The supply center too would have the function, under NAMSSA's supervision, of buying, anywhere, at most advantageous prices, certain supplies to be made available to customers at cost plus five percent.[14]

The first task assigned NSC was the management of depot-level support for components and spare parts for five obsolete aircraft being furnished to certain countries by the United States under MAP. These aircraft were the RF/F-84F, F-86, T-33, C-47, and C-119. On the recommendation of the U.S. Air Force, SHAPE decided to make NSC responsible for supporting two squadrons of Fiat G-91 aircraft to be supplied to Greece and Turkey under U.S. grant aid.

As it developed, the NATO Supply Center came to resemble closely what one might expect to find in the functioning of a national logistics depot organization. It was able to perform all normal depot and supply functions, together with the procurement activities and financial accounting necessary for assessing requirements, and for acquiring, storing, maintaining, and issuing spare parts to user countries. It developed a functional type of organization by which a manager was responsible for each program within a prescribed budget, and such services as data processing, storage, transportation, and finance were centralized and provided for each manager.

Most of the senior members of the staff of NSC were officers on loan from the national military services, though a number were civilian officials. Partly to avoid embarrassing situations where a subordinate member of the staff might be senior in military rank to his supervisor or chief, all members wore civilian attire and they were addressed simply as "Mr." As long as the supply center remained in France a French officer was the commander, but division and project directors represented nearly all the nations participating in the Organization. As of 1963, for instance, the deputy commander was a German, the inspector a Belgian; the director for programs was a Belgian; the director of the procurement division an Italian; director for operations an American, and director of the management division an American. Of the other division, branch, and project heads, it happened that nine were British, six French, six American, five Belgian, five German, four Danish, four Turkish, four Greek, three Norwegian, two Italian, and one Dutch.

A change in organizational concept at NSC in 1962 brought adoption of program management in place of the previous weapon system concept. The change was less in theory—in the idea of single responsibility—than in broadening that responsibility in the funding of programs by arrangement with participating countries, building up stocks as needed, and doing whatever might be necessary within the limits of financial resources and general policy to provide the support desired. Another reorganization in 1964 eliminated the position of director for services, previously only a formality.

The duties of the NSC Procurement Division were to arrange for quality control through government inspection in the respective countries where procurement contracts were being carried out, to make price analyses and studies of contracts, and to negotiate for the free use of government-owned facilities and machine tools by the contractors. The division also negotiated termination agreements. Sometimes it sent survey teams to determine the qualifications of certain firms under contract to maintain a certain type of weapon or equipment. Program managers acted as contracting officer representatives in administering the contracts to the extent deemed desirable by the director of the Procurement Division.

All contracts, generally, were of the fixed-price type. The director of the Procurement Division was authorized to sign contracts in amounts up to $100,000 on his own responsibility, and with the approval of the general manager of NAMSO, he might sign for up to $500,000. Contracts carrying a payment higher than $500,000 required the signature of the general manager.

In the beginning it was assumed that one of the major advantages of procurement through NSC would be to consolidate the smaller requisitions submitted by individual countries into larger orders that would stimulate more competition in bidding by interesting more firms in the proposals, and that would result in more favorable prices because of the greater volume as well. But in practice this had not worked out very well. Requisitions were usually accumulated for as long as three months, but the small amount of consolidation did not justify the delay. Moreover the delay tended to bring further reductions in business and so in opportunities for consolidation. As it turned out, priority items could not wait and routine items did not pay. The fact that participating countries remained free to use or not use NSC undermined in effect the whole concept of consolidated procurement.

After a series of conferences with representatives of the participating countries in 1962, the NMSSA staff arrived at recommendations on stocking and requisitioning policy. For items to be obtained in the United States, the stock objective would be three months' supplies, which consisted of an operating level of two months and a safety level of one month. Allowing an order and shipping time of six months, this gave a stock control level of nine months. The reorder cycle was on the basis of two months, with a reorder point of seven months for items stocked in the continental United States. Annual country and bulk purchases would be replaced by quarterly or monthly buying of stocked items wherever necessary. All repair parts would be obtained from U.S. Army, Europe, or from stocks in the United States except when excess stocks were on hand in one of the countries, or when the item was being manufactured in Europe. Management of inventories would include the establishment of a conventional branch for the management of stocked items and the establishment of segregated storage for those items. Only participating members would share in the inventories and the content would change according to country consumption data, demand data as developed in NSC, and items listed by the Items Selection Committee.[15]

Responsible for receiving, storing, inspecting, and issuing property at the supply center, the Depot Operations Division developed plans for internal operations and finance, provided for periodic counting and identification of stocks, determined the need for warehouse facilities, maintained quality surveillance over its own functions, operated a facility for making boxes and other containers, directed the movement of materials into, within, and from the center, and carried out custom formalities for all deliveries to NSC. In addition, it operated a disposal storage facility for all divisions of NSC. Commercial shipping agents operated an Intransit Point at the depot under Depot Operations Supervision.

One of the most significant as well as most complicated parts of the task of the NATO Supply Center was in arranging for maintenance—i.e., for the servicing to keep in operational condition, repairing, and modification of designated items of equipment, and in the supply of spare parts for these purposes. Indeed the major emphasis from the beginning had been upon this function. A particularly important part of maintenance was carrying out modification work orders. These orders represented changes in the design of an item of equipment for the purpose of overcoming a weakness or improving the performance of the equipment, or in order to facilitate its production. In either case it was desirable to alter earlier models in the hands of troops so that they would conform in design to the newer models in which changes had been incorporated. In the case of the five old aircraft and the F-100 aircraft, the U.S. Air Force prepared what were called "Class IV Modification Kits" for making certain improvements on aircraft, engines, or aircraft ground equipment that would assure greater flight safety or for the urgent correction of deficiencies noted in use of the equipment. Previously the United States had furnished these kits under its grant aid program to countries sharing in the Mutual Assistance Program, but since a number of countries now were no longer to receive U.S. grant aid, they turned to NMSSA to assist them in obtaining the kits.[16]

Whenever a major weapon or other item of equipment had to be repaired or rebuilt or modified, the unit had to use another item if it were to remain fully operational. In order to meet this need, NSC developed a maintenance float. Up to mid-1964 it had been possible to stock about half of the planned goal of 375 end items representing 55 different line items of equipment in the maintenance float. These items had a value of about $11 million.

In addition to the depot at Chateauroux, two other distribution points served the maintenance float system. One was at Merchernich Eifel in Germany, and the other at Vigodarzere in Italy. Whenever one of the included items was to be repaired, the country leased an extra one from a distribution point and then returned it when the repairs had been completed. If the item were to be rebuilt, the distribution center made a direct exchange with the country of a previously rebuilt model. The country paid the cost of rebuilding and transportation, but in this case there was no rental fee.

Always a problem for any major supply system was the matter of item identification and recording. All phases were affected—procurement, storage, distribution, maintenance. As supply officers said, "If you can't identify it, you have lost it." Each country had set up a codification bureau to coordinate the supply and identification of common items among its own land, sea, and air forces. When it came to coordination among fifteen nations, the problem became that much more complex. In the interest of economy and mutual use, standardization, as noted previously, was highly desirable. But efficiency demanded standardization of identification no less than of the equipment itself. Since 1961 codification was a major task of the NSC Research and Data Center. Actually the NATO codification system was developed by the Panel on Codification of Equipment established by the North Atlantic Council in 1957.[17] The Military Agency for Standardization had prepared the groundwork in two standardization agreements (STANAG 3150 covering classification and STANAG 3151 covering identification) that the countries ratified in 1956. In this action the countries adopted the Federal Catalog, which the United States had been developing over an eight-year period. Countries generally used the Federal Catalog System in identifying their own equipment; it was essential for equipment used by two or more countries. Under the NATO system, each item of supply was assigned a uniform classification, a single thirteen-digit stock number.

The NATO codification system provided a uniform identification language among nations as well as among the different armed services. It gave to the inventory manager a means for standardizing and simplifying his procurement, storage, and distribution procedures. He could determine quickly who used an item and who made it, and could thus contribute effectively to cross-servicing. Further, the standardization of identification contributed also to the standardization of equipment itself, for it revealed duplication, the variety of items used for the same or similar purposes, and where different kinds of similar items were being produced. The codification system simplified procurement by helping to eliminate the buying and selling at the same time of the same types of equipment; it facilitated interchange among nations and services, contributed to a reduction in record keeping and storage space, facilitated requirements determination and budgeting, lead to improvement in operations for disposal of excess or surplus property, and contributed to better relations between governments and manufacturers.

Along with its work in codification, the NATO Research and Data Center maintained a Master Index, which made available to nations as well as to program managers and others original identifications, alternatives, and substitutes for all items handled by NSC. Even historical data that had become obsolete and deleted from national catalogs were retained here for cross-reference. From the Master Index the Research and Data Center assisted the depot with identification of items in the depot inventory, compiled project catalogs, constructed "buyers' guides," and edited and amended manufacturers' catalogs.

Each participating county generally maintained liaison officers at Chateauroux to follow through on requisitions, to accept deliveries for shipment to their country, and to assist in coordination. The importance of their role depended to a great degree on the extent to which their country made use of NSC. Norway, for example, preferred to receive its U.S. Military Assistance Program shipments directly from the United States—a more simple and rapid procedure. Germany, on the other hand, preferred to make the greatest possible use of NSC. The Germans found it quicker to go through NSC even for MAP equipment, for when they forwarded their requests to the United States, they had to go first to the machine records center at Mainz, then to the U.S. Depot at Kaiserslautern, then to U.S. Communications zone headquarters (Orleans through 1966), and then to the United States. They found it just as quick to make requisitions on NSC, which then checked on U.S. sources in Europe, and then if necessary, sent directly to the United States. The German air force liaison officer in the period 1963–64 was handling about 500 items a month in following up requisitions and shipments.

As indicated earlier, the NATO Supply Center was intended to be financially self-supporting. The Finance Division operated a commercial-type accounting system subject to audit by the NATO Board of Auditors. Each program manager was said to be "in business by himself." He built his own budget, and then the Finance Division served as his "professional accounting firm." However, he did not operate under a fully developed management fund concept, as did various agencies within the U.S. supply system, and he had no authority, for example, to obtain loans with which to obtain better prices for early payment of purchased items.

The inventory budget was rebuilt by sales, though some funds were needed for spare parts and transportation. The administrative or operational budget included all expenses for the pay of personnel, utilities, maintenance of facilities, and handling of supplies. So long as the U.S. Air Force maintained a base adjacent to the NATO Supply Center, the latter was able to have the use of its buildings rent-free. NSC paid the maintenance cost based upon the ratio of the space that it occupied to the total. Similarly, utilities were shared on a pro rata basis. The center maintained its own trucks and operating equipment. Income to meet these expenses was mainly from the five percent surcharge.

NSC financial statements were given in terms of French francs, though contracts were drawn in dollars and bills to customer nations for materials and services were given in dollars. However, the surcharge was expressed in francs, and administrative costs were payable in francs. Under the administrative budget for 1964, estimated expenditures were F. 26.621.000—an increase of 2.855.600 over the previous year owing to increases in pay and additions to the staff. Cost of "old work" left over from previous years was given as 1.752.000 francs that, with twenty-five percent added as the proportionate share of overhead, made 2.200.000 francs for "old work." Estimated income included F. 18.500.000 from surcharges on sales, 100.000 francs from surcharges on services, 4.800.000 francs as reimbursement for services from SHAPE, and miscellaneous income of 500.000 francs. Profits of 2.200.000 francs from previous years would be applied to finance "old work," but this still left a deficit of 500.000 francs. However, it could be made up from the sale of items on hand no longer authorized to be carried in stock.[18]

Dependence of NSC on the surcharge led to pressure for it to deal in those items which would be most profitable. If it were to have a healthy future, NSC would have to rid itself of the support of obsolete equipment and concentrate on new items for which there would be a demand for parts far into the future. This would not necessarily insure the kind of service most needed at the moment, but it was an inevitable consequence of the policy that required the NATO Supply Center to be self-supporting.

Major Programs

As suggested earlier, the logistic support activities of the NATO Supply Center were organized around several programs, each of which was under the direction of a program manager. Each program in turn might include several projects—a single weapon or piece of equipment being supported, or a specific activity. A rockets and missiles program supported the NIKE (including AJAX and HERCULES), HONEST JOHN, and SIDEWINDER; there was a program for the support of selected aircraft and for the overhaul of jet engines; an electronics program supported the ACE High communications system, the Early Warning System, tactical aircraft beacons (TACAN), and cryptographic machines; there was a program for the calibration of test equipment and for general maintenance service outside other programs, and finally there was a program for brokerage service and disposal of excess and surplus property.

The system worked out by the NATO Supply Center for the support of rockets and missiles set the pattern in a way for all such operations. The program manager was responsible for stock control, including the monitoring of all incoming demands, and for inventory management together with the management of the system of selected assets and the reporting of consumption data. These same responsibilities extended to the maintenance float for rockets and missiles. Further, the manager maintained direct liaison with the customers, and he was responsible for redistribution and cross-servicing, and for the designation of obsolete and excess items in the inventory. Among his many duties he assisted in estimates of depot level maintenance requirements as requested by the member countries and provided technical assistance for them.

The NIKE/HONEST JOHN/SIDEWINDER program manager received direct distribution of all U.S. Department of the Army modification work orders pertaining to those systems. If a modification work order was extensive or complicated, an analysis of it was published in the NSC technical bulletin to assist the countries and the military assistance advisory group or mission and the country in determining the number of modification kits required. The country consolidated its requisitions for modification kits and parts and submitted them, either directly or through the U.S. Military Assistance Advisory Group, to the NATO Supply Center. At NSC the requisitions were edited and screened to make sure that the given modification work order was applicable, and that nomenclature, quantities, and serial numbers were correct. The requisitions then were forwarded to the United States to be filled, and the kits were shipped to NSC for distribution to the countries.[19]

One of the main projects of the rockets and missiles program was the rebuilding of those weapons and their associated ground guidance equipment. The Procurement Division had to locate a suitable source for making the repairs, but it was up to the rockets and missiles program manager in the first place to determine the requirements, on the basis of country requests and experience, and then to maintain contact between the repair facility and the country on operational and technical matters. Country requests might be unprogrammed—that is, they would have to be considered as unforseeable and requiring urgent processing, or they might be foreseen and programmed. All requirements from the various countries were consolidated to the extent possible and processed as a single NATO requirement to the repair facility. As the program just was well established about 1961, most participating countries were coming to NSC with calls for repairs of NIKE-AJAX and NIKE-HERCULES missiles and ground equipment amounting to about $35,000 per year. At that time those items had to be sent to a U.S. ordnance depot for repair or rebuilding, since no European repair source was readily available. NIKE-AJAX bodies, which had to be rebuilt after a two-year fueling period, were sent to the Letterenny Ordnance Depot in the United States, had 154 missiles being rebuilt at one time. The long shipping time and high prices made it desirable to find a repair facility in Europe. In 1962 an initial two-year agreement was signed with a firm in Coventry, England, for all fifth-echelon rebuilding of NIKE-AJAX bodies. Thanks to the development of support for the SHAPE communication system, two year later a rebuild facility was ready in Europe for the radar, director stations, battery and radar control stations making up NIKE ground guidance and control equipment.

Supply policy at NSC for rockets and missiles parts was established in 1962 at two months' operating level, and four months' order and shipping time for items stocked in continental United States. An additional allowance for lead time of two to twenty-four months was necessary for items that would have to be obtained commercially. The status of stock then in NSC was, for items belonging to the NIKE system, 5,600 on hand of an established level of 10,200, and for the HONEST JOHN system, 600 peculiar items on hand of an established level of 1,300. Established levels were based on demand history, covering all requisitions of all countries for the preceding twenty-four months. This appeared to provide a more accurate basis than NSC issue experience because so many items had been issued under substitute stock numbers that it was difficult to determine what the equivalent issues really had been for a given item. At the same time, it was necessary, regardless of demand experience, to keep certain items on hand as "insurance." Nonoperational states reports, required twice each month, and studies of order and shipping time provided the basis for stocking these items.

Expansion of the rebuild program added significantly to the number of line items and the number of requisitions that could be processed. From 1963 to 1964 rebuild demands estimated at 10,000 a year, together with direct exchanges for recoverable repair parts, raised the annual demand count from about 40,800 in 1963 to about 51,000 in 1964. Lack of personnel still made it necessary for the NIKE/HONEST JOHN program manager to set aside any effective control of in-storage modification and maintenance, as well as control of modifications and records of items in the maintenance float, yet he was being given the additional task of advising the governments of participating countries, as they requested, in evaluating their equipment rebuild requirements.

Responsibilities of the manager of the Selected Aircraft/Engine Overhaul program were very similar to those of the manager of the NIKE/HONEST JOHN/SIDEWINDER program. At first the responsibilities of NSC for the support of five obsolete U.S. type aircraft—the RF/F-84F, F-86, T-33, C-47, and C-119—were supposed to be limited to the redistribution of spare parts among participating countries. However, the program never gained any real impetus, mainly because of U.S. restrictions on the transfer of grant-aid matériel. Later, the scope of this program was extended to include receiving and placing country-funded orders for spare parts, which was essentially a brokerage operation. Then the United States and Germany furnished an inventory advance amounting to nearly $40 million. Specific listings of items were to be developed and approved, and then items would be procured and stored for common use. But as it turned out, very few items were preselected, no specific listings were developed for approval of the countries, and commitments for participation and such stock levels as were established were based simply on frequency of demand, regardless of what the end-item application of the spares might be. Later, with the benefit of consultations with member countries, NSC clarified the stockage objectives for these aircraft with the development of a list of 126 specifically chosen, high-value, insurance-type items to be held in common stock for use by selected groups of nations, depending upon the type of aircraft involved. The addition of the F-100 brought to six the number of aircraft being supported under this program.[20]

Several factors contributed to difficulties of supply in the aircraft project: (1) the aircraft, already obsolete, were no longer in production when NSC assumed responsibility for them; (2) inventories in U.S. Air Force depots were running low and were not being replenished; (3) no reliable consumption data were at hand; (4) even if they were, it would have been of little use because of the great variation in the use that countries made of NSC—some would place requisitions for parts covering requirements for two or three years, while others would requisition only as needed; and (5) the limits of NSC's commitments were not well defined.

Maintenance of an inventory for rockets and missiles was easier than for obsolete aircraft, because such an inventory had existed when NSC began operations, there was only one source of supply (i.e., the United States), and the weapons were in large-scale use in the U.S. forces.

Now a major question was whether the F-104G jointly produced in Europe and supported by a weapon system partnership, should be added to the NSC aircraft program for the supply of spare parts. Finally the decision was to support the F-104G under NAMSO, but for this program a special procurement office, the Koblenz Procurement Center (KPC) had been established at Koblenz, Germany, for the coordinated procurement of parts.[21] Earlier the G-91, the first NATO-sponsored aircraft, was brought into the program.

The engine overhaul project, administered as a part of the same program, included two major goals: supplying spare parts to four centralized jet engine overhaul facilities, and receiving orders from the countries for jet engine overhaul and placing these orders on the facilities.[22] Again it was difficult to anticipate the extent to which the various countries would make use of this program. Particularly disturbing was an indication of intent by the U.S. Air Force to obtain spare parts for overhaul of 900 J-57 engines through NSC over a two-year period, fiscal years 1963 and 1964, and to arrange through NMSSA for overhaul service as well, only to have the whole arrangement canceled. In this case it was estimated that the spare parts would amount to about $20,000 for each engine and the cost of each overhaul would be about $4,500. In other words the NSC program manager and other officials saw a prospective $20 million of business vanish, at least for the time being.

The electronics program—that is, the one comprising ACE High, Early Warning, cryptographic machines, and tactical air beacons—was different from the others since it was created for and financed by SHAPE. The supply center maintained liaison officers with SHAPE and with the host countries for these projects.

Planning for support through NMSSS of the ACE High system, including Forward Scatter, Hot Line, and Latina School began in 1958, two years before NSC had been established at Chateauroux. Then it became the policy to support the system by direct supply through NSC. Capital funds for construction of the communications facilities, it will be recalled, had been obtained as a part of the Infrastructure program.[23] Now operational funds were budgeted by SHAPE as a part of military headquarters funds. The NSC prepared the annual budget for logistic support and forwarded it through NMSO and SHAPE to the Military Budget Committee. Representatives from NSC appeared before this committee to justify the budget requests. The budget estimates had to include allowances for spare parts, transportation, and for third- and fourth-echelon maintenance service.[24]

The preparation of these estimates was no easy task. Installations had to be supported in seven different countries. Plans for transportation of parts and components to isolated stations had to anticipate the use of all kinds of transportation, from ski lifts in Norway to camels in Turkey. There was no experience upon which to base requirements for parts, and customs regulations slowed movement of parts across national boundaries. These factors, together with taxes and various local regulations, added to the burden of paperwork. Mobile maintenance teams were organized, one in each of the four regions.

Funding for the support program began in 1961. The program operating at half-capacity by 1962 and was fully operational by early 1964. The first emphasis had to be obtaining and storing items to be stocked and developing consumption data that was likely to vary from region to region and from station to station. Very long lead times were involved in a number of the complex electronic parts. Some 25,000 line items were required for the ACE High System, but no more than 5,000 to 8,000 parts could be stocked. This situation required a well-thought-out process of selection.[25]

Support for the Early Warning radar system involved the management and stocking of about the same number of line items as for the ACE High system. Authorization for Early Warning preceded that for ACE High, but the two systems were developed and became operational about the same time. In the Early Warning case a distinction was made between mechanical spare parts, which were funded through Infrastructure, and electronic parts, which were funded by SHAPE's Military Budget Committee. In order to make provision for emergency repair parts during the interim before support through the NMSSS could be established, the SHAPE Military Budget Committee made a grant of $56,000 to each station, as it opened, for purchasing parts directly as needed. Host countries, responsible for operation of the stations, adopted different policies, according to varied interpretations, for the use of these emergency funds. By the time the NATO Supply Center was able to assume support, Norway and Denmark had committed nearly all of their funds to make up stocks at stations in anticipation of an emergency. Germany, on the other hand, had spent no money since it had had no emergency. The German interpretation was more in keeping with the original intent, although it was recognized that some minimum stocks to cover a foreseen emergency should be authorized.

As with rockets and missiles, modifications of electronic equipment were an important aspect of logistic support. In this case it was the responsibility of SHAPE to propose modifications and the responsibility of the NAMSO, through NSC, to provide kits and to see that the modifications were carried out. However, Denmark reserved the right to perform minor modifications without asking NAMSO, provided of course that the original parts were retained and no new parts were introduced that might undermine logistic support. It was pointed out, for example, that the electric system might be of the wrong voltage for the local power source. The Norwegians suggested that the individual nations, as well as SHAPE, should be able to test equipment and suggest modifications.

Each station of the Early Warning System had an engineer from the Marconi company assigned to it for one year from the time of its opening. Representatives of participating countries sought the extension of the services of an engineer for a longer period. One suggestion was that a country finding itself in need of such assistance might contract for an engineer if then it could be reimbursed through its budgetary allowance. But for this to be done all hiring had to go through NAMSO so that it could be budgeted for payment by SHAPE for all work done on the site.

Similarly, whatever responsibilities NAMSO might assume for support of the Early Warning project would depend upon the availability of funds for specific purposes in the NATO military budget. While the NATO Supply Center would furnish guidance on stock levels as needed, the host countries remained fully responsible for maintaining levels at the agreed amounts—six months' supplies in the depot and three months' in the country—and for keeping stock record accounts of the stations in their territory. Each country was to designate a single central control point for the submission of all requisitions for Early Warning parts going to that country.

Distribution procedures for the Early Warning parts were similar to those for ACE High. The NSC depot consolidated the items going to any country in packages that ordinarily were not to exceed a weight of fifty kilograms. Country liaison representatives at Chateauroux then would arrange for transportation of the supplies to their respective countries. From that point it was up to the country to distribute the parts to the stations. A country would send Early Warning parts outside its own territory to another NATO country as requested by NSC—if this could be done without impairing or endangering the effectiveness of stations on its own territory.[26]

Coordination of support for such a project as Early Warning called for frequent visits to the countries and the sites, meetings at least once each quarter, and constant attention to the buildup of stocks which grew in one year from 400 line items to about 8,000. From 1963 to 1964 this project too was expanded: full support of Link 3 equipment was taken over as an integral part of the system, and the applicable Weapon System Supply List and catalogues had to be prepared for the entire system. Expansion of the warning and control system continued under what came to be referred to as NADGE (NATO Air Defense Ground Environment), of which Early Warning constituted a major element.

As the result of a proposal of the European Communications Security Agency in the spring of 1960, NAMSO became responsible for coordinated support—i.e., in providing spare parts—for cryptographic machines. This new duty insured an adequate holding of spare parts in Europe, assisted the production plans of the sole-source manufacturer, and provided for the redistribution of surplus property among participating countries.

The project started with a three-year plan for a one-time consolidated procurement capitalized with a U.S. credit loan. The value of parts to be procured under this plan was over $101,000. Denmark, Germany, Greece, Luxembourg, Norway, Portugal, and Turkey, as well as SHAPE, agreed to participate. NSC provided centralized warehousing for the times obtained, as well as brokerage service for all the countries using the cryptographic machines. This service included procurement to meet emergency demands, as well as for annual anticipated requirements. During three years, 1962–64, this proved to be an $800,000 business. Still, the size of the "Crypto" project was but a small fraction of that of ACE High or Early Warning.

The project for support of tactical aircraft beacons was also relatively small-scale. It involved simply the supply of spare parts to keep in operation some forty or so aircraft beacons under SHAPE funding. Procedures were similar to those of the other projects under this program manager.

The manager for the maintenance and calibration programs administered two rather different activities. As mentioned above, this program had to do with arrangements for maintenance services not already part of other recognized programs. Over a period of time, NAMSO developed a considerable program in assessing responsibilities for overhaul and repair and in arranging for on-call contracts against which member nations could place their repair orders directly. In addition a procedure was developed for the consolidation of annual repair requirements as well as for meeting emergency demands.

The NSC calibration facility, comprising the Secondary Reference Laboratory at Chateauroux and several mobile teams equipped with secondary transfer calibration equipment, performed an essential service in keeping the missile systems operationally effective and accurate. The mobile teams visited missile sites in the participating countries to provide this service directly, but also to give assistance when requested in developing the capacity to do this work on the part of the countries' own teams. At first the U.S. Army provided most of the technicians for calibration service, but these were largely replaced later by international personnel.[27]

The nature and extent of logistic projects and programs must change frequently to keep pace with modifications and wholesale changes in weapon systems. No firm, consistent policy could be established with respect to the roles of NAMSO and the NSC in the face of these changes. Instead the question rose anew with each change, and each had to be decided on its own merits. In 1964 the North Atlantic Council did create an ad hoc committee to consider the problem of "the integration of logistics support for advanced weapons in peace and war." At that time discussion centered around four weapon systems then being jointly produced in Europe—the Early Warning

System, the F-104G aircraft, and SIDEWINDER and HAWK missiles.[28] The committee recommended that "the Organization and member states concerned with the logistic support of these weapon systems should contact NMSSS (NAMSO), in order to specify the role that (NAMSO) should play in the execution of this support."

This recommendation seemed a pale imitation of any decisive position. Nevertheless, support for Early Warning, the SIDEWINDER missile, and in a special way for the F-104G aircraft, did soon come under NAMSO programs. But the question would remain for other weapon systems. For some of these, the production organization was meant to retain responsibility for the supply of spare parts for perhaps two years or so, and then this would be turned over to NAMSO. On the face of it, this seemed reasonable enough. But, as one staff officer put it, "It just does not make any logistical sense to set up a whole logistic system paralleling [NAMSO] . . . when it is intended in a year or two—about the time the new organization will begin to become effective—that [NAMSO] will take it over anyway—We are no smarter or better, or more clever than they are, but we already have learned some things the hard way."

Actually conversations about transferring support for the HAWK missile to NAMSO went on for nearly two years while the HAWK production management agency did develop its own maintenance supply system, patterned very closely after that of NAMSO. Meanwhile responsibility for calibration of HAWK test equipment was turned over to the NSC.

Another project being brought under NAMSO was support for the NATO Missile Firing Installation (NAMFI), built on Crete. NAMFI was a firing range, scheduled to open in 1967, where missile units from all participating NATO countries could go far training in the firing of their missiles. As a NATO installation, it seemed logical that this should be supported by the NATO Maintenance and Supply Organization, but the question was how? In September 1963 the logistics committee agreed that NAMFI should be treated as a new customer, like SHAPE. The board of directors asked for further consideration by the Finance and Administration Committee. However, the Greek authorities insisted that NAMFI should not be regarded as a separate customer, but that support for it should be arranged through Greece as the host country. Subsequently the Greek view prevailed. According to the Ottawa Agreement and other regulations, clients of the NATO Supply Agency could only be member countries of NAMSO or subsidiary bodies of NATO created under Article 9 of the North Atlantic Treaty. This covered military headquarters such as SHAPE, but NAMFI was held not to be a subsidiary body within the meaning of the Ottawa Agreement. On the other hand, the Multilateral Agreement for NAMFI assigned to Greece as host country extensive responsibilities and functions, including logistic support. Still, under terms of a memorandum of understanding, the NATO Supply Agency did ship fuel, delivered ground equipment, sent technicians, and supported the NIKE system for NAMFI, even though it might be done through the host country.[29]

The Brokerage/Disposition program manager at NSC had responsibility for several programs or projects in connection with disposal of excess and surplus property, and with the procurement and distribution of certain items of supply for member countries. These were items of many kinds not included within any of the other programs.[30]

A major disposal program had been created just to get rid of items not authorized for stockage. In August 1962 there were over 84,000 line items of stocks on hand at Chateauroux, most of which were not authorized. Some of these had been accumulated as a result of an earlier stockage policy, the acceptance of some U.S. Air Force contract termination inventories, purchases of excessive amounts in some instances, and changes in programs. A program aiming at redistribution of excess stocks ran into a U.S. limitation on extending credits for redistributed property, though a modified "cross-support" program, with better financial support, was more successful. This 1963 program included about 1,150 line items a month. A considerably larger activity was the Inventory Disposition Group, which handled about 7,300 line items a month of "old work" in disposing of unauthorized stocks. Added to this was a "Clean-up Project" for processing some 56,000 old brokerage back orders, including 6,000 back orders taken over from the NIKE/HONEST JOHN program.

Brokerage, the procurement of items specifically ordered by member countries, began as a revised system, functioning with the limited semi-manual record system, in May 1963. During 1963, 6,000 monthly requisitions followed closely what had been projected. New tasks added in 1964 for the brokerage program included the verification and certification of supplier invoices, customer billing at supplier invoice prices, verification and certification of shipping agents' transportation bills, and contract administration.[31]

Continuing Problems and Prospects

The early days of the NATO Maintenance Supply Services System were bitterly disappointing for the sponsors.[32] The system's problems so far outweighed its achievements that there was serious doubt about whether it should be continued. The agency lost responsibility for support of the G-91, and except for the F-100 and two U.S. missile systems, it gained no additional responsibility for some time. The whole operation was caught in a vicious circle. Disruptions in the board of directors and poor staffing in the agency and center led to poor supply performance; poor performance in supporting weapons and equipment originally assigned barred the way to new assignments; lack of new assignments led to lack of interest in governments in making the entire program work, and lack of interest in providing staff and resources led to poor supply performance.

Critics blamed much of the poor performance on the board of Directors. Losing sight of the international concept behind the organization, governments appointed to the board men with little experience in military logistics but who seemed most anxious to gain national advantage or to prefer one military service over the others in approving programs and policies. Not only did bickering and ineffectiveness result, but also involvement in operations at the expense of the general manager, who thus found himself unable to manage the activities for which he was supposed to be responsible.

The situation was further aggravated by failures in the supply systems of certain countries. Even a NATO system otherwise beyond criticism could not have been effective in cases where nations failed to anticipate requirements and where individual supply systems never had been geared for the type of support NAMSA and NSC were designed to give. National stockage policy had to take into consideration the factors of administrative and production lead times, periods between supply status reviews, and the depot working stock levels desired in the country. Otherwise no system of procurement and distribution would work.

Member nations delegated neither the resources nor the management functions to the agency necessary for it to be effective. Instead they used the NSC as a limited broker, or department store, only as necessary. They were free to shop around and to order from NSC what they could not find elsewhere. They did not provide good data on resources, consumption, and requirements, and, with the possible exception of Germany, did not commit themselves to regular and exclusive use. The only regular customers were the recipients of U.S. grant aid—because the United States required this aid to go through NSC. But neither was the United States consistent in use of the system, and when it withdrew its aid program from these channels, the whole NATO Maintenance Supply Services System approached total collapse.

On the other hand, the supply agency, required to be self-supporting, tended to deal not in costly and hard-to-get items where it could have been most useful, but in fast-moving items, and it solicited brokerage business calculated to keep it "in the black." The uncertainties of logistical requirements were only compounded in this international agency. All together, it could get no firm requirements, had no reliable data and thus no basis for a reasonable inventory policy, often received rush "blue-streak" orders for items it usually did not have, received little cooperation on the redistribution of excess stocks, was frequently regarded as a more expensive source of supply (though in this matter country representatives probably neglected to allow for the savings in warehousing), developed a low fill rate, and often had long delays on the orders it did fill. With all this, the NATO system turned out to be an addition to, rather than a substitute for, the logistic echelons of the individual nations.

In the decade following the inception of the NATO Maintenance Supply Services System, NAMSO was yet to have a clear-cut mission that could be clearly defined. As often is the case in international structure—and frequently in logistics structure alone, domestically—cross-purposes or varying objectives of different supporters had to be reconciled with each other, as well as with the views of skeptics and opponents in the compromise of diplomatic obscurity. But the lack of a clear definition of purpose continued to underlie many of the shortcomings that were obvious in these efforts at Allied supply support. It never had been clear just what the nature or extent of this support was expected to be. A depot set up on the assumption of handling about 500 transactions a day within a few years was handling 1,200 a day, while in the meantime there had been some question about whether it should continue operations at all.

NAMSO depended not upon any overall, rationalized policy, but upon the pressures of the moment and individual negotiations. It would receive full responsibility for supplying repair parts for one weapons system, while responsibility for another system would remain with a separate organization. One country would rely upon it extensively, while another would have little or no business for it. When, on account of the nature of demands placed upon it or a workload that piled up for lack of staff to cope with it, critics proposed cutting back the organization, they failed to make clear just which functions ought to be curtailed or who else would take up the tasks. Rumors of an impending phase-down discouraged business at one point and uncertainty made it difficult for agencies and countries to plan on definite support.

One of the best and most consistent NAMSO customers was a country that also had one of the best maintenance records. Another, which clearly had not been getting enough parts from the NATO Supply Center to keep its rocket forces operational, either had been getting parts from some other source or had been operating off surplus stocks previously built up, or it was not keeping up its rocket capability. Which of these was the case would not become clear to NATO authorities, however, until the situation reached crisis stage. A third country seldom used the supply center at all, and even had established its own jet engine overhaul facility instead of relying on NSC.

By the nature of things, whenever a country turned to NSC, a crisis already was imminent. In attempting to develop and maintain working stocks, Greece and Turkey, depending upon the U.S. Military Assistance Program for financing needed items, faced a real dilemma. In order to maintain a working stock in their depots of six months' estimated requirements, it was necessary for them to set their maximum levels at thirty months and to set their reorder level at the point where their assets (i.e., stocks plus dues in) fell to twenty-four months. Theoretically, then, a country in this situation would always have at least six months' working stock on hand, allowing for a lead time of eighteen months. On the basis of these assumptions, anything less than these levels eventually would lead to a "no-stock" position. These assumptions appeared to square with NSC experience. Many country requisitions obviously had not been based upon these assumptions. Quantities ordered and the frequency of ordering suggested that in many cases there were no levels at all. Inevitably, if items were stocked neither in NSC nor elsewhere, countries always would be in trouble. But in the case of Greece and Turkey, so long as they were depending upon MAP funds, they had to rely on annual allocations. This operated against their submitting requisitions that might fall for payment during a period not covered by allocated funds.

Perhaps the most important obscurity of all in NAMSO's operations was the matter of wartime versus peacetime. It was not at all clear to what extent peacetime procedures and operations would carry over into a war situation nor what the nature of a wartime mission might turn out to be. It was not a question that had not been raised; it was one having inadequate answers. Even the status of NSC personnel in a time of national mobilization for war was not clear. No one was sure whether French workers would remain, or which or how many nationals of other countries now on the international staff would be transferred by the national authorities. Were supplies to be stored in one place or in several? What would be the priorities for transportation?

The uncertainties of mission, in peace and war, resulted in part from the divided authority administering NAMSO. Its board of directors was certainly answerable to the North Atlantic Council, but the board also had a separate responsibility to each of the thirteen subscriber nations. Another obscurity was in the relation of the U.S. Military Assistance Program to NAMSO and the supply channels for recipient countries. At one point, withdrawals of U.S. MAP support precipitated a crisis in the whole system. There had been the question, moreover, about whether the NATO countries concerned should go through the U.S. Military Assistance Advisory Group in the country or directly through the NATO Supply Center.

Finally, there was a serious division in the early period of operation when control of the supporting U.S. logistical organization at Chateauroux passed from the U.S. Army to the U.S. Air Force (1 January 1961). Cooperation betwen staffs of the two U.S. services was anything but close, and when the Air Force moved in, U.S. Army participation was terminated as rapidly as possible, and with it went the Inventory Control Branch that Army experts had established. This event came at a time when countries were having difficulty in making the NIKE systems operational, which made all the more important the guidance of U.S. Army experts in establishing stock levels. There was a special need for care in the mechanization of the supply process, but the Air Force staff went all-out for rapid mechanization. The new process quickly proved to be too sophisticated to be applied to new systems like the NIKE. Previously, the U.S. Army staff had maintained a close relationship between its Inventory Control and Technical Assistance branches in the interpretation and checking of inaccurate requisitions submitted by supply staffs of NATO countries still unfamiliar with the equipment. Overlooking this situation, the Air Force's mechanized process simply rejected country requisitions if they were not completed in the prescribed manner. Moreover, the Technical Assistance Branch, established to facilitate the introduction of the NIKE and HONEST JOHN systems into NATO countries, was cut back in the cause of financial self-sufficiency.

What further complicated the operation of NSC at the same time was the transition from United States to international staffing, so that even those experts whom the U.S. Air Force had retained were being replaced in large measure by men of little experience from other NATO countries. Even though many rocket and missile techicians of the other countries had been trained in the United States under the Grant Aid program, the countries did not now offer these men for service at the NSC. A proposed transition period of three months for the relief of U.S. personnel proved to be hopelessly inadequate in many cases.

The suspicion arose that the changeover and reassignment of personnel was intended to put an end to technical assistance, possibly in favor of some contractual arrangement. With confidence waning, some investigators were reporting the whole NAMSSS program a failure and were recommending its liquidation. Other counsels prevailed, however, and NAMSO survived to become a fairly thriving activity. Nevertheless it still suffered from the division of authority and lack of definition of mission in peace and war.

However, the fundamental problem of personnel persisted: few officers had had experience in the specialized procedures used, national loyalties conflicted with international responsibilities, pay scales and working conditions needed to correspond to the situation and the requirements, and language was always a handicap in an international agency with frequent personnel turnover.

At every level the question of national responsibility versus interdependence reappeared. In major procurements general effectiveness warred with special national interests, and as in every decision long-term advantages and disadvantages had to be weighed against those of the short term. In day-to-day depot operations, country documents had to be reconciled with NSC documents, since the loss of identity could amount to the effective loss of an item.

In similar vein there remained the nagging question of effectiveness versus cost. Small requisitions for brokerage—"the nickel and dime orders"—were especially difficult to handle. Generally, brokerage requests were not made of NSC unless there already was a problem. Then when NSC accepted the problem—particularly if it was for small orders—it opened itself to criticism. Some kind of annual package or long-term ordering cycle was necessary for effective and efficient action. Here an example might be noted from the U.S. Air Force, which in certain cases ordered a "life of type" package—i.e., it obtained a full set of spare parts estimated to be needed for maintenance for the entire period of serviceability of the item of equipment. The conflict between early performance and cost in procurement was an item of continuous discussion in NSC staff meetings. Throughout NAMSO, and indeed throughout major logistical organizations everywhere, there are those who tend to think logistically and those who tend to think financially. The former wishes to deliver the supplies or to get the aircraft flying and "keep 'em flying." For the latter the main question is "What will it cost?" The measure of efficiency, then, would depend upon which view prevailed in a particular case. In NAMSO the temptation always was to strive to show a profit, to emphasize whatever returned the earliest and most dependable surcharges and service fees, and to curtail those activities showing a deficit. Strictly speaking, NAMSO really should have shown a deficit because it generally dealt in the difficult problems. Its true measure ought to have been the effectiveness of the equipment depending upon its support.

Closely related to the problem of cost and effectiveness was the problem of obsolescence. In stocking parts amounting to a total value of seven to ten million dollars over a period of time, it was inevitable that at some point a large share of those on hand would become obsolete. The commandant had been anxious to be able to return excess items to the United States and receive credit, but this he could not do. Some supply experts estimate that about one-third of the value of the intake into an inventory of military spare parts eventually becomes useless through obsolescence.

One of the most urgent and immediate problems for the staff of the NATO Supply Center was in matching tasks and manpower. Shocked by a growing backlog of work to be done, a review committee in 1962 reported a state of "current confusion" and a "chaotic situation" at NSC. Actually the review committee began its investigations only eight months after the center had come under international management. Less than half the number of the 183 international employees had been assigned. Moreover, the center apparently had been in trouble while under U.S. national management, for in September 1961, only a few weeks after formal transfer to international authority, a special U.S. task force had been organized to help deal with the situation. Surely much of the trouble came from the poorly defined mission alluded to above. The NATO Maintenance Supply System was intended to deal with a "limited number of items . . . at the most 10,000." But there seems to have been no satisfactory provision made for obtaining the other 490,000 items, which would be needed sooner or later as the United States withdrew its direct grant aid support in favor of channeling them through NSC. When, in the course of sixteen months, countries placed 500,000 demands, the result was expected but the staff was inadequate. Additional workers were not authorized and countries were slow in filling the spaces already allotted. Much of the backlog and delays were in brokerage. At the time, the depot was stocking 85,000 items, including parts for HONEST JOHN and NIKE, as agreed by the board of directors. Most of the 272,000 items reported to be "in files" represented brokerage demands. Since these were not in stock, and if the items were not available in U.S. depots, 14 months' administrative and production lead time might be involved. Officials of NMSSA urged that the work backlog should be met by increasing the work force rather than, as some were suggesting, by cutting back on the number of items.

In attacking the backlog itself, the Supply Agency took several steps. It increased the working hours at headquarters from forty to forty-three a week. A commercial accounting system was introduced, management analysis procedures adopted, and planning methods applied to anticipating and dealing with the work load. Some workers were transferred from one section of NSC to another, and additional temporary workers were hired. Still the timely reduction of the backlog of orders depended to a considerable degree upon action by U.S. liaison officers in the U.S. depots.

What perhaps was the most unfortunate aspect of the faulty start of NSC was a tendency to attribute the difficulties to its international character. This provided more ammunition for those opposed to practically any kind of international logistic operation. But over the years NAMSO gained the experience in such cooperation that was perhaps, after all, its greatest justification.

If the role of NAMSO was obscure, it was not because those concerned had not been giving thought to it. It was rather a consequence of a lack of consensus among the nations and the various groups and persons within nations about what the nature of international logistic support should be. To some of the officers at SHAPE, the idea that "logistics is a national responsibility" made no logistical sense as support for Allied military operations in Europe. On the contrary, the SHAPE staff had put forward a plan where country depots would be organized as satellites of NSC and would operate as extensions of the NAMSO system. The NAMSO general manager would be responsible for the effectiveness of the entire system, and the satellite depots could be manned by men of the respective countries. In any case, closely integrated international military operations would require common methods and procedures in the participating countries, whether the proposed satellite depots technically came under NAMSO or remained under exclusive country control. It was clear that the whole logistic support system needed to be under the direction of one responsible person.

SHAPE further proposed establishing specialized depots for particular items, and, finally, a system of regional supply centers. The regional centers would be an extension of the system already established at Chateauroux. SHAPE suggested that at least another depot should be opened in the southeast area, and a third in the north. This was a subject of considerable discussion over a two-year period (1962–64) in a North Atlantic Council ad hoc group and in a NMSSS working group. Most serious attention was on the desirability of a depot in the southeast to serve mainly Greece and Turkey. The Turkish representative on the council was especially anxious for such a development, and the Greek representative, while seeing such a depot as less urgent at that time, concurred in backing a proposed feasibility study. Actually, both Greece and Turkey were then depending upon direct supply from the United States for most conventional aircraft and army conventional weapon parts. Only for the support of NIKE and HONEST JOHN, together with some Early Warning and Forward Scatter requirements, did they depend upon the NATO Supply Center. This meant a regional supply center for the time being was nonessential. But supporters of the project pointed out that, limited though a regional supply center might now be, it could be useful for such activities as support of NAMFI and for onsite calibration and maintenance work, as well as functioning as a regional control point. In the beginning it could perform a limited stock-holding function, with a simple stock recording system, while master recording, billing, and so on, might remain centralized at Chateauroux. Later, attracted by the very existence of the regional supply center, other weapons and forces might be added to its responsibilities.

Discussions about regional supply centers took on new meaning in 1967 with the decision that the NATO Supply Center at Chateauroux, following the removal of NATO military and political headquarters from France, should also be moved out. The French withdrew from the NIKE program, but continued to be a member of NAMSO. They made no demand that NAMSO or the supply center be removed from France. Nevertheless, the other members decided that it would be better to avoid possible pressures in the future by moving out the NATO supply facilities. No one doubted the embarrassment to logistic efficiency that the departure from France entailed, but in the general reorientation and restructuring of NATO, it was only one part.

Two depots, a northern and a southern one, would now replace NSC Chateauroux. The choice for the northern site was relatively easy. Luxembourg offered a facility at Capellen that formerly had served as a mobilization depot for the Luxembourg army. The Luxembourg government required no financial outlay for the site itself, though some effort would be required for adaptation to the NATO needs, particularly for the installation of data processing equipment and a calibration workshop.

Choosing a site for the southern depot was more complicated. Keen competition developed among Italy, Greece, and Turkey to obtain the depot. If it went to Italy, the choice would be between Taranto and Sardinia. If it went to Greece, Eleusis would be the site, and if it went to Turkey, it would be near Izmiz. Meanwhile the NSC stocks at Chateauroux would be moved to Capellen between December 1967 and April 1968. Headquarters for the organization—i.e., the NATO Maintenance and Supply Services Agency— would move from Paris (Neuilly) to the city of Luxembourg. After long studies and negotiations by staff members and national authorities, the southern depot finally went to Taranto, Italy.[33]

The reception given to SHAPE and other proposals for expanding the NATO Maintenance Supply Services System depended to a great extent upon the attitude of the particular person or group toward internationally integrated logistics in general. Some favored any feasible extension of the system as a step toward a full international system of logistic support. Others, for the same reason, but more interested in preserving national and separate responsibilities, opposed such moves.

Attitudes of the nations toward the NAMSO concept, while generally approving, varied from the relative coolness of the French to the unreserved position of the Germans, stated by the federal defense minister as early as 1960:

We should welcome NATO's competence and responsibility for the entire field of logistics. . . . Since the Federal Republic has no national military tasks and our security is inalienable from that of Western Europe, the Federal Republic has fully integrated her fighting forces in the NATO command systems; and she is the only country to have done so in peacetime. . . . We should welcome NATO's assurring competence and responsibility for the entire field of logistics. . . . The Federal Government has been proposing that for years.[34]

Recommendations for improvement in the operation of the system itself had focused on the desirability of developing procedures for meeting one of the major continuing problems mentioned above, the obsolescence of equipment. These suggestions centered mainly on proposals for establishing a true joint inventory system. As the NAMSA logistics staff saw it, the development of an effective inventory system was the principal test for the efforts in NATO to underpin national logistic support activities in the field with a joint procurement, supply, and maintenance system. Recommendations included the following major points: (l) countries should build in the NATO Supply Center a joint inventory for prompt service and commit themselves to using it fully; (2) the joint inventory should mingle the national elements, and the whole mass of matériel should be available for all participants; (3) matériel should be available to users on requisition: the military services of a country should not "procure" from the joint depot, though participating countries should delegate certain procurement functions to it; (4) countries operating a weapon system should organize a weapon-system partnership that should set policies of joint inventory operation and financing, with the NSC providing the management; (5) the purpose and range of joint inventories should be clearly defined, and responsibility clearly divided between them and any backup stocks that partners might want to keep in national depots; (6) the cost of joint inventory operation should be shared among partners on the basis of the likelihood of their requiring deliveries, which might be called their "exposure to stockouts," and of actual deliveries to them—a compromise between paying for the insurance provided by the pool of matériel and paying for the drafts made on it; (7) financial contributions to the original inventory and to inventory expansion might be assessed according to a simple measure of exposure to stockouts; (8) capitalized by the partners, a joint inventory should make provision for the sharing of obsolescence losses by a reduction of the assets to which the partners can lay claim, or by additional financial contributions for the procurement of up-to-date items; and (9) as an important alternative to new procurement, especially for expensive items, recoverable items should be repaired. If done efficiently, the joint inventory should save substantially on procurement and thus add significantly to the economic advantages of the partnership.

The joint inventory principle was in sharp contrast to the brokerage principle. A broker buys for a customer, and the customer buys from the broker. The joint inventory is an extension of a participating nation's own military supply system. The joint inventory procures for the participants a specified type of matériel, but the nations do not buy from it; the national military organizations requisition on the joint inventory as bases do on national depots. The aim of a brokerage system is to sell specific items to customers, and there is a certain pressure to show a profit. The essential aim of a joint inventory system is to provide insurance against stockouts due to unpredictable requirements.

In spite of a sequence of ups and downs, with periods in its earlier years when its very continuation hung in doubt, the NATO Maintenance and Supply Organization by the spring of 1966 appeared to be healthy indeed—at the very time that the future of NATO itself was being most seriously questioned. By this time NAMSO had enough business to keep it going for five years and with a promise of more to come. With a reserve of 30 million francs, it had been able to subsidize some activities and had reduced the transportation handling charge from five to four percent. The regular surcharge of five percent was being held, even though rising costs had been bringing pressures for an increase. The work force at Chateauroux was held below 600.

During the summer of 1967, in spite of difficulties arising out of the impending move from France, NAMSO continued to take on added responsibilities. The first of these was in the storing and distribution of repair parts for the HAWK missle. HAWK common depot tasks were transferred to NSC at the new locations, and NAMSO then would manage these stocks for the HAWK Management Office, which would continue to control the general operations relating to support of this weapon system. Repair parts and certain handling equipment would be moved from the HAWK depot at Chatellerault to the new NSC depots after NSC stocks had been moved to the new locations. Second, NAMSO had entered into a formal agreement with NADGEMO to manage the entire initial twenty-four months' spares for maintenance for the NADGE system. This was a natural addition to the responsibility for the Early Warning-ACE High systems that NAMSO already supported. Third, NAMSO would have responsibility, beginning about 1 January 1968, for follow-up support for BULLPUP. This would be an operation similar to that already in effect for support of the SIDE-WINDER, accomplished under an "instrument of transfer" drawn between the boards of the BULLPUP organization and NAMSSA.

NAMSO had developed a refined supply and maintenance organization with well-established lines of communication with the participating countries, and with well-developed sources of supply both in Europe and America. It comprised an integrated international logistic support system for thirteen countries, each having an equal say and having to agree unanimously on such matters as funding and stockage policy, even though all countries might not be using a particular weapon. Like many of the other procedures and activities in NATO logistics, this was altogether new in military logistics. Although the period 1966–67 had not been a crucial time for decisions on the future of NATO, it was such a juncture for the future of NAMSO. By this time a number of U.S.-produced weapons were being replaced by European-produced weapons such as F-104G, HAWK, SIDE-

WINDER, and so forth. The question was whether the support of these and other advanced weapon systems should be entrusted to NAMSO—the kind of function for which the organization had been created—or whether more specialized and parallel, independent agencies would be set up in each case, or indeed whether each nation would be thrown back entirely on its resources and facilities, supplemented by whatever bilateral agreements it might be able to negotiate.

To a great extent the future of the NAMSO system depended upon the success of the North Atlantic Council in reconciling member nations' widely differing attitudes and conceptions of integrated logistics. The immediate problem was to develop integrated logistic support for advanced weapons in a way that would meet the wartime requirements of Allied Command Europe without sacrificing responsiveness to individual national requirements.

Cooperative Logistic Support Arrangements

In a coalition war, the alternative to a system of integrated logistics or specialized multilateral arrangements is a network of bilateral agreements for specific cooperative logistic arrangements—or else no cooperation at all, in which case the coalition loses an element of mutual strength and thereby the purpose of the coalition. In the event of the liquidation of NATO, or of such logistic structures at NAMSO, then undoubtedly a series of bilateral agreements would succeed the NATO agreements. As a matter of fact, it is undoubtedly true that even with the various NATO logistic organizations, the total advance toward an integrated NATO logistic system had been relatively so limited that currently bilateral cooperative arrangements still were much more significant in the total scale of logistic support. A war situation in these circumstances undoubtedly would see this bilateral approach paramount in the logistics of NATO forces.

Whether this was as it should have been remained open to question. There were those who would have been glad to see NAMSO and its facilities closed down. Holding that a NATO-wide system of integrated logistics was hopeless, they would contend that the best that might be expected would be the appointment of a logistics "monitor" under SACEUR to observe, report, and suggest general guidelines for the various national logistic systems and for the many group and bilateral agreements by which they cooperated. Indeed some logisticians saw the whole NAMSO effort in the support of advanced weapon systems as a step backward because it was built upon traditional depot operations and requisitioning procedures involving weeks or months of administrative lead time and delays in obtaining essential parts for keeping current missile systems operational. Yet the U.S. Air Force had found it more efficient to shortcut traditional supply lines by eliminating area storage points and by having its bases requisition directly on central "wholesale" storage points in the United States for high-priority items to be airlifted.

Thanks to a bilateral arrangement with the United States, the United Kingdom, as early as 1960, was able to obtain resupply of high-priority parts for THOR missiles, for which it had operational responsibility, within fifty to sixty hours. In this case the requisitions went directly to the U.S. Air Force, which had responsibility for logistic support. The Air Force's logistic support manager for THOR was the San Bernardino Air Matériel Area, California. The depot included a control center equipped with electronic data-processing equipment and linked by a high-speed communications network with missile sites, manufacturing plants, storage sites, and various headquarters. It operated on a semiautomatic inventory control system. Daily usage reports into the data processing center would lead to automatic reordering of parts from the manufacturer when they fell to a certain level. High value or special items were airlifted directly from the manufacturer to the missile site.[35]

All countries maintaining forces in Germany had to enter into bilateral agreements of various kinds for the logistic facilities that they needed on German soil. On the other hand, Germany was active in conducting bilateral negotiations for logistic facilities in France, Belgium, and other neighboring countries in order to have storage areas removed from the potential combat zone.[36] While similar in purpose, these facilities lay altogether outside the NATO common infrastructure.

The other side of cooperative logistics had to do directly with supply. The most significant of these agreements were between the United States and Germany, though there were numerous others. These agreements covered different types of supply activities such as programs of military sales, loans, grant aid, and cooperative suppport.

While the United States for a number of years had maintained programs of reimbursable aid according to which its procurement services were put at the disposal of foreign governments for military purchases in the United States, the U.S. Department of Defense in more recent years was pushing programs of military sales as a means of alleviating the problem of gold outflow for the United States. Foreign governments might make purchases through U.S. military assistance advisory groups in the countries, or their agents in the United States might go directly to a U.S. military service or to the manufacturer. A model offsetting agreement was that between the United States and Germany by which Germany agreed to purchase military equipment in the United States to offset dollar expenditures in Germany.

What was termed more specifically *cooperative logistic support* was an arrangement of the United States intended mainly to back up Allied equipment of U.S. design or manufacture with long lead-time maintenance parts. In effect this system paralleled NAMSO, and with similar purpose, but operated outside by a series of bilateral agreements. Advantages claimed for this system were several. It of course provided a means for improving the logistic posture of NATO Allies. It reduced the cost of parts for the Allies, and thus permitted them to assign a larger share of funds for other military purposes. It carried a strong inducement for the standardization of weapons and equipment. It enabled the Untied States to buy in larger quantities at lower unit cost. It provided a greater range of production and for the redistribution of excesses. It cut the cost of converting a high inventory of obsolete items. Finally, it contributed to an easing of the balance-of-payments problem of the United States.[37]

That these benefits were advantages as against no system of cooperation at all is undeniable. But whether they were advantages over a fully integrated multilateral system might be open to serious question. The practical advantage was that bilateral arrangements were often more feasible politically and that they had a certain simplicity in execution as compared to the complexities of multilateral agencies dedicated to satisfying conflicting demands of many nations.

The cooperative logistic support arrangements sponsored by the United States were those by which the United States provided logistic support to another government through its participation in the U.S. Department of Defense logistic system with reimbursement to the United States for the support provided. This method was mainly for the support of weapon systems common to the United States and cooperating government's forces, though in certain instances the United States assisted in developing support systems for weapons not in the active inventory of United States forces. Special types of matériel not ordinarily procured centrally by the military departments and the Defense Supply Agency of the United States were not as a rule provided under cooperative depot supply support arrangements. Negotiations for the sale of U.S. weapon systems or other military matériel were expected to look to the intended use of the matériel and to provision for effective concurrent and follow-on logistic support.

As a matter of stated policy of the United States, matériel and services provided under cooperative arrangements to other countries were to be the same as those for its own forces having the same mission and equipment. The Department of Defense supply system was to be used without modification unless it could be shown clearly that costs would be reduced or combat effectiveness increased by a change. Department of Defense standard procedures such as MILSTRIP (Military Standard Requisitioning and Issue Procedure), including the U.S. system of priorities, and MILSTAMP (Military Standard Transportation and Movement Procedures) applied. Records were to permit prompt determination both of status of supply and financial status.

Formal agreements for cooperative logistic support included two elements—the Procedural Arrangements concluded between the U.S. Department of Defense and the defense ministry of the other country concerned, and the Implementing Procedures worked out by the corresponding armed services.

Cooperative logistics brought mixed advantages for the cooperating nations. Inevitably criticisms accompanied the most extensive of those arrangements, those between the United States and Germany. On the one hand, American logistic installations in Europe found themselves hard-pressed at times as a result of the action of American officials in agreeing to an arrangement allowing the Germans to requisition on U.S. depots. This added to the expense of maintaining backup supplies in order to meet all demands. Some observers suggested too that it may have caused the Germans to lose some of their enthusiasm for integration, since they had complete access to U.S. resources. On the other hand there was growing German resistance to American pressure to purchase quantities of military equipment in the United States as a balance to the dollar expenditures that the United States made in maintaining its forces in Germany.

Battlefield Support

Earlier sections have discussed the deficiency in the planning process when it came to arrangements for wartime logistic support of tactical units in the field. Practices for forces already stationed in Europe and those assigned to NATO commands for maneuvers reflected the inadequacies. Deep uncertainties about tactical and strategic assumptions further confused the situation.

The magnitude of the problem could be seen simply in the vast quantities of supplies that modern fighting forces require. Even without the complications of international support or cooperative arrangements, and even when a national command controlled all of its own resources, the task was formidable enough. According to estimates given in 1967, the U.S. Seventh Army, even in peacetime in Germany, had a daily requirement for over 500 tons of food, 800 tons of fuel, 125 tons of ammunition, and 225 tons of equipment, spare parts, and miscellaneous supplies. It was said that deployment of this force to meet an emergency would require the use of some 120,000 vehicles, which would consume over 750,000 gallons of fuel a day.[38]

The Allied Mobile Force brought into focus the problem of international logistic support for tactical ground units. One of the principal concerns of its commander was the system in each country (Belgium, Germany, Great Britain, Canada, Italy, and the United States) for the supply of spare parts—what in NATO was designated as Class VI supply. National contingents were of battalion size. A central Logistic Support Unit, organized initially by the British, consisted of various quartermaster, ordnance, and transportation units. As expected, it was reemphasized at every opportunity that each nation was responsible for the logistic support of its own contingent. Of course this responsibility might be met by participation in multilateral agencies, by cooperative arrangements with other countries, or by shipments out of the country's own resources. The nations agreed on predetermined levels of accompanying and follow-up supplies. Insofar as possible, each country arranged with the host country for drawing upon local resources for common-user items such as petroleum products. Once the units were deployed, handling and forwarding of supplies was coordinated through the Logistical Support Unit. This unit, in addition to the elements listed above, also included small detachments from each country to help identify and account for national supplies.

Requests for resupply by units went through the Logistical Support Unit and then, if necessary, to the Logistic Coordination Center at Headquarters, Allied Forces Central Europe. The Coordination Center then passed these requirements on to the respective nations to be met by the national authorities. There had been considerable progress in the standardization of supplies and procedures, but it was reported, "You have to experience only one AMF exercise to realize that much remains to be done."[39]

A study group of Western European Union in 1960 urged that the hands of Allied commanders be strengthened by granting them authority over a designated number of days of supplies in the rear areas, in addition to the authority that they had over supplies actually in the combat zone.[40] Little was done in this direction, though without some kind of authority such as this over logistics, command itself can have little real meaning. However, SACEUR did have authority to transfer supplies in the combat zone from the forces of one nation to those of another. Theoretically, it should be possible for SACEUR to transfer supplies out of the forces of a nation, thus creating new requirements for those forces for which the nation would send up more supplies, which in turn might again be transferred in the process of building up supplies for the forces of another nation.

But an irony in the situation was the complete confusion that surrounded the maintenance of supply reserves at certain levels. Traditionally the number of days of supply established as the level of supply for a given area in a given situation has depended upon a calculation of the order and shipping time, together with allowances for administrative and productive lead time needed for resupply. Estimates of possible losses due to enemy actions or other developments ordinarily would give the basis for some additional cushion. Now this whole concept had to some extent been perverted into basing estimates for reserves upon some supposed "nuclear threshold"—according to the number of days that conventional war would be tolerated before the use of nuclear weapons. Beneath this lay the question of international balance of payments. In other words, an economic condition was determining logistics—and strategy—rather than an analysis of military requirements. Great Britain's proposal in September 1966 to cut back further its military spending on the European Continent by $90 million a year again highlighted this situation. It was reported then that NATO representatives still were talking in terms of ninety days of conventional war, with initial reserves on the Continent of thirty days, though all the partners except the United States were far below that level in their actual stocks. Now the British proposed to cut their supply level to ten days in order to save about $40 million a year in foreign currency.[41]

Following this reasoning, it might be suspected that European countries bent on emphasizing the nuclear deterrent and seemingly anxious to avoid conventional war at almost any cost, deliberately held down the supply stocks in order to enforce this position.

Conclusions

Undoubtedly the greatest single problem in supply for NATO forces was spare parts. Even under normal circumstances, the problem was complicated by NATO having to anticipate needs and maintain inventory stocks at levels that would meet demands without incurring the costs of excessive stocks. This was difficult to do because of the lack of experience in maintaining many modern weapons and the frequent modifications in weapons and equipment that made parts obsolete. When several nations were brought into the picture, the problem of spare parts supply became even more complicated.

Although war generally was assumed to bring a big increase in demands for spare parts, this was not necessarily the case. On the contrary, if rockets were being fired, they no longer would need continuous maintenance. Aircraft and other weapons would be lost completely, so that demand would shift to whole replacements.

A more general problem in the support of forces in Europe was the shortage of service troops. It always has been difficult to maintain a realistic ratio of service to combat troops. Pressure to reduce U.S. forces in Europe in order to reduce the gold outflow and to provide replacements for units in Viet Nam always seemed to be directed at service troops and logistic facilities. In this way, it was said, forces could be reduced without cutting down on combat power. But this was clearly a myth. Logistic support is just as necessary as combat forces for combat effectiveness. Moreover, at the same time that the Americans were cutting back their logistic installations in Europe, they were discussing with the Germans the possibility of the latter's drawing supplies from U.S. depots.

Related to this was the question of lines of communication. In particular, the United States was relying mostly on the Bremerhaven line, at first because it was simpler, shorter, and less expensive than the line across France and later because of the anticipated withdrawal of France from active military collaboration. But the north-south line across Germany remained as vulnerable as when the alternate system was opened across France, and commanders in Europe were very reluctant to count on the Bremerhaven line as a wartime line of communication running parallel to a central European front.

Another local complication involved the transfer of facilities. Some people, failing to recognize the international character, at times put the system in jeopardy. But it was important not to attempt to shortcut normal international procedures. When the United States had some depots in France that it wanted to hand over to the Germans, some officers would simply do just this. But these depots were held by special agreement with the French. If the Americans wanted to transfer them to the Germans, they had to hand them back to the French, and then let the French negotiate a new agreement with the Germans.

The real test of a logistics system is how and whether it can stand the shock of war. The NATO supply system remained rudimentary. Whether it, even with great expansion, could meet the needs of war even in its limited field remained doubtful. Yet it was providing invaluable experience in international logistics. Conceivably it could serve as the nucleus of a far more complete system, which could be of the greatest significance for the mutual security of the North Atlantic Allies in time of crisis.

Notes

1. For a review of planning and economic mobilization, see chap. 5.

2. In French the designation was *Système OTAN d'Approvisionnement et de Réparation.* This might suggest a broader mission in terms of general supply as well as of repair, whereas the implication of the English designation, more in keeping with the stated mission at the time, was that the organization was to be concerned only with the supply of spare (repair) parts for maintenance.

3. See L. A. Wear, "An International Venture in Collective Logistics," *Supplies: Journal of the Institute of Public Supplies,* (February 1966): 18–19; "Saving Time and Money," *NATO Letter,* March 1961, 13–17; NATO Press Release MI (58) 1, 16 April 1959; K. Claude Rupert, "International Logistics Is Becoming a Fact," *NATO's Fifteen Nations* (December 1962–January 1963): 71–72.

4. Charter of the NATO Maintenance and Supply Organization (NAMSO), NM (64) BOD/60 (Final), 18 March 1968.

5. Air Commodore E. J. Smith, NMSSS Presentation, Neuilly, 1964.

6. NAMSO, General Organization NM (66) BOD/24 (Final) Series 100, 12 October 1966.

7. Rules of Procedure of the Board of Directors and Its Subsiding Bodies, NM (64) BOD/53 (Final), 29 September 1964, Directive 130.

8. General Principles Governing the Organization of the NATO Supply Center, NM (64) BOD/7, 11 February 1964, Subseries 140.

9. Redistribution of Stocks, NM (69) BOD/37, 9 September 1963, Directive 222.

10. NATO Press Release (59) 10, 28 June 1959.

11. Report on Review of Concept and Methodology of Brokerage Programme, NM (70) LOG/8, 22 May 1970; Brokerage Operations (Supply), NM (64) BOD/3 (Final) 12 February 1964, Directive 212.

12. Establishment of the NATO Supply Center as a part of the NATO Maintenance and Supply Organization, P & P Directive 142, 3 March 1960.

13. Recruitment Policy for International Staff, NM (64) BOD/46, 9 December 1964, 8 December 1967.

14. Handbook of Missions and Tasks entrusted to NAMSA, NM (68) BOD/30, 15 October 1968.

15. Choice and Management of Stocks, NM (64) BOD/5, 11 February 1964, Directive 213.

16. "Programmed and Unprogrammed Repair and Overhaul Services," NM (68) BOD/14, 16 July 1968; NAMSA Maintenance Manual NR 235-1.

17. *The NATO Codification System* (Paris; 1960) 1, A-1; NMSSA Supply Manual, NMSSA Instruction 225-1.

18. Financial Regulations of NAMSA, NM (66) BOD/37, 16 July 1968, amended 8 July 1969; Pricing Policy NM (64) BOD/58, 29 September 1964, amended 11 December 1969.

19. NIKE/HONEST JOHN Programme NM (66) BOD/3, 24 February 1966, amended 10 December 1968, Directive 341; NAMSA Supply Manual NR 225-1; NAMSA Maintenance Manual 235-1; SIDEWINDER Programme, 18 October 1967, Amended 14 October 1969, Directive 342.

20. Programmed and Unprogrammed Repair and Overhaul Services, NM (68) BOD/14, 16 July 1968, Siewxricw 231; Maintenance Float, NM (68) BOD/13, 15 October 1968.

21. F-104 Procurement Programme, NM (65) BOD/22, 3 May 1965, Amended 10 December 1968, Directive 321; General Provisions for F-104 Saks Dir. 711, 10 December 1968.

22. Four-Year Programme for Spare Parts Support of Jet Engine Overhaul, NM (64) BOD/76, 9 December 1964, Amended 18 October 1967.

23. See chap. 8.

24. Agreement between SHAPE and NAMSA on Supply and Maintenance Support of ACE Communications System, NM (66) BOD/59, 11 December 1969.

25. See Long-Term Forecasts for Programmes, NM (66) BOD/7, 24 February 1966, Directive 610.

26. Early Warning System Logistic Support, NM (67) BOD/19, 18 October 1967, amended 11 December 1969.

27. Calibration Services, NM (63) BOD/65, 11 December 1963, amended 8 December 1966, Directive 231.

28. See chap. 9.

29. Support of NAMFI (NM (63) BOD/DS/29).

30. Excess and Surplus, NM (69) BOD/46, 14 October 1969.

31. For later revisions, see "Report on Review of Concept and Methodology of Brokerage Programme," NM (70) LOG/8, 22 May 1970.

32. This section is based on personal interviews and on-site visits at the NATO Maintenance and Supply Services Agency, Neuilly-sur-Seine, France, July 1962 and July 1964, and at the NATO Supply Center, Chateauroux, France, July 1962.

33. Note by the chairman, Additional Information Concerning the Activation of the Southern Depot, NM (69) BOD/6, 11 March 1969; Study of the Feasibility of Activation of Taranto as a Depot Site, NM (68) BOD/31, 20 August 1968. On the relocation of NAMSO Headquarters to Luxembourg City, see Note by the Chairman, Recommendations of the Permanent Committees Concerning Relocation of NAMSO, NM (67) BOD/47, 9 October 1967; Logistics Committee and Finance and Administration Committee, Status of Transfer of NAMSO, NM (67) LOG/30-F&A/30, 14 September 1967; memo for Chairman NAMSO, NAMSO Relocation, 19 July 1967, AG/67/31; Relocation Budget, Logistics Committee and Finance and Administration Committee, NM (67) LOG/19-F&A/24, 18 July 1967; NAMSA Relocation, NM (67) LOG/21-F&A/25, 13 July 1967; Transfer of NAMSO, NM (67) LOG/19-F&A/24, 17 July 1967; Note by Chairman, NAMSO Relocation, NM (67) BOD/33, 30 June 1967.

34. F. Strauss, Radio Address, 2 March 1960, Bonn.

35. Samuel E. Anderson, "Aerospace Power and Logistics," *NATO's Fifteen Nations* 5 (Winter 1960): 15.

36. See WEU Doc. 180, 25 October 1960, Appendix.

37. Department of Defense Instruction 2000.8, 14 February 1964, Cooperative Logistic Support Arrangments.

38. Carl H. Amme, Jr., *NATO Without France* (Stanford, Calif., 1967), 87.

39. Maj. Gen. G. W. Brown, "NATO's Allied Mobile Force," *Army,* August 1966, 47.

40. WEU Doc. 180, 25 October 1960, Appendix.

41. Bernard D. Nossiter, "NATO Nations Far Apart on Timing of a A-Trigger," *Washington Post,* 7 September 1966, A10.

Part 4
Conclusions

13
NATO Strategy and Logistics
Problems and Potentials

The nuclear dilemma was at the heart of most of the controversy about NATO's strategy during its first twenty years, and, by implication, about logistic plans and policies. Logistic plans and preparations for a conventional war must be diametrically opposed to those assumed for a nuclear war. The major strategic dispute was between advocates of "massive retaliation," who urge a deterrence posture, and advocates of "flexible response," who accept conventional warfare as a realistic alternative to immediate nuclear retaliation. Between these two philosophies are other arguments about, for instance, selection of targets for nuclear war, counterforce (military targets, enemy missiles) versus countercity strategies, the feasibility of a "pause" in nuclear strikes, to what extent and at what point the flexible response should include the use of tactical nuclear weapons, whether the nuclear threshold should be high or low, and the manner of possible escalation, under what circumstances, to all-out nuclear war.

Yet, even when the popularity of the massive retaliation doctrine was at its height, various steps already taken in cooperative logistic efforts—including most of the infrastructure program—clearly indicated that the Alliance intended to support its forces in Europe as something more than a tripwire to trigger nuclear weapons.[1]

In its posture for conventional war, Allied Command Europe emphasized a "forward strategy." Certainly this was in keeping with its mission of defending Western Europe, but if it were to be effective, the forces on the ground and the means of logistic support needed to be better disposed to protect such a key area as the Ruhr, and to block the Baltic approaches. On the other hand, everyone needed to recognize the advantages of the Atlantic Ocean both as an arena for strategic nuclear strikes and as an avenue for logistic support.

A basic difficulty in strategic and logistic planning was in the divergent thrusts of Allies and of separate nations. As members of the Military Committee or of the International Military Staff and as members of the staffs of the major commands, Allied officers proceeded on the basis of requirements growing out of the strategic assumptions. At the same time, some of these same men or their colleagues in the various national defense establishments were at work planning for their national forces and for contributions to NATO on the basis of their estimates as to what their governments thought they could afford. At last the council in its ministerial meeting at Ottawa in May 1963 tried to come to grips with this problem when it asked that the council's permanent session undertake studies of strategy, force requirements, and the resources needed and available to meet them. These studies led to the development of the five-year force goals and the five-year planning cycles.[2]

Still the dilemma of NATO strategy, growing alike out of differences in assessing the chief military threat—whether it be the sizable Soviet conventional forces or the Soviet nuclear weapons, or indeed whether in the next decade or two it would be the Chinese nuclear capability—and of the proper response whatever the provocation, continued to overshadow logistic planning.[3] A lack of firmness in strategic decisions and policy led to vagueness in logistic plans and policies.

Indisputably the departure of the French from the international military staffs and the French withdrawal from general logistic cooperation left a serious gap in strategic and logistic planning and in the logistic dispositions in the vital center of the Alliance. It is not clear whether France or the Alliance suffered more. It was a bizarre situation, as Henry Kissinger noted, "where neutrals enjoy most of the protection of allies and allies aspire to have the same freedom of action as do neutrals."[4]

Whatever else it did, the French initiative inspired a spate of discussion on the future of the Alliance, though it should be noted that this had been going on for several years previously. Streams of essays and oratory by scholars, political leaders, and military men, however, had resulted in little action. There was frequent reference to the "malaise of the Alliance," observations that "NATO is in the doldrums," and that "NATO is in danger of becoming unravelled," but nobody seemed to be able to do very much about it.[5]

Inspired perhaps by the stresses in the Alliance growing out of the Suez crisis of 1956 and then by the Berlin crises of 1958 and 1961, but also by their own concern about the weaknesses that they recognized, a large number of writers in the late 1950s and early 1960s gave serious attention to these issues. In an especially thoughtful analysis, Helmut Schmidt, a leading spokesman on defense policy in the West German Bundestag, urged that "Europe is defensible," and "stability is policy." Looking ahead, in 1960 he saw major tasks for NATO in developing a coordinated military analysis of various proposals for disengagement in Central Europe, implications of German reunification for defense policies, meeting possible future pressures on Berlin, dealing with questions of arms control and disarmament, and further standardization in major items of military equipment.[6]

Already by that time Hans Kohn was seeing as the single greatest obstacle to Atlantic unity and democracy "self-centered nationalism and imperial gloire."[7] *The Times* of London was sounding a similar note. Holding that NATO had lost much of its relevance because "the threat of massive Russian assault, if it ever existed, had disappeared," the newspaper went on to say:

> The need is for a completely integrated alliance strategy to take the place of the declining power of [NATO] and the militarily ineffective central and Southeast Asia Treaty Organizations. The suggestion that this world strategy might be formulated and directed within the existing framework of NATO meets the inevitable objection that it would be impossible to persuade some of the European allies to make common cause in the defense of the Middle East and the Far East. If this is really so . . . then the time may have come for a completely new alignment of allies.[8]

J. William Fulbright, chairman of the U.S. Senate Committee on Foreign Relations, believed that "the single most useful step toward the strengthening of NATO as a meaningful instrument of Atlantic partnership would be the elevation of the NATO Council to the stature of a genuine organ of policy coordination."[9] George W. Ball, American Under Secretary of State, granted that a major problem of NATO was that of broadening participation in the management of nuclear defenses, though he still saw the solution lying in the acceptance of the multilateral nuclear force proposal. But then he went on to agree that NATO should "extend its concern to the larger question of Free World policy if it is to fulfill its purpose as the central arrangement for the defense of the Free World."[10] In another thoughtful comment, Kurt Birrenbach foresaw the evolution of the North Atlantic Council into a real "Atlantic Council" with the kind of authority envisaged in the Declaration of Paris prepared by a citizens' convention in January 1962.[11] Still another view for a future role for NATO was for it to serve as an instrument for common negotiations with the East European countries of the Warsaw Pact.[12]

In later discussions, Eugene Rostow pointed to the value of NATO in providing a framework for realistic policy in the national interest on the part of the United States as well as of European nations. He warned against a possible revolt of American opinion on the part of a people weary of carrying the world's burdens in the face of heavy criticism at home and abroad. Although he granted that national interest forms the rational basis for a nation's foreign policy, Rostow knew that public opinion would not always support measures in the national interest. As he wrote, "Many of the voices now criticizing our actions in Vietnam were raised in the same terms, and with the same vehemence, against President Truman's policies in Iran, Turkey, Greece, and Berlin. After Korea, a comparable revolt of opinion led to the Geneva Conference of 1954, and to Suez, and laid the foundation for our present troubles in Vietnam and Laos."[13] He went on to conclude, "I agree . . . that the passage of time, the revival of Europe and Japan, and the changing contours of world politics require us not to defend NATO foot by foot, committee by committee, but to rethink the bases of our policy, and if necessary to imagine entirely new structures for our alliance, which we agree in regarding still indispensable to security and desirable to the possibility of progress."[14]

Alastair Buchan developed an imaginative scheme for restructuring the Alliance for "crisis management" that went far toward meeting the suggestions and criticisms of those who would extend the functions of NATO into a broader role in the coordination of world strategy. Starting with the fundamental assumption that American power was paramount in the Western world and that it ought to be frankly recognized that the United States was not going to give over the basic decision-making on matters of its foreign and military policies to some supranational authority, he proceeded to develop a system that would bring an international element into American decision-making, on the one hand, and would at the same time develop European institutions for making decisions and coordinating activity on matters more strictly European in nature.[15]

Interestingly enough, it was for General André Beaufré, a leading interpreter of French strategic doctrine, to make some of the most meaningful concessions in the direction of American-European partnership. So far as the structure of NATO was concerned, he would have reorganized it on a three-level concept. The highest level would be that of the Alliance itself, with headquarters in Washington. The second level would be the European. Then there would be an embryonic European Defense Community, with headquarters, perhaps, at Paris. SHAPE would come under a European commander and would become essentially a European headquarters, with U.S. representation only by a liaison team. There would be a German commander in Germany, an Italian commander in Italy, and so on. Finally there would remain at the third level the national forces that each country would continue to maintain, but that presumably would be available for joint operations in a common cause.[16] It should be noted, however, that the cadre for an "embryonic European Defense Community" already existed. The instrument for developing a European side to the military dumbbell was at hand. It was Western European Union, revitalized in the first place to fill the breach caused by the death of the European Defense Community Treaty in 1954. A revival and reconstruction of Western Union, formed by the Brussels Pact of 1948, WEU was extended to include Germany and Italy as well as Britain, France, and the Benelux countries. It was mainly an instrument for guaranteeing British cooperation with the continental powers and for supervising certain armaments restrictions, including a prohibition against nuclear weapons, on Germany. But in addition it did a great deal of general planning work in European security and toward improving the effectiveness of NATO.

Writing as the deputy assistant secretary of state for Atlantic Affairs in the spring of 1966, J. Robert Schaetzel suggested that in organizing European-North American relations, the only two alternatives to the Kennedy concept of partnership with a uniting Europe were the old system of treating with individual nation-states and a federated Atlantic Union, neither of which held much hope in the current world. Both of these approaches would leave the United States in a dominant position. Feelings of true equality could develop only with a united Europe. And the lack of prospect of immediate success, he asserted, should not be permitted to halt the effort. Looking to the example of Cavour and the unification of Italy, Schaetzel pointed out that thirty to forty years of frustration and defeat preceded the final success.[17] Addressing the twelfth NATO Parliamentarians Conference in November 1966, the current secretary-general said that "the two-pillar approach . . . launched by President John Kennedy's great political talent and insight, is still the most positive and far-reaching idea so far in the Atlantic relations field."[18]

Finally, some experts held that the best future for NATO was to remain essentially on its present course. NATO's secretary-general in 1963, in looking at the major problems of the Alliance, contended that improvement was to be found not so much in changing the machinery as in a will to make it work. It was his impression that the civil side of the organization, in political consultation, was working fairly well, and so was the military. Less satisfactory was the bringing of the civil and the military together.[19]

Harald von Rickhoff of Carleton University, Ottawa, argued persuasively for continuing more or less on the present path. He warned that attempts to broaden the functions of the council to worldwide policy-making, or to attempt to endow it with true political authority, could very well lead to the disintegration of the whole system, for it had been the maintenance of a nonsupranational political structure, with preservation of each nation's protective veto, that had permitted the integrated military commands to flourish. Matters of economic relations and aid to less developed countries had better be left to OECD and other agencies organized for the purpose, he insisted, rather than to set up competing projects under the auspices of NATO that would be more likely to be counterproductive both to economic and to security policies. Furthermore, multiple approaches, with the acceptance of disagreement as normal, he thought, should be the rule in East-West relations, rather than in attempting to throw any NATO cloak of diplomatic uniformity over the western partners. Indeed he saw the whole "preoccupation with ambitious blueprints of what NATO ought to be instead of what it is" as promoting an unnecessary air of pessimism by constantly stressing the discrepancy between desire and performance. Moreover, the NATO membership already was too disparate to offer any hope of unity or federation in any way to permit the early development of a European counterpart for a dumbbell. At the same time he argued for a continuation of NATO as a security arrangement on the grounds that the joint planning and maintenance of an integrated Allied force in a forward position in Europe substantially exceeded any formal but unfortified commitment in deterrence value, and that the option for a conventional response to a limited provocation in Europe could better be supported by an integrated Allied force than by separate national conventional forces. But, he went on, what might prove to be the most valuable contributions of NATO in the future might be its internal effects in developing a controlling function, and this and other of its aspects might further the development of a "security community," defined as a group of nations having become sufficiently integrated by formal and informal practices and institutions to allow the expectation of peaceful change for a long period.[20]

General Beaufré observed in 1967 that Europe was the most stable of the major areas of the world in the sense of being free from internal strife, involvement in war, and of the stress of international tensions,[21] though this estimate was subject to some revision within the next several months (and particularly in France). He attributed this revision largely to the continuing aftermath of decolonization on the other continents and somewhat related disturbances involving the United States and Latin America. But surely, on the other side of the ledger, considerable credit had to be given to NATO as a stabilizing influence in Europe. Aside from von Rickhoff and a few others, writers and political leaders generally had neglected what already had become a significant new role for NATO quite apart from its original purpose. A special aspect of this resulted in what amounted to a guarantee against German adventurism or any temptation for the West Germans to force a unilateral solution of the German unification problem.

Since the Government of the Federal Republic had deliberately tied to NATO its military planning, as well as the disposition of its forces, NATO in itself had operated as a stabilizing influence in central Europe. In addition, the presence of American and other Allied forces in Germany served further as an informal restraint against any future "Drang nach osten." But their presence was far easier to justify as a part of a NATO collective effort rather than simply as a bilateral arrangement. There was some evidence, moreover, that signs of a possible revival of extreme German nationalism had appeared strongest at times and places when Allied forces had been reduced, or when there had been a serious discussion of possible withdrawal of troops. For these reasons it may well be that the Russians, for all of their denunciations, secretly welcomed the existence of NATO and the presence of Allied troops on German soil.[22]

Although NATO was valued as a deterrent against attack, and although it provided integrated military headquarters in order to make effective the early conduct of coalition warfare, and although it contributed to the growth of a true security community and to stability in Europe, one of NATO's most important contributions to military effectiveness had been almost completely neglected except by specialists in the field and by a group of planners in Western European Union. This benefit, is some ways potentially the most significant of all at this point, was the advancement of cooperative logistics.

While progress in NATO logistics appeared meager in comparison with any fully developed logistic system of a major military power, it was notable when viewed as the tentative beginning of a unique international system. Most notable of all in a series of significant steps was the common infrastructure program for the construction of facilities. The standardization program had only fair success, but the adoption of the NATO cartridge, a system of highway and bridge classification, the classification of fuel oil and gasoline, systematized marking and handling of patients in medical evacuation, and dozens of instances of harmonizing equipment and identifying items all demonstrated how significant these efforts might be.

At the same time the efforts at combined production, themselves depending to an extent upon standardization, had some measure of success. Yet in terms of total logistic requirements and national armaments programs, these too had been small. Some successful aircraft, some missiles, and a few other items, but nothing, with the possible exception of the F-104 aircraft, was produced in the mainstream of military equipment. Early in the history of the alliance, some of the obstacles to the integration of military production were pointed out. These observations did not seem very convincing, but the fact remained that cooperative production had not progressed far.

It was said, as it is always said when proposals for closer logistic collaborations are offered, that responsibility for equipment is a national prerogative. Why was this point so often reemphasized? It was said that the geographical expanse of the Alliance, extending as it did over such diverse terrain and climatic conditions, made the requirements of the participating nations so different that integrated programs were not practical. But this criticism ignored the vast areas over which forces of member nations were deployed and the great diversity already necessary within each national arsenal—whether that of the United Kingdom in supporting forces from Great Britain to Singapore to Hong Kong, or of Portugal from Iberia to southern Africa and the Azores, and of the United States from Germany to Southeast Asia. It was said that the immediate problem of recreating European industrial production in 1949 made any idea of completely reorganizing European defense production, with the necessary retooling and the retraining of workers, out of the question. But this retraining was done in the process of restoring national defense industries, and surely it is infinitely more difficult to integrate armaments industries *after* they have been rebuilt independently than it would have been before.[23]

If the possibility of developing a NATO-wide production plan was remote at the outset, and remained so, the later achievements in integrated national production projects for modern weapons were rather startling in comparison with the meager results of earlier efforts at more conventional items. The greatest results were in areas where there was a clear advantage to sharing a costly undertaking, and where the project made use of, rather than threatened the position of, major national industries and industrial organizations.

Transportation was the element of NATO logistics that had had the benefit of perhaps the most extensive and detailed planning of all, though this was an area where results in terms of actual logistic coordination in practice had been least visible—with the one important exception of the operation of the very substantial NATO pipeline system.

In its own logistic operations in Europe in the 1960s, the U.S. Army had introduced a large number of procedures that could be adapted in developing support for the forces of other nations or in developing certain common procedures for a system integrated to some degree. A revival of the World War II-type "Red Ball Express" provided the framework for possible future expansion of a going trailer-transfer, line haul relay system of motor transportation for delivery of supplies.[24] Adoption of a "Roll-on/Roll-off" system for shipping loaded trailers directly from New York to Europe, to be driven directly onto the piers over ramps carried on specially designed ships, provided in effect a trans-Atlantic ferry where the costly and time-consuming activities of loading cargo into ships' holds and of discharging it with special machinery could be avoided, and where pilferage could be almost eliminated. A "New Offshore Discharge Exercise" system (NODEX) was an organized an systematized way for unloading supplies over the beaches by small craft and amphibious vehicles operating from ships one to two miles offshore. An "Electronic Manifest System" had cut five days in the time taken for delivery of manifests for essential cargo arriving from the United States. Under a procedure called "Economic Order Quantity" (EQR), certain items having a value of less than one dollar were ordered only in lots of $1,000 worth or a twelve-months' supply; applied to some 30,000 line items, the number of requisitions being handled was reduced by fifty to sixty percent. On the other hand, items of very high cost were taken out of automatic processing and were given close personal attention. This practice permitted frequent personal attention to a high percentage of the dollar value of the inventory, while applying to only .4 percent of the line items regularly stocked. For supplying spare parts to units of the U.S. Seventh Army, a new direct requisitioning procedure made it possible to obtain delivery within three and one-half days on ninety-five percent of the parts available, and all parts could be delivered within seven days; under former requisitioning procedures it had taken twenty-three days. An aerial support center coordinated the forwarding of supplies by airplane—including parachute drops.[25] These and other procedures that developed out of the U.S. Army's experience in Europe would be available for broader application should the necessity arise, though the removal of the United States installation resulted in dislocation of the headquarters and communications machinery that had been developed, and made any future organization of a wartime system in central Europe far more difficult than it otherwise would have been. NATO logistic procedures in general, nonetheless, and the procedures particularly of the NATO Supply Center, bore the unmistakable imprint of United States logistics. In terminology, in the use of the federal catalogue, in the institution of standardized requisitioning and inventory procedures, not to mention the high percentage of U.S.-type equipment in the international supply lines, the American influence had been paramount.

Generally it was assumed that since "logistics is a national responsibility," and since there were no existing military forces organized on an international basis—other than the small Allied Mobile Force and the Standing Naval Force Atlantic—there could be no general, unified NATO supply system. The NATO Maintenance and Supply Organization showed what could be done by a NATO agency in a limited field, but this was a long way from a general system of international supply. Many questioned the desirability even if the feasibility of such a system could be established. Yet the experience of two world wars and Korea demonstrated the basic necessity of international cooperation in matters of supply in coalition warfare. And if war ever should come again to Europe it hardly could be anything else than a coalition effort. In a way, then, it seemed that a coordinated supply system for the Alliance was as important as the Alliance itself. Those who opposed further development of international machinery for mutual support did so on the ground that future war in Europe of the kind assumed by such structure was altogether unlikely. Yet they supported the continued maintenance and modernization of their own national forces. If they were so confident that peace in Europe was assured, why did they not eliminate their own forces and their own logistic machinery? On the other hand, those who accepted the notion that a strong Allied military posture was desirable or even essential for maintaining stability and security in Europe were unwilling to see that posture include a general system of international supply. The need for integrated Allied military headquarters was accepted. The need for military forces to be organized and earmarked for the NATO commands was accepted. But the need of a logistic system to make those forces effective was left as a matter of individual "national responsibility."

In matters of military preparedness, peoples generally overemphasize the importance of troops at the expense of matériel. But if one element of the military enterprise is to suffer, it would be better to have some kind of coordinated or integrated logistic system with less operational planning than the reverse. Mobilization depends more upon matériel than upon manpower. Men can be collected in a matter of days or weeks. It takes months or years to equip them. All the strategic and operational planning that can be generated will come to naught if there is no logistic substance to give them life. When operational plans are put into effect it already is too late to develop logistic plans. A more rapid and meaningful response to a major attack in Europe could be made, even if all the operational headquarters had been abolished, if at the same time there had been developed a general system of supply, with adequate and well-positioned stockpiles in reserve, with a communications system remaining intact, than ever could be the case if the elaborate and well-organized military headquarters had to face a crisis with empty hands.

Those who worked most closely with the problem never ceased to worry about the logistic deficiencies of NATO defense. One high comander said very frankly, "Logistics as a national responsibility does not make any military sense." General Hans Speidel, commander of Allied Land Forces Central Europe, made a plea for six steps to strengthen NATO: (1) Organizational reform; (2) land MRBM's in Europe; (3) firm command and control procedures; (4) air reinforcement to give greater mobility; (5) uniform training and tactical aims, and (6) unified logistics.[26]

A leading member of the British Parliament wrote, "It is no use having international forces under one command unless there is an international logistics system to support them under the same command. . . . I do not see any alternative to tackling the logistics problem on a NATO-wide basis."[27] Echoing a contention of years, the NATO Parliamentarians' Conference in 1963 recommended "that the alliance take all possible steps to increase still further co-ordination of research, development and production within the framework of NATO, and to organize an integrated logistics system."[28]

Again, Liddell Hart had reemphasized the importance of logistic coordination in these terms:

> The weakest spot of any force is its administrative area. . . . This weakness has increased with technical progress. . . . That complexity, and weakness, would be vastly multiplied in any force composed of national contingents intent to maintain their "national character"—each requiring different rations to feed its men; different calibres of ammunition to feed its weapons; different spare parts and tools; and each functioning on a different staff-system.[29]

Probably the most thoroughgoing consideration of the question of an integrated system of logistics, with particular focus on the central European area, was under the auspices of Western European Union. In January 1957 members of the WEU Committee on Defence Questions and Armaments visited Headquarters, Allied Forces Central Europe, and heard this comment from General Valley, then commander-in-chief:

> The nationalisation of the logistics system gives the central European army such rigidity and sluggishness that it would be difficult, for example, in the event of the enemy attack being concentrated on one particular axis, to move divisions from one section to another. . . . In the field of logistics the C-in-C can only advise, co-ordinate, and generally help countries. Under these circumstances the Supreme Commander is at a great strategic and tactical disadvantage (apart altogether from numbers) as compared with an enemy who can switch his divisions wherever they are needed.[30]

A little over a year later the committee's rapporteur (Fens) reported upon a further visit to AFCENT: "The problem of command has remained unchanged. . . . Logistics in any case remain a purely national responsibility in peace and in war. In these circumstances it is difficult to see in what sense a NATO commander can be said to 'command' the forces assigned to him."[31] Again in 1960 the bureau and the Rapporteur (Goedhart) of the WEU Committee on Defense Questions and Armaments visited AFCENT. Again they were impressed by the "serious limitations resulting from the logistics system of the assigned forces being a national responsibility in peace, the Allied commander's authority in this field being restricted even in war to certain areas and to special circumstances. These limitations make the lateral movement of units from one part of the front to another difficult, and could imperil defence operations in this command."

After further discussions of the problem, the Rapporteur prepared a commentary for the committee in which he said:

> It is impossible in a rational organization to separate the operational control of forces from the control of their supplies—yet this is the present situation. The lives of the soldiers are entrusted to allied commands, while material bought with the taxpayer's money may not pass from national control.
>
> Your Rapporteur calls on the Committee to endorse his demand for proper authority in the field of logistics to be given to allied commanders without delay. This should comprise full authority over all logistic resources in war, irrespective of their location, and adequate authority to plan and inspect stockpiles in peace.[32]

He went on to say that if defense resources are to be made effective, and if the greatest return on defense expenditures is to be realized, then "a completely integrated logistics system is required." This would mean "NATO stockpiles in NATO depots, with NATO transport to move stocks to any combat area." A number of practical obstacles—not the least of which was the lack of standardization—stood in the way of achieving such a system. But it was a matter of such importance that obstacles would have to be overcome. Common production and support of various new weapons was an encouraging development, and it was suggested that the NATO common infrastructure system should be extended to provide depot sites and facilities. The procedures applied to the pipeline system for the distribution of fuel might be used as well for the distribution of equipment and ammunition. Further, it was pointed out that depots for the support of forces in Central Europe still were badly sited, and those of Germany in particular were in a vulnerable area. It was suggested that NATO support depots should be disposed in great depth—including sites in Spain to be negotiated for by NATO, and that they should be stocked with a ninety-day level of supplies (a goal previously accepted by the North Atlantic Council for national depots) to be financed by common funding, as was done for infrastructure.

Clearly the committee, after all its deliberations and on the basis of studies spread over a period of several years, agreed with these views. By a unanimous vote of 14 to 0 it accepted the report, which, most significantly, included a statement of a draft recommendation that included the following:

> Noting that while member governments, in assigning national forces to NATO Command, have entrusted the lives of their soldiers to allied commanders, they have not transferred sufficient control over materials, to enable these commanders to employ their forces efffectively;
>
> • • • • •
>
> Recognizing that defence in modern war requires a fully integrated and flexible logistics system adapted solely to the dictates of geography and military capabilities, where national frontiers have no part;

Welcoming the progress made in producing a common NATO pipeline system for the supply of standardized fuels, yet recalling the long history of otherwise fruitless efforts in NATO to establish a satisfactory logistics system,

Recommends to the Council

1. That as a matter of urgency allied commanders be given adequate control in peace and full control in war over all logistic resources earmarked for forces assigned to their command;
2. That the logistics system of the allied forces be integrated beginning with common depots for new equipment standard to all forces, such as missiles, warheads and electronics, and expanding as more modern equipment is introduced, while the existing national systems correspondingly contract as older non-standard equipment is withdrawn;
3. (i) That military stockpiles, which must provide equally for the requirements of nuclear or more limited war, be brought up to the planning levels for the first 90 days, the cost being shared equitably among the countries of the alliance;

   (ii) That adequate stocks of food and medical supplies be provided for the civilian population.
4. That common NATO stockpiles be sited in accordance with allied military requirements, appropriately distributed in depth from the territory east of the Rhine to areas well in the rear, possibly including the territory of non-member countries of the Alliance, and that agreements on the establishment of common NATO depots be negotiated not by individual States but by NATO itself.[33]

Thus this group was urging a principle that in NATO, logistics should be a "national responsibility" only in the sense that each nation should be responsible for meeting the requirements of its share. In calling for fulfillment of the ninety-day level of supplies, the committee was basing its assumption of requirements on United States experience factors in arriving at the following breakdown of daily requirements for a division slice (including army support and tactical air units):

	Metric tons	Percent of Daily Requirement
Food and medical supplies	180	9
Individual and unit (clothing and equipment and special purpose supplies)	480	24
Petroleum products	330	16
Ammunition and explosives	1,040	51
Total	2,030	100

The move toward an integrated logistics system had especially strong support from the German representatives. Indeed, several months earlier the German delegation at a meeting of NATO defense ministers had been urging steps such as these.[34] On 1 December 1960 the Assembly of Western

European Union adopted the resolution of the Committee on Defence Questions and Armaments without serious dissent. A British member of the assembly did record his opposition a little later, not to the general idea of an integrated logistic system, but to several specific points in the resolution. Noting that he had not wished to force a division at the time of the vote, he nevertheless opposed the resolution on the following grounds: (1) That it would be better to make a selection, each on its merits, of military depots in Western Europe to be placed under NATO authority, rather than so placing them all; (2) that stockpiling a ninety-day level of supply would be costly and it would tend to delay modernization and standardization; (3) that cost-sharing on the basis of GNP was not the best method of financing, for greater consideration should be given to types of currency and balance of payments, and (4) bases or depot sites in nonmember countries should be negotiated for by a selected member acting as agent for NATO rather than by NATO itself.[35] Earlier the *Economist* of London had expressed an opinion that "NATO solidarity has not so far evolved that an integrated NATO supply system has any chance of success yet."[36] This was the kind of advice that may have been realistic, but it was the kind that, if taken, probably would have stopped most of NATO's notable achievements.

A more serious critic offering this kind of advice was a U.S. Air Force colonel, K. Claude Rupert, who, as a veteran of dealing with problems of international logistics in the policy branch of the SHAPE logistics division, had come away with the conclusion that such a system as that advocated by Western European Union was completely beyond reach. Pointing to some of the improvements that had been made for coordinating logistic policy at SHAPE since the WEU resolution had been adopted, but which improvements had little to do with the logistic situation in central Europe with which the report and recommendation had been concerned, he turned to a direct attack upon the proposals: "The demand for an integrated logistics system is fanciful and ill-advised," he wrote, "a 'magical solution' proposed by 'neo-logisticians.' "[37]

Maybe it was impractical even to think of an integrated system of logistics in the North Atlantic Alliance, but the fact was that logistic arrangements for support of Allied forces in battle remained chaotic, and if the paleologisticians could come up with a better and less fanciful and magical solution for the problem, they needed to do so. They were so busy being practical that the commander had been left virtually empty-handed for all those years. Fortunately the system had not been put to trial by combat, and its weaknesses had not been fully exposed.

Patiently, Rupert reminded us that in a nation there is a central authority over logistics—as over strategy—in the general staff and the defense ministry, with budgetary and financial responsibility, while there was no such authority in NATO, although such authority over strategy, to a degree, was granted to SACEUR. Since national forces have remained under their own national commanders up to army group-tactical air force level, "the support of such forces traditionally and quite properly still remains the responsibility of the individual nations. It follows that the geographical grouping of the national forces for tactical reasons has generated some interdependence of these forces, which in turn has resulted in bilateral and multilateral support agreements based upon reasonable economic and financial considerations."[38]

But how could it be supposed that such an arrangement could be satisfactory in meeting the situation in AFCENT where the forces of nine nations were or would be deployed on the territory of five of them? If an emergency arose in Denmark and SACEUR wanted to rush reserves from the center, must the commander first check a chart to see if Belgium, the Netherlands, and the United Kingdom each had agreements with Germany and Denmark for logistic support?

The Achilles heel of NATO (if the position of France be taken as a major chink in its armor) undoubtedly has been its logistic system, but the achievements gained in those formative years indicated what could be done to repair this deficiency. The fact that the United States did have cooperative logistic arrangements with Germany for common access to depots suggested that it would not take a great extension either of doctrine or technology to extend this approach to a NATO-wide basis.

On the other hand, one should never forget that logistic effectiveness is a relative matter, and in appraising NATO's logistic deficiencies, one should note that the logistic problems of the Soviet Union with respect to possible military operations in Central and Western Europe were, at least in some respects, immeasurably greater. It might be said that the more complete Russian domination of Eastern Europe during those years had resulted in a greater degree of standardization on the part of forces of the Warsaw Pact, but that was about the end of any advantage. The great distances from principal industrial centers to potential battle areas, the relatively fewer railroads and the very awkward change of gauge at the Soviet frontier, the poor roads, and the general vulnerability of long lines of communication extending through potentially hostile countries, not to mention the industrial inferiority of the Soviet Union in comparison with Western Europe and the United States, all put the Soviet Union at a distinct logistic disadvantage in any conventional military contest with the NATO allies. To mention logistic deficiencies in NATO was rather to emphasize a comparison with what might be, rather than any general disadvantage vis à vis a potential enemy. But it was the very industrial strength of the NATO countries, where most of the countries could make very substantial contributions to meeting military requirements for supplies and equipments, that made cooperation more difficult but also more rewarding. If all NATO forces relied on the United States for weapons and equipment to the extent that the Warsaw Pact nations depended upon the Soviet Union, then the problems of standardization, cooperative agreements, or an integrated support system would not arise. The question was whether the strength deriving from such multiple sources could be fully mobilized in the most effective way.

If there were no plan and war should come, the Allies would be driven to some kind of integrated logistic system, probably operated by the United

States. This would have all the disadvantages of a system set up in the rush of emergency conditions, and it would lose the advantages of diplomatic strength that an impressive indication of Allied unity arising from a free association of logistic efforts might provide.

Perhaps it was expecting too much even to entertain a hope that there could be any farreaching integration of Allied logistics in peacetime. Perhaps the best that could be done would be to set up a pilot program and make plans for further integration so that if there should come a conflict of the kind that such measures would support, steps would have been taken toward effecting them. Yet to the extent that current military strategy and policy relied upon existing alert forces, logistics had to be concerned to a large degree with the support of such forces. The distinction between peacetime and wartime support of military forces always must assume the prospect of war. But such a distinction had even less reasonable justification in the circumstances of the middle and late twentieth century.

When it came to facing squarely the problem of wartime logistic support of Allied forces in Europe, there appeared to be only three ways, with variations on each, for going about it. One would be to "satellite" Allied forces on the supply systems of the major nations. The specific character would depend upon the nature and extent of standardization, size and disposition of forces, and the nature of the combat. This would mean that France, Germany, Italy, and Great Britain would be prepared to support a substantial number of troops and naval units on or near its own territory, in addition to its own, and the United States would provide substantial general support for forces in those countries, as well as for those in the north and in the southeast. The second possible method of support would be to develop an international, integrated system. This plan would permit maximum flexibility in facilitating the movement of troops from area to another, but it also was the most remote in terms of an early enough general acceptance to make it really effective when needed. The third way would be simply to accept the oft-repeated principle, "Logisitcs is a national responsibiity," depend upon each nation to set up its own system, and let it go at that. This was the most simple plan, but how complicated it would be to make it work for large Allied forces!

Over the years a great deal of discussion among NATO officers and officials, and among officials of the Allied governments, centered on the question of developing closer coordination of logistics. Of many suggestions for improvement, the defense ministers have put major emphasis on these four: (1) creation of logistic centers within major Allied commands; (2) common storage of major items and repair parts and common maintenance facilities for all advanced weapons; (3) an integrated depot superstructure; and (4) joint use of training facilities. Yet years of discussion and recommendations did not result in an integrated system, beyond a very limited degree, for distributing supplies to Allied forces.

Implicit in nearly every discussion of NATO policy and structure was a certain restlessness against a supposed American domination of the Alliance. Ronald Steil accurately wrote, "while Europeans may deplore de Gaulle's methods, they secretly applaud his audacity."[39]

Yet the thrust of United States policy since World War II had been exactly to the contrary. United States support for European economic recovery, United States support for a united Europe, and indeed United States support of the North Atlantic Alliance itself had had the effect of *adding* to the weight of European contributions to the common efforts, not of diminishing them.

General George C. Marshall's initial suggestion, in his address as secretary of state at Harvard University in June 1947, for what later became known as the "Marshall Plan," carried a plea for European economic cooperation:

> It is already evident that before the United States Government can proceed much further in its efforts to . . . help start the European world on its way to recovery, there must be some agreement among the countries of Europe as to the requirements of the situation, and the part those countries themselves will take in order in give proper effect to whatever action might be undertaken by this Government. . . . The initiative, I think, must come from Europe. . . . The program should be a joint one, agreed to by a number of, if not, all European nations.[40]

Marshall's speech certainly was not aimed at keeping Europe in a permanent state of economic inferiority, and it certainly was not an approach aiming to "divide and rule" the European nations.

In the act giving practical effect to the Marshall Plan, the Congress of the United States included this significant policy statement:

> Mindful of the advantages which the United States has enjoyed through the existence of a large domestic market with no internal trade barriers, and believing that similar advantages can accrue to the countries of Europe, it is declared to be the policy of the people of the United States to encourage these countries through a joint organization to exert sustained common efforts . . . which will speedily achieve that economic cooperation in Europe which is essential for lasting peace and prosperity.[41]

In the amendments of April 1949 to the Economic Cooperation Act, this statement was added: "It is further declared to be the policy of the people of the United States to encourage the unification of Europe."

On the specific question of integrated logistics, it would be difficult to be more explicit than was the Congress in the 1959 amendments to the Mutual Security Act:

> The Congress believes it essential that this Act should be so administered as to support concrete measures to promote greater political federation, military integration, and economic unification in Europe, including coordinated production and procurement programs participated in by the members of the North Atlantic Treaty Organization to the greatest extent possible with respect to military equipment and materials to be utilized for the defense of the North Atlantic area.[42]

The Alliance itself was not really necessary if its essential purpose was to assure United States support of the Western European countries in case of attack against them. This could be done as well with a series of bilateral agreements (as with Spain), or with no agreements at all. It was so obviously in the interest of the United States not to permit a Russian takeover of Western Europe that few doubted that American power would counter any such attempt in any case. The significance of a formal alliance, then, was in assuring the machinery for effective *European* participation in the common defense.

In this design, it might be hoped (from the American point of view) that the experience of Allied cooperation in World War I might have more to offer than that of World War II. If American preponderance ever was evident, it was in the later stages of the Second World War. Then on a large part of the western front in Europe and in the Pacific there was standardization of equipment because it was American. There was common procedure—largely American. Behind the combat zones were depots filled with supplies—mostly American, and transportation to deliver them—mostly American. Only the British and Commonwealth forces had any kind of supply system of their own, and only they had equal status in top-level strategic planning.

This situation made control relatively easy. From the American point of view this method would be the easy way in a future crisis, and if something better is not developed, it may have to come to that again. But the drive of the United States has been, in spite of difficulties, for *multiple* participation on a basis of equality among the nations. If General De Gaulle really were concerned about American domination, he would have been well advised to preserve France's position of logistic indispensability. More that than, he should have been moving swiftly toward a more closely integrated logistic system involving all the European powers, and facilitated by the entry of Britain, Denmark, and Norwy into the European Economic Community, in order to free all of Europe from such a large measure of logistic dependence upon the United States. The North Atlantic Alliance remained "the most important instrument for West Europeans to influence American policy and strategy."[43]

The North Atlantic Council itself defined possible future area of tasks for the Alliance in terms of the special groups set up to study, (1) East-West relations; (2) interallied relations; (3) general defense policy; and (4) relations with other countries.[44]

A 1967 study on national security and international operations for a subcommittee of the Committee on Government Operations of the U.S. Senate concluded with this statement:

> The founders of the Atlantic Alliance were forward-looking in 1949. Their successors should be equally forward-looking today. The future is filled with challenges no one of the Allies can handle in isolation, and that neither North America nor Western Europe can meet alone.
>
> Today's political leaders—executive and legislative—have solemn

duties. Theirs is the main responsibility to assure the common defense, to advance the cause of a genuine European settlement, and to provide for stability in Europe as a basis for a peaceful international society. They must inspire the oncoming generation of young people to do its best in the unfinished work of the Alliance.

For today as yesterday the need for the Alliance is fresh and compelling; it is difficult to imagine a hopeful future which does not rest on the stability and steadiness of our association, and, of course, especially on the steadiness of American policy.[45]

Effective logistics is at the heart of a realistic system of defense. Whatever grand designs or bold schemes that may be offered to achieve this for the North Atlantic Alliance, the achievements already attained should be kept in mind. How out of reach it would have seemed in 1949 if someone had suggested the broad system of common infrastructure that was later achieved! Who could have foreseen such a vast pipeline system functioning so well, a NATO Supply Center giving effective support for aircraft and missiles? Who could have predicted such thorough planning in certain aspects of transportation? Who could have suggested the imaginative projects in coordinated production that were to be accomplished? Indeed, who could have hoped for the effectiveness of staff work that would be performed by Germans and Frenchmen and Belgians and Danes and Greeks and Turks, and all the others, working together as a unit? Future security and stability will depend to a considerable extent upon the achievements of NATO already recorded. The question now is whether the imagination of contemporary leaders will still be able to match the full potential of their own peoples in concert.

Notes

1. See Henry E. Eccles, *European Logistics, 1956,* George Washington University Logistics Research Project no. ONR 41904 (Washington, D.C., 1956).

2. Dirk V. Stikker, "The Long, Rough Road," *NATO Letter,* December 1963, 3–9.

3. See Robert Strausz-Hupé and William R. Kintner, *Building the Atlantic World* (New York, 1963), 74ff.

4. Henry A. Kissinger, *The Troubled Partnership* (New York, 1965), 18.

5. J. B. Duroselle, "The Future of the Atlantic Community," in *The Atlantic Nations: Converging or Diverging? Prospects for 1975* (Boulogne-sur-Seine, 1966), 45–46. Cf. Robert Kleinman, *Atlantic Crisis: American Diplomacy Confronts a Resurgent Europe* (New York, 1964); J. Robert Schaetzel, *The Unhinged Alliance: America and the European Community* (New York, 1975); Lothar Rühl, "The Nine and NATO," in *Dilemmas of the Atlantic Alliance,* ed. Peter Christian Ludz et al. (New York, 1975), 213–52.

6. Helmut Schmidt, *Defense or Retaliation,* trans. Edward Thomas (Edinburgh, 1962), 125–61; 175–216.

7. Hans Kohn, "Western Europe and Atlantic Unity," *Current History,* September 1960, 153.

8. "Is NATO Becoming Irrevelent?" *The Times* (London), 6 April 1964.

9. Quoted in Livingston Hartley, "Atlantic Partnership—How?" *Orbis* 8 (Spring 1964): 147. See also Richard H. Rovere, "Letter from Washington," *New Yorker,* 11 April 1964, 149–55.

10. George W. Ball, "NATO and World Responsibility," *Atlantic Community Quarterly* 2 (Summer 1964): 208–18.

11. Kurt Birrenbach, "Partnership and Consultation in NATO," *Atlantic Community Quarterly* 2 (Spring 1964): 62–71.

12. See, e.g., Betty Goetz Lall, "A NATO-Warsaw Detente?" *Bulletin of the Atomic Scientists* 20 (November 1964): 37–39.

13. Eugene Rostow, "Possible Futures for the Atlantic Community," in *The Atlantic Nations: Converging or Diverging? Prospects for 1975* (Boulogne-sur-Seine, 1967), 84.

14. Ibid., 97.

15. Alastair Buchan, *Crisis Management: The New Diplomacy,* The Atlantic Papers, NATO Series 2 (Boulogne-sur-Seine, 1966).

16. André Beaufre, "European Aspects of the NATO Crisis," *NATO Letter,* May 1967, 27; "General Beaufre's Solution to the NATO Crisis," *NATO Letter,* March 1967, 26.

17. J. Robert Schaetzel, "The Necessary Partnership," *Foreign Affairs,* 44 (April 1966): 417–33.

18. Manlio Brosio, "The Hard Tasks of the Alliance," *NATO Letter,* December 1966, 5.

19. Stikker, "The Long, Rough Road," 3–9.

20. Harald von Rickhoff, "The Changing Function of NATO," *International Journal* 21 (Spring 1966): 157–72. The definition of a "security community" is from Karl Deutsch, *Political Community and the North Atlantic Area* (Princeton, N.J., 1957), 5.

21. André Beaufre, "La Drôle Paix," *Le Figaro,* 26 August 1967, 1.

22. Cf. von Rickhoff, "The Changing Function of NATO," 161.

23. See Ernest H. Meili, "Nations United for Peace—NATO Infrastructure," *Signal,* December 1959, 25.

24. See the author's *Across the Face of France* (Lafayette, Ind., 1963), 131–41.

25. Maj. Gen. Henry R. Westphalinger, "U.S. Army Communications Zone, Europe," *Army Information Digest,* December 1962, 9–16.

26. *Frankfurter Allgemeine Zeitung,* 8 April 1964.

27. F. W. Mulley, *The Politics of Western Defence* (London, 1962), 198, 200.

28. "NATO Parliamentarians' Conference Resolutions," *NATO Letter,* December 1963, 23.

29. B. H. Liddell Hart, *Deterrent or Defense* (New York, 1960), 242.

30. Western European Union Doc. 38, par. 8.

31. Western European Union Doc. 87, par. 42.

32. "State of European Security: Logistics in Allied Forces Central Europe," Assembly of Western European Union, Doc. 180, 25 October 1960, 3.

33. Ibid, 1–2.

34. Ibid., appendix.

35. John H. Hallett, M.P., letter to the editor of *The Times* (London), 5 December 1960.

36. "NATO and WEU; Those Bases Again," *The Economist,* 2 April 1960, 26.

37. K. Claude Rupert, "International Logistics is Becoming a Fact," *NATO's Fifteen Nations,* December 1962–January 1963, 69–70.

38. Ibid.

39. Ronald Steel, *The End of Alliance* (London, 1964), 81.

40. U.S. Senate, Committee on Foreign Relations, *A Decade of American Foreign Policy: Basic Documents, 1941–1949* (Washington, 1950), 1269.

41. Economic Cooperation Act of 1948, Section 102 (a).

42. Mutual Security Act of 1954 as amended (1959), Sec. 105, b, 1.

43. Curt Gasteyger, *Europe in the Seventies,* Institute of Strategic Studies, Adelphi Papers no. 37 (London, 1967), 15.

44. NATO Press Release (67)3, 13 April 1967.

45. U.S. Senate, Committee on Government Operations, Subcommittee on National Security and International Operations, *The Atlantic Alliance: Unfinished Business,* 90th Cong., 1st sess., 1967. Committee Print.

Glossary

ABC. U.S.A., Britain, Canada (regional grouping for standardization).

ACE. Allied Command Europe.

ACE High. Allied Command Europe signal communication system.

ACEMF. Allied Command Europe Mobile Forces.

ACITCE. Authority for the Coordination of Inland Transportation in Central Europe.

ACofS. Assistant Chief of Staff.

ACTISUD. Authority for the Coordination of Inland Transportation in Southern Europe.

AFBALTAP. Allied Forces Baltic Approaches (Colvrä, Denmark).

AFCENT. Allied Forces Central Europe (Fontainebleau, Brunssum).

AFMED. Allied Forces Mediterranean (Malta).

AFNORTH. Allied Forces Northern Europe (Oslo).

AFSOUTH. Allied Forces Southern Europe (Naples).

AGARD. Advisory Group for Aeronautical Research and Development.

AGF. Army Ground Forces.

AGO. Adjutant General's Office.

Airborne early warning and control. An airborne radar station providing early warning and control facilities.

Airhead. 1. A designated area in a hostile or threatened territory that, when seized and held, ensures the continuous air landing of troups and matériel and provides the maneuver space necessary for projected operations. 2. A designated location in an area of operations used as a base for supply and evacuation by air.

ANF. Proposed Atlantic Nuclear Force.

Army service area. The territory between the Corps rear boundary and the Combat Zone rear boundary. Most of the Army administrative establishment and service troops are usually located in this area.

ASF. Army Service Forces.

Basic load (ammunition). That quantity of ammunition which is authorized and required by each nation to be on hand within a unit or formation at all times. It is expressed in terms of rounds for ammunition items fired by weapons, and in other units of measure for bulk allotment and other ammunition items.

BENELUX. Belgium, Netherlands, Luxembourg.

Bilateral infrastructure. Infrastructure that concerns only two NATO members and is financed by mutual agreement between them (e.g., facilities required for the use of forces of one NATO member in the territory of another).

Block-stowage loading. A method of loading whereby all cargo for a specific destination is stowed together. The purpose is to facilitate rapid off-loading at the destination, with the least possible disturbance of cargo intended for other points.

BOCCA. Board for the Coordination of Civil Aircraft.

Broadfields. Listings of categories of matériel and characteristics of equipment in use by armies and air forces of NATO members.

BULLPUP. Air to surface missile.

Bundesbahn. German Federal Railways.

CAPC. Civil Aviation Planning Committee.

CEPO. Central Europe Pipeline Office.

CEPPC. Central Europe Pipeline Policy Committee.

CEWP. Central European Wagon Pool.

CINCEUR. Command in Chief, Europe.

CINCHAN. Allied Commander-in-chief Channel; one of the major NATO commanders.

CINCUSAREUR. Commander in Chief, U.S. Army, Europe.

CISMISH. Interministerial Committee for the Installation of SHAPE.

CIVLOGEX. Logistic training exercise for civilian agencies.

Combined common user items. Items of an interchangeable nature that are in common use by two or more nations.

COMINTSE. Committee on Inland Transportation Southern Europe (Rome).

Commercial loading. The loading of personnel and/or equipment and supplies for maximum use of space. Sometimes called "Administrative Loading."

Commodity loading. A method of loading in which various types of cargoes are loaded together, such as ammunition, rations, or boxed vehicles, in order that each commodity can be discharged without disturbing the other.

Common infrastructure. Infrastructure essential to the training of NATO forces or to the implementation of NATO operational plans that, owing to its degree of common use or interest and its compliance with criteria laid down from time to time by the North Atlantic Council, is commonly financed by NATO members.

Communications zone. Rear part of theater of operations (behind but contiguous to the combat zone) that contains the lines of communication, establishments for supply and evacuation, and other agencies required for the immediate support and maintenance of the field forces.

Cross-servicing. That servicing performed by one service or national element for other services or national elements and for which the other services or national elements may be charged.

DCofS. Deputy Chief of Staff.

DELWU. (Delegation to Western Union) U.S. delegation to the Military Committee of the Five Powers.

DSA. Defense Supply Agency.

Economic mobilization. The process of preparing for and carrying out such changes in the organization and functioning of the national economy as are necessary to provide for the most effective use of resources in a national emergency.

ECA. Economic Cooperation Administration: the agency set up to administer the Marshall Plan.

EEC. European Economic Community (the "Common Market").

EFTA. European Free Trade Association.

EQR. Economic Order Quantity; a procedure for ordering low-value items only in large lots.

ERP. European Recovery Program: the Marshall Plan.

Emergency fleet operating base. A base providing logistic support for fleet units operating in an area for limited periods of time.

EUCOM. European Command.

FACC. Foreign Assistance Coordinating Committee.

FAFLO. French-American Fiscal Liason Office.

FEBA. Forward edge of the battle area. The foremost limits of a series of areas in which ground combat units are deployed, excluding the areas in which the covering or screening forces are operating, designated to coordinate fire support, the positioning of forces, or the maneuver of units.

FINABL. France, Italy, Netherlands, Germany, Belgium (regional grouping for standardization).

Force de Frappe. French nuclear force.

FM. Field manual.

Forward Scatter. Long-range high-frequency tropospheric radio communication (a part of ACE HIGH)

G-1. Personnel section of division or higher staff.

G-2. Intelligence section of division or higher staff.

G-3. Operations and training section of division or higher staff.

G-4. Supply section of division or higher staff.

HAWK. A surface-to-air missile.

HLG. High-level Group.

HONEST JOHN. Surface-to-surface missile.

HUCO. Hughes NADGE Consortium.

ICAF. Industrial College of the Armed Forces (Ft. McNair, Washington, D.C.)

INF. Intermediate-range nuclear forces.

Infrastructure. A term used in NATO generally applicable for all fixed and permanent installations, fabrications, or facilities for the support and control of military forces.

Inventory control. That phase of military logistics which includes managing, cataloging, requirements determination, procurement, distribution, overhaul, and disposal of matériel. Synonymous with Material Control, Material Management, Inventory Management and Supply Management.

ITD. International Transit Declaration.

JAAF. Joint Action Armed Forces.

JAMAG. Joint American Military Advisory Group.

JCS. Joint Chiefs of Staff.

JUSMAPG. Joint United States Military Advisory and Planning Group.

Joint staff. A staff formed of two or more of the services of the same country.

KPC. Koblenz Procurement Center.

LCC. Logistics Coordinating Center (SHAPE).

Level of supply. The quantity of supplies or materials authorized or directed to be held in anticipation of future demands.

LNO. Limited nuclear options.

LOC. Line of communication, a principal supply line.

LOGEX. Training exercise in logistics.

Logistics. The science of planning and carrying out the movement and maintenance of forces. In its most comprehensive sense, those aspects of military operations that deal with 1. design and development, acquisition, storage, movement, distribution, maintenance, evacuation and disposition of material; 2. movement, evacuation, and hospitalization of personnel; 3. acquisition or construction, maintenance, operation, and disposition of facilities; and 4. acquisition or furnishing of services.

MAAG. Military Assistance Advisory Group.

MACE. Surface-to-surface missile.

Major NATO Commanders. Major NATO Commanders are Supreme Allied Commander Atlantic (SACLANT), Supreme Allied Commander Europe (SACEUR), and Allied Commander-in-Chief Channel (CINCHAN).

Marshall Plan. Program of United States for European economic recovery after World War II.

MAS. Military Agency for Standardization (London, Brussels).

Materials handling. The movement of materials (raw materials, scrap, semi-finished) to, through, and from productive processes; in warehouses and storage; and in receiving and shipping areas.

MATS. Military Air Transport Service.

MDAP. Mutual Defense Assistance Program.

M-Day. The term used to designate the day on which mobilization is to begin.

MEE. Minimum essential equipment.

MFNG. Military Facilities Negotiating Group.

MILSTAMP. Military Standard Movement Procedure.

MILSTRIP. Military Standard Requisitioning and Inventory Procedures.

MLF. A proposed multilateral force of missile-carrying surface vessels manned by mixed crews.

Mobile support group (naval). Provides logistic support to ships at an anchorage; in effect, a naval base afloat; although certain supporting elements may be located ashore.

Movement control. The planning, routing, scheduling, and control of personnel and supply movements over lines of communication; also an organization responsible for these functions.

MSA. Mutual Support Agency.

MSP. Mutual Security Program.

MSTS. Military Sea Transportation Service.

NADGE. NATO Air Defense Ground Environment.

NADGEMO. NADGE Management Office.

NAMSA. NATO Maintenance and Supply Agency.

NAMSO. NATO Maintenance and Supply Organization.

NAMSSS. NATO Maintenance Supply Services System.

National infrastructure. Infrastructure provided and financed by a NATO member in its own territory solely for its own forces (including those forces assigned to or designated for NATO).

National Territorial Commander. A national commander who is responsible for the execution of purely national functions in a specific geographical area. He remains a national territorial commander regardless of any Allied status that may be assigned to him.

NATO-unified product. A standardized product that is used or is fully suitable for use by all NATO nations for a given end use.

Naval augmentation group. A formed group of escort vessels employed to augment the through escort of convoys when passing through areas known or suspected to be threatened by enemy forces.

NETSO. North Europe Transshipment Organization.

NIKE. A family of two-staged surface-to-air missiles.

NMSS. NATO Maintenance and Supply System.

NODEX. New Offshore Discharge Exercise. A system for unloading supplies over the beaches by small craft and amphibious vehicles.

NPG. Nuclear Planning Group.

NSC. National Security Council.

NSC. NATO Supply Center.

Ocean manifest. A detailed listing of the entire cargo loaded into any one ship showing all pertinent data that will readily identify such cargo.

OCMH. Office of the Chief of Military History.

OEEC. Organization for European Economic Cooperation.

Operational interchangeability. Ability to substitute one item for another of different composition or origin without loss in effectiveness, accuracy, and safety of performance.

PBEIST. Planning Board of European Inland Surface Transport.

PBOS. Planning Board for Ocean Shipping.

Petroleum intersectional service. An intersectional or interzonal service in a theater of operations that operates pipelines and related facilities for the supply of bulk petroleum products to theater Army elements and other forces as directed.

Pipe line. In logistics, the channel of support or a specific portion thereof by means of which material or personnel flow from sources of procurement to their point of use.

Planning factor. A properly selected multiplier, used in planning to estimate the amount and type of effort involved in a contemplated operation. Planning factors are often expressed as rates, ratios, or lengths of time.

Preload loading. The loading of selected items aboard ship at one port prior to the main loading of the ship at another.

PTT. Postes, Téléphones, et Télégraphs (France).

QMC. Quartermaster Corps.

Red Ball Express. Trailer-Transfer line rehaul relay system of motor transportation for delivery of supplies.

Replacement factor. The estimated percentage of equipment or repair parts in use that will require replacement during a given period due to wearing out beyond repair, enemy action, abandonment, pilferage, and other causes except catastrophes.

Required supply rate. The amount of ammunition expressed in terms of rounds per weapon per day for ammunition items fired by weapons, and in terms of other units of measure per day for bulk allotment and other items, estimated to be required to sustain operations of any designated force without restriction for a specified period.

Roll-on/roll-off. System for shipping loaded trailers directly, from U.S. to Europe, to be driven onto the piers and over ramps carried on specially designed ships.

SAC. Strategic Air Command.

SACEUR. Supreme Allied Comander Éurope.

SACLANT. Supreme Allied Commander Atlantic (Norfolk).

SATCOM. Satellite communications system.

Selective loading. The arrangement and stowage of equipment and supplies aboard ship in a manner designed to facilitate issues to units.

SEP. Selective employment options.

SERGEANT. Ground-to-ground missile.

SHAPE. Supreme Headquarters Allied Powers Europe (Rocquencourt, near Paris; Casteau, near Brussels).

Shore party (beach group). A task organization of the landing force formed for the purpose of facilitating the landing and movement off the beaches of troops, equipment, and supplies; for the evacuation from the beaches of casualties and prisoners of war; and for facilitating the beaching, retraction, and salvaging of landing ships and craft. It comprises elements of both the naval and landing forces.

SIDEWINDER. Air-to-air missile.

Slice (Division). Total strength of a combat division, together with its appropriate share of supporting forces.

Slice (Infrastructure). Program for a given year of development of NATO's common infrastructure.

SNCF. Société Nationale des Chemins de Fer (French national railroads).

SOF. Status of forces agreement.

SOLOG. Standardization of operations and procedures agreement.

SOP. Standing operating procedure.

STANAG. Standardization agreement (NATO) The record of an agreement among several or all of the member nations to adopt like or similar military equipment, ammunition, supplies, and stores; and operational, logistic and administrative procedures.

STEG. Staatliche Erfassungsgesellshaft für offentliches Gut m.b.H. (a German public corporation).

TACAN. Tactical aircraft beacons.

Tactical control. The detailed and, usually, local direction and control of movements or maneuvers necessary to accomplish missions or tasks assigned.

TCC. Temporary Council Committee.

TIF. International Transport Declaration.

TRAPIL. Société des Transports Pietroliers par Pipeline (a French semipublic corporation).

Unit loading. The loading of troop units with their equipment and supplies in the same vessels.

UNRRA. United Nations Relief and Rehabilitation Administration.

USAGG. U.S. Army Group, Greece.

USAREUR. U.S. Army, Europe.

USCINCEUR. U.S. Commander in Chief, Europe.

USEUCOM. U.S. European Command (successor to EUCOM).

USFA. U.S. Forces in Austria.

USFET. U.S. Forces, European Theater.

WDGS. War Department General Staff.

Western Union. The organization developed by the five powers (Belgium, France, Luxembourg, the Netherlands, and the United Kingdom) who had signed the Brussels Pact in 1948.

WEU. Western European Union. The redesignation of Western Union with the adherence of Germany and Italy to the Brussels Pact.

Bibliography

NATO Documents

A. NATO Information Service (London, Paris, Brussels)

NATO Press Communiqué (65) 2, 16 December 1965.
NATO Press Release (65) 19, 27 November 1965.
NATO Press Release (66) 3, 16 December 1966.
NATO Press Release (67) 3, 13 April 1967.

B. NATO Maintenance and Supply Organization (Luxembourg City)

"ACE Tropospheric Forward Scatter Communications System Logistic Support." NM (67) BOD/52, Directive 361, 8 December 1967. Amended 11 December 1969.

"Additional Information Concerning the Activation of the Southern Depot." NM (69) BOD/6, 11 March 1969.

"Agreement Between SHAPE and NAMSA on the Supply and Maintenance Support of the ACE Tropospheric Forward Scatter Communication System." NM (66) BOD/59, 8 December 1966. Amended 11 December 1969.

"Brokerage Operations (Supply)." NM (64) BOD/3 (final), Directive 212, 12 February 1964.

"Calibration Services." NM (63) BOD/65, Directive 231, 11 December 1963. Amended 8 December 1966.

"Charter of the NATO Maintenance and Supply Organization (NAMSO)." NM (64) BOD/60 (final), 18 March 1968.

"Choice and Management of Stocks." NM (64) BOD/5, Directive 213, 11 February 1964.

"Early Warning System Logistic Support." NM (67) BOD/19, 18 October 1967. Amended 11 December 1969.

"Establishment of the NATO Supply Center as a Part of the NATO Maintenance and Supply Organization." P&P Directive 142, 3 March 1960.

"Excess and Surplus." NM (69) BOD/46, 14 October 1969.

"F-104 Procurement Programme." NM (65) BOD/22, 3 May 1965. Amended 10 December 1968.

"Financial Regulations of NAMSA." NM (66) BOD/37 (final), 8 July 1969, 16 July 1968.

"Four-Year Programme for Spare Parts Support of Jet Engine Overhaul." NM (64) BOD/76, 9 December 1964. Amended 18 October 1967.

"General Principles Governing the Organization of the NATO Supply Center." NM (64) BOD/7, Subseries 140, 11 February 1964.

"Handbook of Missions and Tasks Entrusted to NAMSA." NM (68) BOD/30, 15 October 1968.

"Long-Term Forecasts for Programmes." NM (66) BOD/7, Directive 610, 24 February 1966.

"Maintenance Float." NM (68) BOD/13, 15 October 1968.

"Memo for Chairman NAMSO, sub.: NAMSO Relocation." AG/67/31, 19 July 1967.

"Mutual Emergency Support Procedures." NM (69) BOD/35.

"NAMSA Maintenance Manual." NR 235-1.

"NAMSA Relocation." NM (67) LOG/21-F&A/25, 13 July 1967.

"NAMSO—General Organization." NM (66) BOD/24 (final), Series 100, 12 October 1966.

"NAMSO Relocation." NM (67) BOD/33, 30 June 1967.

"NIKE/HONEST JOHN Programme." NM (66) BOD/3, 24 February 1966.

NMSSA Instruction 225-1. NMSSA Supply Manual, amendment no. 1, 1 January 1964. Five 1–Five 10.

"Policies to Govern NAMSA Procurement." NM (64) BOD/99, Subseries 250, 9 July 1964. Revised 28 March 1968.

"Programmed and Unprogrammed Repair and Overhaul Services." NM (68) BOD/14, 16 July 1968.

"Recommendations of the Permanent Committees Concerning Relocation of NAMSO." NM (67) BOD/47, 9 October 1967.

"Recruitment Policy for International Staff." NM (64) BOD/46, 9 December 1964. Revised 8 December 1967.

"Redistribution of Stocks." NM (69) BOD/37, Directive 222, 9 September 1963.

"Relocation Budget, Logistics Committee and Finance and Administration Committee." NM (67) LOG/19–F&A/24, 18 July 1967.

"Report on Review of Concept and Methodology of Brokerage Programme." NM (70) LOG/8, 22 May 1970.

"Revised Agreement Between SHAPE and NAMSA for Logistic Support." NM (66) BOD/58, Directive 770, 18 October 1967.

"Rules of Procedure of the Board of Directors and Its Subsiding Bodies." NM (64) BOD/53 (final), Directive 130, 29 September 1964.

"Sidewinder Programme." Directive 342, 18 October 1967. Amended 14 October 1969.

"Study of the Feasibility of Activation of Taranto as a Depot Site." NM (68) BOD/31, 20 August 1968.

"Transfer of NAMSO." NM (67) LOG/19–F&A/24, 17 July 1967.

C. North Atlantic Council and Related Organs (Brussels)

Armaments Committee, Basic Agreements. "Methods of the NATO BULLPUP Production Organization." Working paper AC/74-WP/22, 17 December 1963.

———. "Methods of the NATO HAWK Production Organization." Working paper AC/74-WP/19, 12 December 1963.

Final Communiqués, Conferences of Defense Ministers of NATO member countries.

Final Communiqués, Ministerial Sessions of North Atlantic Council.

Logistics Committee and Finance and Administration Committee. "Status of Transfer of NAMSO." NM (67) LOG/30-F&A/30, 14 September 1967.

The North Atlantic Treaty and Related Documents. SRE special publication.

Technical Secretariat on Codification of Equipment. "The NATO Codification System." Paris, 1960, 1, A-1.

D. *Supreme Allied Command, Europe (Casteau, Belgium)*

Annual reports, Supreme Allied Commander, Europe.

Brief prepared by SHAPE Office of Public Information; Consortium of SHAPE Architects and Engineers, Group Alpha, SOBEMAP, ELECTROBEL, Gibbs and Hill, Inc., Scheduling Progress Report no. 34, 14 July 1967.

E. *Western European Union (Fontainebleau)*

"Recommendations on the State of European Security Aspects of Western Strategy." Anthony Duynstee, Rapporteur. Assembly of Western European Union, 1 December 1964. Reprinted in *The Atlantic Community Quarterly* 2 (Winter 1964–65): 683–84.

"State of European Security: Logistics and Allied Forces Central Europe." Assembly of Western European Union, Document 180, 25 October 1960.

"State of European Security (Navies in the Nuclear Age)." Lord Kennet, Rapporteur. Assembly of Western European Union, Document 269, 1963 (draft).

Western European Union Document 38, par. 8.

Western European Union Document 87, par. 42.

NATO Publications

A. *Periodicals*

Aspects of NATO (pamphlet series on specific topics including "AGARD," "Defense Production and Infrastructure," and "Pipelines for NATO")

The Atlantic Alliance and the Warsaw Pact

Man's Environment and the Atlantic Alliance

Pocket Guide to NATO

NATO Background Information Notes

NATO: Facts about the North Atlantic Treaty Organization (Annual)

NATO Facts and Figures (Annual)

NATO Handbook (Annual)

NATO Letter (Monthly)

NATO Review (Monthly)

Why NATO?

B. *Articles and Monographs*

"AFCENT Leaves France for The Netherlands." *NATO Letter,* March 1967.

Barnes, L. W. C. S. "The NATO Small Arms Ammunition Panel." *NATO Letter,* November 1963, 22–24.

Beaufre, André. "European Aspects of the NATO Crisis." *NATO Letter,* May 1967, 27.

Beretty, Dominque. "AIRCENT—Seven Nations, One Command." *NATO Letter,* June 1964, 14–18.

Brosio, Manlio. "The Hard Tasks of the Alliance." *NATO Letter,* December 1966, 5.

———. "Past and Future Tasks of the Alliance: An Analysis of the Harmel Report." *NATO Letter,* March 1968, 8–13.

———. "The Substance and Spirit of the Alliance." *NATO Letter,* December 1965, 2–10.

"Building a New Shape at Casteau." *NATO Letter,* January 1967, 14–17.

Garrett, Johnson. "An Alliance Goes into the Construction Business." *NATO Letter,* February 1965, 2–10.

Goodman, Elliott R. "The Duynstee Plan." *NATO Letter,* July–August 1965, 2–9.

Hinterhoff, E. "Protecting the Flanks of the Alliance." *NATO Letter,* January 1965, 10–13, 16–17.

Hodder, John S. "NATO's Mobile Force in Action." *NATO Letter,* September 1964, 11–19.

"A Look at Allied Command Channel." NATO Letter, January 1966, 17–21.

Lord Ismay. *NATO's First Five Years.* Paris: NATO, 1955.

Madre, Jean de. "SHAPE's Fifteen Years at Rocquencourt." *NATO Letter,* April 1967, 17–23.

Meili, E. H. "Defense Production and Infrastructure." *NATO Letter,* April 1959, 25–28.

"NATO Parliamentarians' Conference Resolutions." *NATO Letter,* December 1963, 23.

Parker, T. W. "NATO Military Development, 1949–1959." *NATO Letter,* April 1959, 5–9.

Rossum, Els van. "Welcome to Brunssum." *NATO Letter,* March 1967.

"Saving Time and Money." *NATO Letter,* March 1961, 13–17.

Sington, Anne. "French Link in a NATO Communications System." *NATO Letter,* April 1965, 10–17.

———. "A NATO Airfield in Greece." *NATO Letter,* March 1965, 16–19.

———. "NATO Defensive Installations in Norway." *NATO Letter,* January 1966, 2–9.

———. "NATO Missile Sites in Germany." *NATO Letter,* June 1965, 14–20.

"NATO Pipelines in Turkey." *NATO Letter,* July–August 1965, 18–22.

———. "NATO 'SATCOM.'" *NATO Letter,* March 1968, 14–21.

———. "NATO Settles Down to Work in Brussels." *NATO Letter,* December 1967, 14–23.

———. "NATO's Air Defense—A Child's Guide to NADGE." *NATO Letter,* April 1967, 10.

Smeeton, R. M. "Oceans to Defend." *NATO Letter,* March 1963, 7–11.

"Statement of Chancellor Erhard to Fifth Bundestag, November 10, 1965." *NATO Letter,* January 1966, 24.

Stikker, Dirk V. "The Long, Rough Road." *NATO Letter,* December 1963, 3–9.

Stone, J. C. "NATO Cooperation in Research, Development, and Production," *NATO Letter,* October 1969, 22–25.

Stone, John. "Equipment Standardization and Cooperation." *NATO Review* 22 (August 1974): 26–28.

Sunder, Richard. " 'Deep Furrow,' An Effective Defense of Greece and Turkey." *NATO Letter,* December 1965, 21–24.

———. "Goodbye to Fontainebleau." *NATO Letter,* March 1967.

"The Transfer of SHAPE to Belgium." *NATO Letter,* December 1966, 12–13.

Van Lynden, Rear Adm. (Ret.) Count R. W. "NATO's Silent Service." *NATO Review* 22 (October 1974): 25–29.

Government Documents and Publications

A. *Department of the Army*

Annual Reports of the Secretary of the Army.

The Army Almanac. Washington, D.C.: Office of the Chief of Military History, 1950.

"Army Foreign Military Aid." Supply Planning Branch, G-4, 1 June 1953.

"Army Progress Report 16-A, Financial Statement." December 1952.

"Basic Policies of the Department of the Army." DA-PB-50, 1953.

"Correspondence." Foreign Military Aid Branch, G-4, Historical Files.

"Criteria for Determining Supply and Financing Responsibility for Assistance to European Production of Military Equipment, Offshore Procurement." Office of the Director for Mutual Security, DMA D-2/2a, 18 February 1953.

Documents on French Line of Communications. Plans Office, Theaters Branch, G-4, 1950–51.

"Foreign Procurement." Historical Summary, Procurement Division, G-4, 13 December 1951. Purchases Branch, Procurement Division, 1951–53.

"Global Mission of the Quartermaster Corps." Historical Summary, Quartermaster Corps, September 1951–December 1952.

Handbook on the Soviet and Satellite Armies. DA pamphlet 30-50-1, March 1953.

Historical Summary. Deployments Branch, G-3, 1951–52.

———. Europe and Middle East Branch, G-3, 1951–52.

———. G-4, 1951–52.

———. Office of the Chief Signal Officer, 1951–52.

Larkin, Lt. Gen. T. B., director of logistics, to director of plans and operations, disposition form: "Continuation of MAP and inclosed staff study," 22 December 1949, AC of S G-4, Department of the Army.

"Logistics Policies and Priorities." 1 November 1952, AC of S G-4, Department of the Army.

"Memo for the Record." Conference in Office of the Assistant Secretary of the Army, 3 November 1949.

"Memoranda of Important Actions." G-4, G4/B1 36480, 1950.

"Messages," Department of the Army, Commander in Chief, U.S. European Command, April 1953.

"Organization and Method of Work of the Army Board, MAS." MAS (Army) (63) 339, 16 July 1963.

"Reports of Critical Problems," G-4, 1951–52.

"Russian Combat Estimate." Staff Study, 'G-3, AGF, Plans. April 1942. Copy in AGO Historical Records section.

"Supply Supplement to the Troop Program and Troop List." 1 August 1950.

Transportation Corps Notes, March 1951.

Westphalinger, Henry R. "U.S. Army Communications Zone, Europe." *Army Information Digest,* December 1962, 9–16.

Young, Brig. Gen. Mason J. "Our New European Supply Line." *Army Information Digest,* October 1951, 56ff.

Zimmerman, Colonel. Interview, 3 June 1953.

B. *Congressional Documents*

Mutual Defense Assistance Act of 1949.

Mutual Security Act of 1954. As amended 1959.

Semiannual Reports to Congress on the Mutual Defense Assistance Program.

House. Committee on Foreign Affairs. *Mutual Defense Act of 1949: Hearings.* 81st Cong., 1st sess., 1949.

———. *Mutual Security Act Extension. Hearings.* 82d Cong., 2d sess., 1952.

———. *Mutual Security Act Extension.* 83d Cong., 1st sess., 1953.

House. *Department of Defense Appropriations for Fiscal Year 1967, Hearings on H.R. 15941, Part 1.* 89th Cong., 2d sess., 1966.

House. *Message of the President of the United States Transmitting Recommendations for the Enactment of Legislation Authorizing Military Aid to the Nations of Western Europe, July 25, 1949.* 81st Cong., 1st sess., 1949. H. Doc. 276.

Public Law 621. 81st Cong., serial 3809.

Senate. Committee on Foreign Relations. *Mutual Security Act of 1952: Hearings.* 82d Cong., 2d sess., 1952.

Senate. Committees on Foreign Relations and Armed Services. *Mutual Security Act of 1951: Hearings.* 82d Cong., 1st sess., 1951.

Senate. Committee on Government Operations. Subcommittee on National Security and International Operations. *The Atlantic Alliance: Basic Issues.* 89th Cong., 2d sess., 1966.

———. *The Atlantic Alliance: Allied Comment.* 89th Cong., 2d sess., 1966.

———. *The Atlantic Alliance: Future Tasks of the Alliance.* 90th Cong., 2d sess., 1968. Committee Print.

———. *The Atlantic Alliance: Hearings.* 89th Cong., 2d sess., 1966.

———. *The Atlantic Alliance: Unfinished Business.* 90th Cong., 1st sess., 1967. Committee Print.

Senate. *Convention on Relations with the Federal Republic of Germany, and Related Conventions.* 82d Cong., 2d sess. S. Exec. Doc. Q&R.

Senate. Subcommittee on Foreign Relations. *Economic and Military Assistance to Free Europe: Hearings.* 82d Cong., 1st sess., 1951.

C. *Department of Commerce*

"Foreign Aid by the U.S. Government. Basic Data Through December 31, 1952."

D. Department of Defense

Bell, John O. Lecture. Industrial College of the Armed Forces, 13 February 1950. L50–91.

"Cooperative Logistic Support Arrangements." Instruction 2000.8, 14 February 1964.

"Department of Defense Operations Under MDAP." December 1952.

"General Procedure for Furnishing Military Assistance to Foreign Governments." Special Regulations 795-200 series.

"History of Joint American Military Advisory Group."

Messages, Secretary of Defense-Acting Secretary of Defense, April 1953.

"Military Assistance and Foreign Military Sales Facts." May 1967.

"NATO Infrastructure." Fact Sheet no. 243-52, 29 December 1952.

"Operations under the Mutual Defense Assistance Program." June 1952 and May 1953.

Palumbo, M. Dominic. "An Analysis of Western Co-production of Weapons of United States Origin." Industrial College of the Armed Forces, Washington, D.C., 1966.

Reports of the Secretary of Defense (annual and semiannual).

Seminar. Industrial College of the Armed Forces, 17 December 1951.

E. Department of State

Ball, George. "The Nuclear Deterrent and the Atlantic Alliance." *Department of State Bulletin* 49 (May 1963): 736–39.

Bradshaw, Mary E. "Military Control of Zone A in Venezia Biulia." *Department of State Bulletin* 16 (June 1947): 1257–72.

Foreign Aid by the United States Government, 1940–1951.

Germany 1947–1949. The Story in Documents. Pub. no. 3556, March 1950.

Howard, Harry N. "Some Recent Developments in the Problems of the Turkish Straits, 1945–1946." *Department of State Bulletin* 16 (January 1946): 143–51, 167.

Messages and Despatches, Department of State-American Embassy, Rome. 1951.

Messages, Department of State-American Embassy, Paris. May 1953.

Mill, Edward W. "One Year of the Philippine Republic." *Department of State Bulletin* 16 (June 1947): 1280 ff.

NATO: North Atlantic Treaty Organization. Its Development and Significance. Pub. no. 4630, August 1952.

Occupation of Germany, Policy and Progress. Pub. no. 2783, August 1947.

Occupation of Japan, Policy and Progress. Pub. no. 2671.

Rusk, Dean. "The State of the North Atlantic Alliance." *Department of State Bulletin* 49 (August 1963): 190–98.

Schaetzel, J. R. "Tides of Change." *Department of State Bulletin* 49 (March 1963): 322–28.

The United States and the United Nations. Report Series No. 7. Report by the President to Congress for the Year 1946. Pub. no. 2735.

F. France

Couve de Murville, Maurice. "Speech before the French National Assembly on April

14, 1966." Speeches and Press Conferences no. 244A, French Embassy. French Press and Information Service, New York.

de Gaulle, Charles. Press Conference Held in Paris at the Elysée Palace on 21 February 1966. Speeches and Press Conferences no. 239, French Embassy. French Press and Information Service, New York.

————. "Third Press Conference, 5 September 1960." French Embassy, French Press and Information Service, New York.

France Air and Space. New York: French Press and Information Service, 1963.

"French Memoranda on NATO Delivered on March 8 and 10 and March 29 and 30, 1966." French Affairs no. 192, and "Third French Memorandum on NATO Handed to the Ambassador of the United States on April 22, 1966." French Affairs no. 192A, and French Embassy, French Press and Information Service, New York.

Pompidou, Georges. "Statements on Foreign Policy before the French National Assembly on April 13 and 20, 1966." Speeches and Press Conferences nos. 243A and 245A, French Embassy. French Press and Information Service, New York, 22 April 1966, French Affairs no. 192A.

G. *Library of Congress*

The United States and Europe: A Bibliographical Examination of Thought Expressed in American Publication During 1959. Washington, D.C.: Library of Congress.

H. *The President*

Executive Orders of the President. 10300, 1 November 1951; 10368, 30 June 1953.

I. *United Kingdom*

Earl of Home. "Speech Delivered at Wilton Park, 18 February 1963." Copy in Institute for Strategic Studies, London.

Wilson, Harold. "Britain and the ANF." (Extracts from statement in the House of Commons, 16 December 1964.) Printed in *Survival,* March–April 1965, 52–54.

J. *U.S. Arms Control and Disarmament Agency*

World Military Expenditures and Arms Transfers, 1967–76 Publication 98, July 1978.

K. *U.S. Military Commands*

Annual Narrative Reports, European Command.

Command Reports, European Command.

"Establishment of Communications through France, 1950–1951." Historical summary, European Command.

Lay, Elizabeth S. "Berlin Airlift, January 1, 1930–September 1949." Occupation Forces in Europe Series, HQ, European Command, Historical Division.

Lucas, Joanne M. "Exchange of Troops and Facilities, United States and French Zones, 1950–1951." HQ, U.S. Army Europe, Historical Division.

"Military Government, Austria." Report of the U.S. Commissioner, 16 February 1947.

"Military Government of Germany." Monthly Reports of Military Governor, U.S. Zone. (Copy in Army Library.)

Occupation. U.S. Forces European Theater. (Pamphlet printed in Germany c. 1947.)

"Quarterly Report on Germany." Office of the U.S. High Commissioner for Germany, September–December 1949.

"Selected Data on the Occupation of Japan." General Headquarters, Supreme Commander Allied Powers and Far East Command.

"Summary of Remarks by Lt. Gen. W. B. Palmer, Deputy Chief of Staff for Logistics." HQ, U.S. Army Europe, 14 June 1954. (Copy in Office of Chief of Military History.)

Books and Monographs

Acheson, Dean. Address. Adelphi Papers no. 5. London: Institute for Strategic Studies, 1963.

———. *Present at the Creation.* New York: W. W. Norton, 1969.

Amme, Carl H., Jr. *NATO Without France.* Stanford, Calif.: Hoover Institution on War, Revolution, and Peace, 1967.

Aron, Raymond. *The Great Debate: Theories of Nuclear Strategy.* Garden City, N.Y.: Doubleday, 1965.

Beaufre, André. *Introduction à la Stratégie.* Paris: A Colin, 1963.

Birrenbach, Kurt. *The Future of the Atlantic Community: Toward European-American Partnership.* New York: Praeger, 1963.

Brown, Neville. *Strategic Mobility.* New York: Praeger, 1964.

Buchan, Alastair. *Crisis Management: The New Diplomacy.* The Atlantic Papers, NATO Series 2. Boulogne-sur-Seine: Atlantic Institute, 1966.

———. *NATO in the 1960s.* Rev. ed. New York: Praeger, 1963.

Bull, Hedley. *Strategy and the Atlantic Alliance: A Critique of U.S. Doctrine.* Princeton University Center for International Studies, Policy Memorandum no. 29. Princeton, N.J., 1964.

Campbell, John C. *The United States in World Affairs 1945–1947.* New York: Harper & Bros. for the Council on Foreign Relations, 1947.

Carmoy, Guy de. *L'Alliance Atlantique Disloquée.* Paris: Association Français pour la Communauté Atlantique, 1966.

Cerny, Karl H., and Henry W. Briefs, eds. *NATO in Quest of Cohesion.* New York: Praeger for Hoover Institution on War, Revolution, and Peace, 1965.

Clay, Lucius D. *Decision in Germany.* Garden City, N.Y.: Doubleday, 1950.

Defense in the Cold War: The Task for the Free World. London: Royal Institute of International Affairs, 1950.

Deutsch, Karl. Political Community and the North Atlantic Area. Princeton, N.J.: Princeton University Press, 1957.

———, Lewis J. Edinger, Roy C. Macridis, and Richard L. Merritt. *France, Germany, and the Western Alliance.* New York: Charles Scribner's Sons, 1967.

Duchêne, François. *Beyond Alliance.* Boulogne-sur-Seine: Atlantic Institute, 1965.

Duroselle, J. B. "The Future of the Atlantic Community." In *The Atlantic Nations: Converging or Diverging? Prospects for 1975.* Boulogne-sur-Seine: Atlantic Institute, 1966.

Dyer, George C. *Naval Logistics.* Annapolis, Md.: U.S. Naval Institute, 1960.

Eccles, Henry E. *European Logistics, 1956.* George Washington University Logistics Research Project no. ONR 4l904. Washington, D.C.: George Washington University, 1956.

Eisenhower, Dwight D. *Crusade in Europe*. Garden City, N.Y.: Doubleday, 1948.

Ely, Louis B. *The Red Army Today*. Harrisburg, Penn.: Stackpole Co., 1951.

Fedder, Edwin H., ed. *Defense Politics of the Atlantic Alliance*. New York: Praeger, 1980.

Gallois, Pierre. *Stratégie de l'Age Nucléaire*. Paris: Calman-Levy, 1960.

Goldstein, Walter. *The Dilemma of British Defense*. Mershon Pamphlet Series no. 3. Columbus: Ohio State University Press, 1966.

Hutchison, Sir James. Paper, 6 July 1959, in files of the Institute for Strategic Studies, London.

James, Robert Rhodes. *Standardization and Common Production of Weapons in NATO*. Defense, Technology, and the Western Alliance no. 3. London: Institute for Strategic Studies, 1967.

Kissinger, Henry A. *Nuclear Weapons and Foreign Policy*. New York: Harper & Bros., 1957.

———. *The Troubled Partnership: A Reappraisal of the Western Alliance*. New York: McGraw-Hill, 1965.

Kleinman, Robert. *Atlantic Crisis: American Diplomacy Confronts a Resurgent Europe*. New York: W. W. Norton, 1964.

Knorr, Klaus. *A NATO Nuclear Force: The Problem of Management*. Princeton University Center for International Studies, Policy memorandum no. 26. Princeton, N.J., 1963.

Leighton, Richard M., and Robert W. Coakley. *Global Logistics and Strategy, 1940–1943. The United States Army in World War II*. Washington, D.C.: Office of Chief of Military History, 1953.

Liddell Hart, B. H. *Deterrent or Defense*. New York: Praeger, 1960.

Lowe, George E. *The Age of Deterrence*. Boston: Little, Brown & Co., 1964.

Ludz, Peter C., et al. *Dilemmas of the Atlantic Alliance*. New York: Praeger, 1975.

Major Problems of United States Foreign Policy, 1948–49. Washington, D.C.: Brookings Institution, 1949.

Major Problems of United States Foreign Policy, 1949–50. Washington, D.C.: Brookings Institution, 1950.

McCune, George M., and Arthur L. Grey, Jr. *Korea Today*. Cambridge, Mass.: Harvard University Press, 1950.

Meade, E. Grant. *American Military Government in Korea*. New York: King's Crown Press, 1951.

Miksche, Ferdinand O. *Failure of Atomic Strategy*. New York: Praeger, 1958.

The Military Balance, 1967–1968. London: Institute of Strategic Studies, 1967.

Mulley, F. W. *The Politics of Western Defense*. New York: Praeger, 1962.

Orvik, Nils, and Niels J. Haagerup. *The Scandinavian Members of NATO*. Adelphi Papers no. 23. London: Institute for Strategic Studies, 1965.

Pollock, James K., and James H. Meisel. *Germany under Occupation: Illustrative Materials and Documents*. Ann Arbor: University of Michigan Press, 1947.

Millis, Walter, ed. *The Forrestal Diaries*. New York: Viking Press, 1951.

Rostow, Eugene. "Possible Futures for the Atlantic Community." In *The Atlantic Nations: Converging or Diverging? Prospects for 1975*. Boulogne-sur-Seine: Atlantic Institute, 1966.

Rostow, Eugene, and Edgar S. Furniss. *The Western Alliance: Its Status and Prospects*. Columbus: Ohio State University Press, 1965.

Schaetzel, J. Robert. *The Unhinged Alliance: America and the European Community*. New York: Harper & Row, 1975.

Schmidt, Helmut. *Defense or Retaliation*. Translated by Edward Thomas. Edinburgh: Oliver and Boyd, 1962.

Schmitt, Hans A., ed. *U.S. Occupation in Europe After World War II. Papers and Reminiscences from the April 23–24, 1976, Conference Held at the George C. Marshall Research Foundation, Lexington, Virginia*. Lawrence, Kans.: Regents Press of Kansas, 1978.

Schütze, Walter. *European Defense Cooperation and NATO*. Paris: Atlantic Institute, 1969.

Schwartz, Harry. *The Red Phoenix: Russia Since World War II*. New York: Praeger, 1961.

———. *Russia's Soviet Economy*. New York: Prentice-Hall, 1951.

Slessor, John. *Command and Control of Allied Nuclear Forces: A British View*. Adelphi Papers no. 22. London: Institute for Strategic Studies, 1965.

Stanley, Timothy W. *NATO in Transition*. London: Pall Mall, 1965.

Stebbins, Richard. *The U.S. in World Affairs, 1949*. New York: Harper & Bros. for the Council on Foreign Relations, 1950.

Steel, Ronald. *The End of Alliance: America and the Future of Europe*. London: André Deutsch, 1964.

The Strategic Balance, 1967–1968. London: Institute for Strategic Studies, 1967.

Strausz-Hupé, Robert, and William R. Kintner. *Building the Atlantic World*. New York: Harper & Row, 1963.

Tassigny, LeLattre de. *Histoire de la Première Armée Française, Rhin et Danube*. Paris, 1949.

Taylor, Maxwell. *The Uncertain Trumpet*. New York: Harper & Bros., 1960.

Truman, Harry S. *Memoirs*. 2 vols. Garden City, N.Y.: Doubleday, 1956.

Turner, Gordon E., and Richard D. Challener. *National Security in the Nuclear Age*. New York: Praeger, 1960.

Younger, Kenneth. *Changing Perspectives in British Foreign Policy*. London: Oxford University Press, 1964.

Wilcox, Francis O., and H. Field Haviland, Jr. *The Atlantic Community: Progress and Prospects*. New York: Praeger, 1963.

Wolfe, Roy I. *Transportation and Politics*. New York: D. Van Nostrand Co., 1963.

Zink, Harold. *American Military Government in Germany*. New York: Macmillan Co., 1947.

Articles and Periodicals

A. Newspapers and News Magazines

Christian Science Monitor
Daily Telegraph (London)
Diplomat (Geneva)
The Economist

Financial Times (London)
Frankfurter Allgemeine Zeitung
Le Monde
Lloyds Daily List
Manchester Guardian
Newsweek
The New York Herald Tribune (European edition)
The New York Times
Paris-Match
The Reporter
Time Magazine
The Times (London)
U.S. News and World Report
The Washington Post

B. Specific Articles

Aron, Raymond. In *Le Figaro,* 22 April 1966, 1.

Allen, Frederick Lewis. "This Time and Last Time." *Harper's Magazine,* March 1947, 195 ff.

"Air Transport and Cargo Facilities Within the NATO Countries." *NATO's Fifteen Nations* 6 (January 1961): 84–85.

Amme, Carl H., Jr. "Nuclear Control and the Multilateral Force." *Proceedings of the U.S. Naval Institute* 91 (April 1965): 24–35.

Anderson, Samuel E. "Aerospace Power and Logistics." *NATO's Fifteen Nations* 5 (Winter 1960): 9–19.

Badurina, Besislav. "France's Military Policy." *Review of International Affairs* 15 (October 1964): 17–18.

———. "NATO's Nuclear Policy." *Review of International Affairs* 15 (December 1964): 8–10.

Baldwin, Hanson. "Taking Stock of Europe's Nuclear Defenses." *The Reporter,* 25 April 1963.

Ball, George W. "NATO and World Responsibility." *Atlantic Community Quarterly* 2 (Summer 1964): 208–18.

Beaufre, André. "La Drôle Paix." *Le Figaro,* 26 August 1967, 1.

———. "The Sharing of Nuclear Responsibilities—A Problem in Need of a Solution." *International Affairs* 19 (July 1965): 411–19.

Beddington-Behrens, Edward. "Using the Multi-national Idea." *European Review* 15 (Spring 1964): 7–9.

Besson, Frank S., Jr. "Logistics and Transportation in the Defense of Western Europe." *National Defense Transportation Journal* 12 (March–April 1956): 54–57, 64–65.

Birrenbach, Kurt. "Partnership and Consultation in NATO." *Atlantic Community Quarterly* 2 (Spring 1964): 62–71.

Bissell, Richard M. "Foreign Aid. What Sort? How Much? How Long?" *Foreign Affairs* 31 (October 1952): 15–38.

"Bonn to Review Defense Policy." *New York Times,* 8 July 1967, 1, 6.

Bowie, Robert. "Strategy and the Atlantic Alliance." *International Organization* 17 (Summer 1963): 719–20, 730–31.

———. "Strategy and the Western Alliance." *International Organization* 17 (Summer 1963): 709–19.

Brodie, Bernard. "Strategic Implications of the North Atlantic Pact." *Yale Review* 39 (Winter 1950).

Brown, G. W. "NATO's Allied Mobile Force." *Army*, August 1966, 47.

Brown, Seyom. "An Alternative to the Grand Design." *World Politics* 17 (January 1965): 232–42.

Brunn, Robert R. "NATO to Assess Strength." *Christian Science Monitor*, 27 May 1963.

———. "NATO's Next Step." *Christian Science Monitor*, 27 May 1963, 1.

Buchan, Alastair. "The Changed Setting of the Atlantic Debate." *Foreign Affairs* 43 (July 1965): 574–86.

———. "The Multilateral Force." *International Affairs* 60 (October 1964): 628–37.

———. "NATO after Nassau." *Air Force College Journal* (Canada)(1963): 45–49.

———. "NATO and the American-European Strategic Relationship." Address given at RAND Corporation, 15 November 1963. Copy in Institute for Strategic Studies, London.

———. "The Reform of NATO." *Foreign Affairs* 40 (January 1962): 165–82.

Carpenter, d'Armee M. "Current Comment." *General Military Review* (July 1963): 287.

Church, Frank. "NATO—Reappraising American Policy." *Survival* 5 (September–October 1963):232–37.

"Civilian Uses for the NATO Pipelines." *Financial Times* (London), 8 August 1963.

Coffe, Josef I. "A NATO Nuclear Deterrent?" *Orbis* 8 (Fall 1964): 584–94.

Collins, J. Lawton. Statement. *U.S. Army Combat Forces Journal* 3 (July 1941): 41.

Colonna, Guido. "NATO—The Unfolding Alliance—The State of the Alliance." *Atlantic Community Quarterly* 2 (Fall 1964): 397–407.

Cook, Don. "French to Veto Plan for NATO Strategic Study. *New York Herald Tribune* (European ed.), 24 July 1963.

———. "M. Seydoux Informe l'O.T.A.N. de l'Opposition de la France." *Le Monde*, 26 July 1963.

———. "Plan to Study NATO Resources and Aims." *Financial Times* (London), 31 July 1963.

———."Strategy and Sentiment." *New York Herald Tribune* (European ed.), 13 July 1963.

Dawson, Raymond H. "What Kind of NATO Nuclear Force?" *Annals of the American Academy of Political and Social Science* 304 (January 1964): 30–31.

Denny, Sir Michael M. "The Atlantic in a World War—What Does it Mean?" *Journal of the Royal United Service Institution* 100 (August 1956): 351–63.

Deutermann, H. T. "International Navy: A Decade of Unity." *NATO's Fifteen Nations* 10 (April 1962): 32–34.

Doty, L. L. "NATO Working Group Supports U.S. Plan for Mixed Nuclear Fleet." *Aviation Week and Space Technology*, 21 September 1964, 25.

———. "U.S. Pressure Delays NATO Target Buy." *Aviation Week and Space Technology*, 2 November 1964, 23.

"Dutch ASW Aircraft Selection Seen Critical in NATO Plans." *Aviation Week and Space Technology,* 11 March 1968, 17.

Duynstee, A. E. M. "The European Aircraft Industry Must Be Integrated." *NATO's Fifteen Nations* 11 (August–September 1966): 23–24.

Dyott, R. B. "Radio Communication by Tropospheric Scatter." *New Scientist,* 16 July 1959, 72–73.

Dziuban, Stanley W. "NATO Infrastructure: Marvel of Military Construction Achievement." *NATO Journal* (April 1962): 18–22, and Part 2 (May–June 1962): 26–32.

Eden, Anthony (Lord Avon). Interview on CBS Television, 27 December 1964, printed in *Freedom and Union,* October 1961, 3–5.

Erler, Fritz. "The Alliance and the Future of Germany." *Foreign Affairs* 63 (April 1965): 442ff.

Etherington, R. A. "The Container Ship Revolution." *European Review* 7 (Summer 1967): 30–32.

Eyraud, Michel. "L'Alliance Atlantique: Court Terme et Moyen Terme." *Stratégie* (January–March 1966): 102–29.

"Facing the Iron Curtain: How Good is Western Defense?" *U.S. News and World Report,* 30 December 1963, 54–60.

Felix, Fremont, and S. B. Newan. "The New Shape of SHAPE." *Military Engineer,* July–August 1967, 258–60.

Fink, Donald E. "NATO Acts To Counter Two-Way Threat." *Aviation Week and Space Technology,* 18 March 1968, 100, 105–6.

————. "NATO Members Move To Bolster the Alliance." *Aviation Week and Space Technology,* 25 November 1968, 21.

Finney, John W. "ULSL to Aid Britain on German Costs." *New York Times,* 27 April 1967, 1, 28.

Fontaine, André. "The ABC of MLF." *The Reporter,* 31 December 1963, 10–14.

"France Abandons Joint Air Project." *New York Times,* 6 July 1967, 1, 2.

Franks, H. George. "The Great Achievement of Infrastructure." *NATO's Fifteen Nations* 4 (April 1959): 130–42; also 5 (1960): 24–33.

Fraser, Blair. "Can We Succeed in NATO Without Really Trying?" *Atlantic Community Quarterly* 3 (Spring 1965): 50–55.

Gallois, Pierre. "The Case for France." *Diplomat,* April 1966.

————. "U.S. Strategy and the Defense of Western Europe." *Orbis* 7 (Summer 1962): 27ff.

Gallois, Pierre, and Paul Stehlin. "Après la Rupture, seron-nous plus en danger qu'aujourd'hui?" *Paris-Match,* 16 April 1966, 56–69.

Gasteyger, Curt, *Europe in the Seventies,* Institute of Strategic Studies, Adelphi Papers no. 37 (London, 1967), 15.

Gill, W. T. "European Cooperation in Britain's Aerospace Industry." *NATO's Fifteen Nations* 11 (August–September 1966): 27–31.

"GM Chosen to Help Make New Tank." *New York Herald Tribune* (Paris ed.), 24 July 1964, 1.

Goodman, Elliot R. "Five Nuclear Options for the West." *Atlantic Community Quarterly* 2 (Winter 1964–65): 57–87.

Gordon, Lincoln. "NATO in the Nuclear Age." *Yale Review* 48 (March 1959): 321–35.

Grossner, Alfred. "France and Germany in the Atlantic Community." In *The Atlantic Community: Progress and Prospects,* edited by Francis O. Wilcox and H. Field Haviland, Jr., 46–50. New York: Praeger, 1963.

"A Guide to U.S. Army Equipment in Operational Use or Development." *Army,* October 1967, 130–31.

Hartley, Anthony. "The British Bomb." *Encounter* 12 (May 1964): 22–34.

Hartley, Livingston. "Atlantic Partnership—How?" *Orbis* 8 (Spring 1964): 141–52.

Hassel, Kai-Uwe von. "Detente through Firmness." *Foreign Affairs* 42 (January 1964): 189 ff.

———. "The Search for Consensus: Organizing Western Defense." *Foreign Affairs* 43 (January 1965): 209–16.

Healey, Denis. "Britain under Labor." *NATO's Fifteen Nations* 9 (June–July 1964): 31.

———. "Turning Point for NATO." *New Republic,* 24 April 1961, 144–47.

Heilbrunn, Otto. "NATO and the Flexible Response." *Military Review* 45 (May 1965): 22–26.

Hilton, Michael. "NATO in the Doldrums." *Daily Telegraph,* 13 December 1963.

Hoag, Malcolm. "Rationalizing NATO Strategy." *World Politics* 17 (October 1964): 121–42.

Hoefling, John A. "The Army and the C-54." *Army,* January 1968, 67–71.

Hoffmann, Stanley H. "Discord in the Community." *International Organization* 17 (Summer 1963): 521–49.

Hollingsworth, Clare. "U.S. Puts Pressure on NATO Partners; Five-Year Package Deal Urged." *Manchester Guardian,* 5 June 1963.

Huizinga, J. H. "Which Way Europe?" *Foreign Affairs* 43 (April 1965): 485–500.

"Is NATO Becoming Irrelevant?" *The Times* (London), 6 April 1964.

Kalijarvi, Thorsten V., and Francis O. Wilcox. "The Organizational Framework of the North Atlantic Treaty." *American Journal of International Law* 64 (January 1950): 155–61.

King, James E. "NATO: Genesis, Progress, Problems." In *National Security in the Nuclear Age,* edited by Gordon E. Turner and Richard D. Challener, 143–72. New York: Praeger, 1960.

Kissinger, Henry A. "Coalition Diplomacy in a Nuclear Age." *Foreign Affairs* 42 (July 1964): 528–32, 539, 540–41, 544.

———. "NATO's Nuclear Dilemma." *The Reporter,* 28 March 1963, 22–26.

Kohl, Wilfrid L. "Nuclear Sharing in NATO and the Mutilateral Force." *Political Science Quarterly* 80 (March 1965): 88–109.

Kohn, Hans. "Western Europe and Atlantic Unity." *Current History,* September 1960, 153.

Kolcum, Edward H. "Czech Crisis Spurs Bid To Toughen NATO." *Aviation Week and Space Technology,* 2 September 1968, 18–19.

Lall, Betty Goetz. "A NATO-Warsaw Detente?" *Bulletin of the Atomic Scientists* 20 (November 1964): 37–39.

Liddell Hart, B. H. "The Defense of West Germany and the Baltic." *Marine Corps Gazette,* February 1964, 18–22.

———. "NATO—Sword or Shield?" *Ordnance* 47 (July–August 1964): 43–46, 65.

Locksley, Norman. "NATO's Southern Exposure." *U.S. Naval Institute Proceedings* 88 (November 1962): 41–54.

Luchsinger, Fred. "France's A-Force." *Swiss Review of World Affairs* 14 (January 1965).

Luns, J. M. A. H. "Independence or Interdependence." *International Affairs* 18 (January 1964): 10–20.

Luthey, Herbert. "De Gaulle: Pose and Policy." *Foreign Affairs* 43 (July 1965): 571–72.

Maffre, John. "Military Deals Balance Trade." *Washington Post,* 26 March 1967, 33.

Magathan, Wallace C. "West German Defense Policy." *Orbis* 8 (Summer 1964): 292–315.

Margerison, Tom. "Lemnitzer's Awkward Army." *Sunday Times Colour Magazine* (London), 9 June 1963, 7–9.

———. Interview with General Lemnitzer. *Sunday Times* (London), 6 October 1963.

McNamara, Robert. "American Strategy Now." *Survival* 7 (May–June 1965): 98.

———. "McNamara on BMD." *Survival* 9 (April 1967): 108–14, 121.

McQuade, Lawrence C. "NATO's Non-nuclear Needs." *International Affairs* 18 (January 1964): 11–21.

Meili, Ernest H. "Nations United for Peace—NATO Infrastructure." *Signal,* December 1959, 12–13, 25.

Middleton, Drew. "Britain Backs Land Force Over NATO's Mixed Fleet." *New York Times* (Int. ed.), 23 June 1964, 1, 2.

———. "Soviet Re-equips Force in Germany." *New York Times,* 1 September 1952, C-4.

Miksche, Ferdinand Otto. "The European Shield." *NATO's Fifteen Nations* 7 (August–September 1962): 15–22.

———. "Tactical Nuclear Weapons and the Defense of Western Europe." *Military Review* 44 (June 1964): 35–42.

Montjamont, Pierre de. "Le Départ du 'SHAPE.'" *La Revue des Deux Mondes,* 1 April 1967, 322–34.

Mooney, Richard E. "Paris and London Will Build a Swing-Wing Jet." *New York Times,* 17 January 1967, 3.

Moore, James E. "NATO Today." *Army,* August 1964, 29–33.

Morgenthau, Hans J. "The Crisis of the Alliance." In *NATO in Quest of Cohesion,* edited by Karl H. Cerny and Henry W. Briefs, 125–27. New York: Praeger, 1965.

Mulley, Frederick W. "NATO's Nuclear Problems: Control or Consultation." *Orbis* 8 (Spring 1964): 21–35.

Murphy, Charles V. "NATO at a Nuclear Crossroads." *Fortune,* December 1962, 84–87.

"Must We Reform NATO?" *Politique Etrangère.* Reprinted in *Survival* 8 (January 1966): 2–8.

Nanes, Alan S. "NATO's Strategic Dilemmas." *Current History* 39 (September 1960): 133–38.

"NATO and the Defense of Europe." *Il Giornale d'Italia,* 9 June 1965. Reprinted in *Survival* 7 (October 1965): 266–67.

"NATO—Reform." *Der Spiegel,* 28 February 1966; *The Times* (London), 22 February 1966.

"NATO Shifts Procuring Plans to Meet Military Needs." *Aviation Week and Space Technology,* 6 March 1967, 94.

Nossiter, Bernard D. "NATO Nations Far Apart on Timing of A-Trigger." *Washington Post,* 7 September 1966, A-10.

O'Donnell, James P. "We're All Fouled Up in France." *Saturday Evening Post,* 11 April 1953, 40–41.

Oldfield, Barney. "The F-104S Salutes Leonardo da Vinci." *NATO's Fifteen Nations* 11 (August–September 1966): 78–84.

Owen, Henry. "NATO Strategy: What Is Past Is Prologue." *Foreign Affairs* 43 (July 1965): 682–90.

———. "What the Multilateral Force Could Achieve." *European Review* 4 (Autumn 1964): 12–14.

Owen, Kenneth. "Still Hope for F-111 Offset Deals." *The Times* (London), 15 September 1967, 1.

Palewski, J. P. "Bilan d'une Alliance." *Politique Entrangère,* no. 2 (1964): 117–30.

Perret, L. "Cooperation Industrielle Aeronautique en Europe." *Revue Militaire d'Information* (May 1963): 57–63.

"Pipelines for NATO." *The Review* 45 (September–October 1965): 41, 106, 109.

Planchais, Jean. "Le Retrait de l'Esadre Française de l'Atlantique a des Raisons Politique et Technique." *Le Monde,* 18 July 1963.

Pleven, René. "France in the Atlantic Community." *Foreign Affairs* 39 (October 1959): 29–30.

Regelin, K. "Multilateral Confusion." *Interavia* 19 (1964): 14–61.

Rickhoff, Harald von. "The Changing Function of NATO." *International Journal* 21 (Spring 1966): 157–72.

Ridsdale, P. G. M. "Military Infrastructure—The Backbone of NATO." *NATO's Fifteen Nations* 7 (August–September 1962): 38–47.

Rostow, Eugene V. "A New Start for the Alliance." *The Reporter,* 25 April 1963, 23–29.

———. "Prospects for the Alliance." *Atlantic Community Quarterly* 3 (Spring 1965): 34–42.

Rovere, Richard H. "Letter from Washington." *The New Yorker,* 11 April 1964, 149–55.

Rühl, Lothar. "The Nine and NATO." In *Dilemmas of the Atlantic Alliance,* edited by Peter Christian Ludz et al., 213–52. New York: Praeger, 1975.

Rupert, K. Claude. "International Logistics Is Becoming a Fact." *NATO's Fifteen Nations* 7 (December 1962–January 1963): 69–70.

[Rusk.] "Dean Rusk Répond à 20 Questions de Paris-Match." *Paris-Match,* 16 April 1966, 42–45.

Schaetzel, J. Robert. "The Necessary Partnership." *Foreign Affairs* 44 (April 1966): 417–33.

Schelling, Thomas C. "Wie neu ist die 'neue Strategule' der Vereington Staaten?" *Europ-Archiv,* 15 February 1963, 551–64.

Schmidt, Dana Adams. "F-111 Deal in Jeopardy." *New York Times,* 14 September 1967, 20.

Schumann, Maurice. "Revising the NATO Treaty." *Atlantic Community Quarterly* 2 (Summer 1964): 230–32.

Scott, Stanley L. "The Military Aid Program." *Annals of the American Academy of Political and Social Science* 278 (November 1951).

"Senate Votes Defense Bill; Curb on British Accepted." *New York Times*, 14 September 1967, 1.

Shabecoff, Philip. "All F-104 Flights Halted by Bonn." *New York Times*, 7 December 1966, 15.

———. "Europeans Join in Jet Venture." *New York Times*, 10 July 1964.

"Shaping SHAPE." *The Bulletin: The Belgian Weekly in English*, 16 December 1966, 17–19.

Silard, John. "The Case Against the MLF." *Bulletin of the Atomic Scientists* 20 (September 1964): 18–20.

Sington, Anne. "NATO Communications Net Completed." *Military Review* 27 (February 1964); *Le Figaro*, 18 November 1963.

Slessor, John. "Control of NATO Nuclear Capacity." *Atlantic Community Quarterly* 2 (Fall 1964): 469–71, and 3 (Spring 1965): 56–63.

Smallman, W. A. "Mobility and Logistics." General Military Review (March 1960): 392–409.

Somers, Herman Miles. "Civil-Military Relations in Mutual Security." *Annals of the American Academy of Political and Social Science* 288 (July 1953): 9–10.

Sommer, Theo. "For an Atlantic Future." *Foreign Affairs* 43 (October 1964): 112–25.

"Southern Shield." *NATO's Fifteen Nations* 8 (February–March 1963): 72–80.

Spaak, Paul-Henri. "A New Effort to Build Europe." *Foreign Affairs* 43 (January 1965): 208 ff.

Spineili, Altiero. "Europe and the Nuclear Monopoly." *Atlantic Community Quarterly* 2 (Winter 1964–65): 595 ff.

Stanley, Timothy W. "NATO's Strategic Doctrine." *Survival* 11 (November 1969): 344–45.

Stehlin, Paul. "French Thoughts on the Alliance." *Military Review* 44 (January 1965): 28–34.

Stikker, Dirk V. "Britain's Role in NATO." *Financial Times* (London), Defense Supplement, 23 March 1964, 29.

———. "NATO—The Shifting Western Alliance." *Atlantic Community Quarterly* 3 (Spring 1965): 7–17.

———. "Weakest Link in NATO." *Life International*, 20 December 1965.

Strauss, Franz-Josef. "Europe, America, and NATO: A German View." *Survival* 4 (January–February 1962): 5–8.

Strausz-Hupé, Robert. "The Crisis in Political Leadership." In *NATO in Quest of Cohesion*, edited by Karl H. Cerny and Henry Briefs, 138–43. New York: Praeger, 1965.

Suire, Colonel. "Logistique et Stratégie in Climat Nucléaire." *Revue Militaire d'Information*, May 1963, 15–23.

Sulzberger, C. L. "Let Us Not Try to Dodge on NADGE." *New York Times* (Int. ed.), 10 April 1963.

———. "Pentagon Hits NATO Air Plan Europe." *New York Herald Tribune* (Paris ed.), 17 April 1963.

Taylor, Edmond. "This Long NATO Crisis." *The Reporter*, 21 April 1966.

———. "What Price MLF?" *The Reporter*, 3 December 1964, 12–14.

Taylor, John W. R. "European Bombers: 1966." *NATO's Fifteen Nations* 11 (August–September 1966): 47–48.

———. "European Fighters: 1966." *NATO's Fifteen Nations* 11 (August–September 1966): 38–44.

Thomson, David. "General de Gaulle and the Anglo-Saxons." *International Affairs* 19 (January 1965): 11–21.

Vailuy, Jean. "Danger de Mort." *Revue Militaire Générale* (January 1961): 3–12.

Vandevanter, Elliott, Jr. "The Politics of Integration." *NATO's Fifteen Nations* 12 (April–May 1967): 23.

Verax, Carmiro. "La Vie Politique." *La Revue des Deux Mondes,* 1 April 1967, 461–66.

Verrier, Anthony. "British Defense Policy under Labor." *Foreign Affairs* 42 (January 1964): 291 ff.

Wear, L. A. "An International Venture in Collective Logistics." *Supplies: Journal of the Institute of Public Supplies* (February 1966): 18–19.

Whipple, Sidney B. "AFNORTH: NATO's Left Flank." *NATO's Fifteen Nations* 9 (April–May 1964): 60–68.

White, Theodore D. "New Era in NATO." *Newsweek,* 29 October 1962, 27–28.

Willoughby, Frank. "Communications and Electronics in Allied Command Europe." *NATO's Fifteen Nations* 6 (January 1961): 41–46, and (March 1961): 53–56.

Winchester, James H. "NATO's Fuel Pipeline Almost Complete; Invaluable Logistic Support System." *NATO's Fifteen Nations* 7 (August–September 1962): 83–86.

Witze, Claude. "The Case for a Common Defense Market." *Air Force/Space Digest International* (January 1966): 4–5.

Wright, Jerauld (SACLANT). "NATO's Naval Forces: The Future." *NATO's Fifteen Nations* 7 (Spring 1959): 114–21.

Wynn, Humphrey. "AAFCE: Europe's Air Defense." *Flight International,* 15 March 1962, 397–402, 418.

Young, Wayland. "MLF—A West European View." *Bulletin of the Atomic Scientists* 20 (November 1964): 19–21.

Zavald, A. P. "SACLANT Communications." *NATO's Fifteen Nations* 8 (February–March 1963): 62–66.

Zitzewitz, Horst V. "Vorwartsverteidigung am Eisernen Vorhang." *Wehrkunde* (February 1964): 63–68.

Index